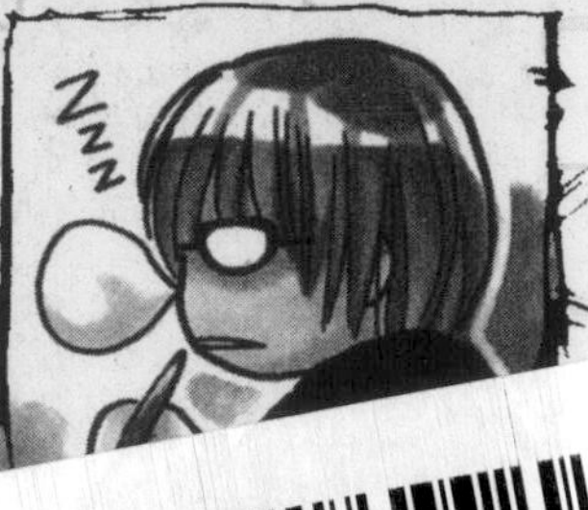
ZZZ

I [illegible] sleepy while I'm working:

1) [illegible]wash my face and brush my teeth

2) Exercise in my living room

3) Eat ice cream

4) Take a break and talk to my assistants

One of the above usually works. If not, I give in and go to bed. (I once worked for two days straight without sleeping, and I accidentally drew Sven where I was supposed to draw Eve.) Lack of sleep is very frightening...

—Kentaro Yabuki, 2003

Kentaro Yabuki made his manga debut with ***Yamato Gensoki***, a short series about a young empress destined to unite the warring states of ancient Japan and the boy sworn to protect her. His next series, ***Black Cat***, commenced serialization in the pages of ***Weekly Shonen Jump*** in 2000 and quickly developed a loyal fan following. ***Black Cat*** has also become an animated TV series, first hitting Japan's airwaves in the fall of 2005.

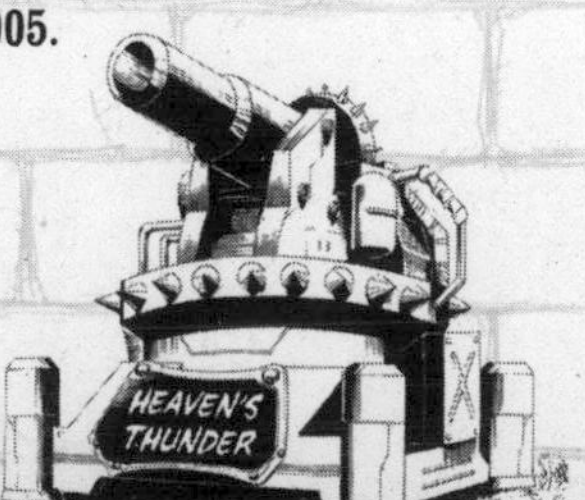
HEAVEN'S THUNDER

BLACK CAT VOL. 13
The SHONEN JUMP Manga Edition

STORY AND ART BY
KENTARO YABUKI

English Adaptation/Kelly Sue DeConnick
Translation/JN Productions
Touch-up Art & Lettering/Gia Cam Luc
Design/Courtney Utt
Editor/Jonathan Tarbox

Editor in Chief, Books/Alvin Lu
Editor in Chief, Magazines/Marc Weidenbaum
VP of Publishing Licensing/Rika Inouye
VP of Sales/Gonzalo Ferreyra
Sr. VP of Marketing/Liza Coppola
Publisher/Hyoe Narita

Printed in the U.S.A.

Published by VIZ Media, LLC
P.O. Box 77010
San Francisco, CA 94107

SHONEN JUMP Manga Edition
10 9 8 7 6 5 4 3 2 1
First printing, March 2008

THE WORLD'S
MOST POPULAR MANGA

www.viz.com

www.shonenjump.com

SHONEN JUMP MANGA EDITION

BLACK CAT

ブラック・キャット

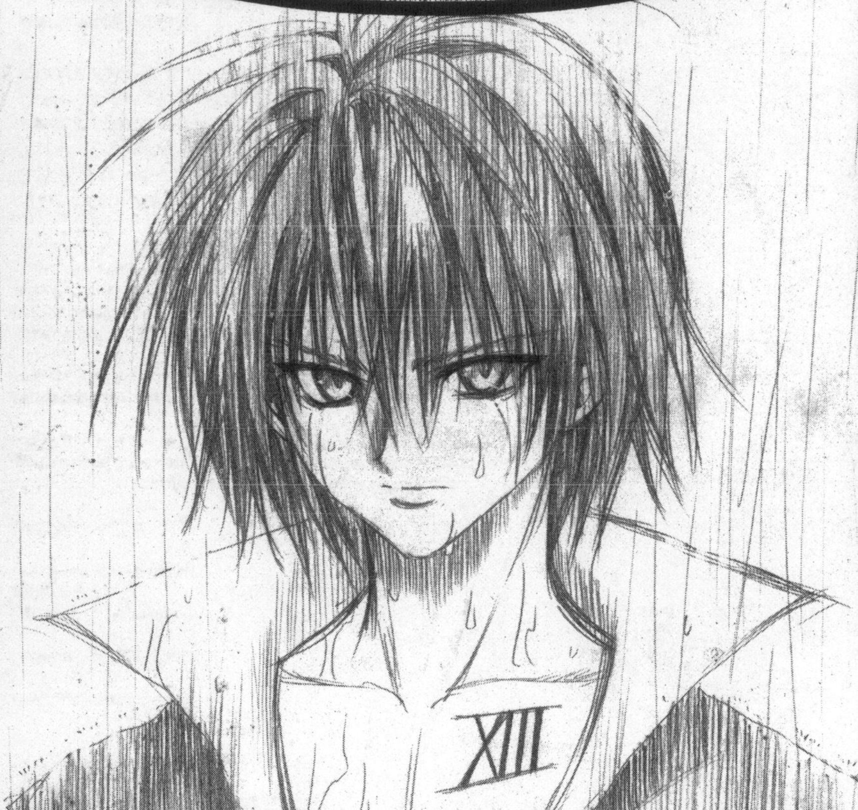
XIII

VOLUME 13

DEAR FRIEND

STORY & ART BY **KENTARO YABUKI**

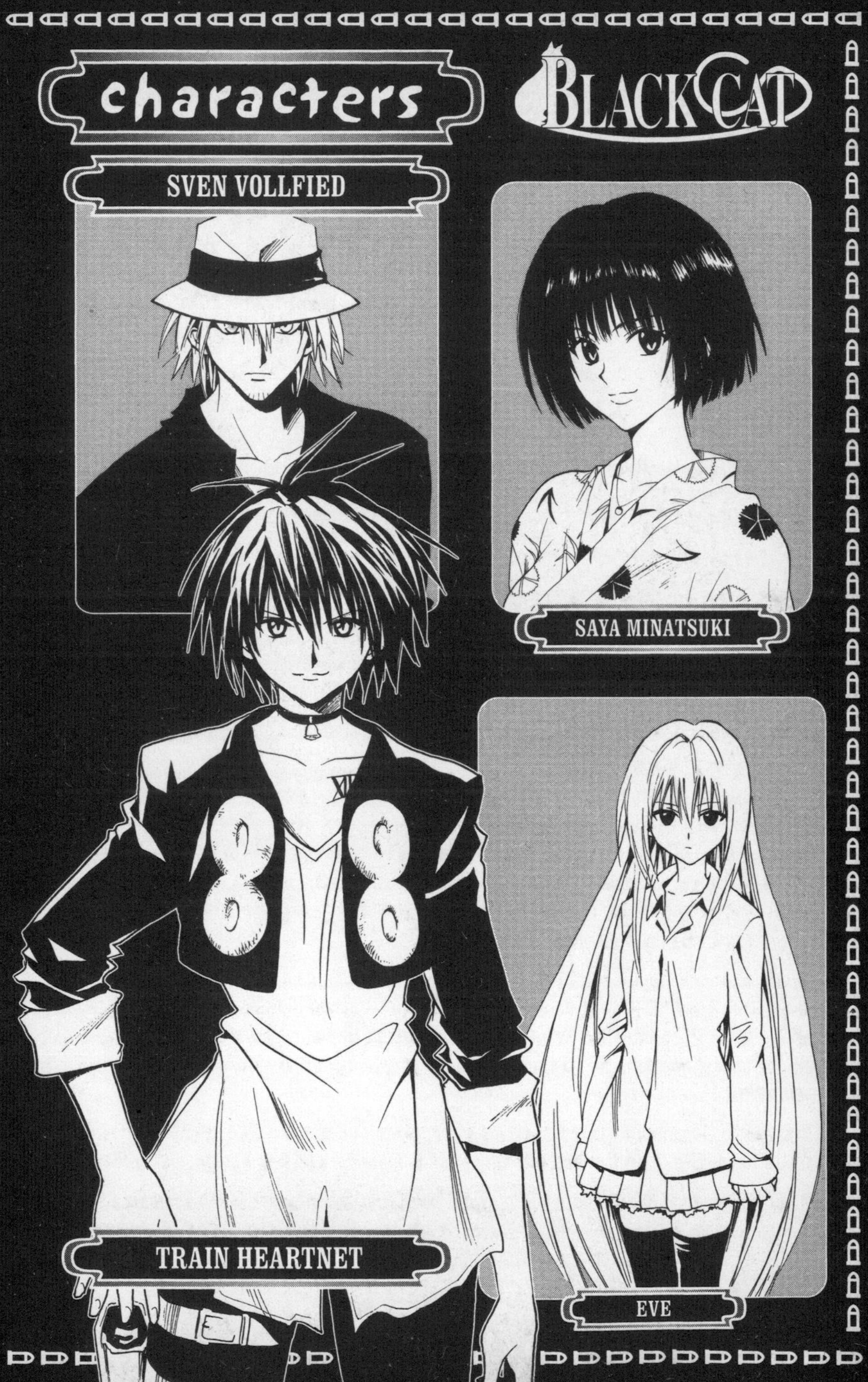
characters
BLACK CAT
SVEN VOLLFIED
SAYA MINATSUKI
TRAIN HEARTNET
EVE

DR. TEARJU

RINSLET WALKER

No. I SEPHIRIA

CREED DISKENTH

No. II BELZE

A fearless "eraser" responsible for the deaths of countless powerful men, Train "Black Cat" Heartnet was formerly an assassin for the crime syndicate Chronos. Train betrayed Chronos and was supposedly executed for it, but two years later he lives a carefree life, working with his partner Sven as a bounty hunter ("sweeper") while pursuing Creed Diskenth, the man who murdered Train's beloved friend Saya. The two sweepers are allied with sexy thief-for-hire Rinslet Walker and Eve, a young girl (and experimental living weapon) whom they rescued from a nanotech lab.

When Creed attempts to kill Sven, Train takes the bullet and winds up infected by a nanotech weapon called LUCIFER. It doesn't kill him, but it causes his body to de-age, reverting to that of a small child. When Sven approaches Rinslet for help, he learns of a Dr. Tearju, who might know how to "cure" Train. As it turns out, Tearju is also the woman responsible for Eve's birth!

Meanwhile, Kyoko deserts the Apostles of the Stars and is pursued by the Chrono Numbers. Train intercedes to protect her, but his small size makes wielding his gun very difficult.

Train and friends finally reach Dr. Tearju's home, but there they come under attack from the Apostles of the Stars. Train changes back to his normal size and attains a new power, "Rail Gun," which he uses to overcome their attackers. Eve decides that Creed is too dangerous to walk free and tries to convince everyone that he should be their next target.

VOLUME 13 DEAR FRIEND

CONTENTS

CHAPTER 114	Time of Decision	7
CHAPTER 115	The Sweeper Woman	29
CHAPTER 116	The Price of Freedom	49
CHAPTER 117	Reflect Shot	69
CHAPTER 118	One Last Act of Courage	89
CHAPTER 119	Dear Friend	109
CHAPTER 120	To the Café	129
CHAPTER 121	Man of Fists	149
CHAPTER 122	Flash Fists	169

Chapter 114: Time of Decision

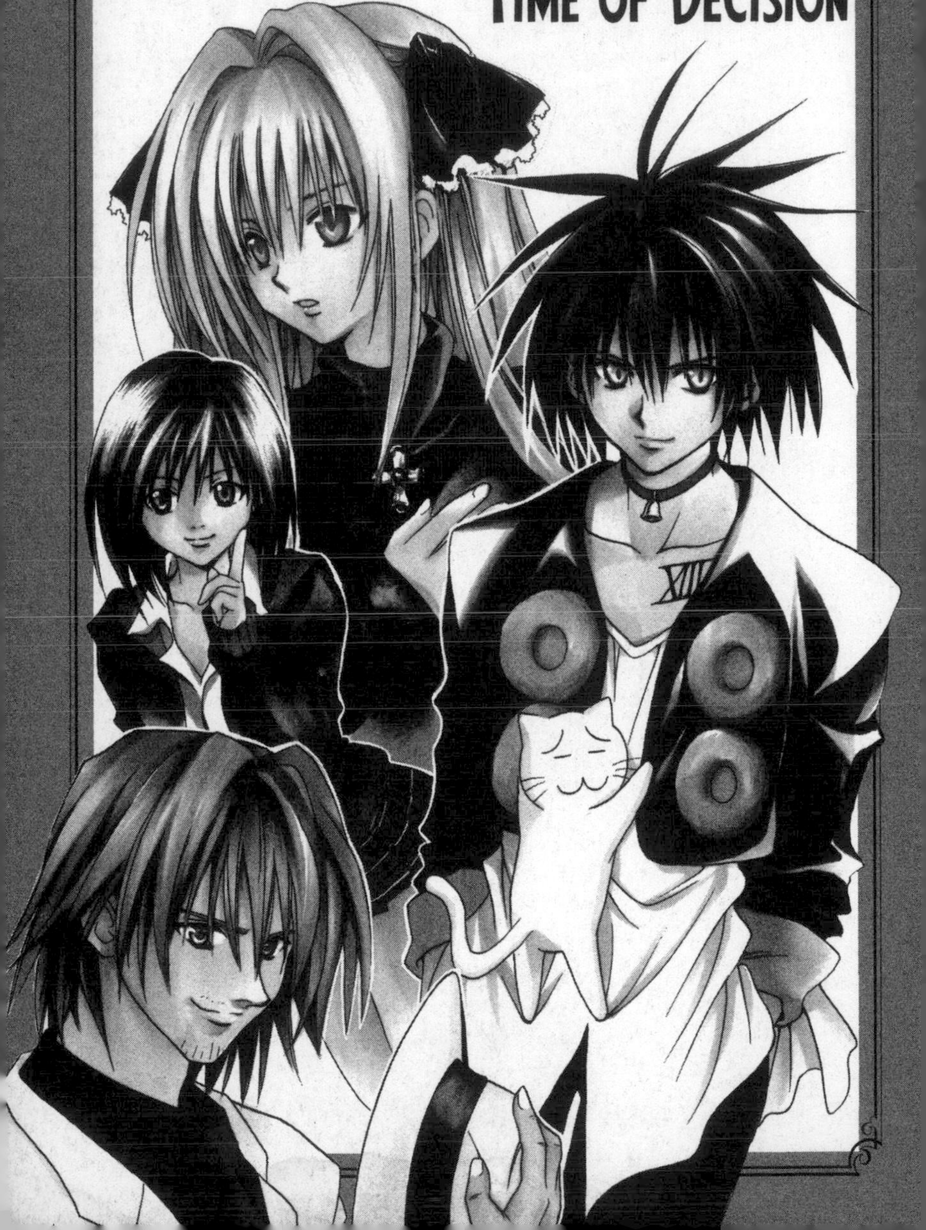

ブラック・キャット
BLACK CAT

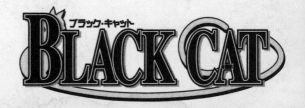

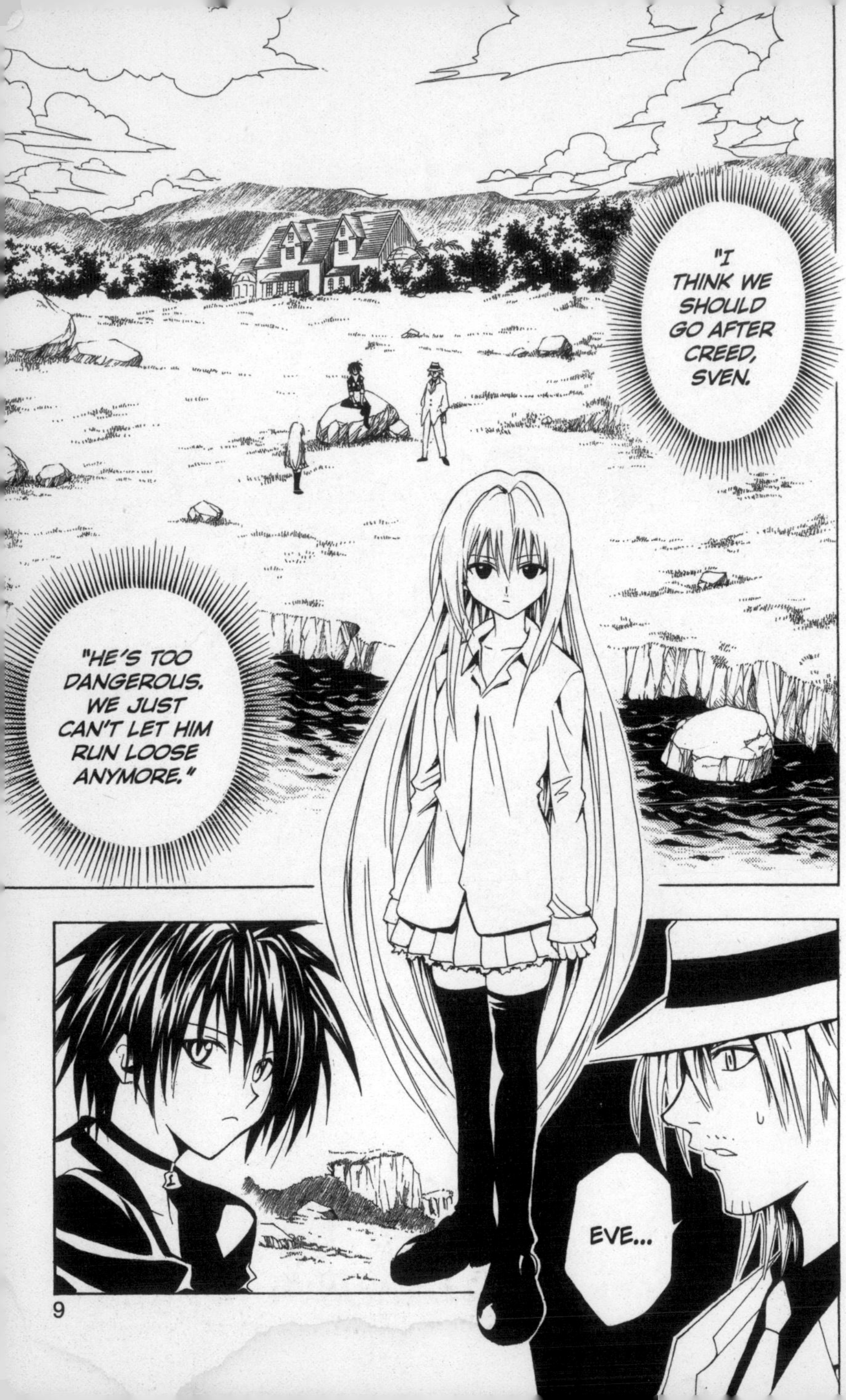
"I THINK WE SHOULD GO AFTER CREED, SVEN.
"HE'S TOO DANGEROUS. WE JUST CAN'T LET HIM RUN LOOSE ANYMORE."
EVE...

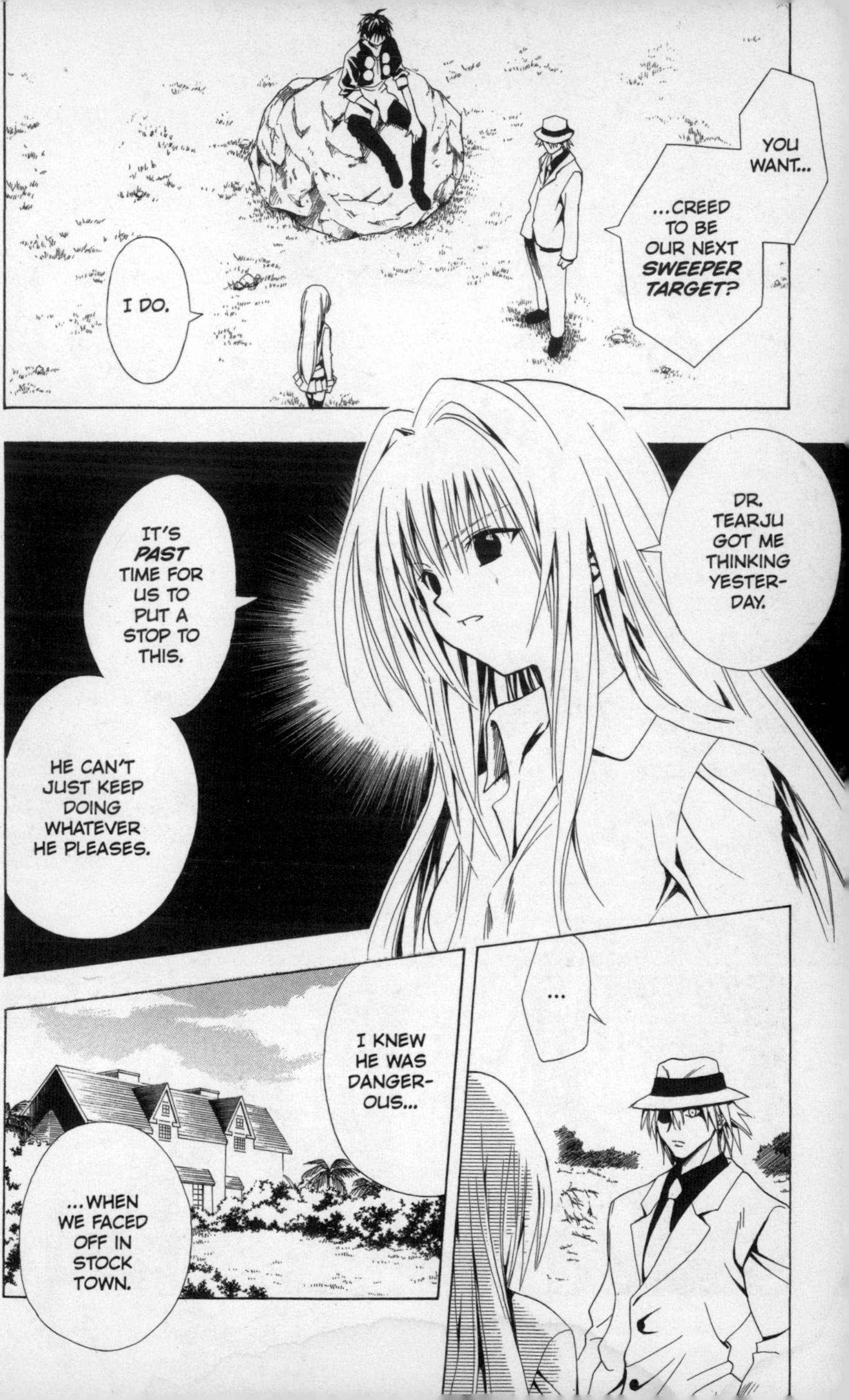
YOU WANT...
...CREED TO BE OUR NEXT *SWEEPER TARGET?*
I DO.
DR. TEARJU GOT ME THINKING YESTERDAY.
IT'S *PAST* TIME FOR US TO PUT A STOP TO THIS.
HE CAN'T JUST KEEP DOING WHATEVER HE PLEASES.
...
I KNEW HE WAS DANGEROUS...
...WHEN WE FACED OFF IN STOCK TOWN.

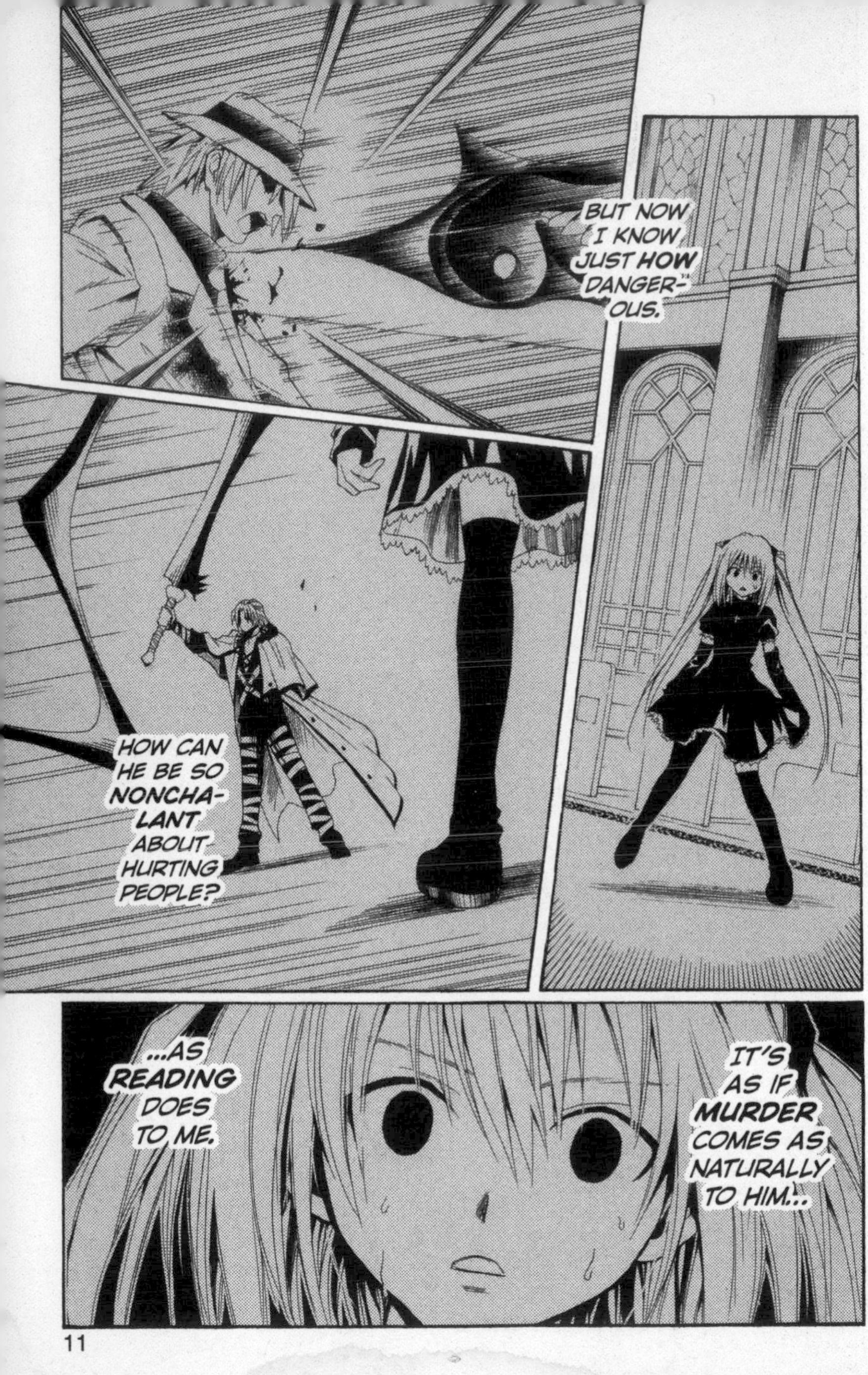
BUT NOW I KNOW JUST HOW DANGER-OUS.
HOW CAN HE BE SO NONCHA-LANT ABOUT HURTING PEOPLE?
IT'S AS IF MURDER COMES AS NATURALLY TO HIM...
...AS READING DOES TO ME.

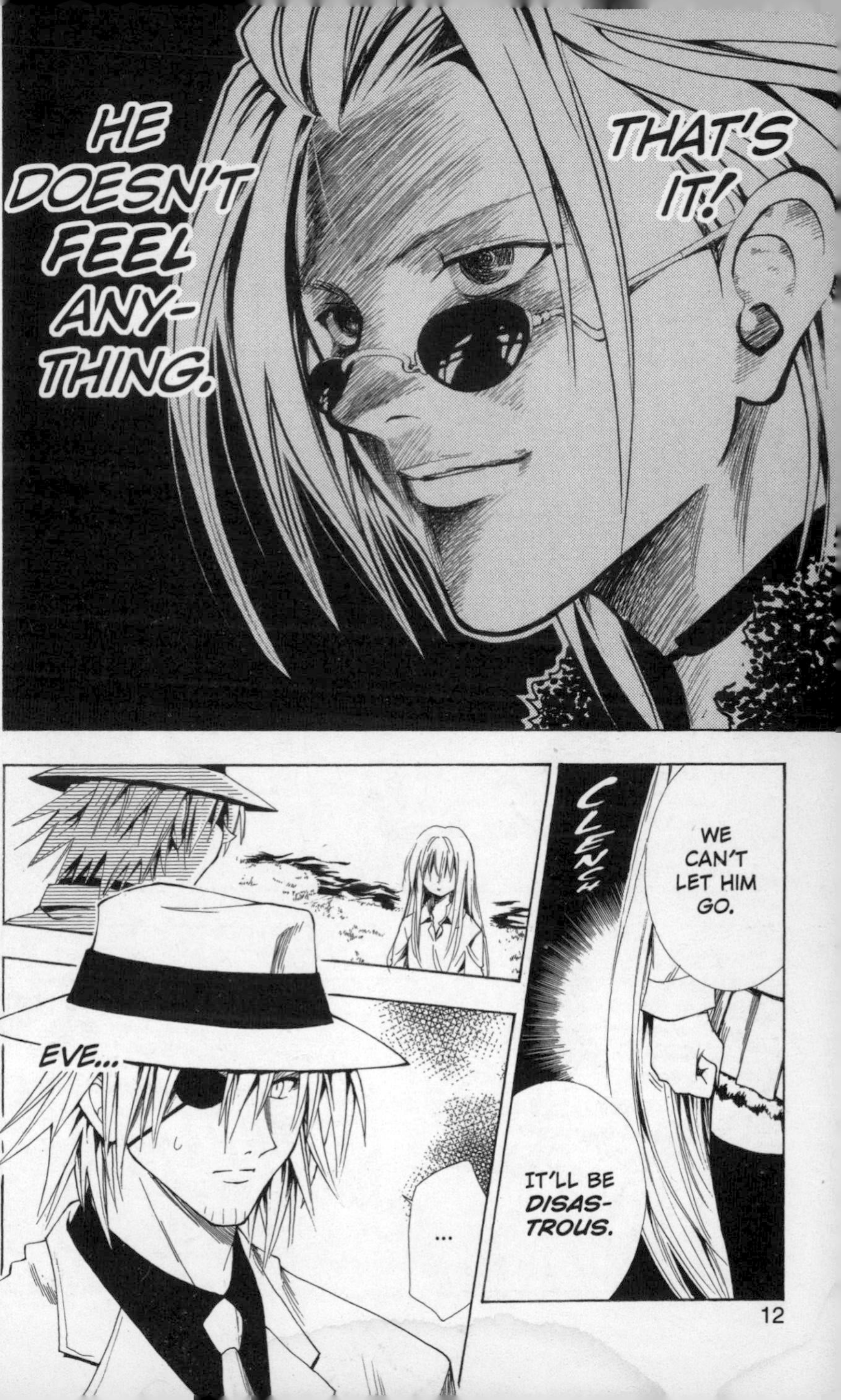
THAT'S IT!
HE DOESN'T FEEL ANY-THING.
CLENCH
WE CAN'T LET HIM GO.
IT'LL BE DISAS-TROUS.
EVE...
...

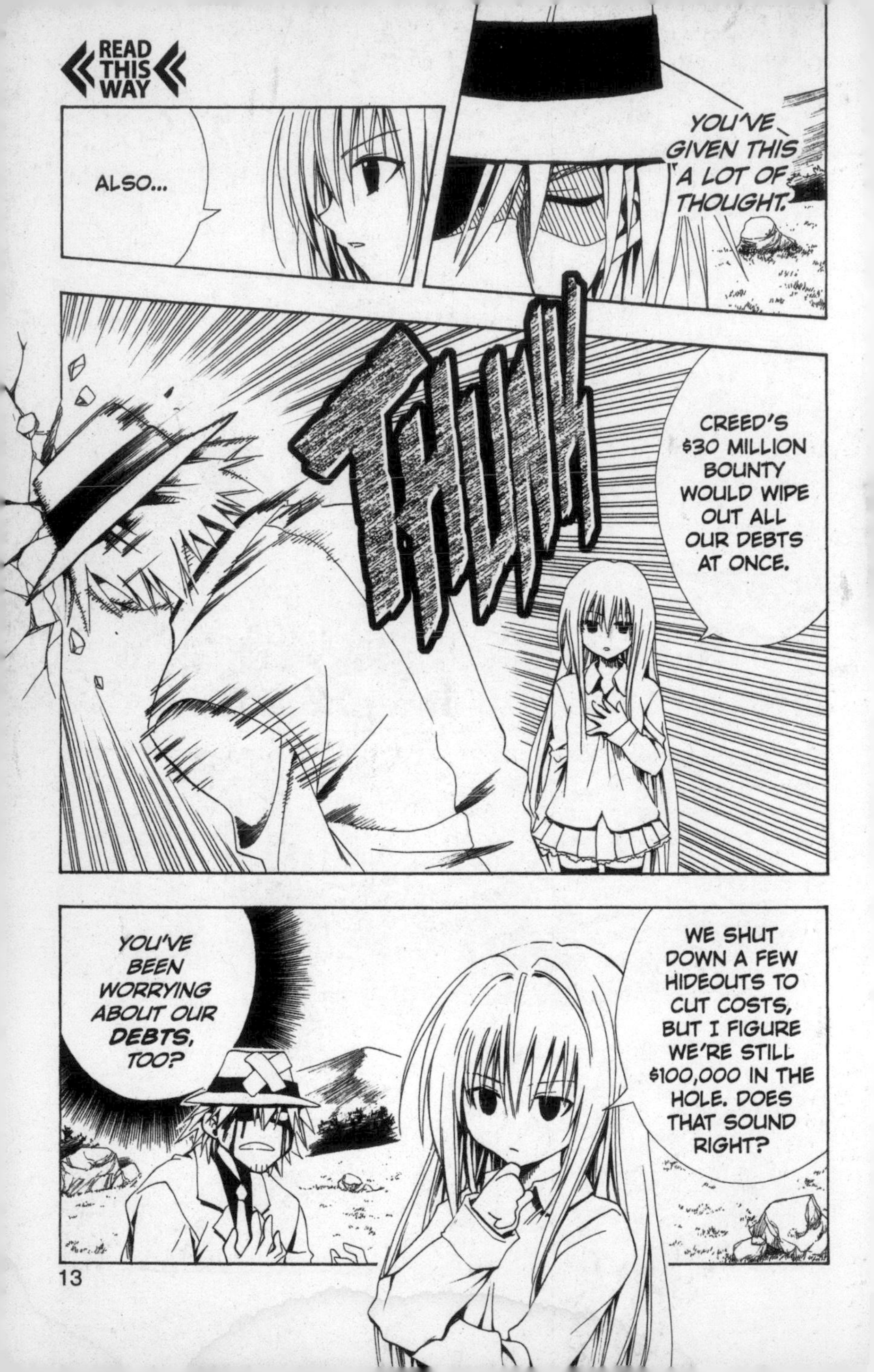
READ THIS WAY
YOU'VE GIVEN THIS A LOT OF THOUGHT.
ALSO...
THUNK
CREED'S $30 MILLION BOUNTY WOULD WIPE OUT ALL OUR DEBTS AT ONCE.
WE SHUT DOWN A FEW HIDEOUTS TO CUT COSTS, BUT I FIGURE WE'RE STILL $100,000 IN THE HOLE. DOES THAT SOUND RIGHT?
YOU'VE BEEN WORRYING ABOUT OUR DEBTS, TOO?

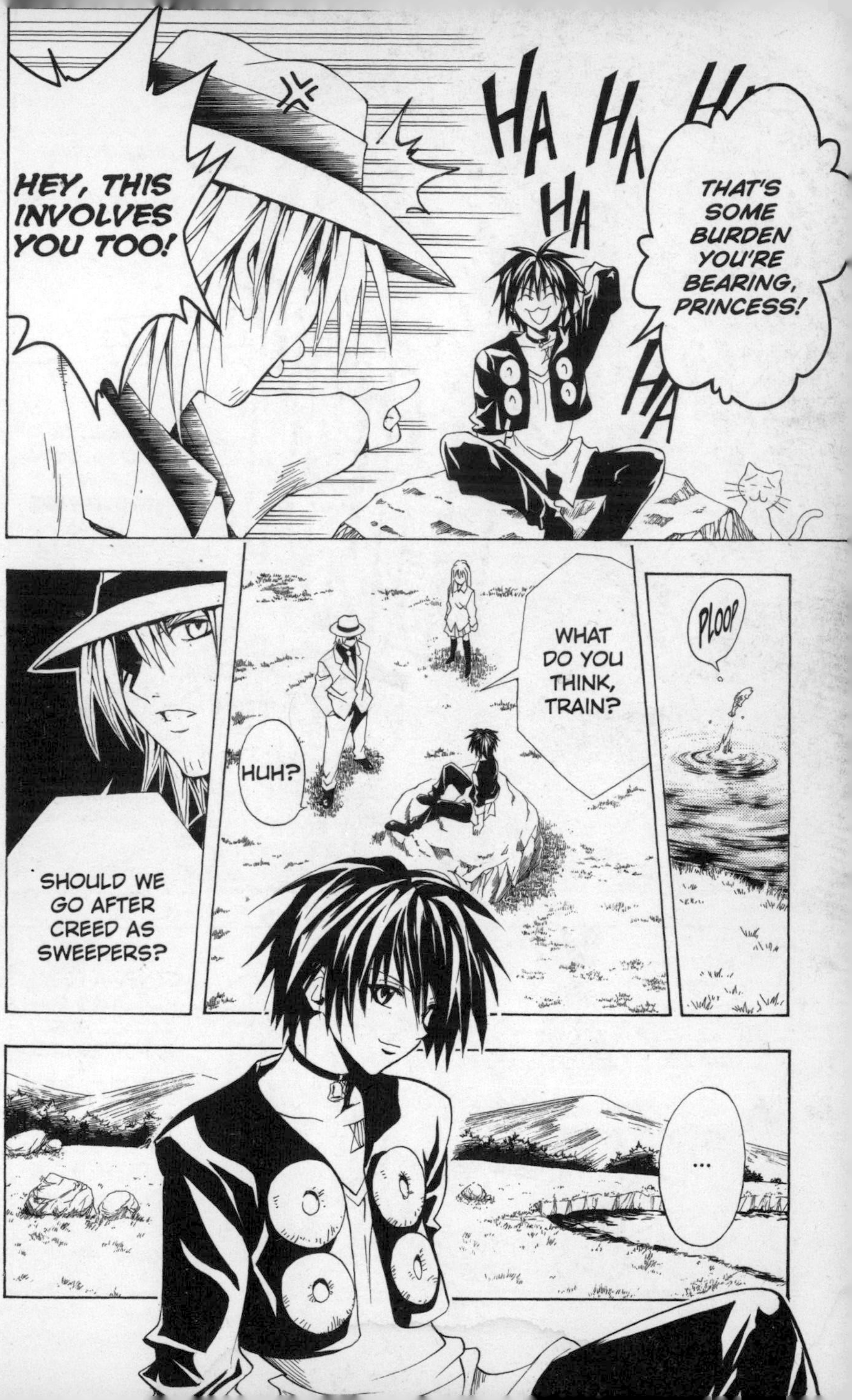
HA HA HA HA HA
THAT'S SOME BURDEN YOU'RE BEARING, PRINCESS!
HEY, THIS INVOLVES YOU TOO!
PLOOP
WHAT DO YOU THINK, TRAIN?
HUH?
SHOULD WE GO AFTER CREED AS SWEEPERS?
...

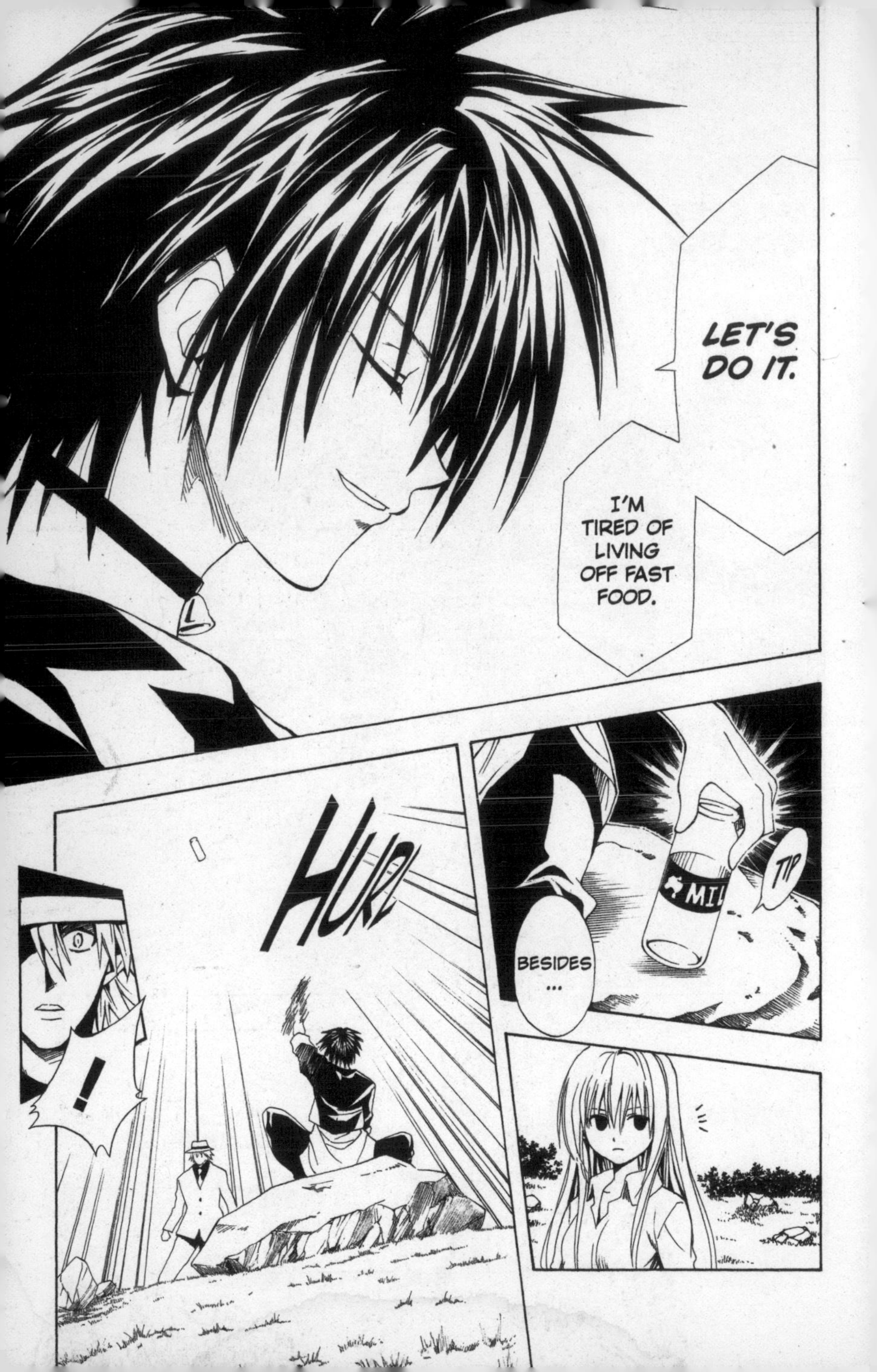
LET'S DO IT.
I'M TIRED OF LIVING OFF FAST FOOD.
TIP
BESIDES ...
HURL
!

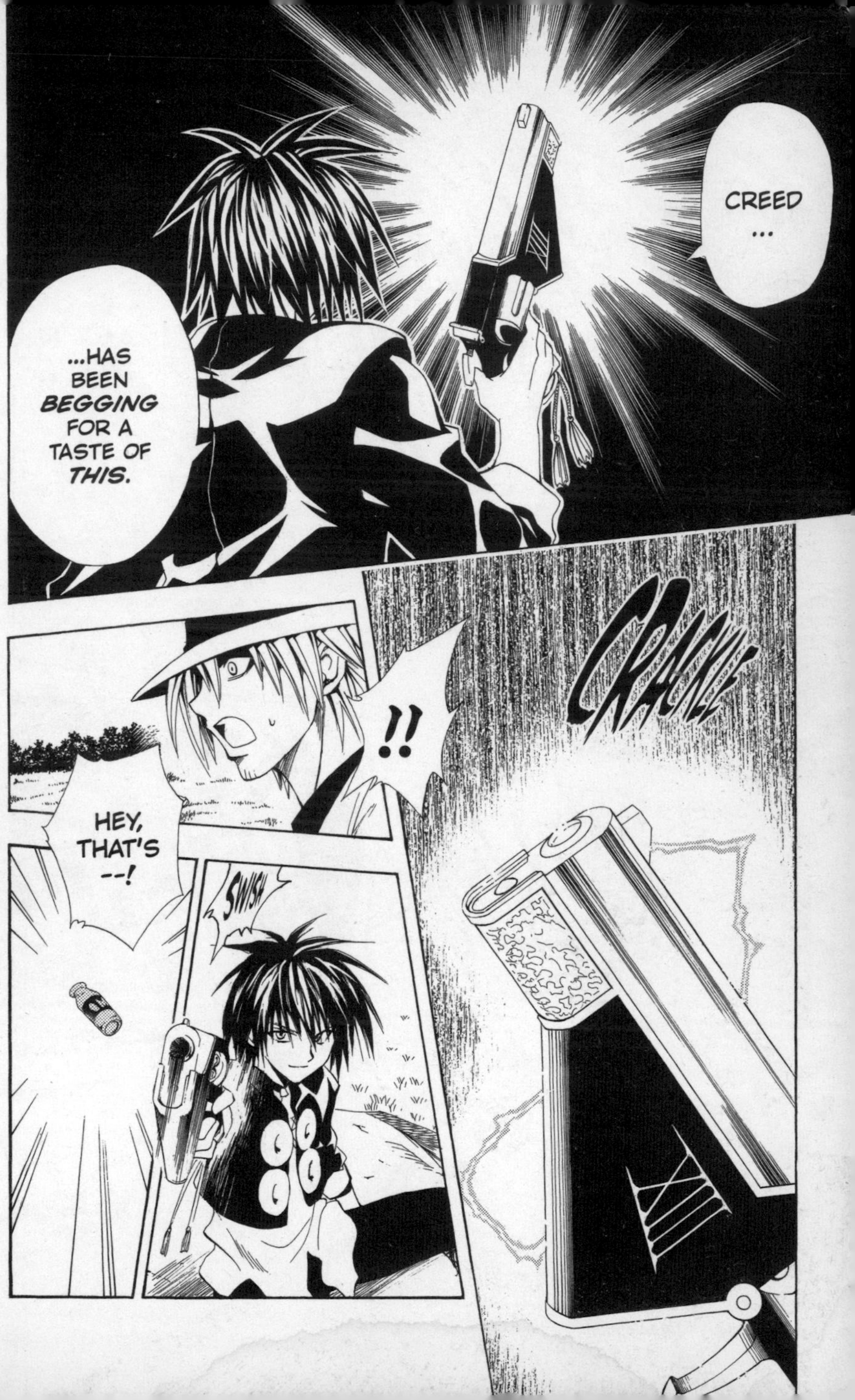
CREED ...
...HAS BEEN *BEGGING* FOR A TASTE OF *THIS.*
CRACKLE
!!
HEY, THAT'S --!
SWISH

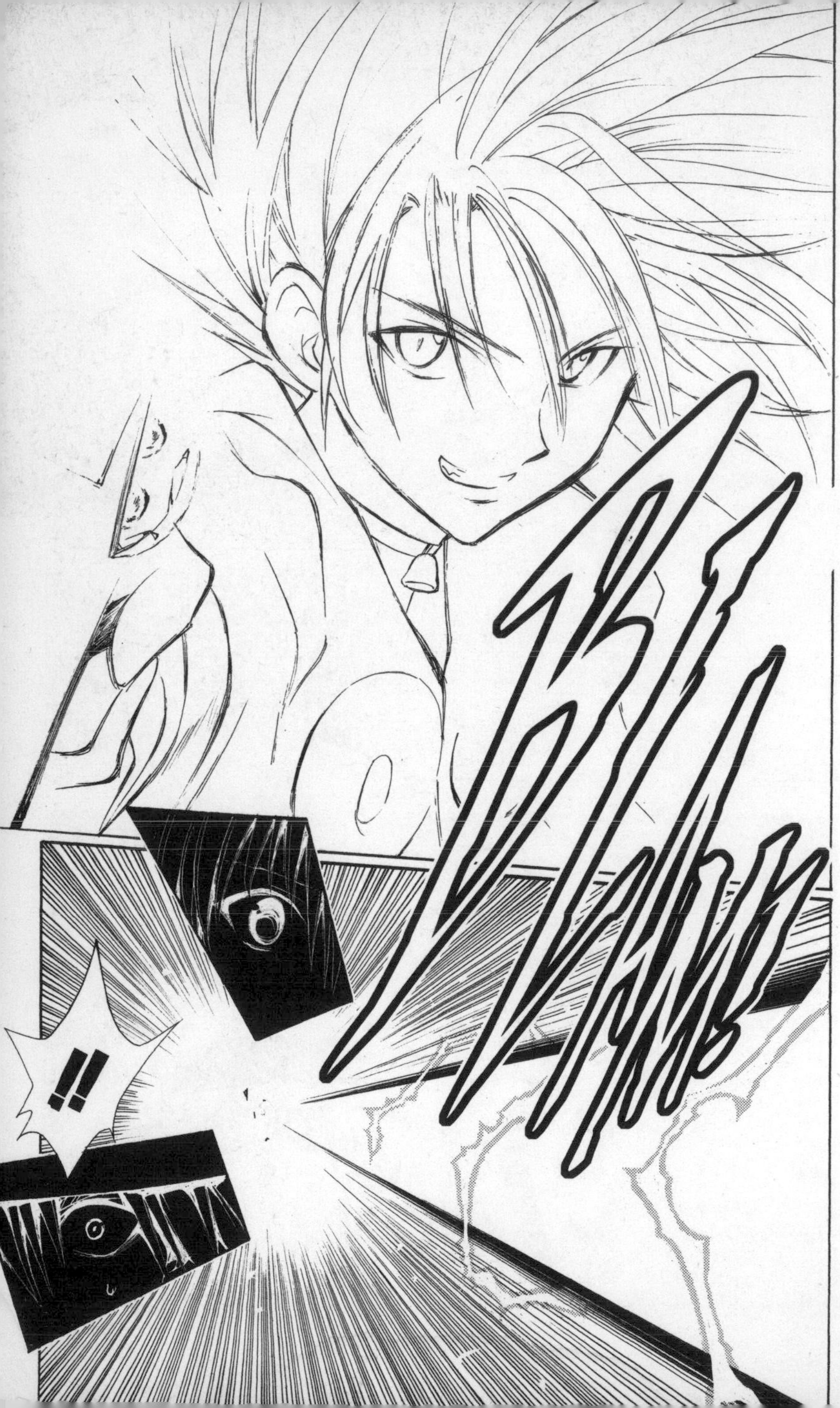
!!

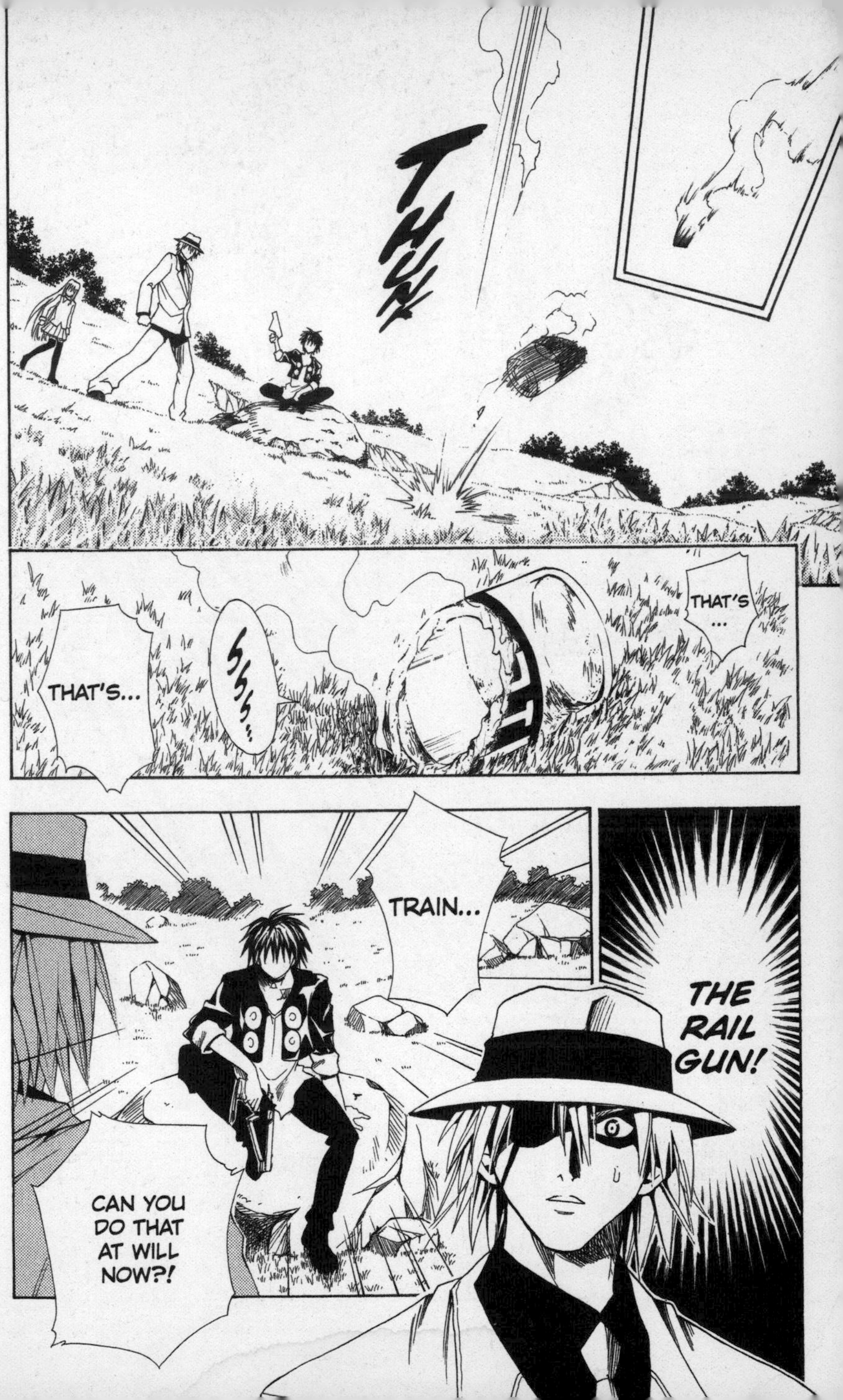
THUNK
THAT'S...
SSSS..
THAT'S...
THE RAIL GUN!
TRAIN...
CAN YOU DO THAT AT WILL NOW?!

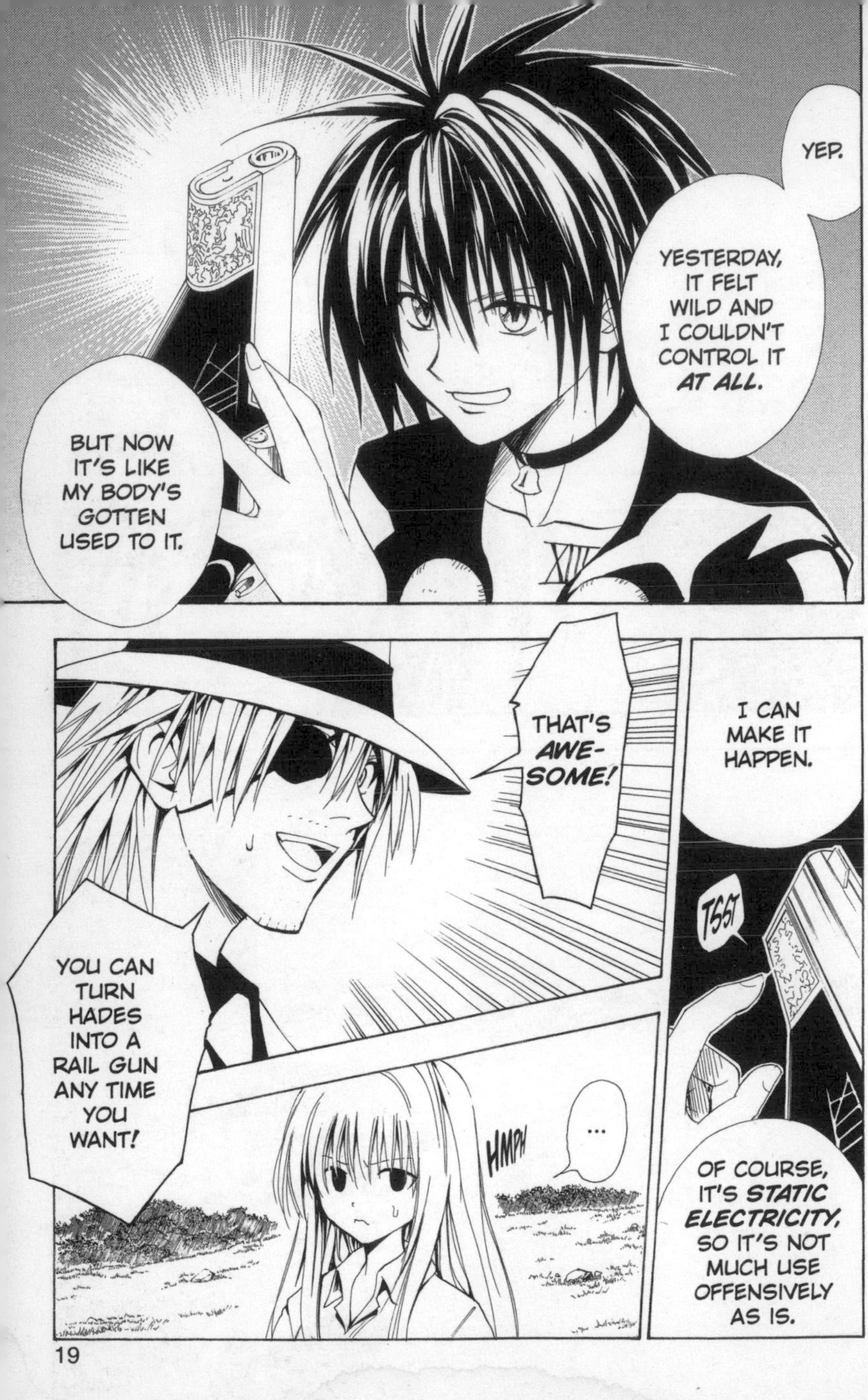
YEP.
YESTERDAY, IT FELT WILD AND I COULDN'T CONTROL IT *AT ALL.*
BUT NOW IT'S LIKE MY BODY'S GOTTEN USED TO IT.
I CAN MAKE IT HAPPEN.
TSST
OF COURSE, IT'S *STATIC ELECTRICITY,* SO IT'S NOT MUCH USE OFFENSIVELY AS IS.
THAT'S *AWE-SOME!*
YOU CAN TURN HADES INTO A RAIL GUN ANY TIME YOU WANT!
HMPH
...

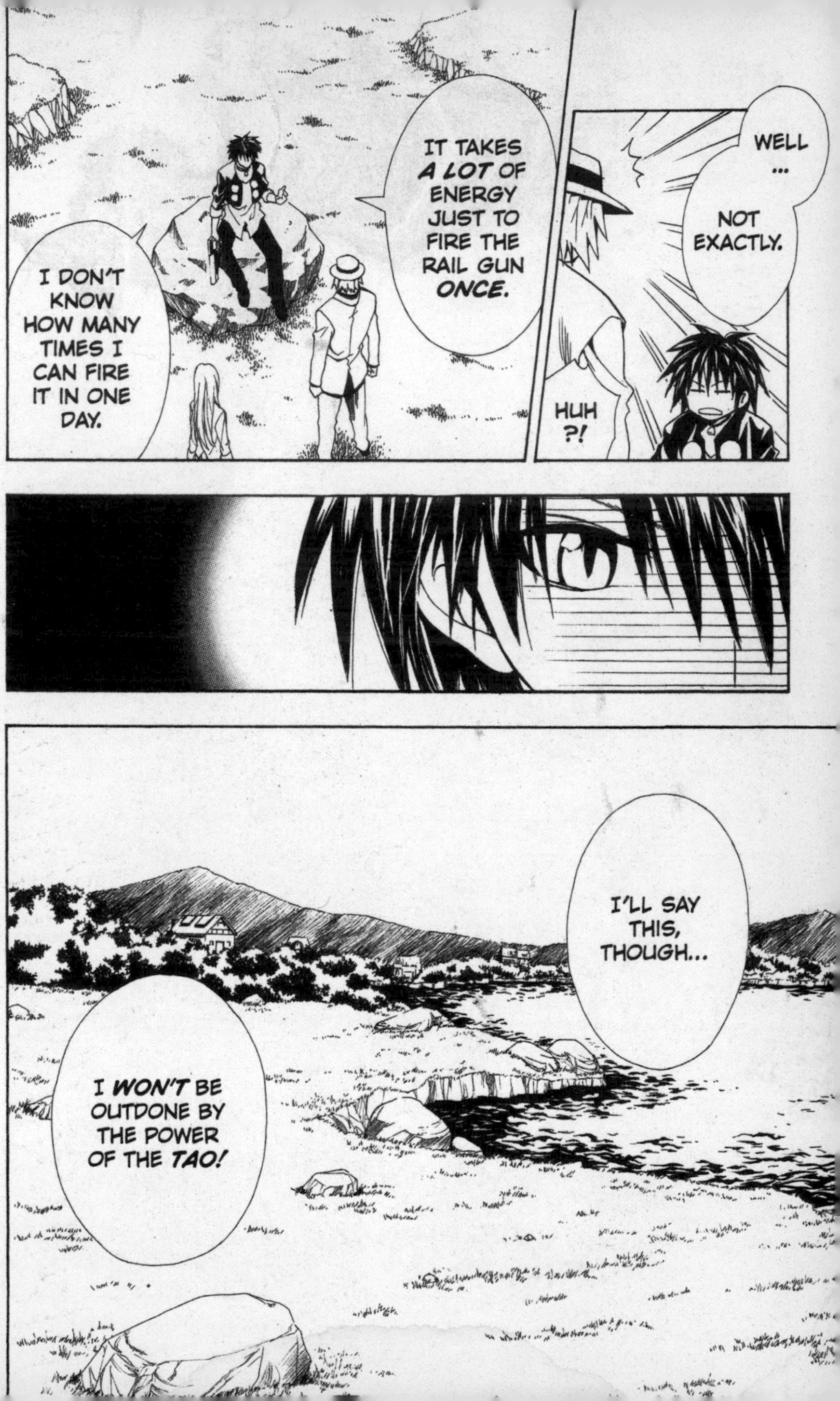
WELL ... NOT EXACTLY.
HUH ?!
IT TAKES *A LOT* OF ENERGY JUST TO FIRE THE RAIL GUN *ONCE.*
I DON'T KNOW HOW MANY TIMES I CAN FIRE IT IN ONE DAY.
I'LL SAY THIS, THOUGH...
I *WON'T* BE OUTDONE BY THE POWER OF THE *TAO!*

READ THIS WAY

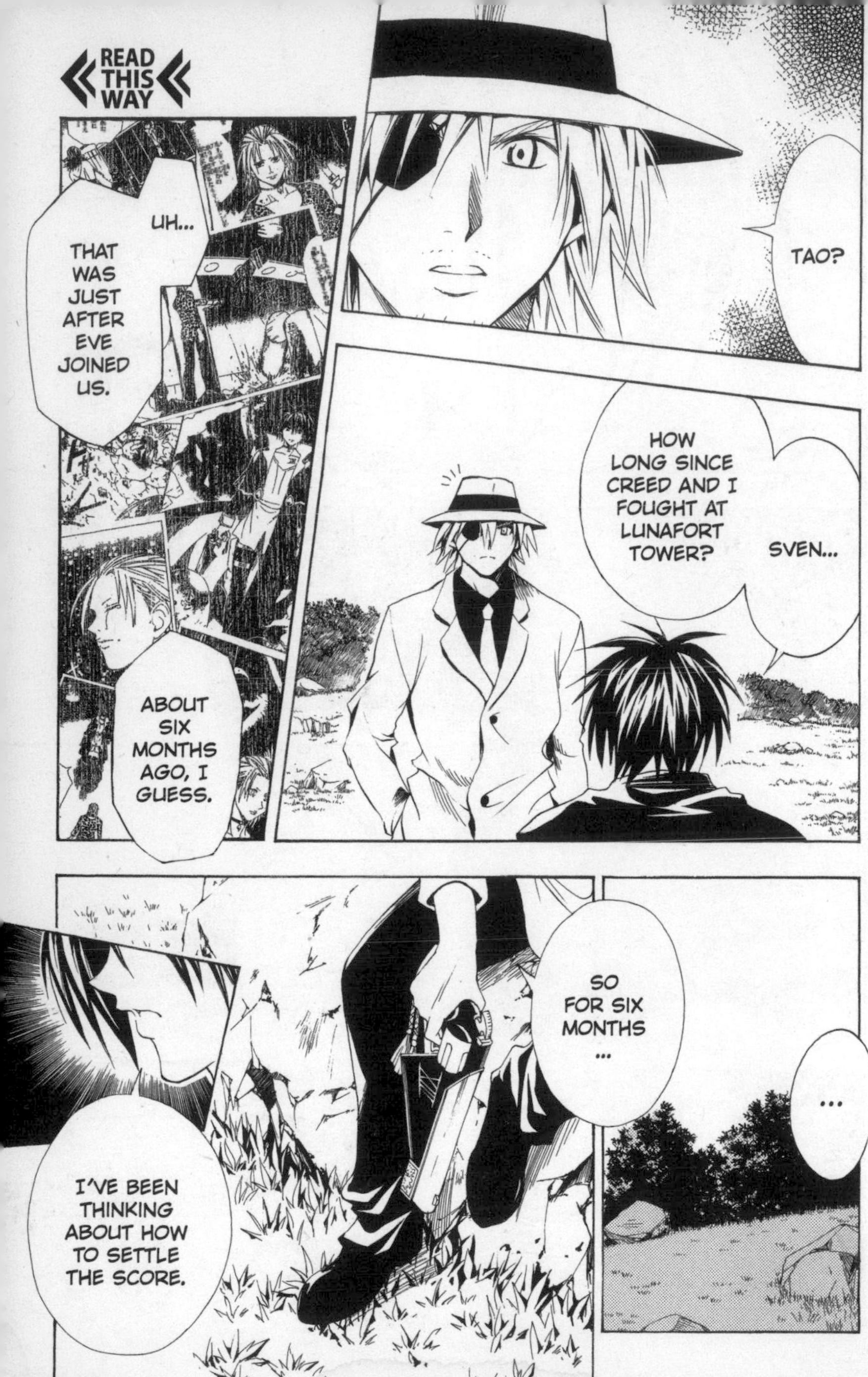
TAO?
SVEN...
HOW LONG SINCE CREED AND I FOUGHT AT LUNAFORT TOWER?
UH... THAT WAS JUST AFTER EVE JOINED US.
ABOUT SIX MONTHS AGO, I GUESS.
...
SO FOR SIX MONTHS ...
I'VE BEEN THINKING ABOUT HOW TO SETTLE THE SCORE.

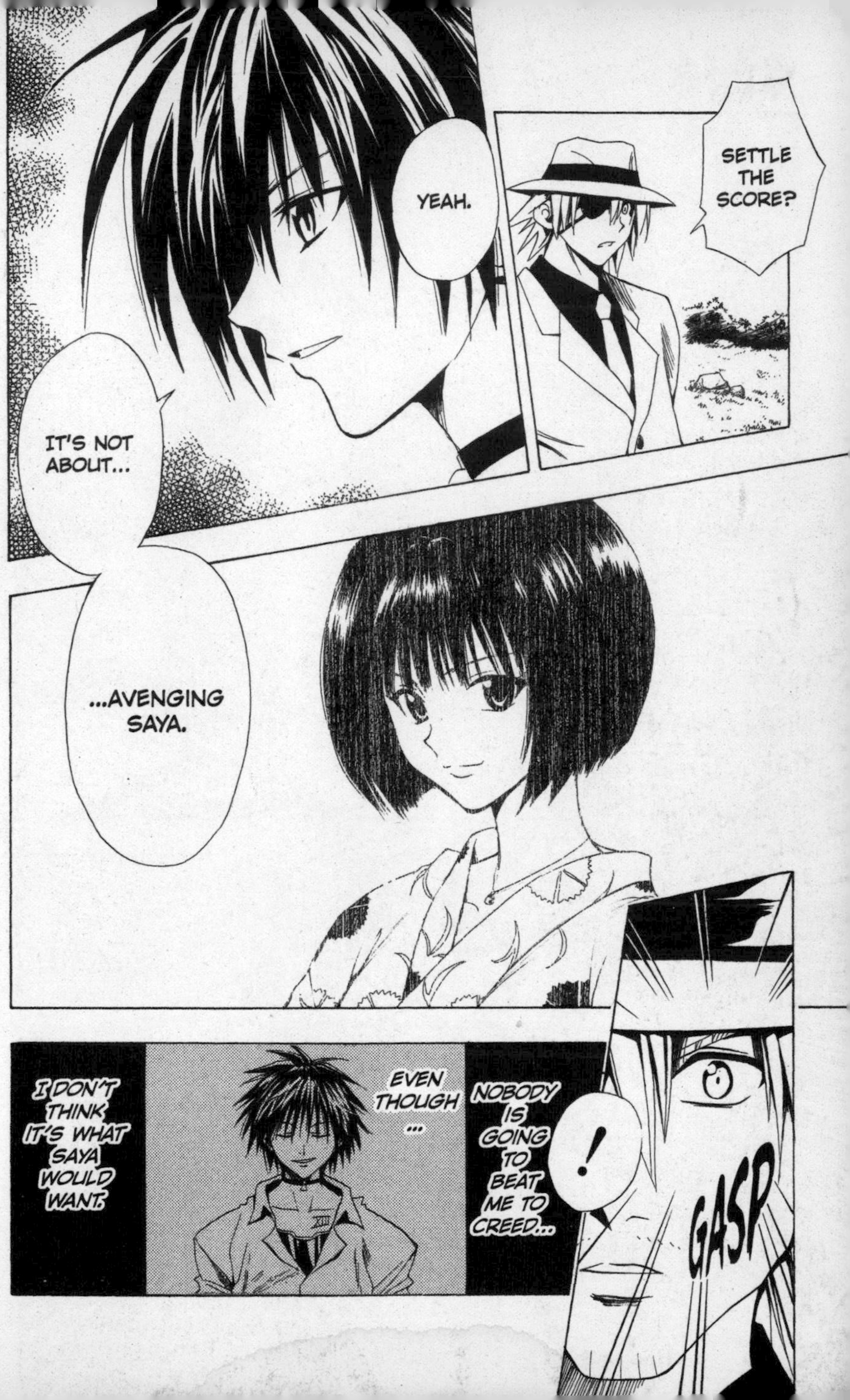
SETTLE THE SCORE?
YEAH.
IT'S NOT ABOUT...
...AVENGING SAYA.
!
GASP
NOBODY IS GOING TO BEAT ME TO CREED...
EVEN THOUGH ...
I DON'T THINK IT'S WHAT SAYA WOULD WANT.

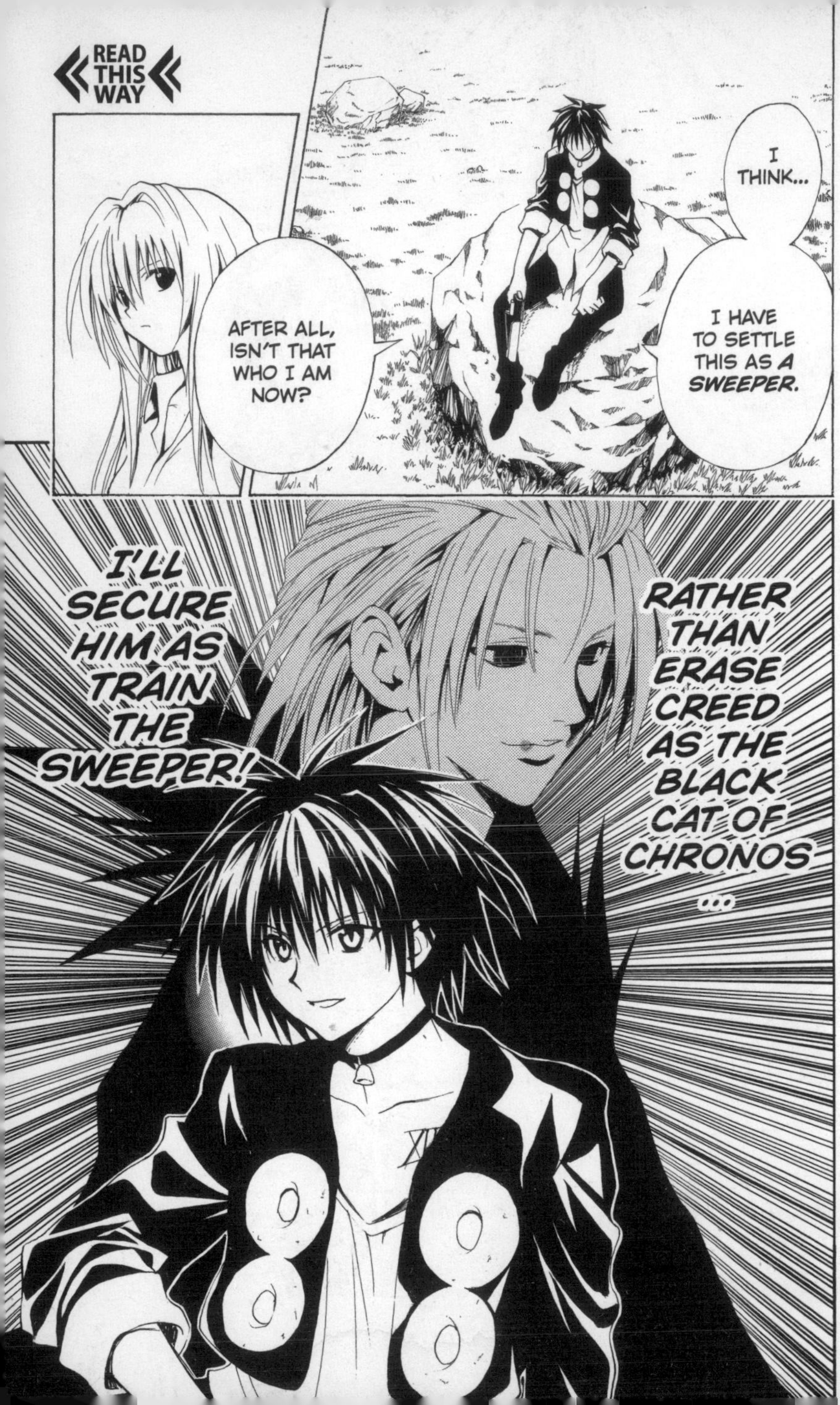
READ THIS WAY
I THINK...
I HAVE TO SETTLE THIS AS A SWEEPER.
AFTER ALL, ISN'T THAT WHO I AM NOW?
RATHER THAN ERASE CREED AS THE BLACK CAT OF CHRONOS...
I'LL SECURE HIM AS TRAIN THE SWEEPER!

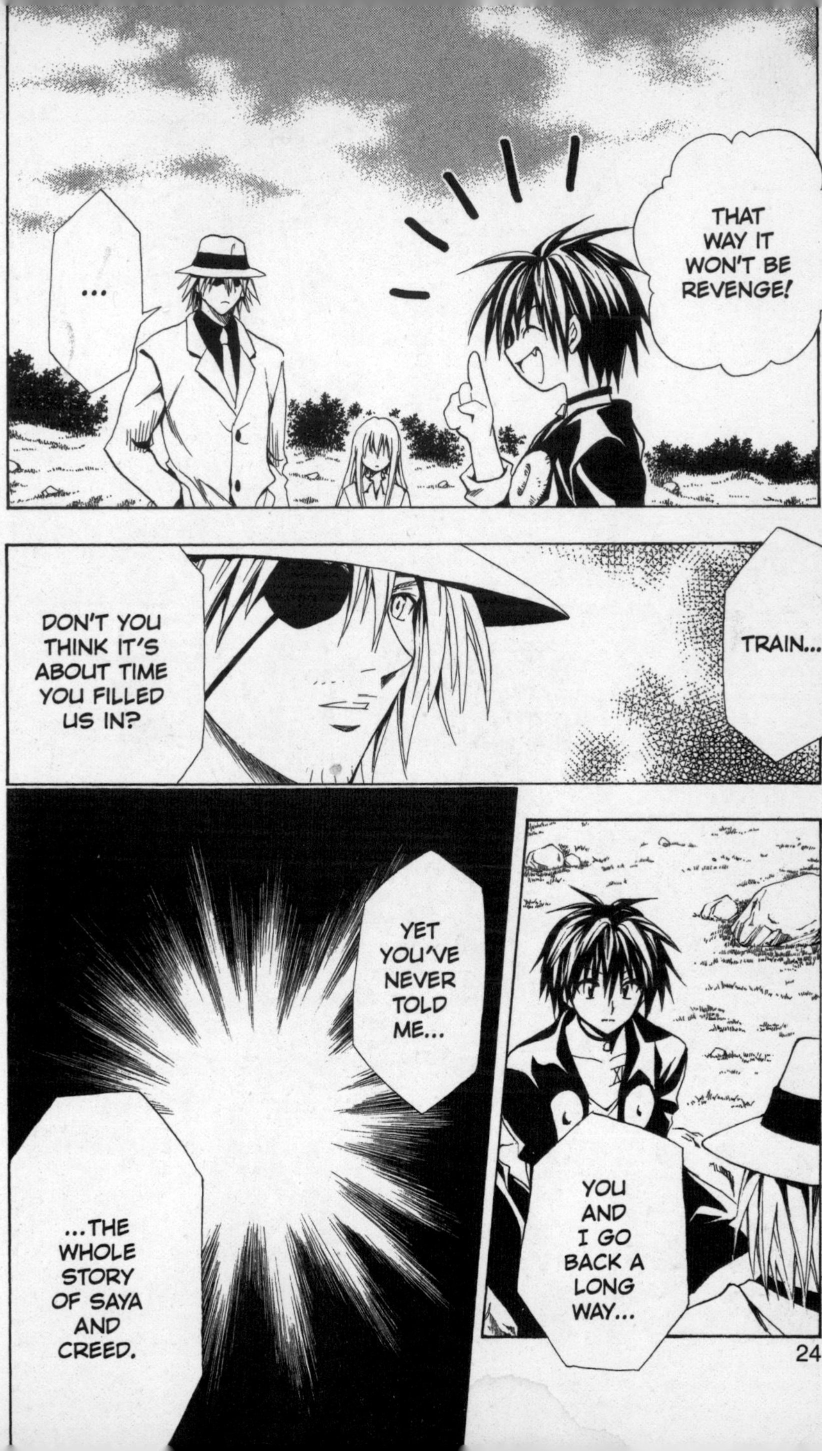
THAT WAY IT WON'T BE REVENGE!
...
TRAIN...
DON'T YOU THINK IT'S ABOUT TIME YOU FILLED US IN?
YOU AND I GO BACK A LONG WAY...
YET YOU'VE NEVER TOLD ME...
...THE WHOLE STORY OF SAYA AND CREED.

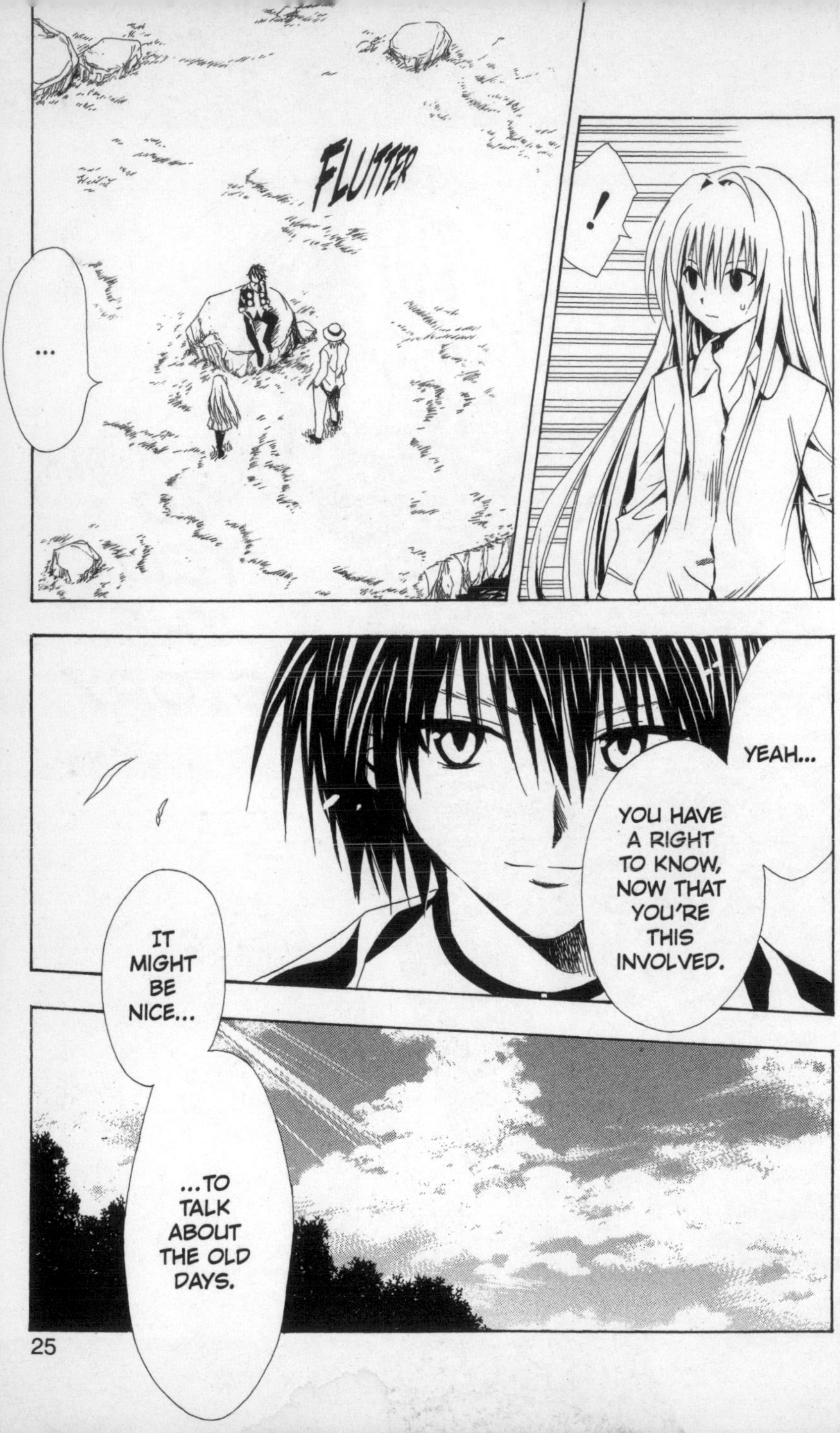
!
FLUTTER
...
YEAH...
YOU HAVE A RIGHT TO KNOW, NOW THAT YOU'RE THIS INVOLVED.
IT MIGHT BE NICE...
...TO TALK ABOUT THE OLD DAYS.

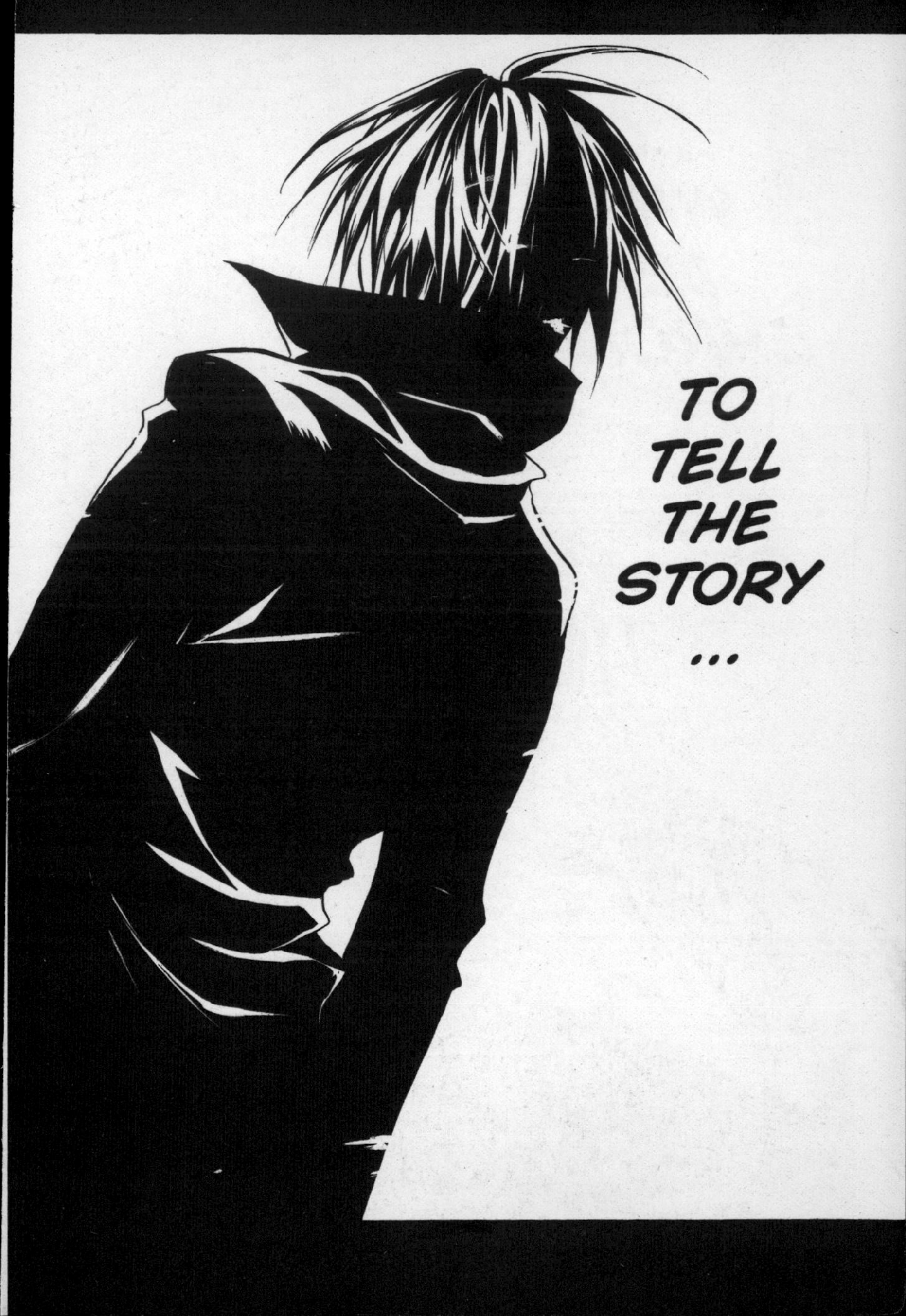
TO TELL THE STORY ...

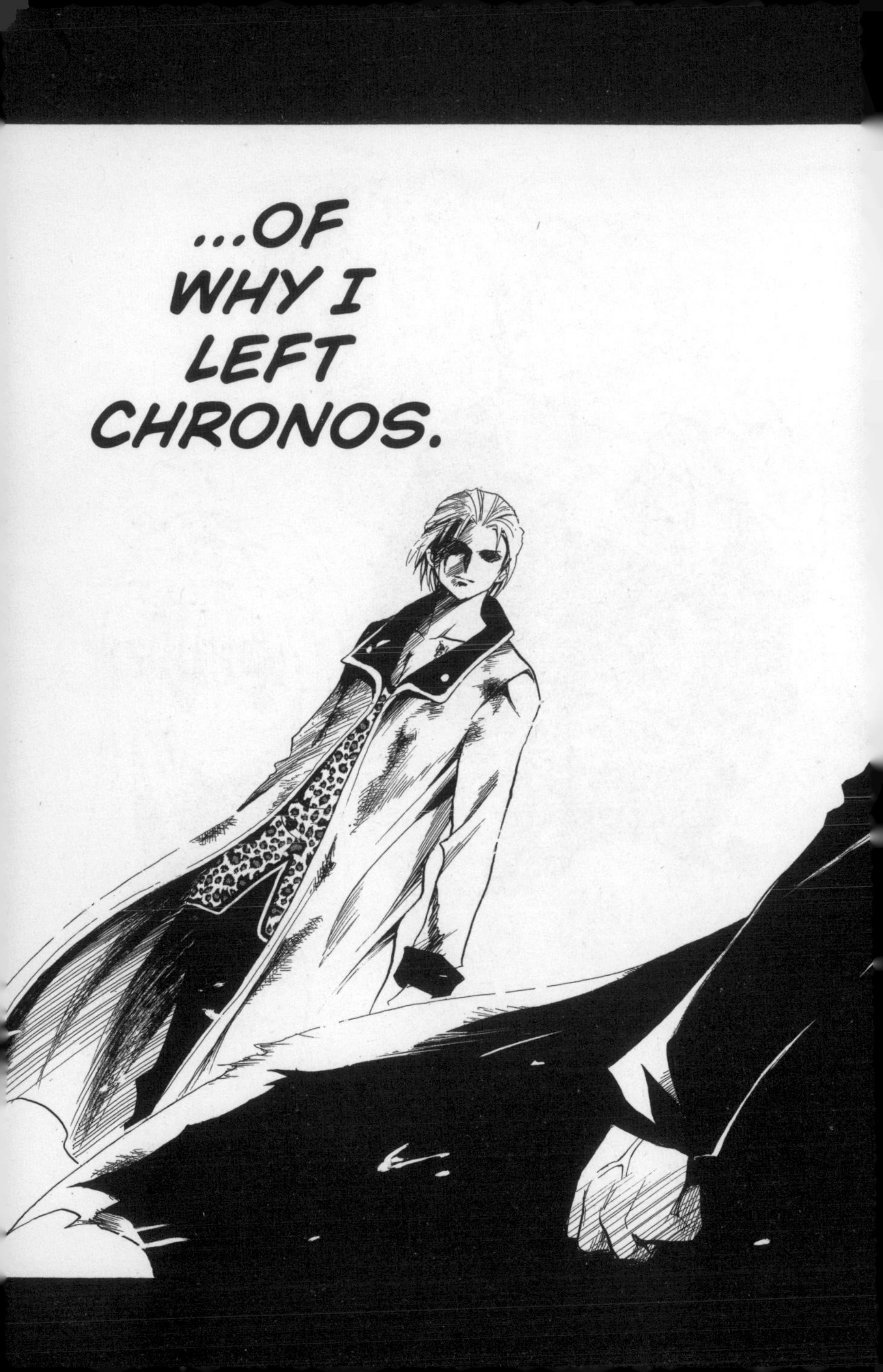
...OF WHY I LEFT CHRONOS.

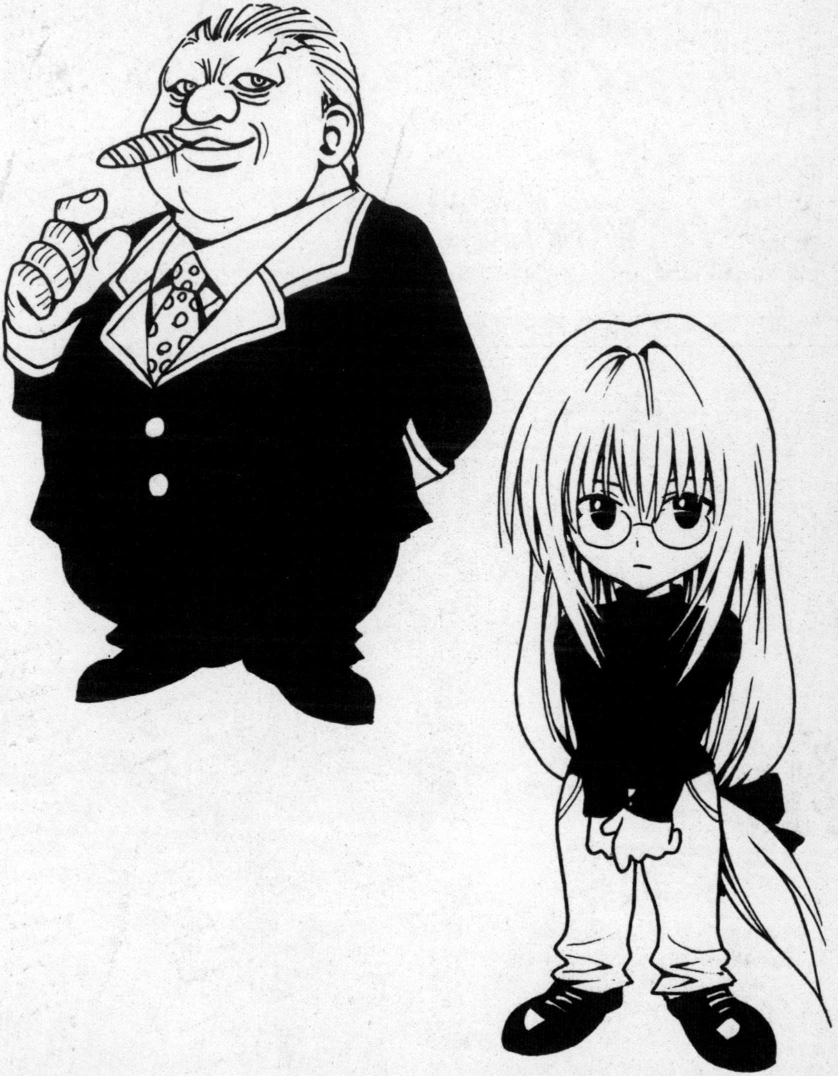

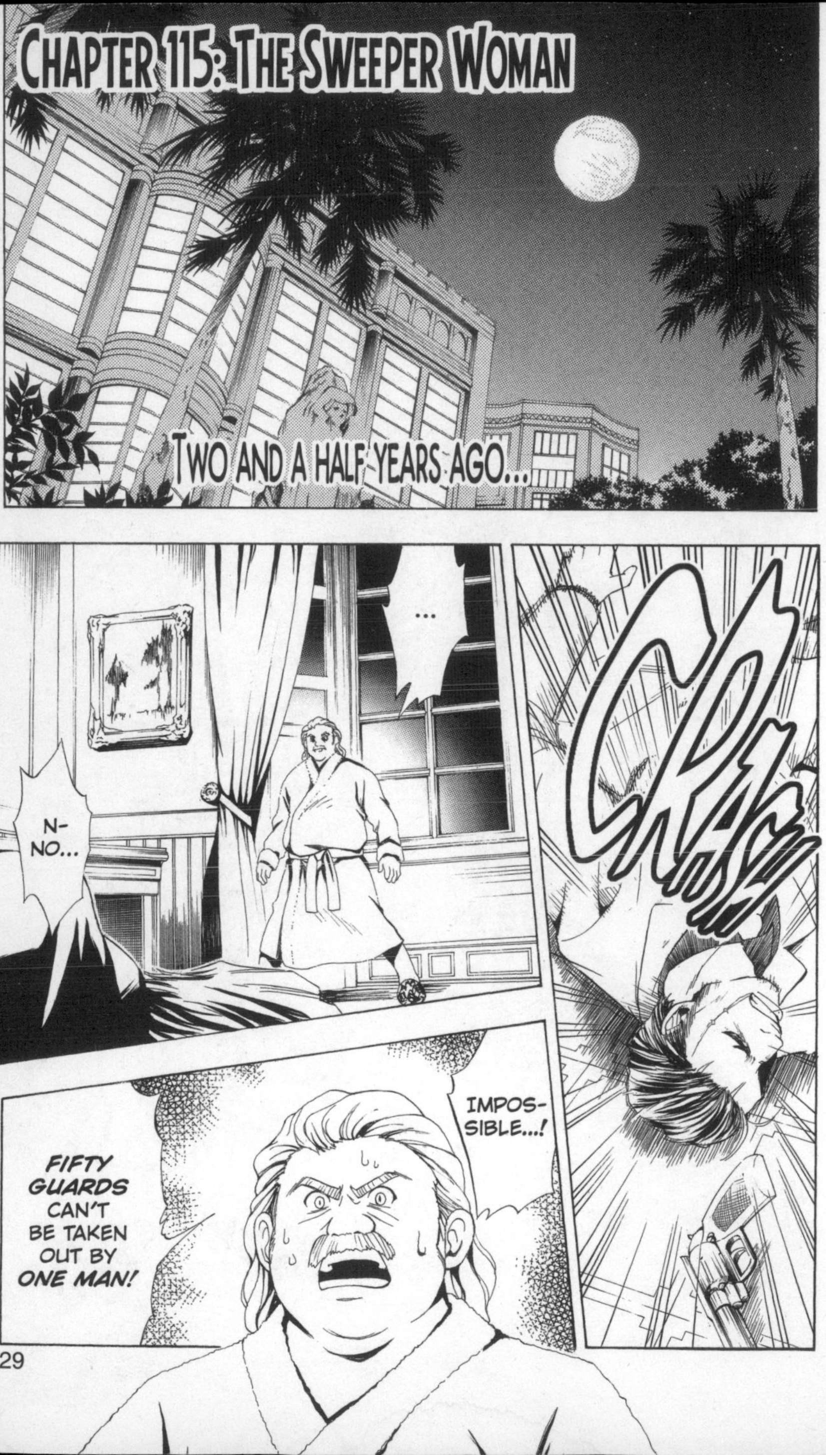
Chapter 115: The Sweeper Woman
Two and a half years ago...
...
N-NO...
IMPOSSIBLE...!
FIFTY GUARDS CAN'T BE TAKEN OUT BY ONE MAN!

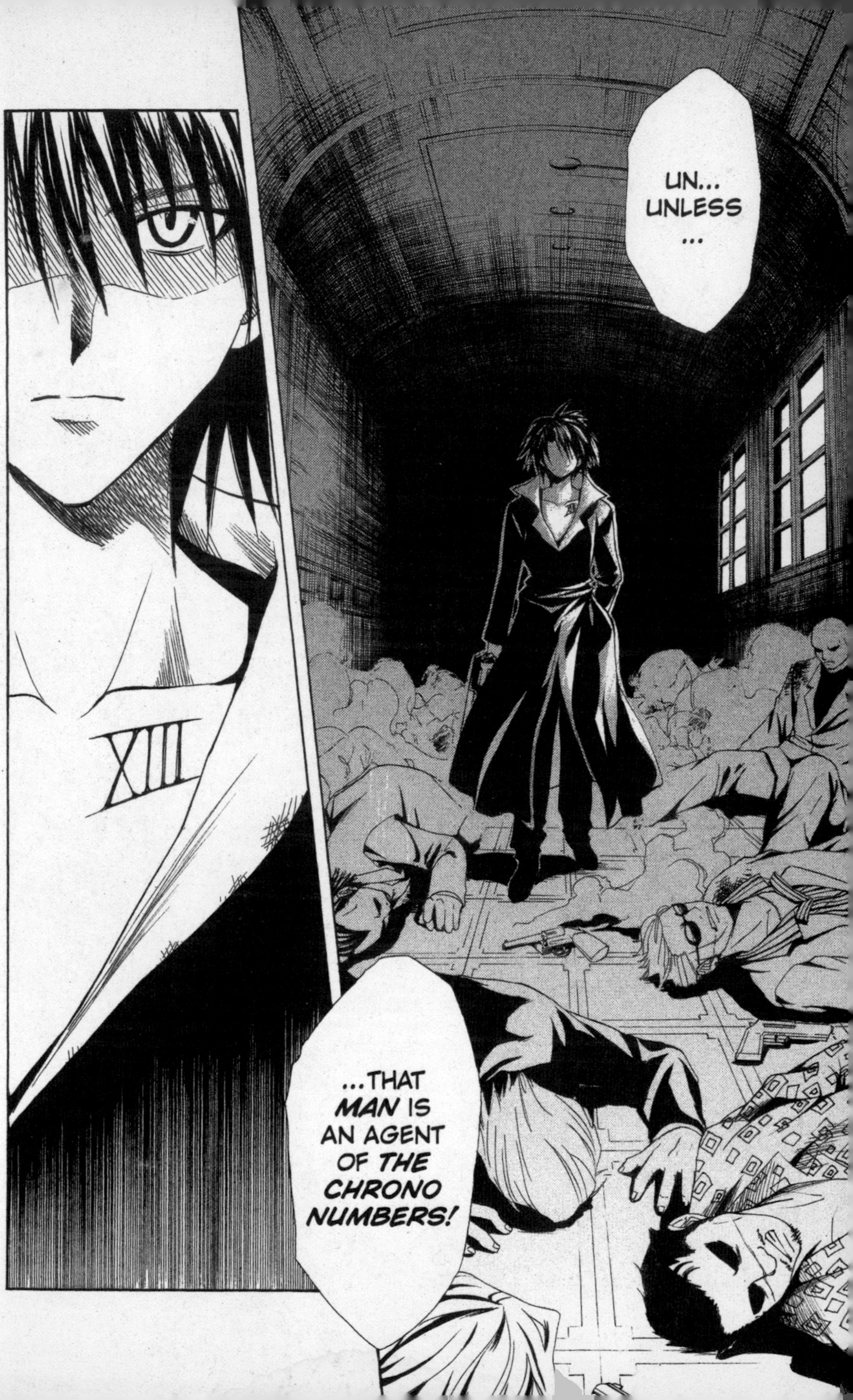
UN... UNLESS ...
...THAT *MAN* IS AN AGENT OF *THE CHRONO NUMBERS!*
XIII

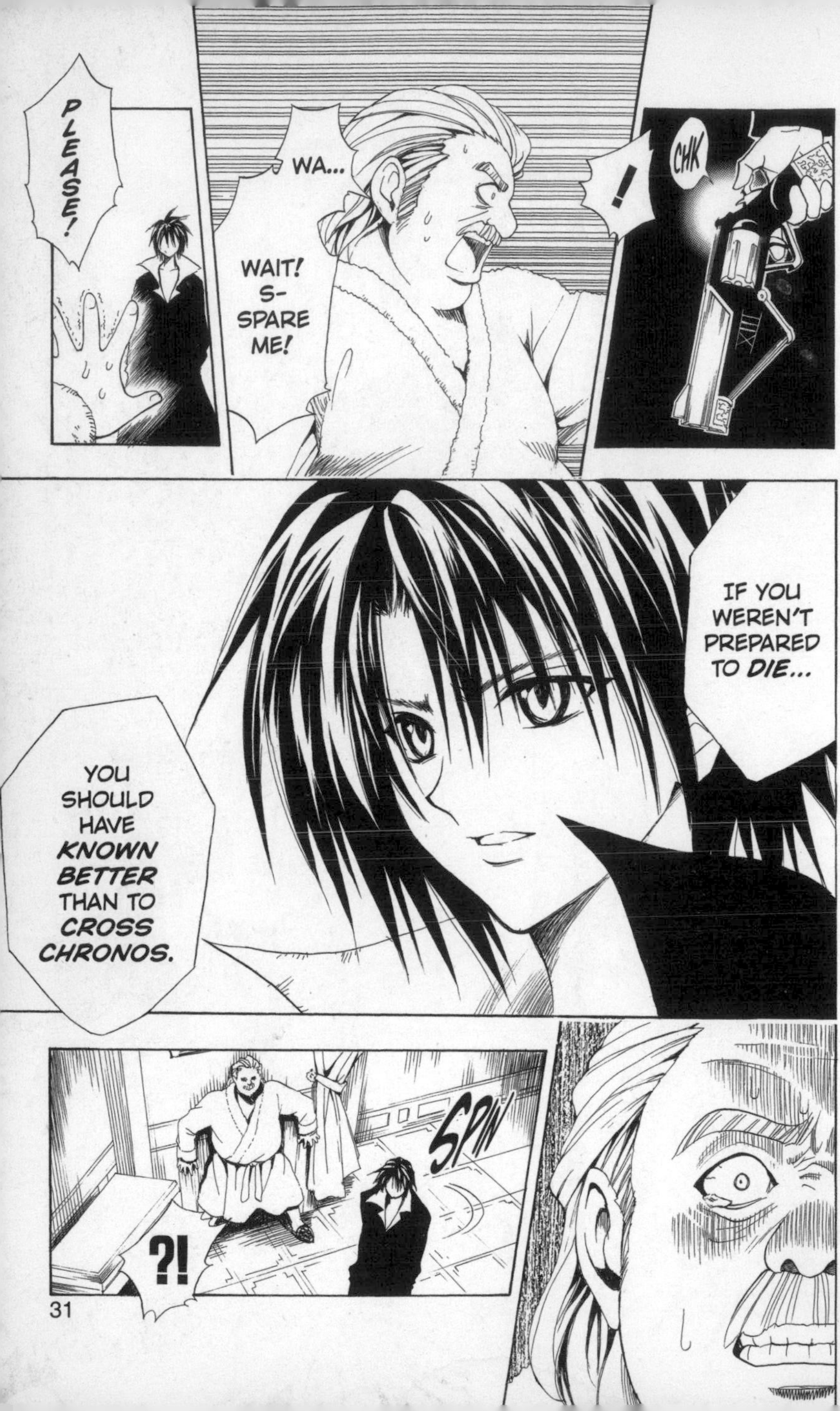
CHK
!
WA...
WAIT! S-SPARE ME!
PLEASE!
IF YOU WEREN'T PREPARED TO DIE...
YOU SHOULD HAVE KNOWN BETTER THAN TO CROSS CHRONOS.
SPIN
?!

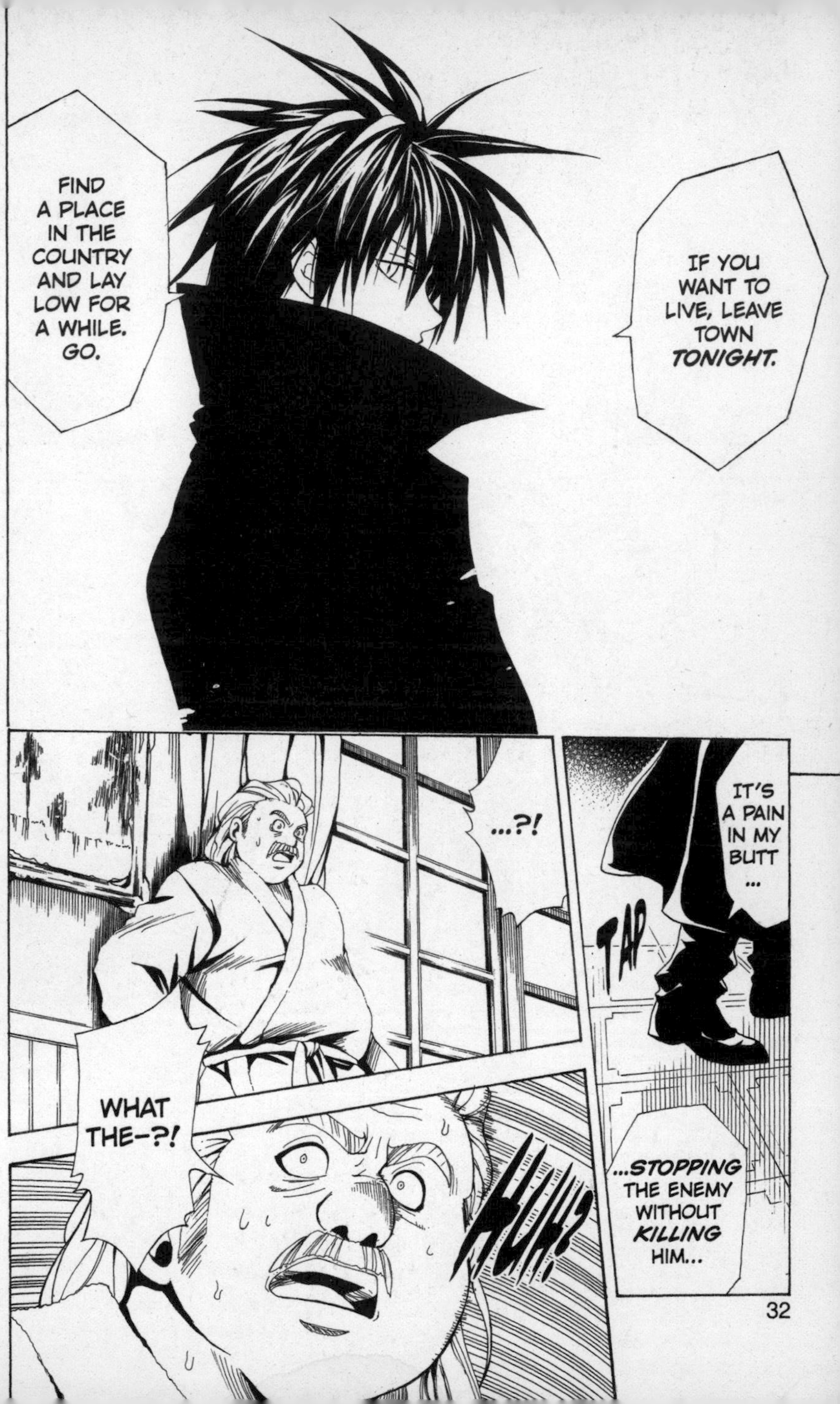
IF YOU WANT TO LIVE, LEAVE TOWN *TONIGHT.*
FIND A PLACE IN THE COUNTRY AND LAY LOW FOR A WHILE. GO.
IT'S A PAIN IN MY BUTT ...
TAP
...*STOPPING* THE ENEMY WITHOUT *KILLING* HIM...
...?!
WHAT THE-?!
HUH?!

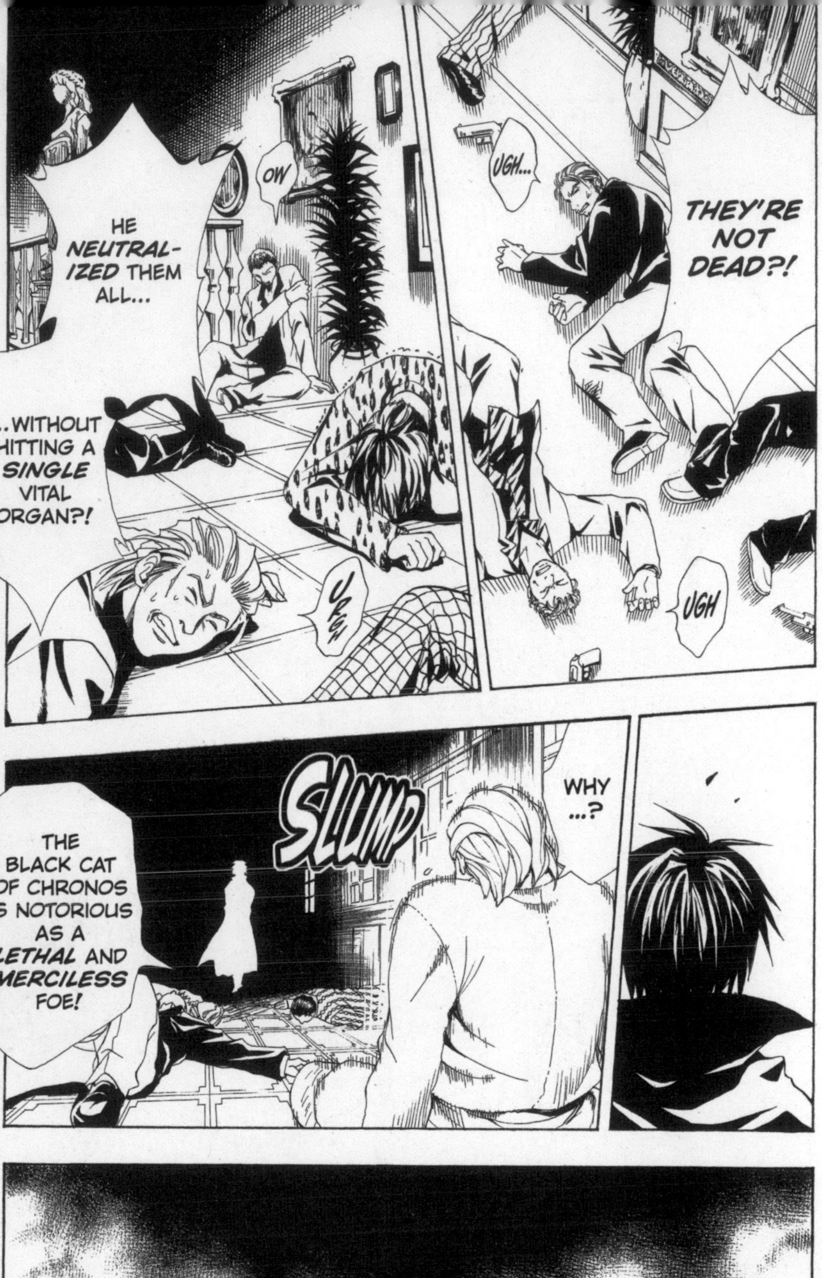

UGH...
THEY'RE NOT DEAD?!
UGH
OW
HE NEUTRALIZED THEM ALL...
...WITHOUT HITTING A SINGLE VITAL ORGAN?!
URGH
WHY ...?
SLUMP
THE BLACK CAT OF CHRONOS IS NOTORIOUS AS A LETHAL AND MERCILESS FOE!

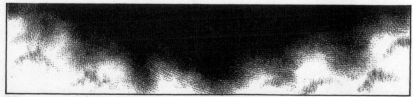

Chapter 115: The Sweeper Woman

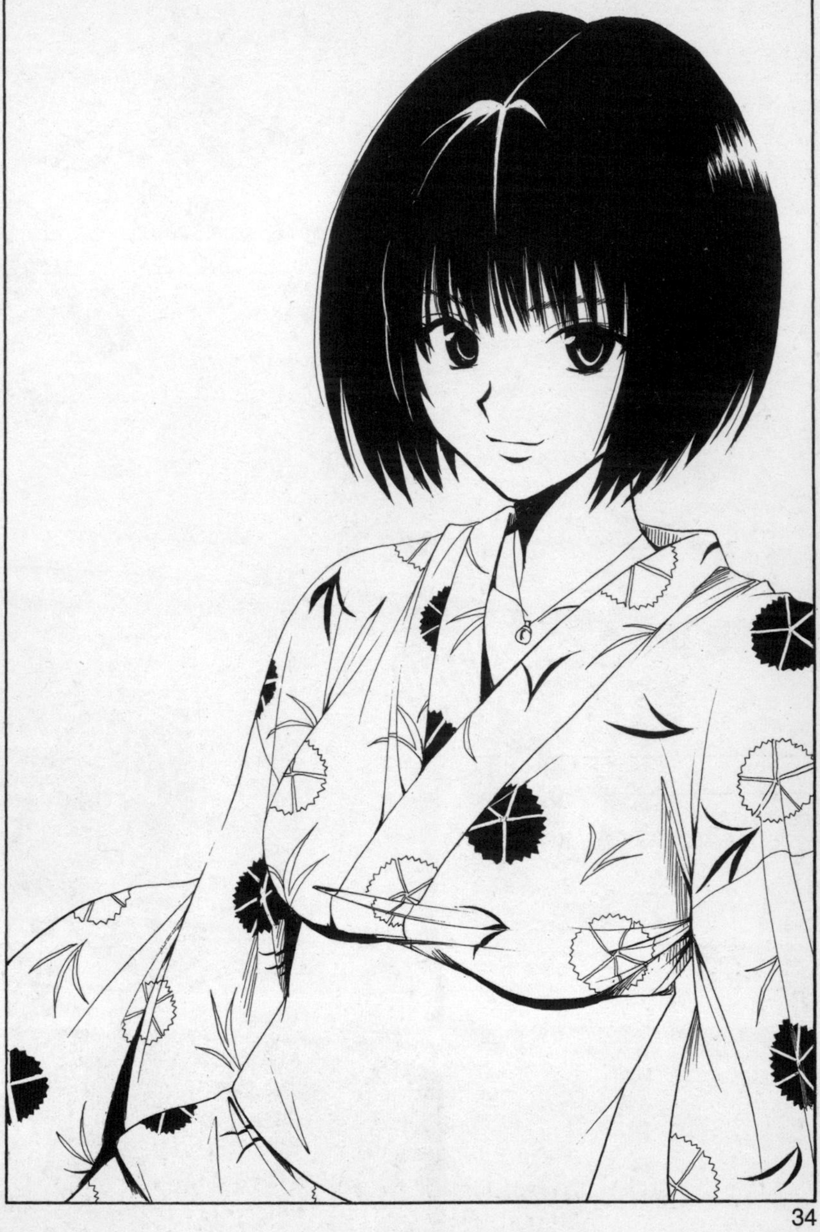

READ THIS WAY

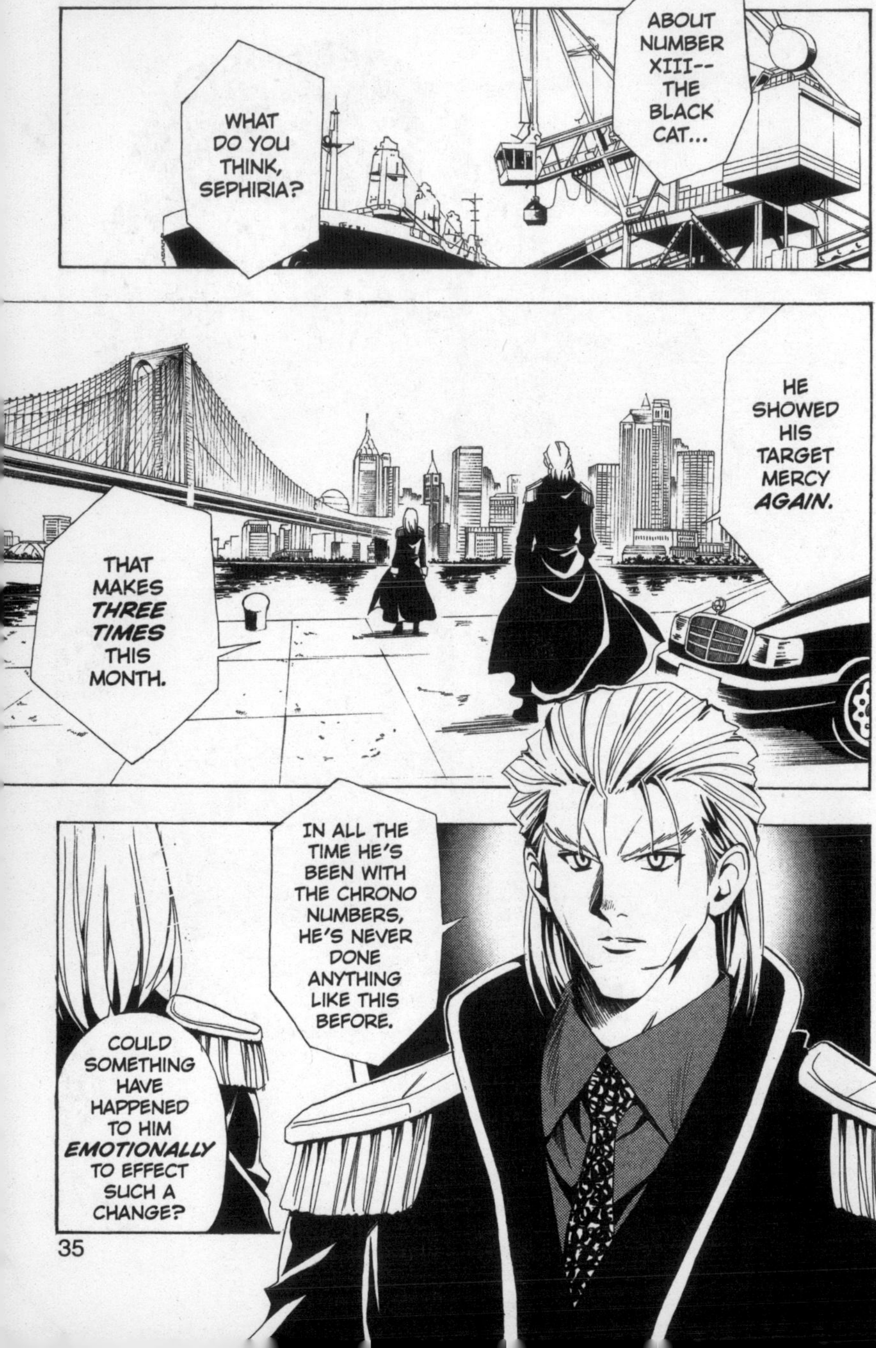
ABOUT NUMBER XIII-- THE BLACK CAT...
WHAT DO YOU THINK, SEPHIRIA?
HE SHOWED HIS TARGET MERCY *AGAIN.*
THAT MAKES *THREE TIMES* THIS MONTH.
IN ALL THE TIME HE'S BEEN WITH THE CHRONO NUMBERS, HE'S NEVER DONE ANYTHING LIKE THIS BEFORE.
COULD SOMETHING HAVE HAPPENED TO HIM *EMOTIONALLY* TO EFFECT SUCH A CHANGE?

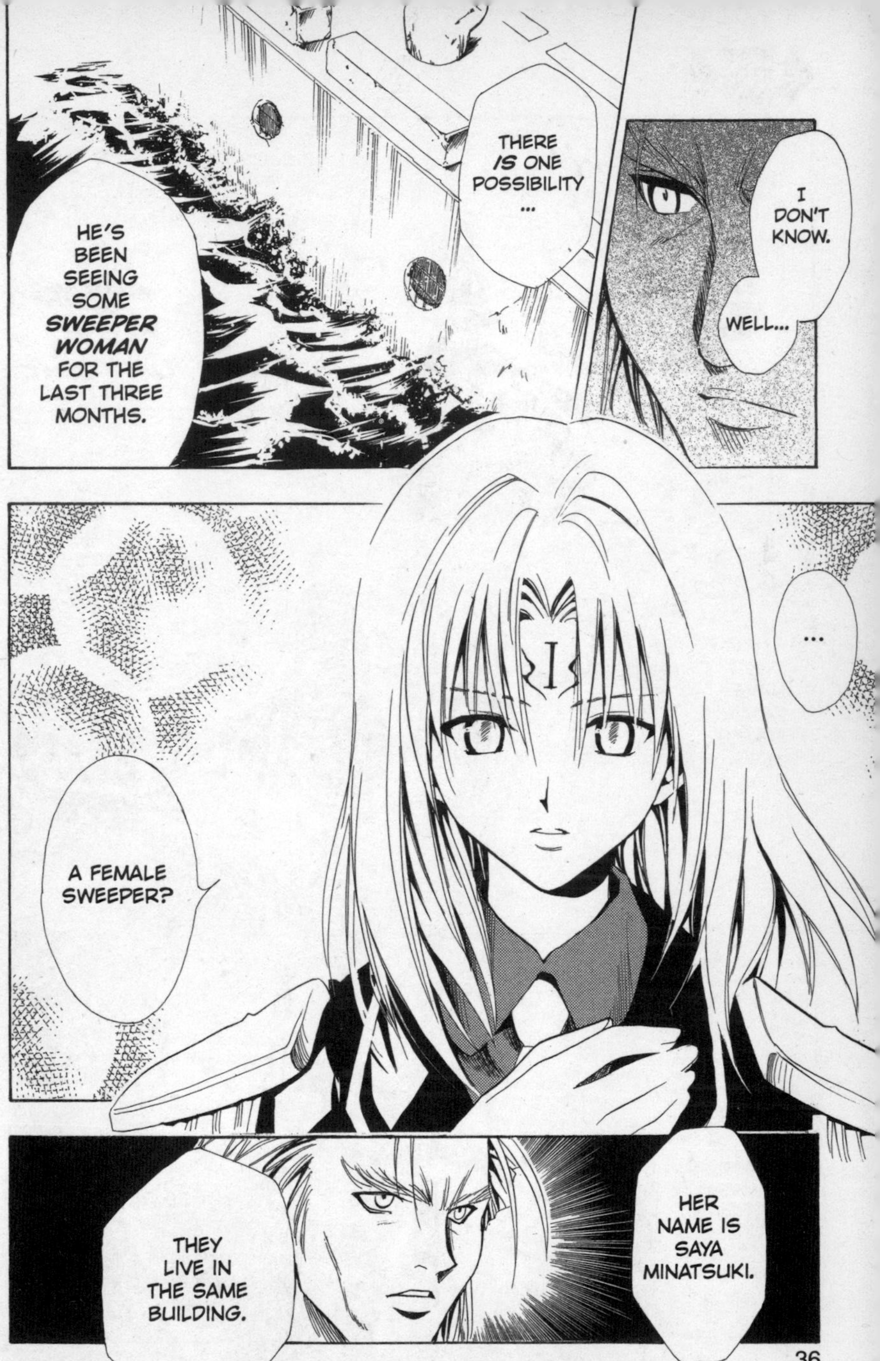
I DON'T KNOW.
WELL...
THERE IS ONE POSSIBILITY...
HE'S BEEN SEEING SOME SWEEPER WOMAN FOR THE LAST THREE MONTHS.
...
A FEMALE SWEEPER?
HER NAME IS SAYA MINATSUKI.
THEY LIVE IN THE SAME BUILDING.

READ THIS WAY

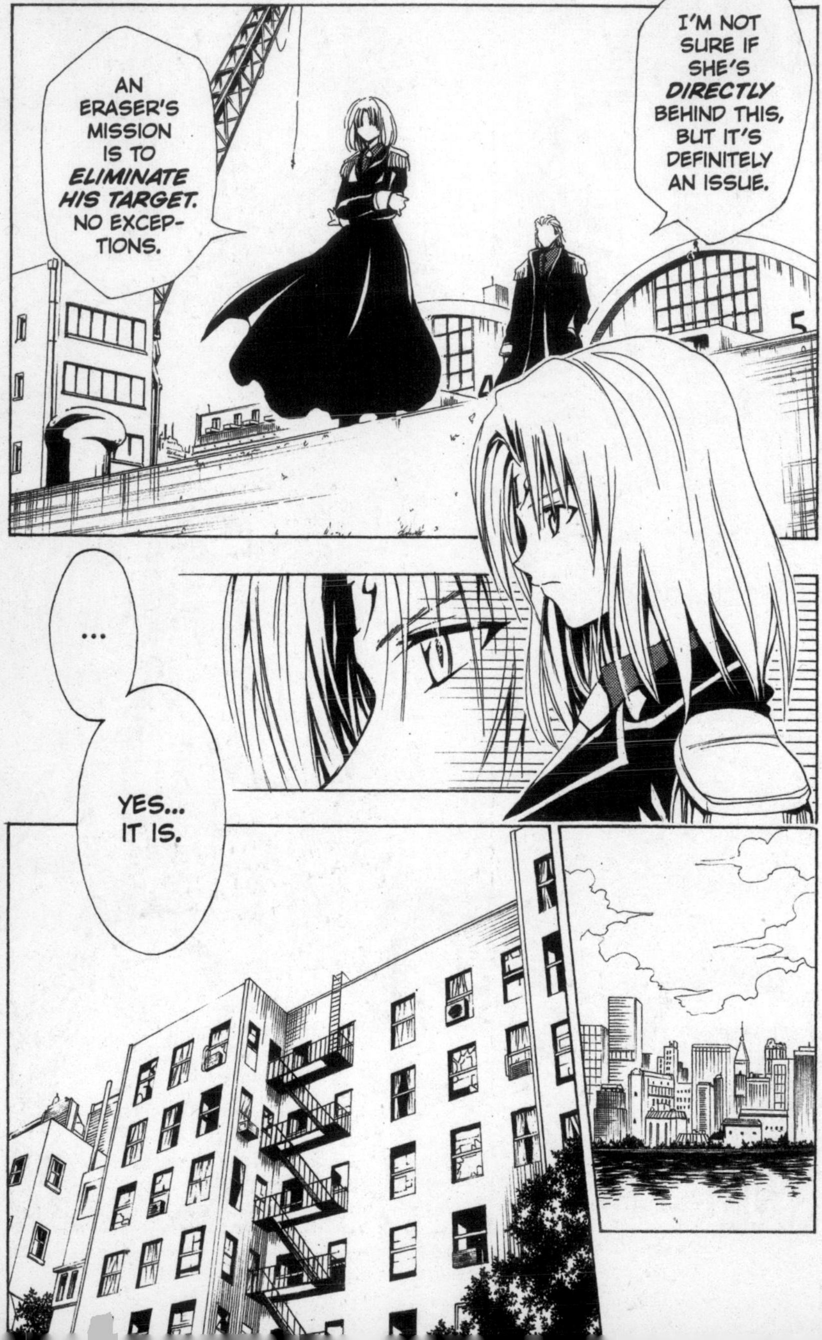
I'M NOT SURE IF SHE'S *DIRECTLY* BEHIND THIS, BUT IT'S DEFINITELY AN ISSUE.
AN ERASER'S MISSION IS TO *ELIMINATE HIS TARGET.* NO EXCEP-TIONS.
...
YES... IT IS.

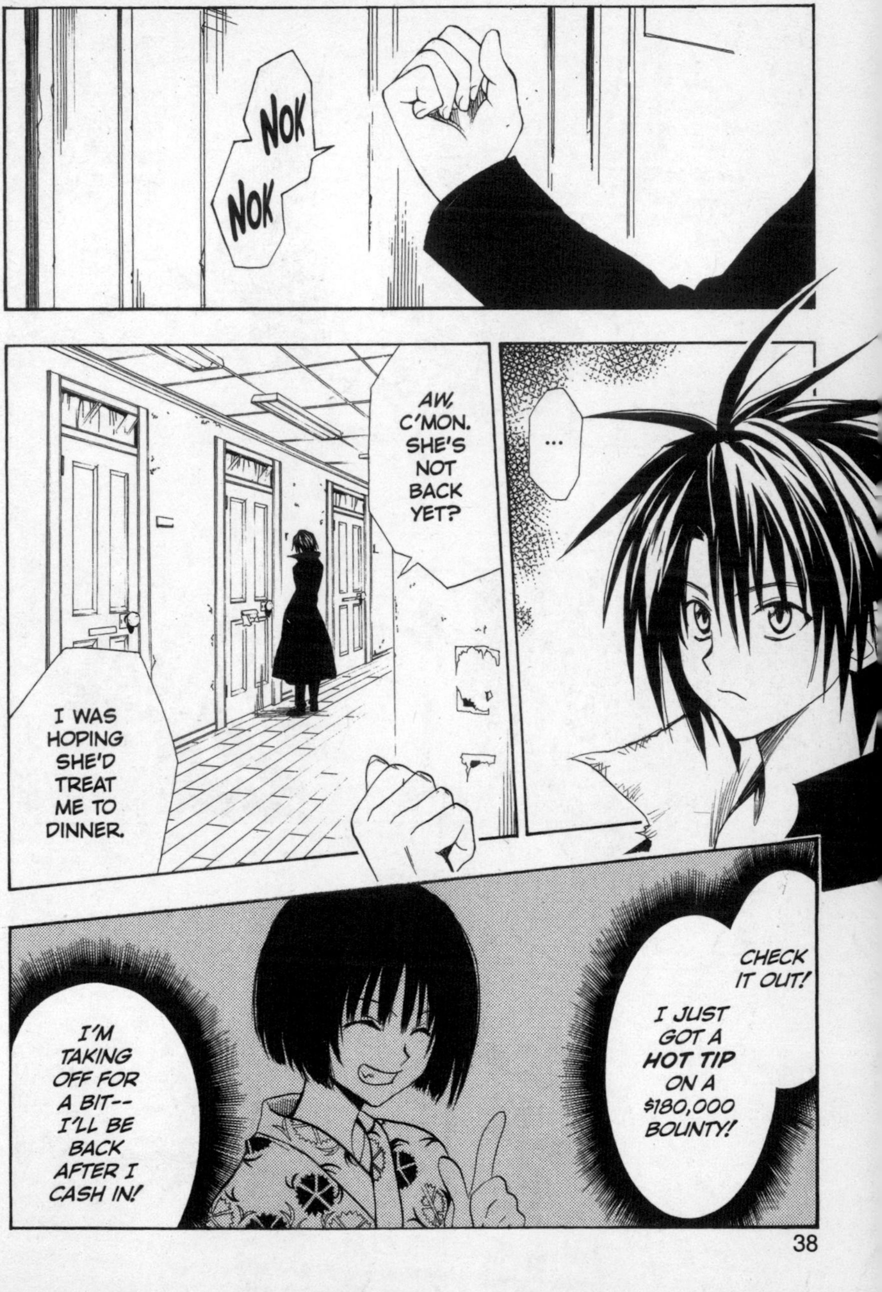
NOK
NOK
...
AW, C'MON. SHE'S NOT BACK YET?
I WAS HOPING SHE'D TREAT ME TO DINNER.
CHECK IT OUT!
I JUST GOT A HOT TIP ON A $180,000 BOUNTY!
I'M TAKING OFF FOR A BIT-- I'LL BE BACK AFTER I CASH IN!

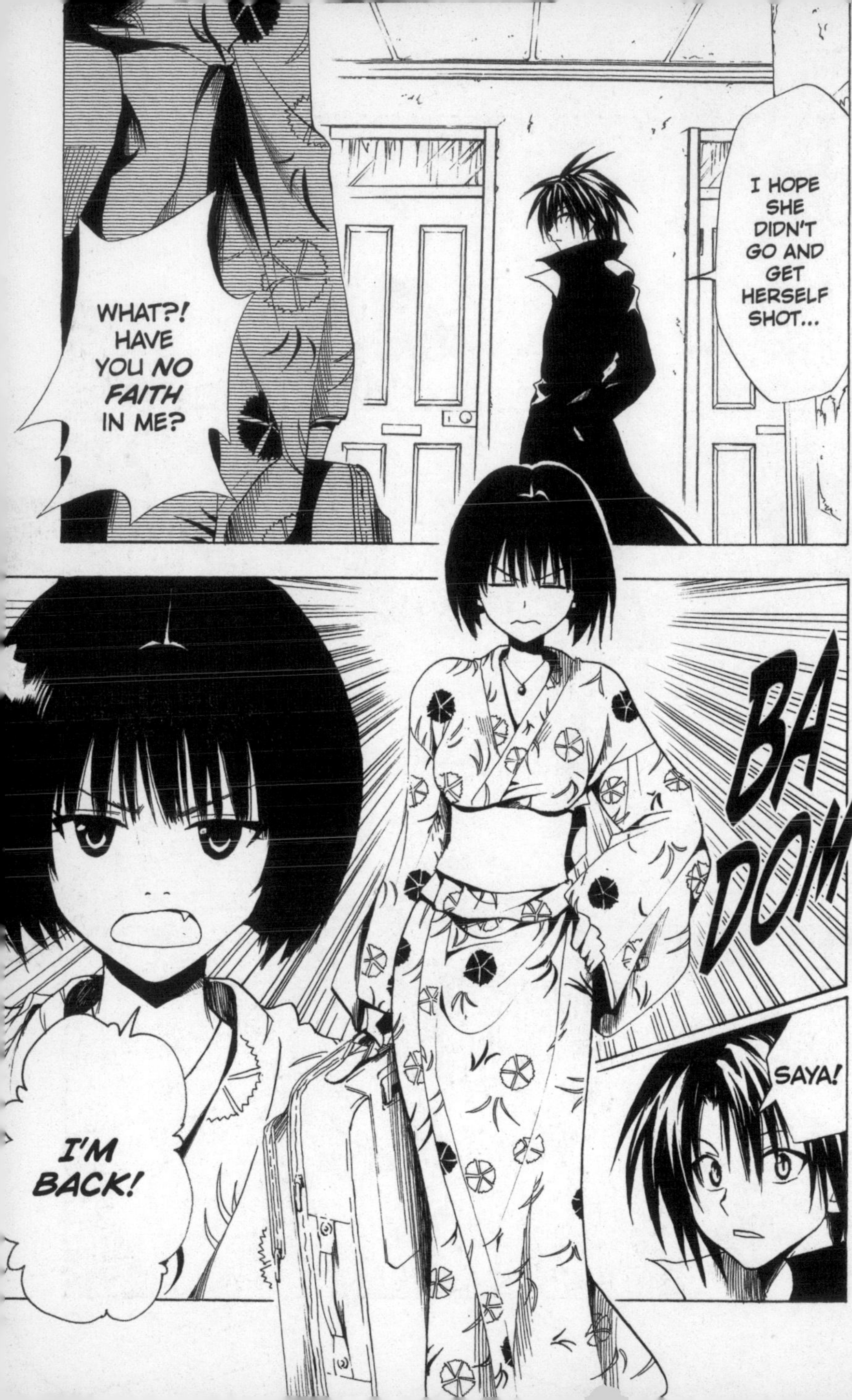
I HOPE SHE DIDN'T GO AND GET HERSELF SHOT...
WHAT?! HAVE YOU *NO FAITH* IN ME?
BA DOM
SAYA!
I'M BACK!

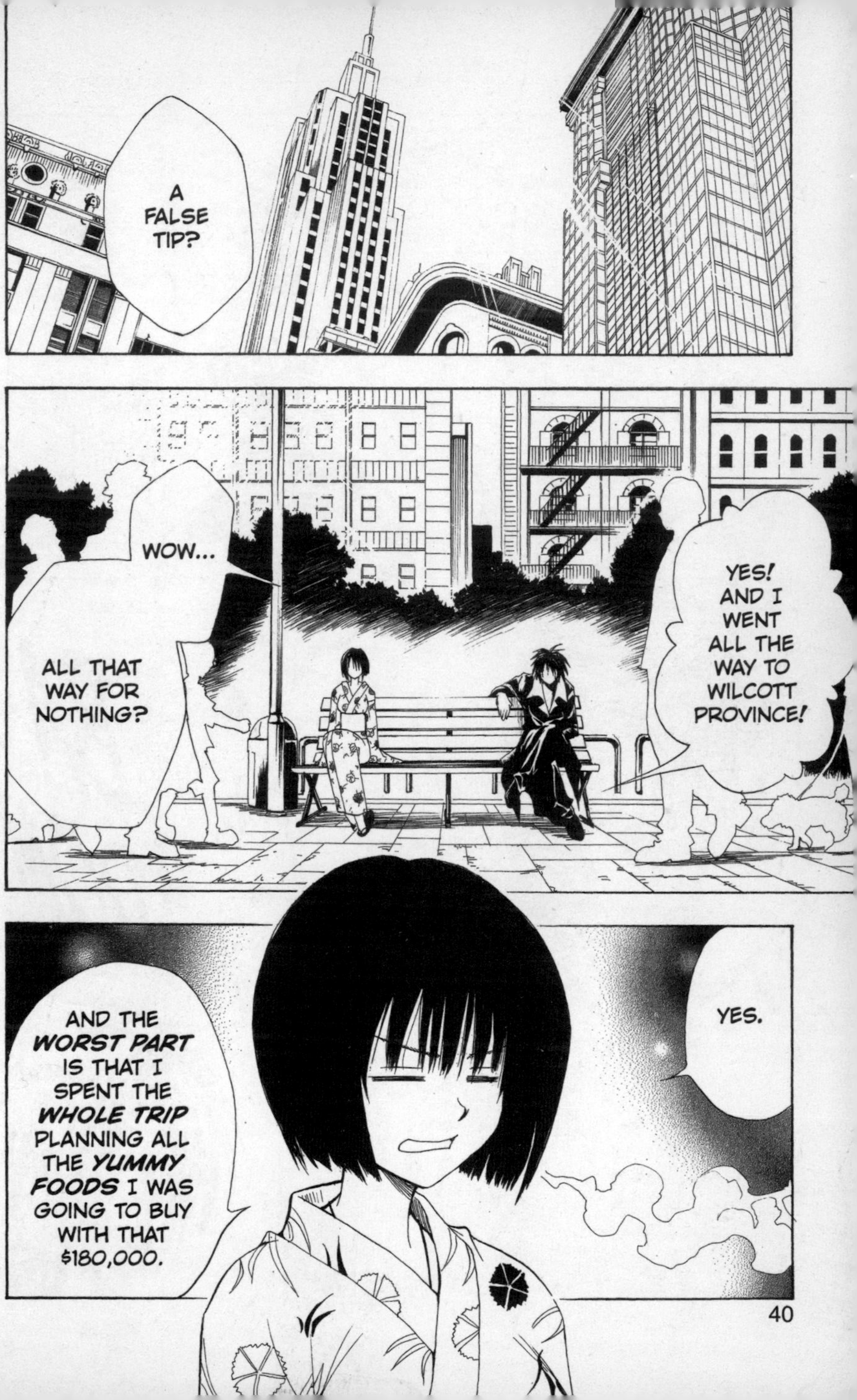
A FALSE TIP?
YES! AND I WENT ALL THE WAY TO WILCOTT PROVINCE!
WOW...
ALL THAT WAY FOR NOTHING?
YES.
AND THE *WORST PART* IS THAT I SPENT THE *WHOLE TRIP* PLANNING ALL THE *YUMMY FOODS* I WAS GOING TO BUY WITH THAT $180,000.

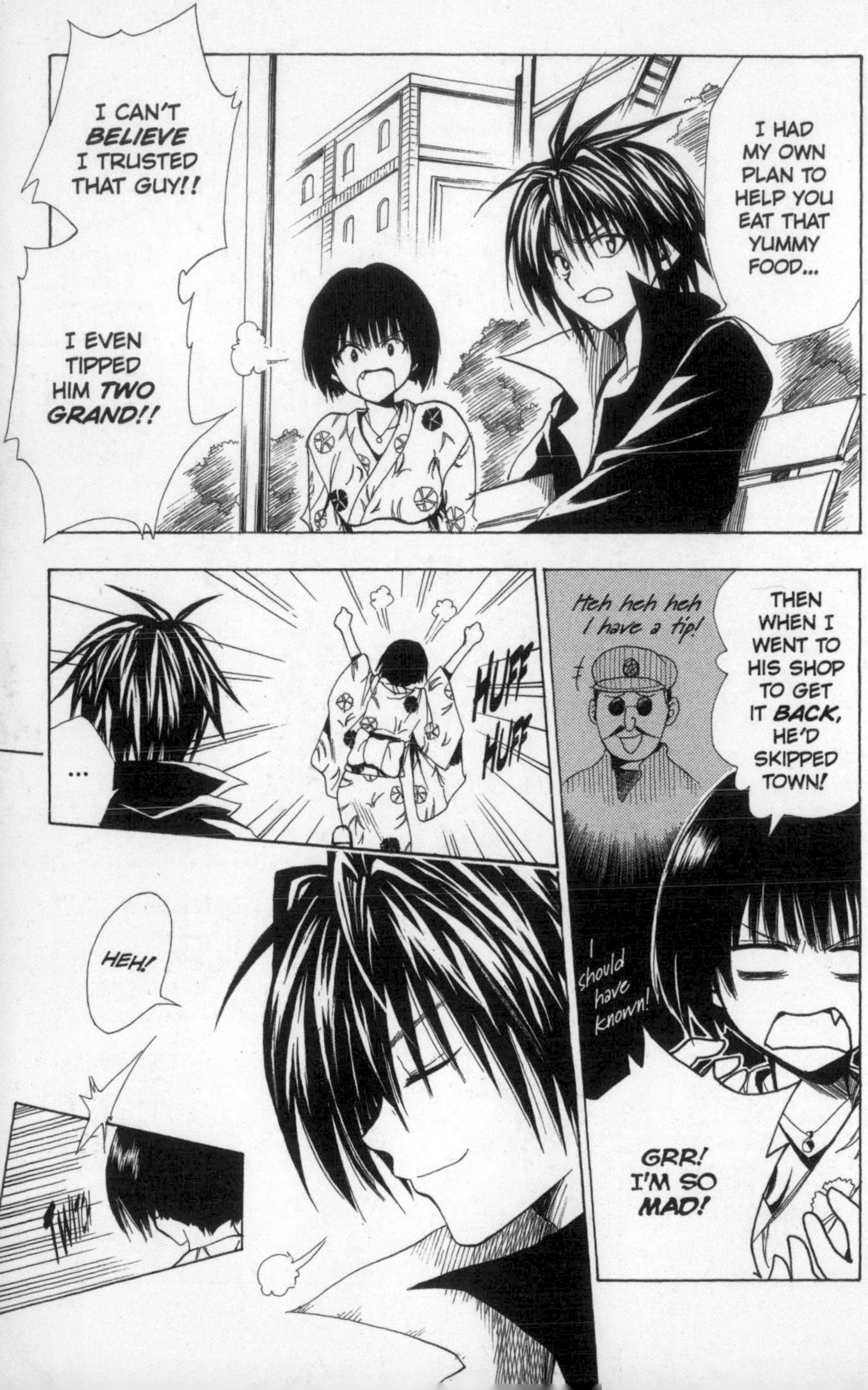
I HAD MY OWN PLAN TO HELP YOU EAT THAT YUMMY FOOD...
I CAN'T *BELIEVE* I TRUSTED THAT GUY!!
I EVEN TIPPED HIM *TWO GRAND!!*
THEN WHEN I WENT TO HIS SHOP TO GET IT *BACK,* HE'D SKIPPED TOWN!
Heh heh heh I have a tip!
HUFF HUFF
...
I should have known!
GRR! I'M SO *MAD!*
HEH!
TWITCH

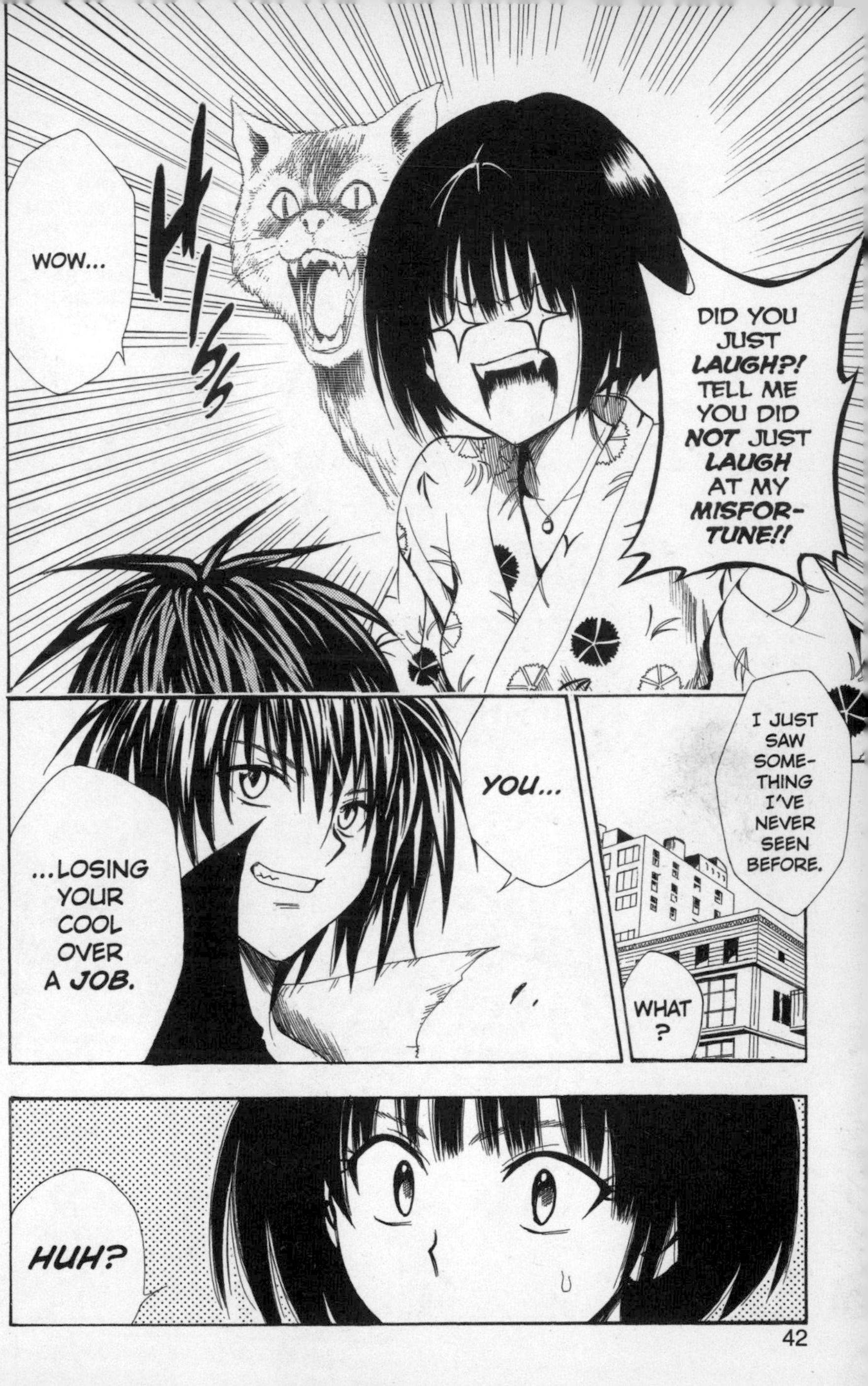
DID YOU JUST ***LAUGH?!*** TELL ME YOU DID ***NOT*** JUST ***LAUGH*** AT MY ***MISFORTUNE!!***
WOW...
I JUST SAW SOMETHING I'VE NEVER SEEN BEFORE.
WHAT?
YOU...
...LOSING YOUR COOL OVER A ***JOB.***
HUH?

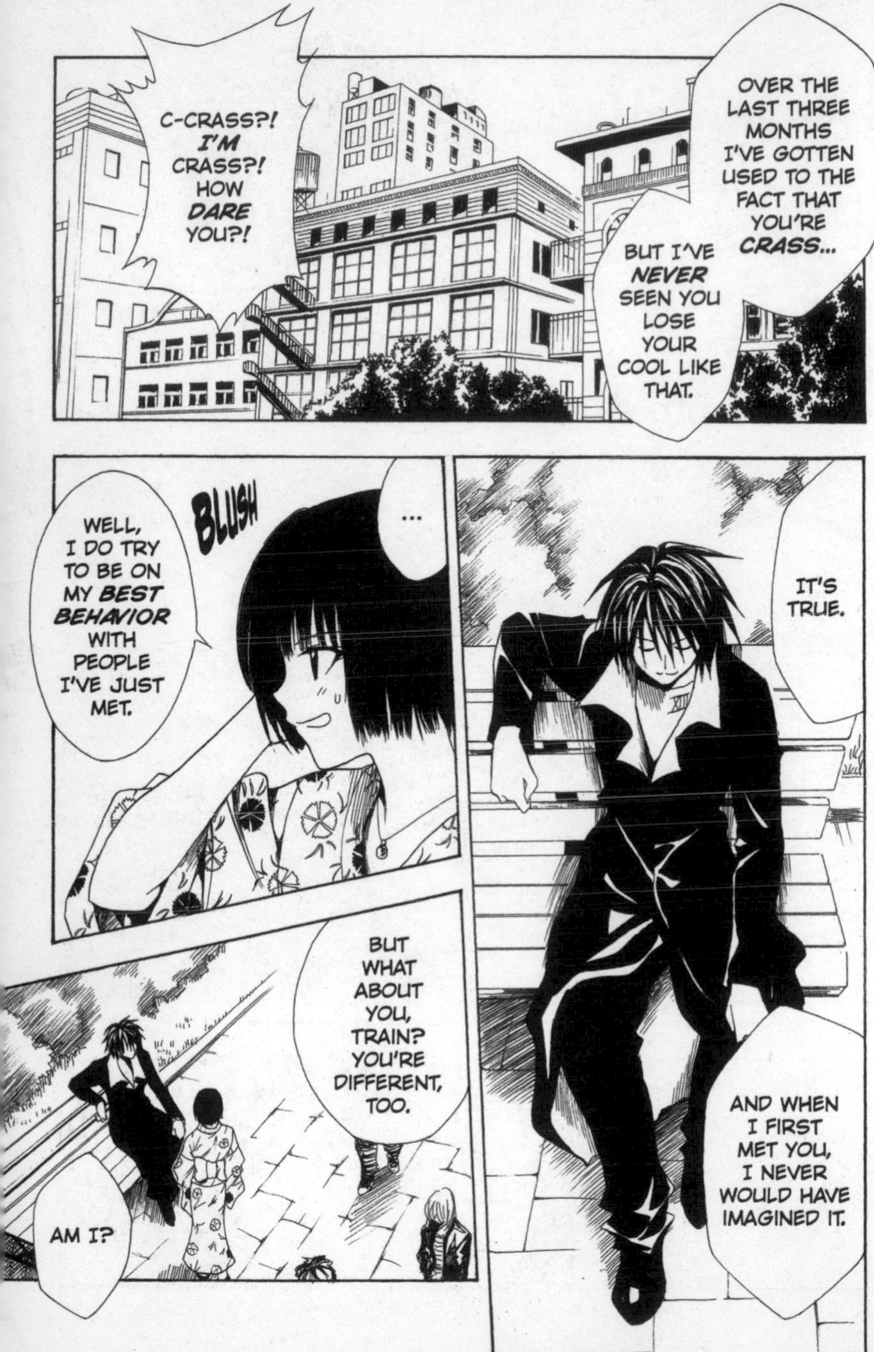
OVER THE LAST THREE MONTHS I'VE GOTTEN USED TO THE FACT THAT YOU'RE *CRASS...*
BUT I'VE *NEVER* SEEN YOU LOSE YOUR COOL LIKE THAT.
C-CRASS?! *I'M* CRASS?! HOW *DARE* YOU?!
IT'S TRUE.
AND WHEN I FIRST MET YOU, I NEVER WOULD HAVE IMAGINED IT.
...
BLUSH
WELL, I DO TRY TO BE ON MY *BEST BEHAVIOR* WITH PEOPLE I'VE JUST MET.
BUT WHAT ABOUT YOU, TRAIN? YOU'RE DIFFERENT, TOO.
AM I?

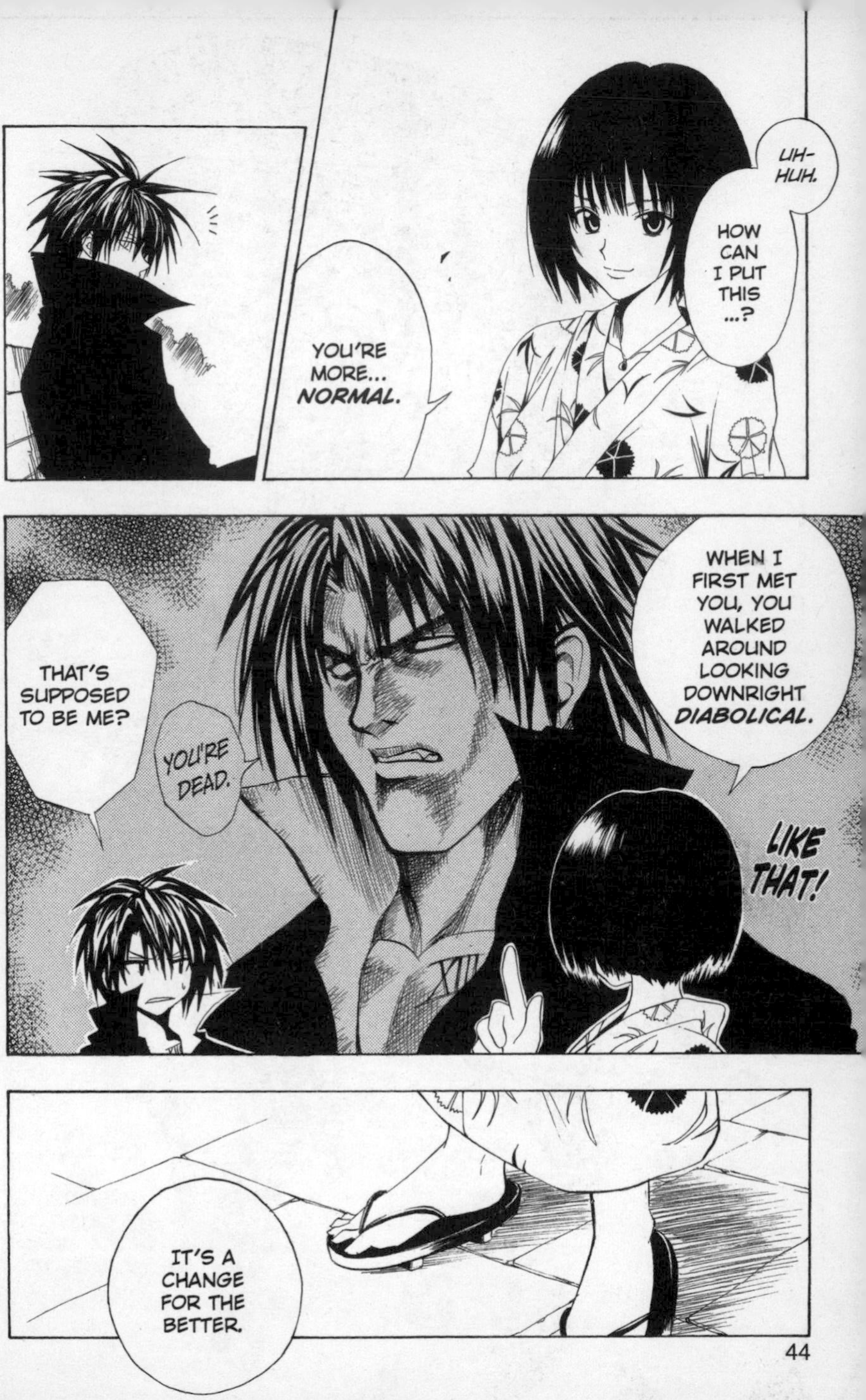
UH-HUH.
HOW CAN I PUT THIS ...?
YOU'RE MORE... NORMAL.
WHEN I FIRST MET YOU, YOU WALKED AROUND LOOKING DOWNRIGHT DIABOLICAL.
LIKE THAT!
YOU'RE DEAD.
THAT'S SUPPOSED TO BE ME?
IT'S A CHANGE FOR THE BETTER.

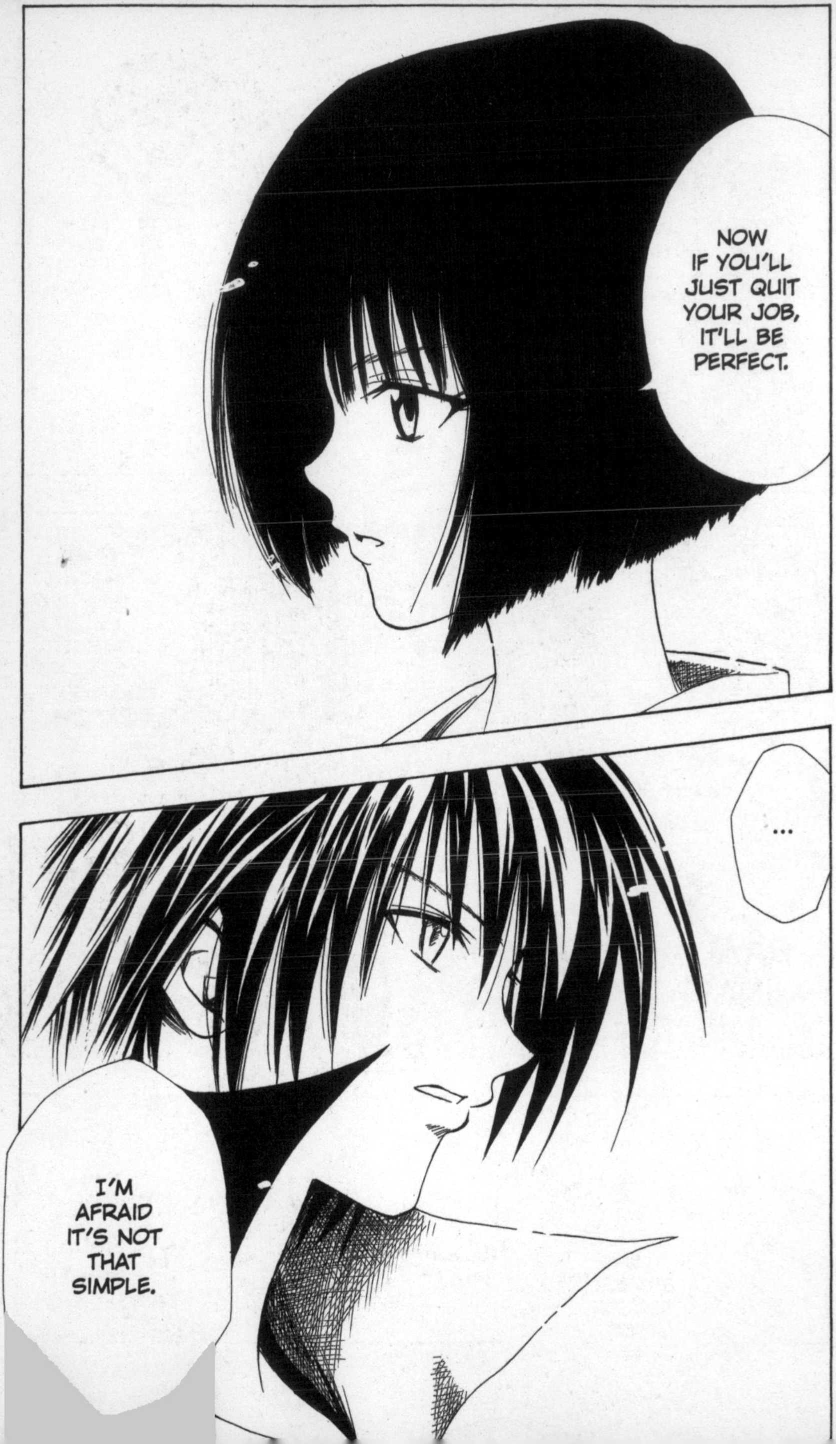
NOW IF YOU'LL JUST QUIT YOUR JOB, IT'LL BE PERFECT.
...
I'M AFRAID IT'S NOT THAT SIMPLE.

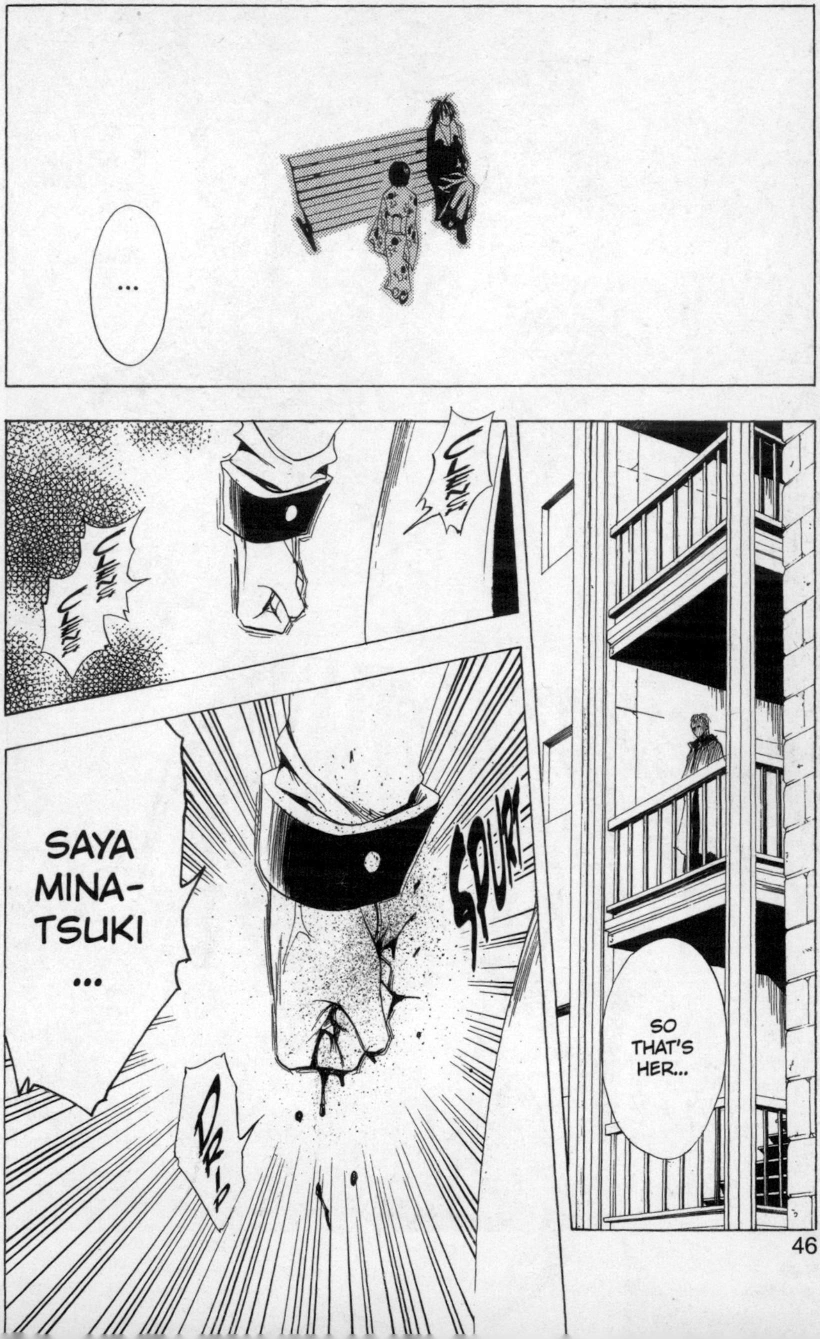
...
SO THAT'S HER...
CLENCH
CLENCH CLENCH
SAYA MINATSUKI ...
SPURT
DRIP

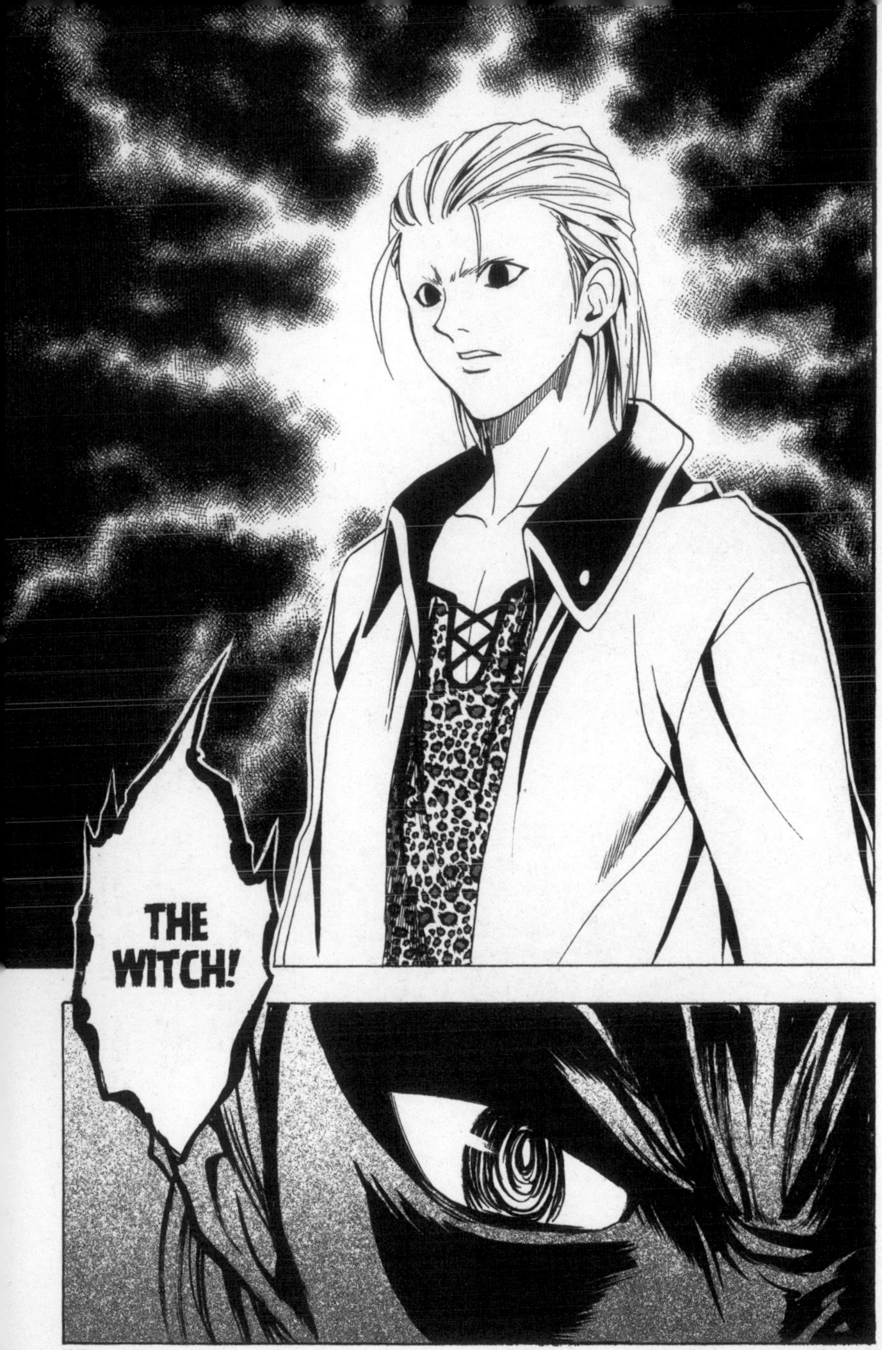
THE WITCH!

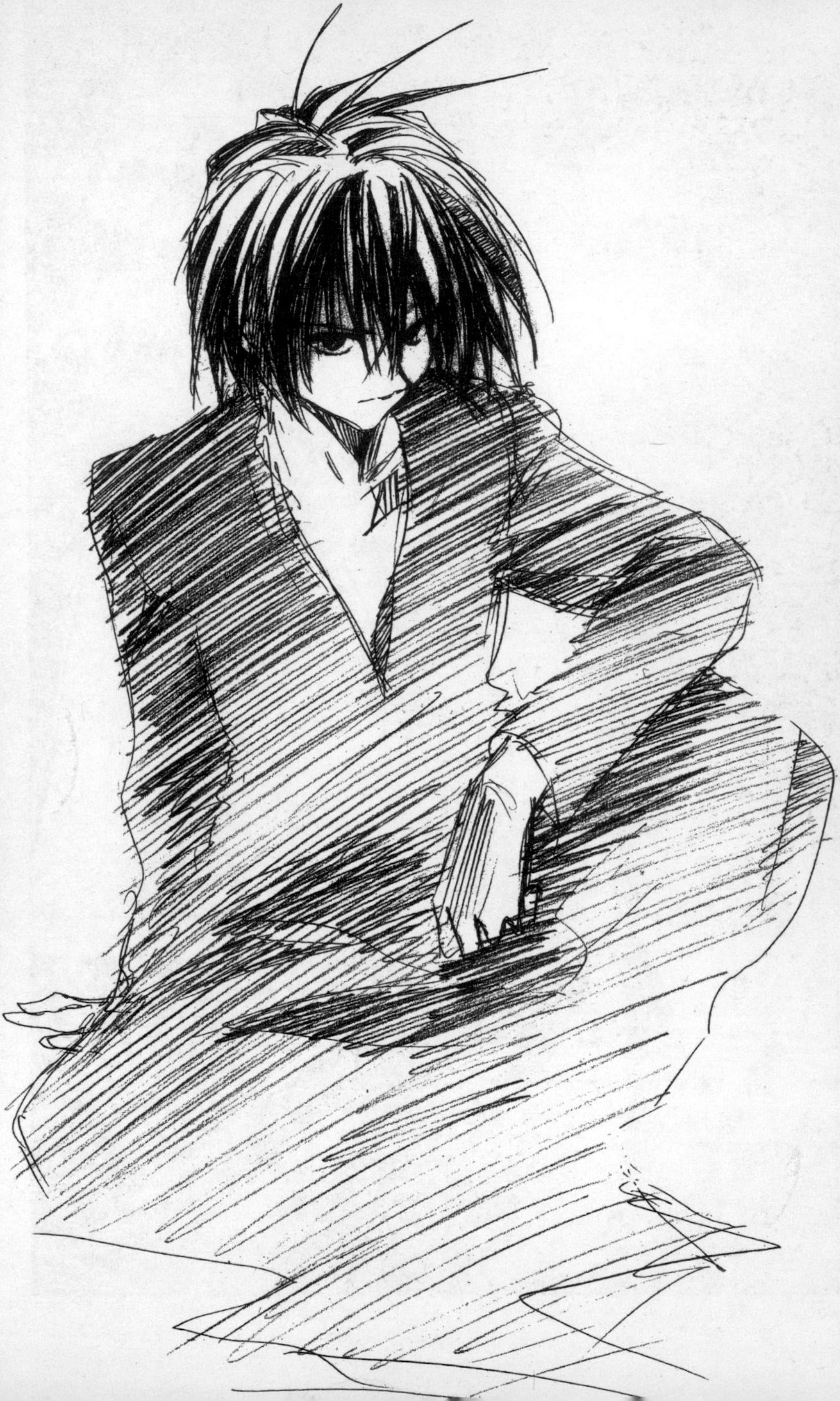

Chapter 116: The Price of Freedom

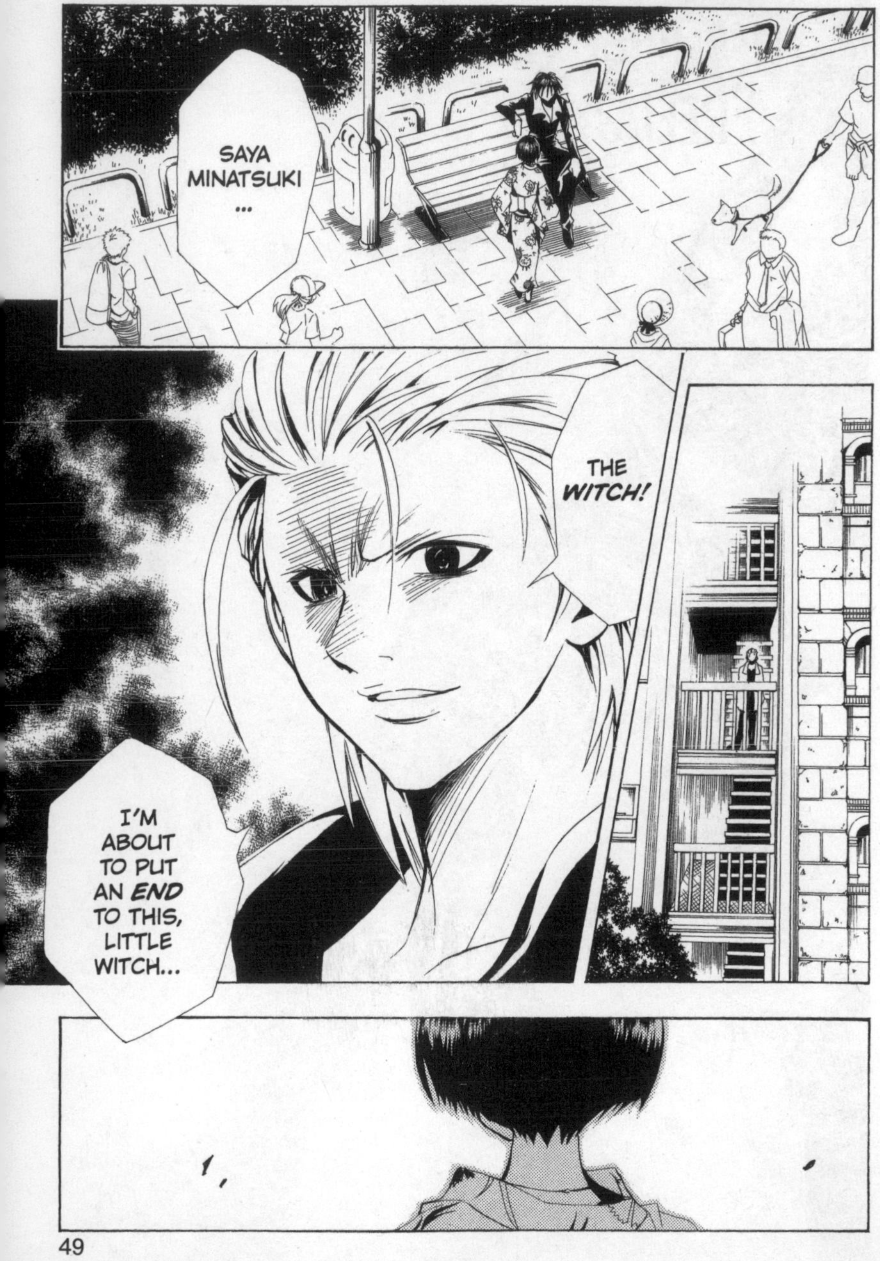
SAYA MINATSUKI ...
THE *WITCH!*
I'M ABOUT TO PUT AN *END* TO THIS, LITTLE WITCH...

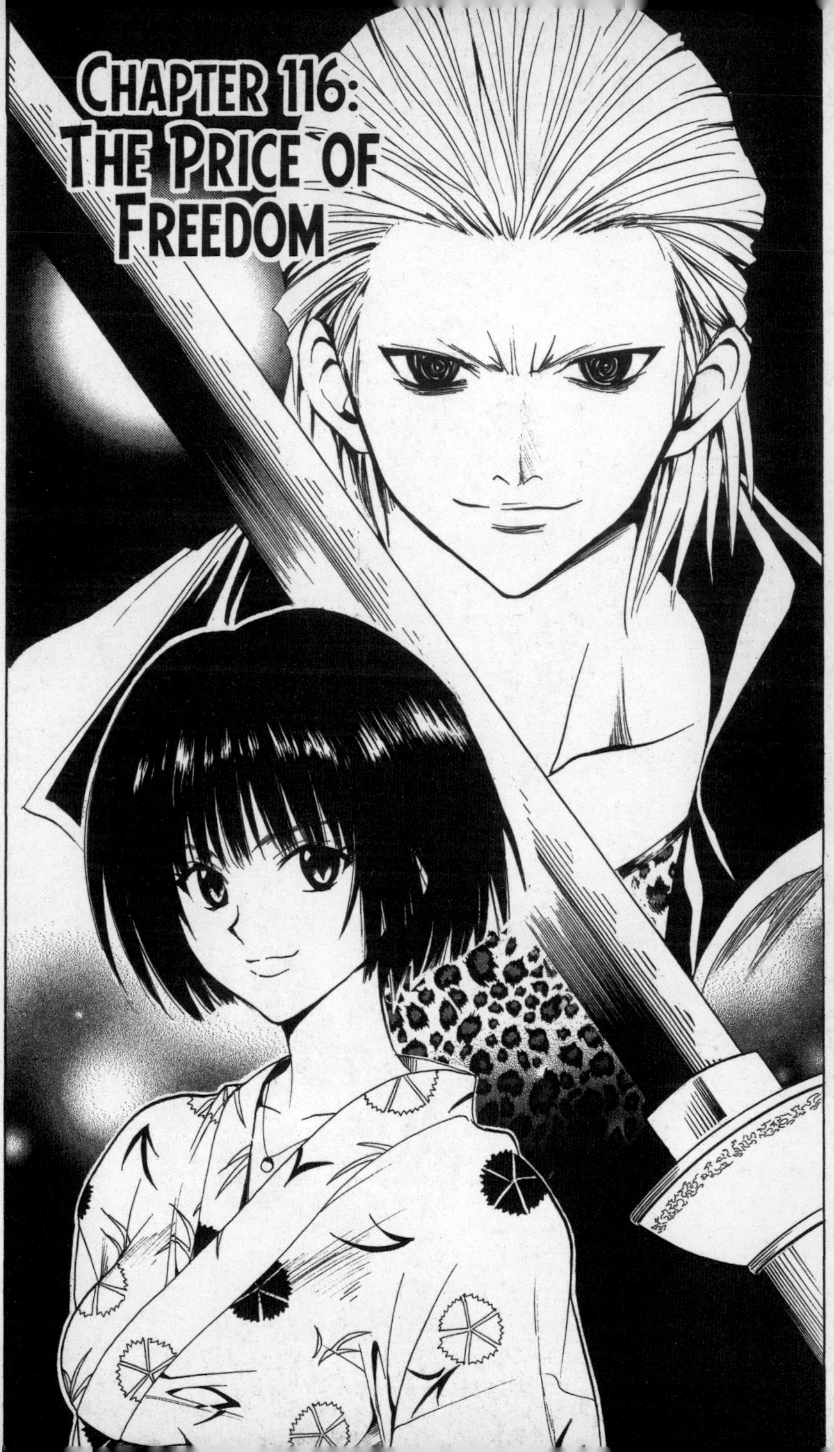
Chapter 116:
The Price of
Freedom

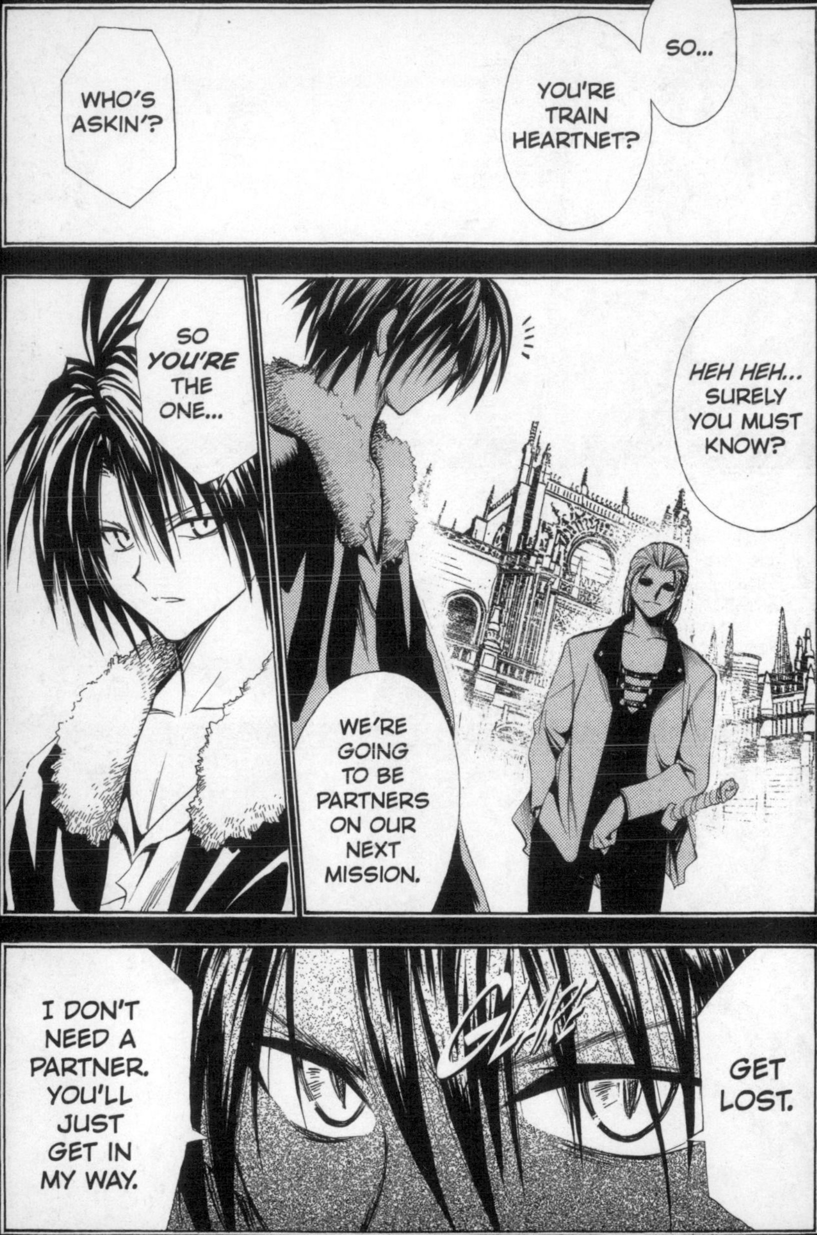
SO...
YOU'RE TRAIN HEARTNET?
WHO'S ASKIN'?
HEH HEH... SURELY YOU MUST KNOW?
WE'RE GOING TO BE PARTNERS ON OUR NEXT MISSION.
SO *YOU'RE* THE ONE...
GET LOST.
I DON'T NEED A PARTNER. YOU'LL JUST GET IN MY WAY.

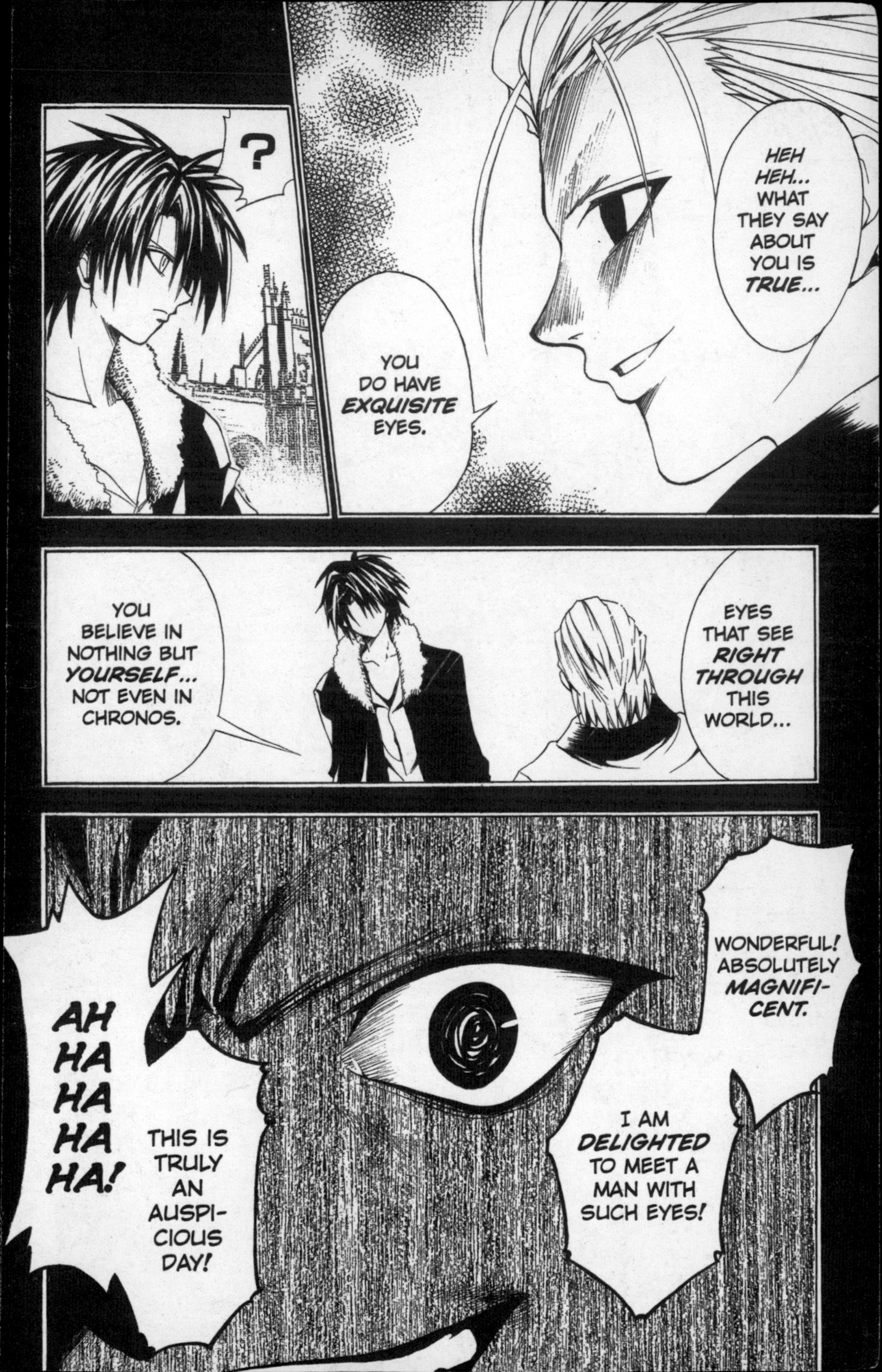
HEH HEH... WHAT THEY SAY ABOUT YOU IS TRUE...
YOU DO HAVE EXQUISITE EYES.
?
EYES THAT SEE RIGHT THROUGH THIS WORLD...
YOU BELIEVE IN NOTHING BUT YOURSELF... NOT EVEN IN CHRONOS.
WONDERFUL! ABSOLUTELY MAGNIFI-CENT.
I AM DELIGHTED TO MEET A MAN WITH SUCH EYES!
THIS IS TRULY AN AUSPICIOUS DAY!
AH HA HA HA HA!

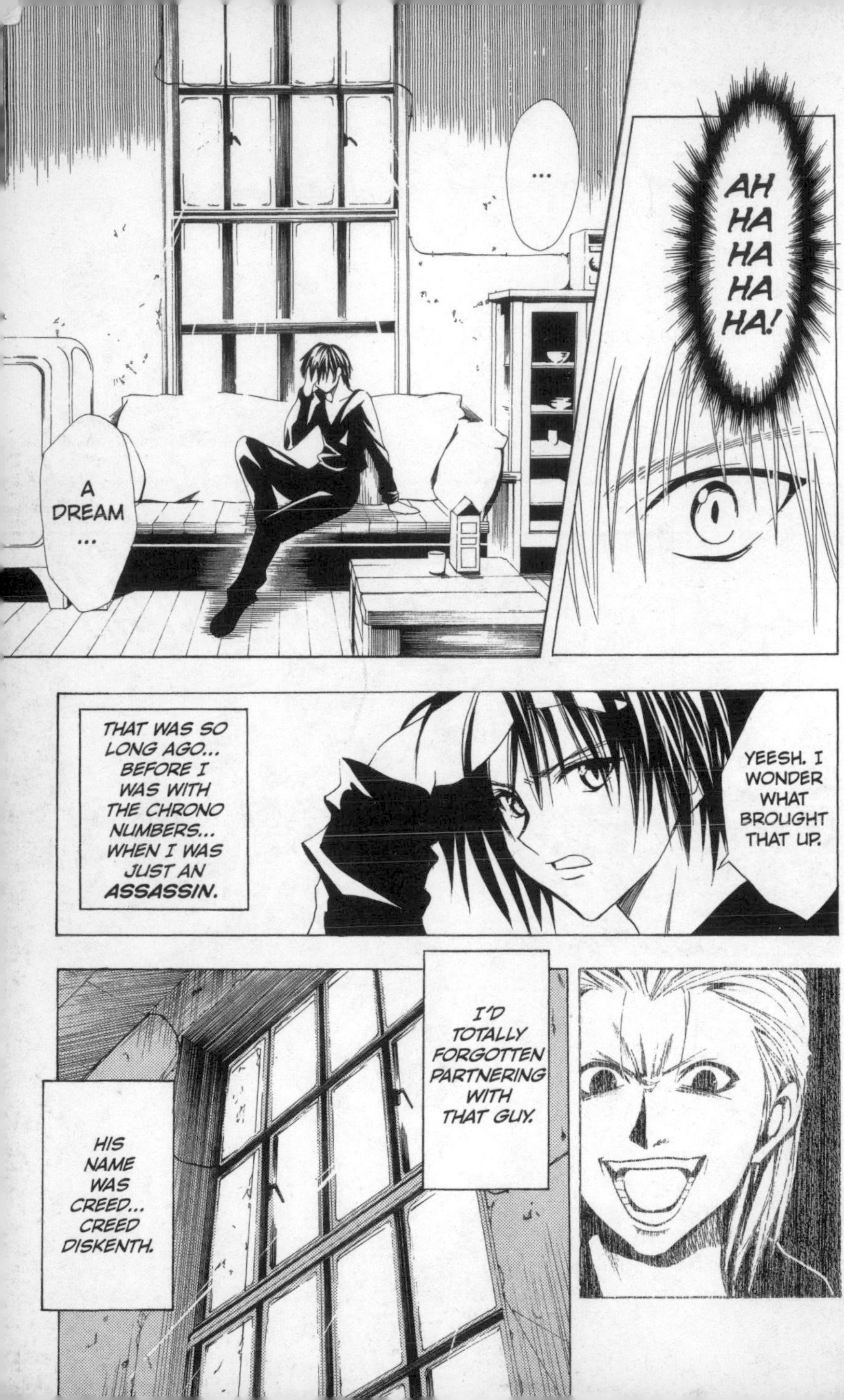
AH HA HA HA HA!
...
A DREAM ...
YEESH. I WONDER WHAT BROUGHT THAT UP.
THAT WAS SO LONG AGO... BEFORE I WAS WITH THE CHRONO NUMBERS... WHEN I WAS JUST AN ASSASSIN.
I'D TOTALLY FORGOTTEN PARTNERING WITH THAT GUY.
HIS NAME WAS CREED... CREED DISKENTH.

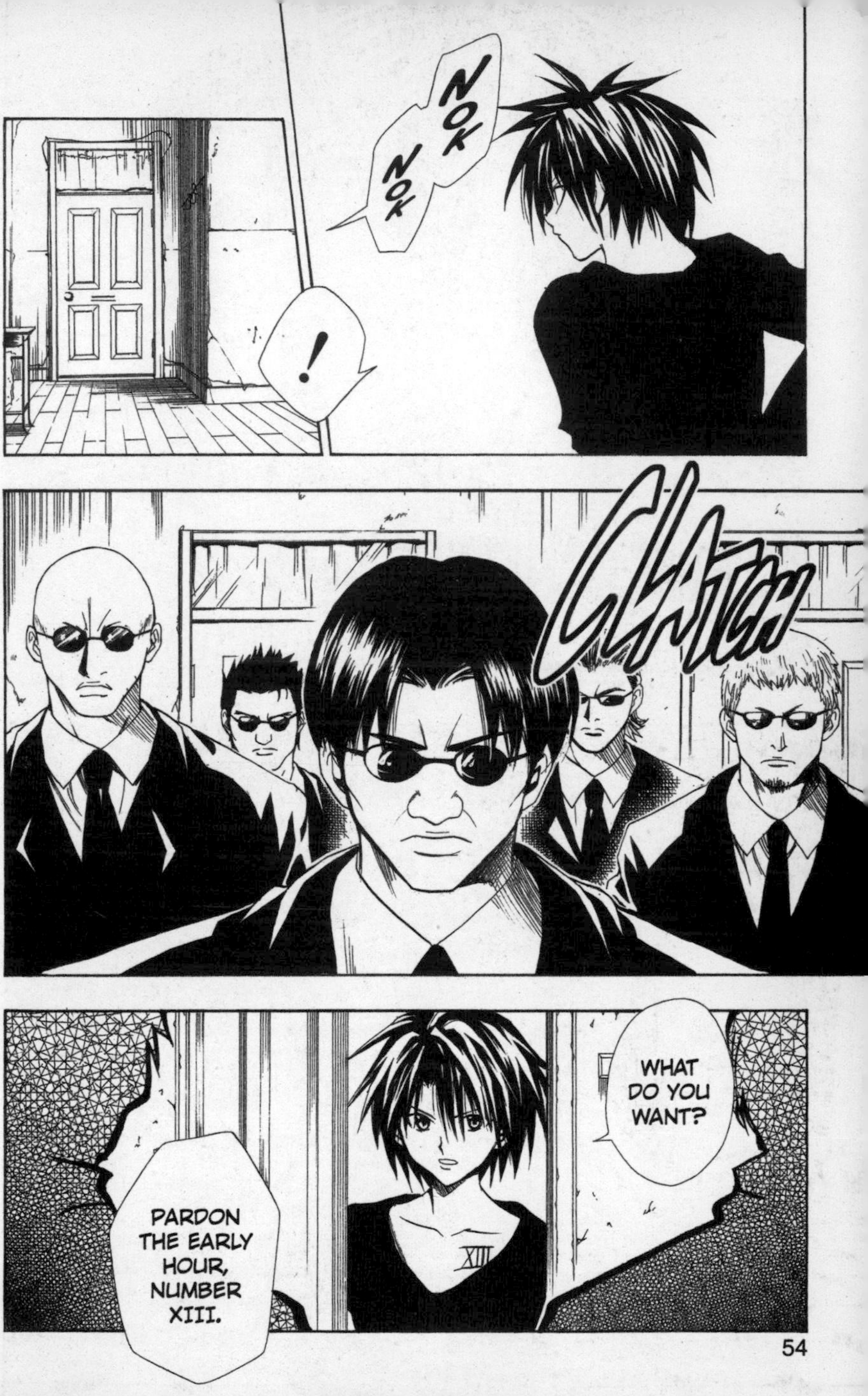
NOK NOK
!
WHAT DO YOU WANT?
PARDON THE EARLY HOUR, NUMBER XIII.

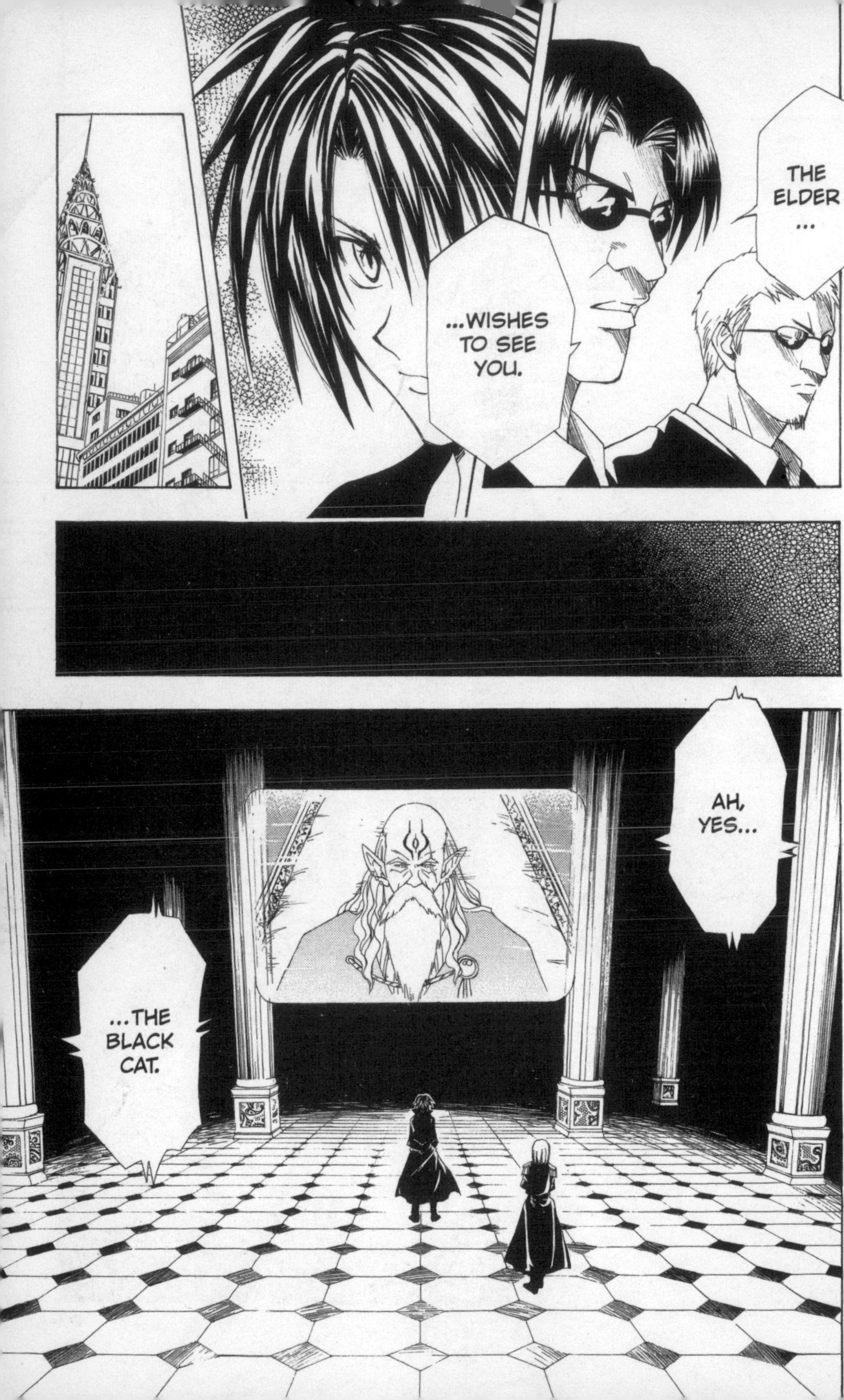
THE ELDER ...
...WISHES TO SEE YOU.
AH, YES...
...THE BLACK CAT.

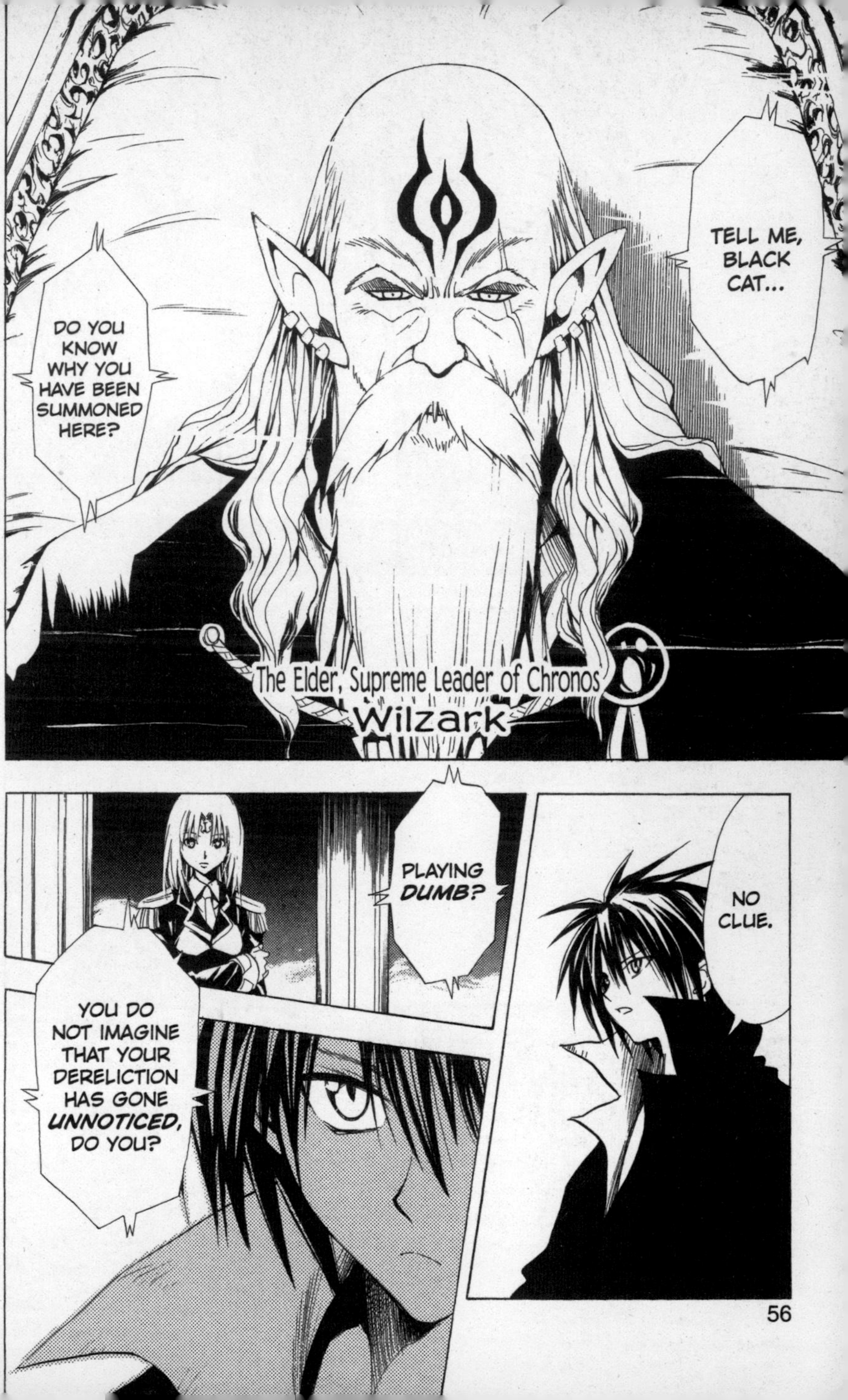
TELL ME, BLACK CAT...
DO YOU KNOW WHY YOU HAVE BEEN SUMMONED HERE?
The Elder, Supreme Leader of Chronos
Wilzark
NO CLUE.
PLAYING *DUMB?*
YOU DO NOT IMAGINE THAT YOUR DERELICTION HAS GONE *UNNOTICED,* DO YOU?

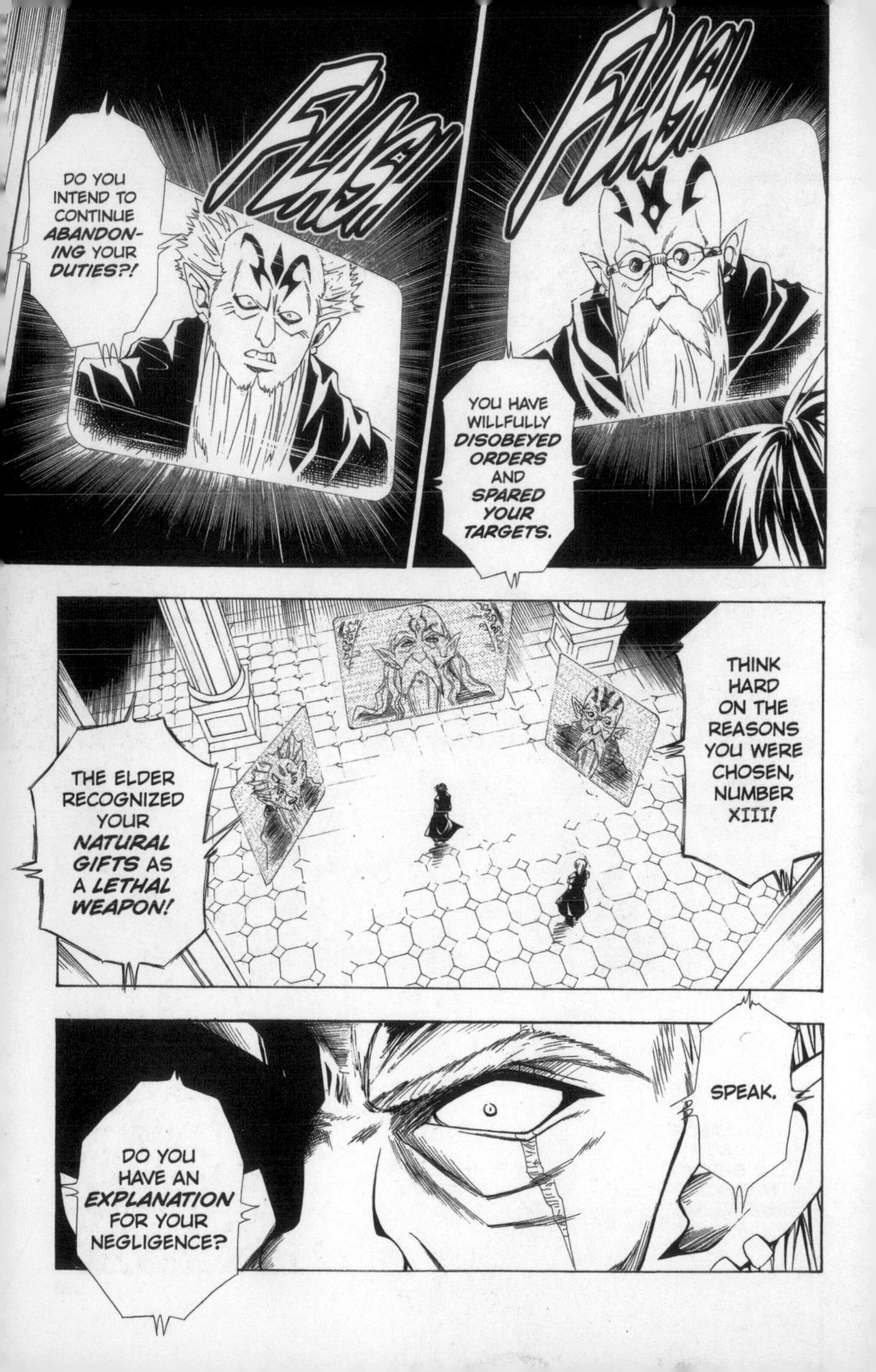
YOU HAVE WILLFULLY DISOBEYED ORDERS AND SPARED YOUR TARGETS.
DO YOU INTEND TO CONTINUE ABANDONING YOUR DUTIES?!
THINK HARD ON THE REASONS YOU WERE CHOSEN, NUMBER XIII!
THE ELDER RECOGNIZED YOUR NATURAL GIFTS AS A LETHAL WEAPON!
SPEAK.
DO YOU HAVE AN EXPLANATION FOR YOUR NEGLIGENCE?

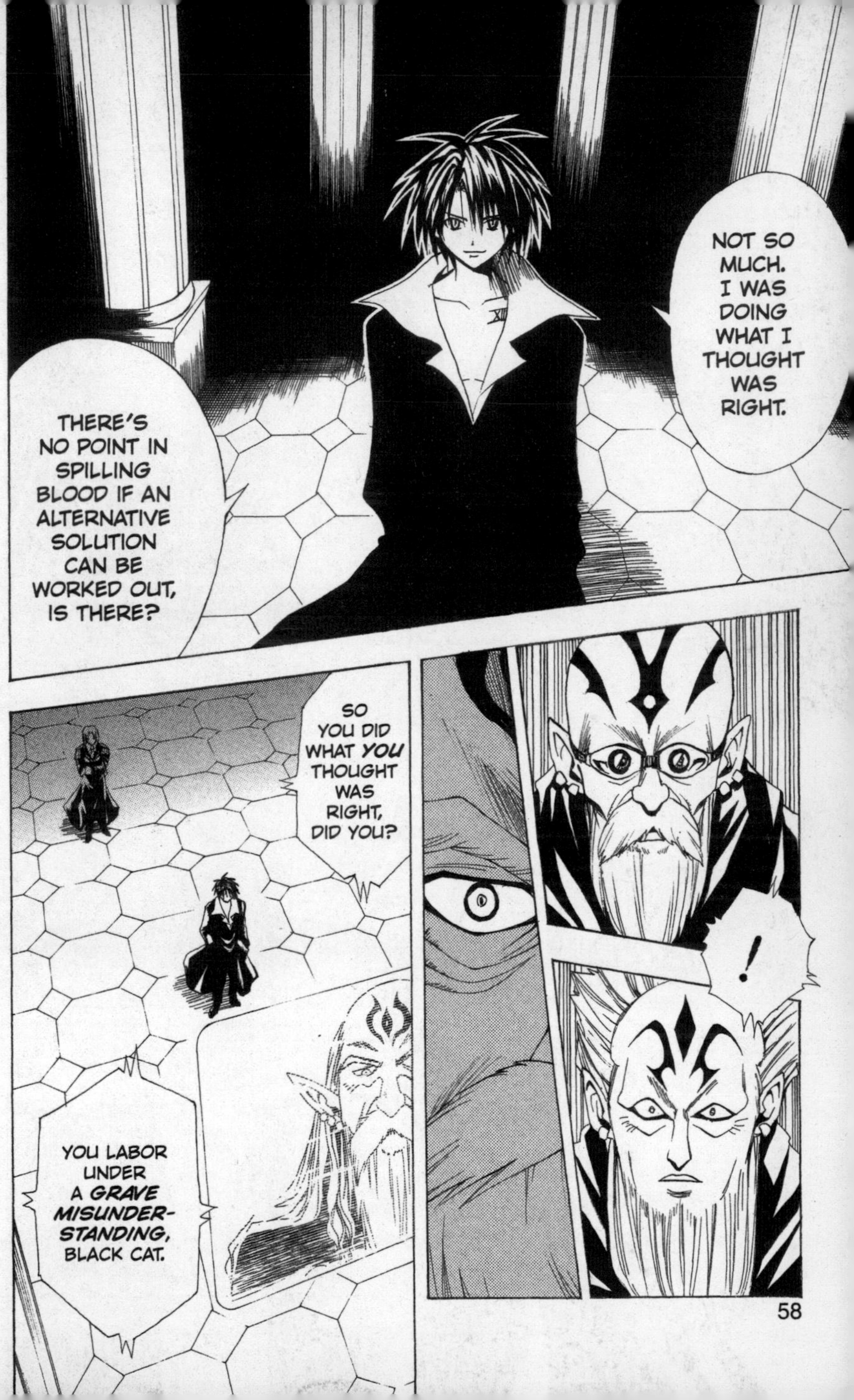
NOT SO MUCH. I WAS DOING WHAT I THOUGHT WAS RIGHT.
THERE'S NO POINT IN SPILLING BLOOD IF AN ALTERNATIVE SOLUTION CAN BE WORKED OUT, IS THERE?
!
SO YOU DID WHAT *YOU* THOUGHT WAS RIGHT, DID YOU?
YOU LABOR UNDER A ***GRAVE MISUNDER-STANDING***, BLACK CAT.

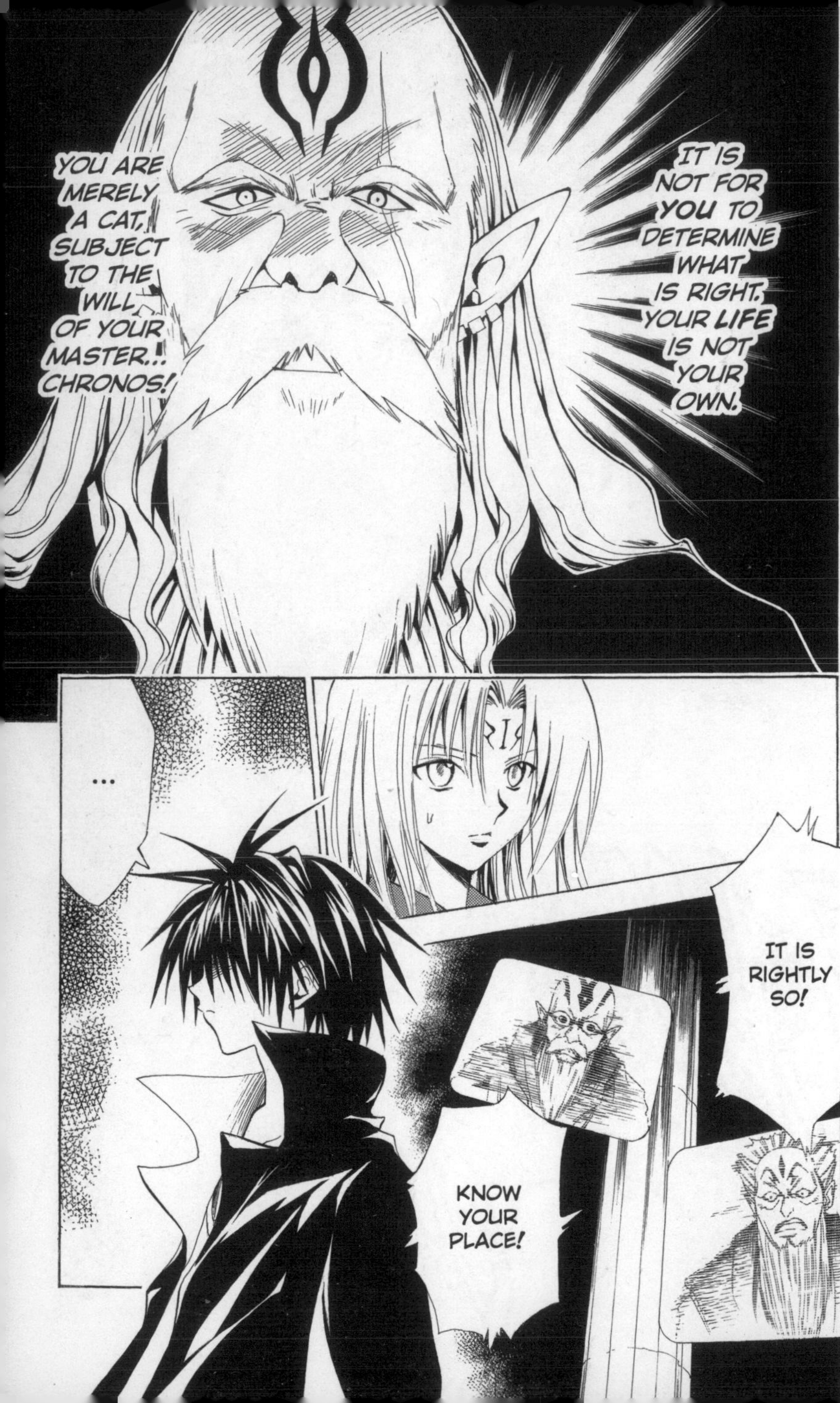
IT IS NOT FOR YOU TO DETERMINE WHAT IS RIGHT. YOUR LIFE IS NOT YOUR OWN.
YOU ARE MERELY A CAT, SUBJECT TO THE WILL OF YOUR MASTER... CHRONOS!
IT IS RIGHTLY SO!
KNOW YOUR PLACE!
...

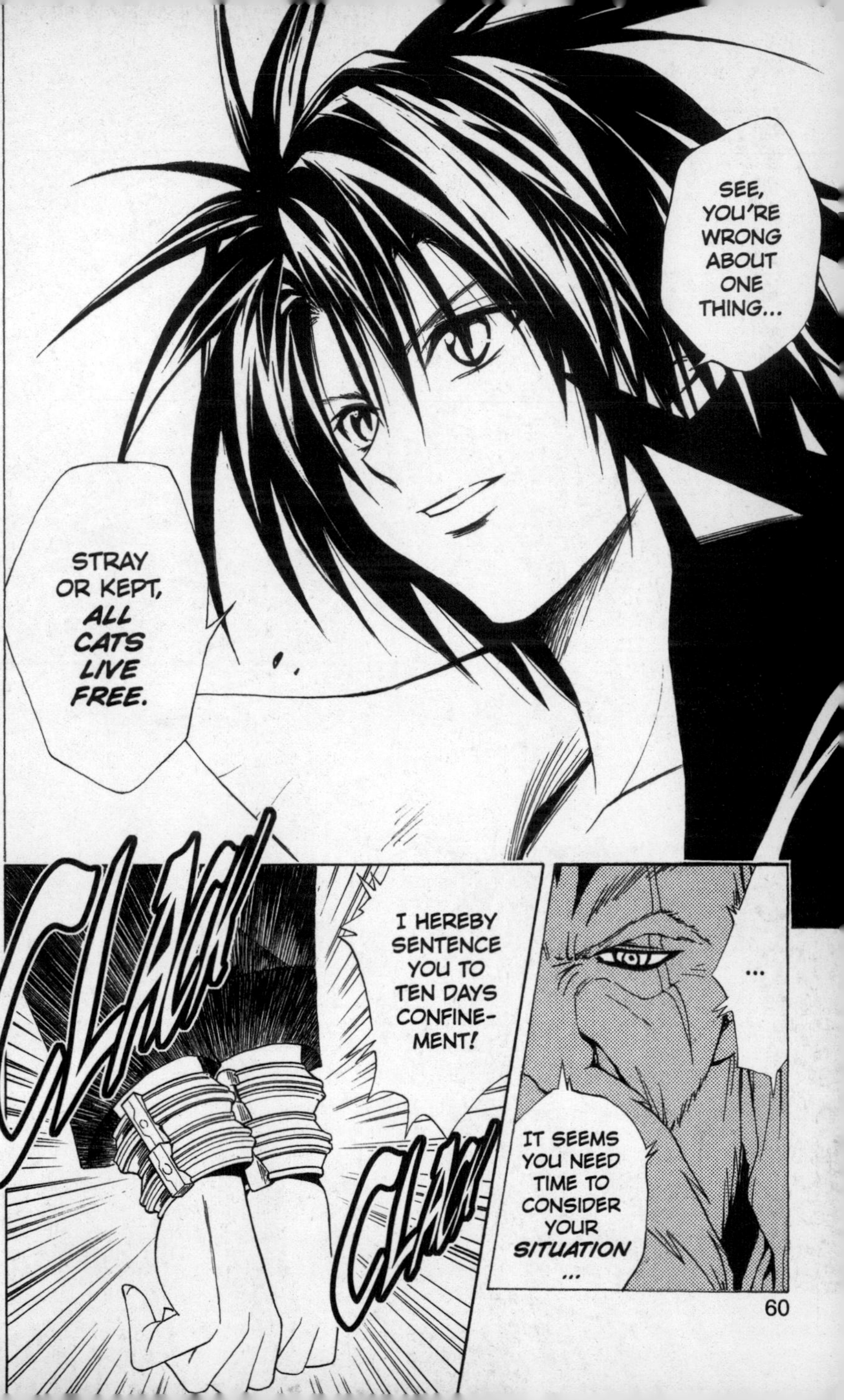
SEE, YOU'RE WRONG ABOUT ONE THING...
STRAY OR KEPT, ***ALL CATS LIVE FREE.***
...
IT SEEMS YOU NEED TIME TO CONSIDER YOUR ***SITUATION*** ...
I HEREBY SENTENCE YOU TO TEN DAYS CONFINE-MENT!

READ THIS WAY

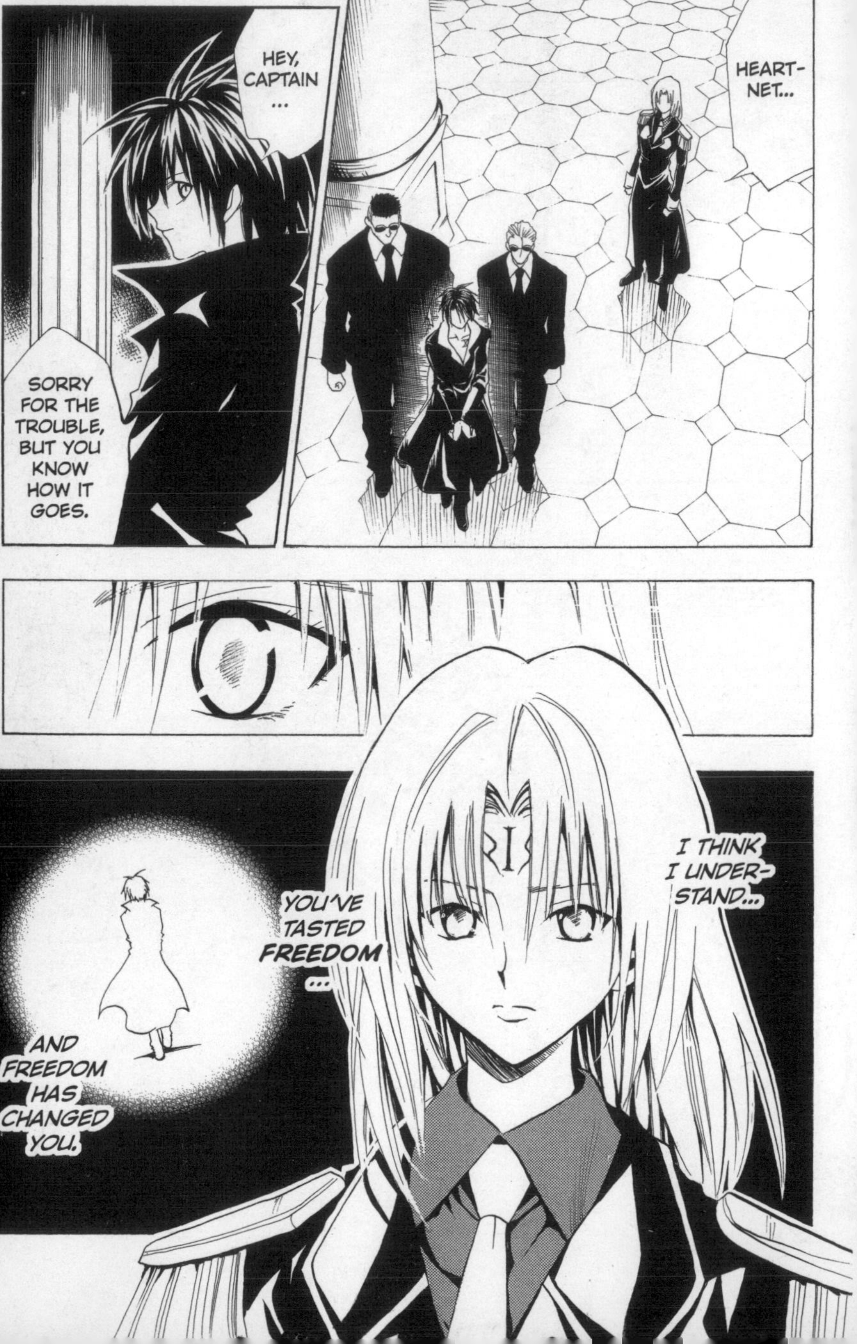

HEART-NET...
HEY, CAPTAIN ...
SORRY FOR THE TROUBLE, BUT YOU KNOW HOW IT GOES.
I THINK I UNDER-STAND...
YOU'VE TASTED FREEDOM ...
AND FREEDOM HAS CHANGED YOU.

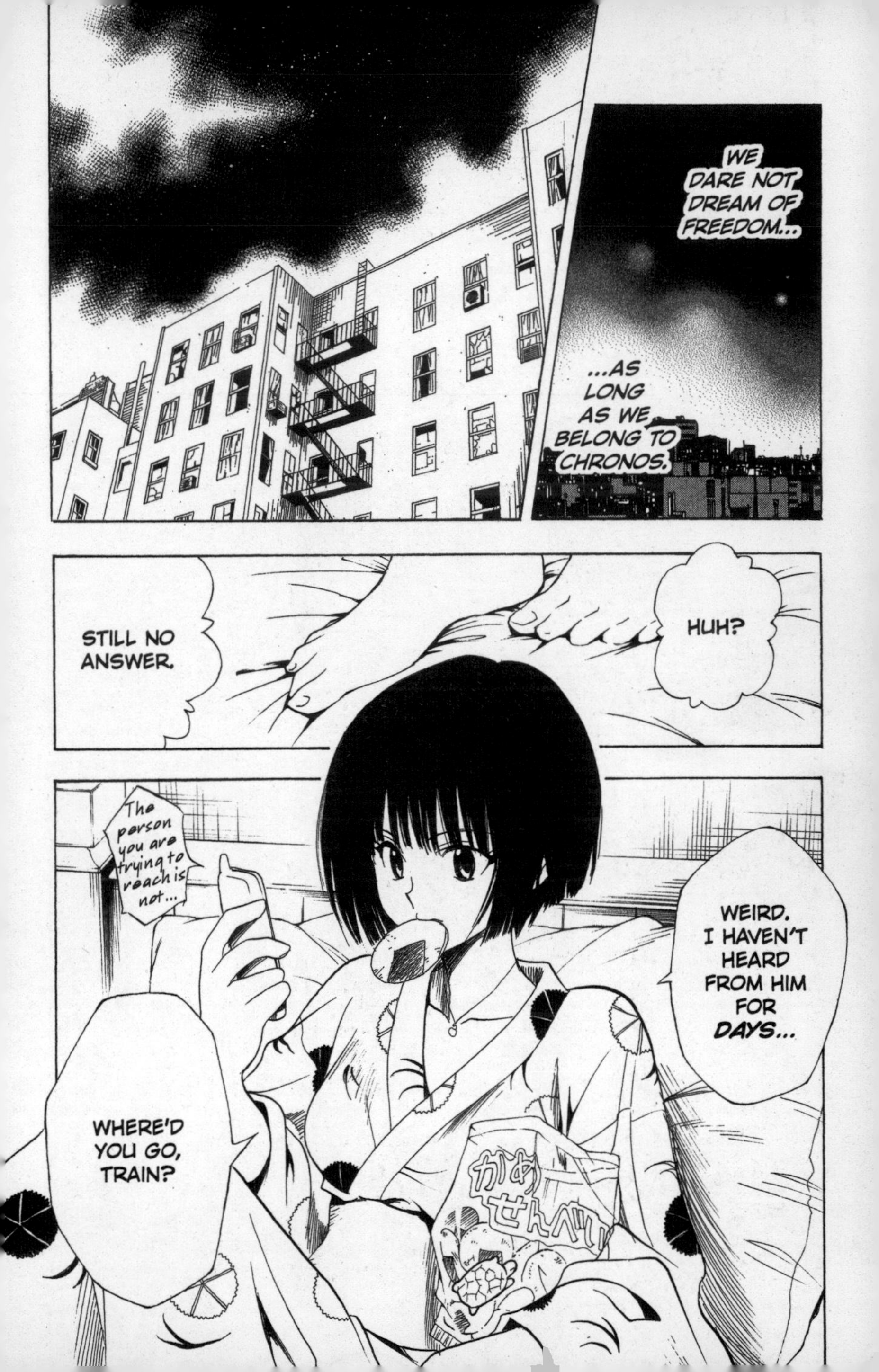
WE DARE NOT DREAM OF FREEDOM...
...AS LONG AS WE BELONG TO CHRONOS.
HUH?
STILL NO ANSWER.
WEIRD. I HAVEN'T HEARD FROM HIM FOR DAYS...
The person you are trying to reach is not...
かめせんべい
WHERE'D YOU GO, TRAIN?

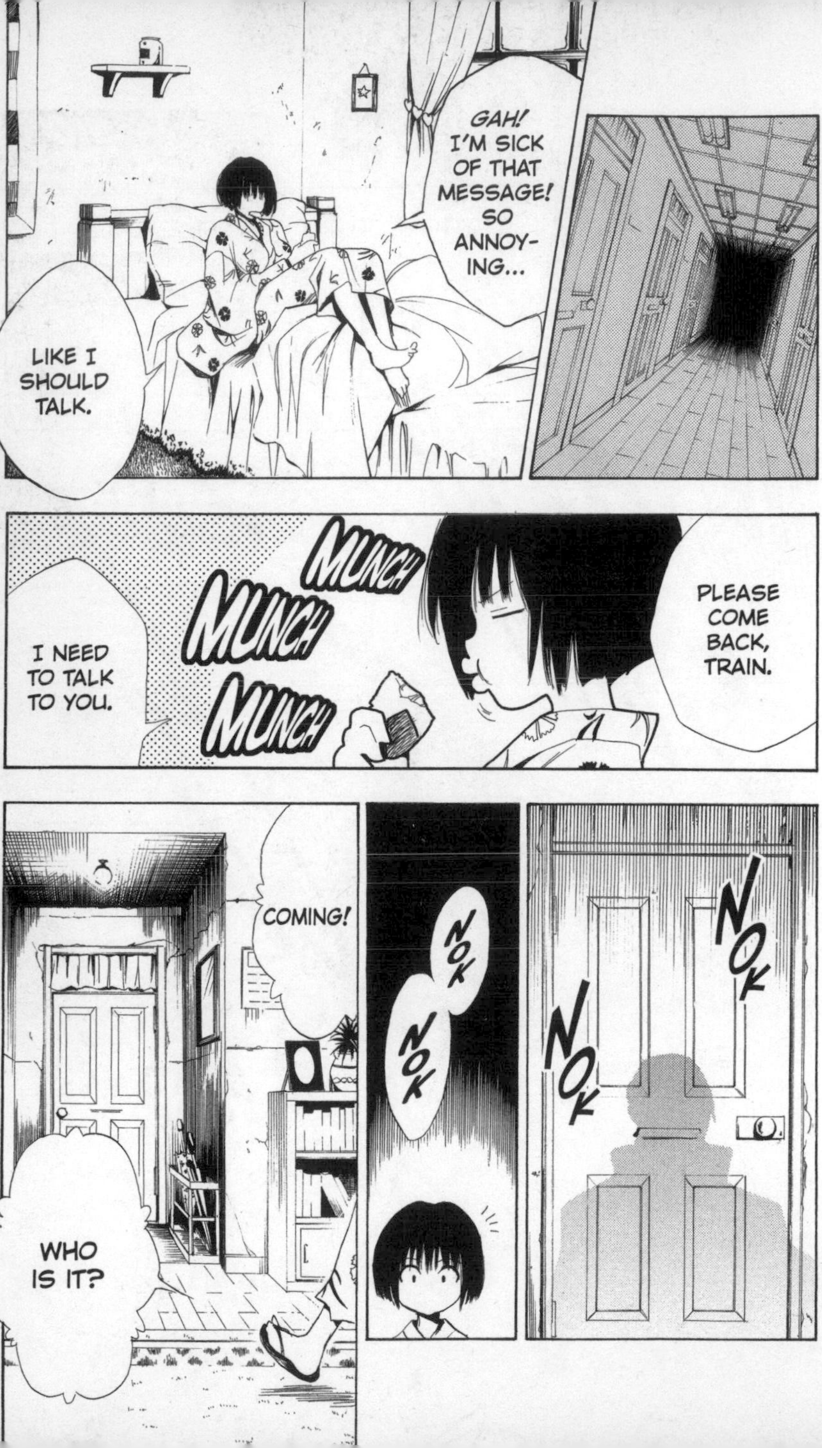
GAH! I'M SICK OF THAT MESSAGE! SO ANNOY-ING...
LIKE I SHOULD TALK.
PLEASE COME BACK, TRAIN.
MUNCH
MUNCH
MUNCH
I NEED TO TALK TO YOU.
NOK
NOK
NOK
NOK
COMING!
WHO IS IT?

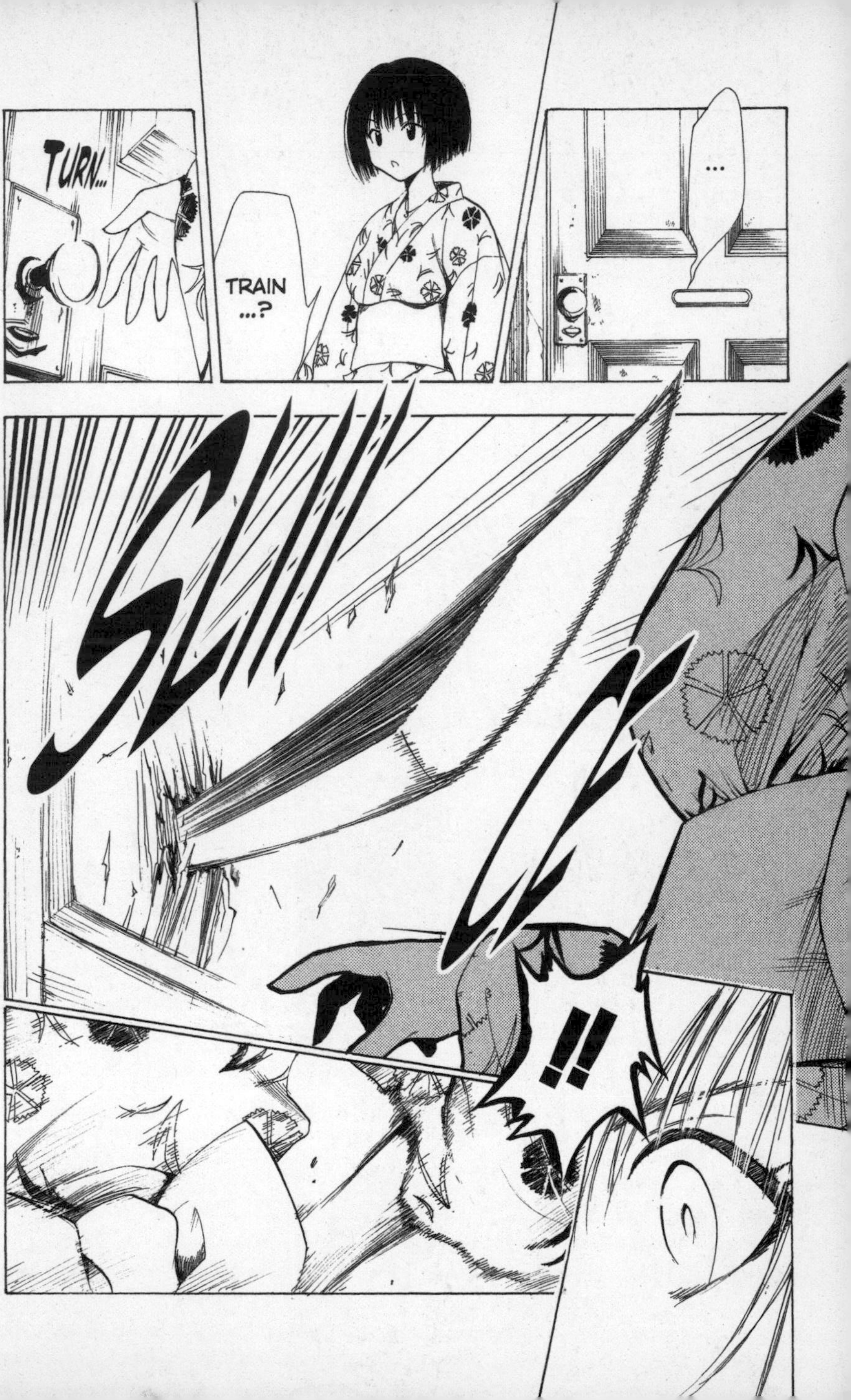
...
TRAIN ...?
TURN...
!!

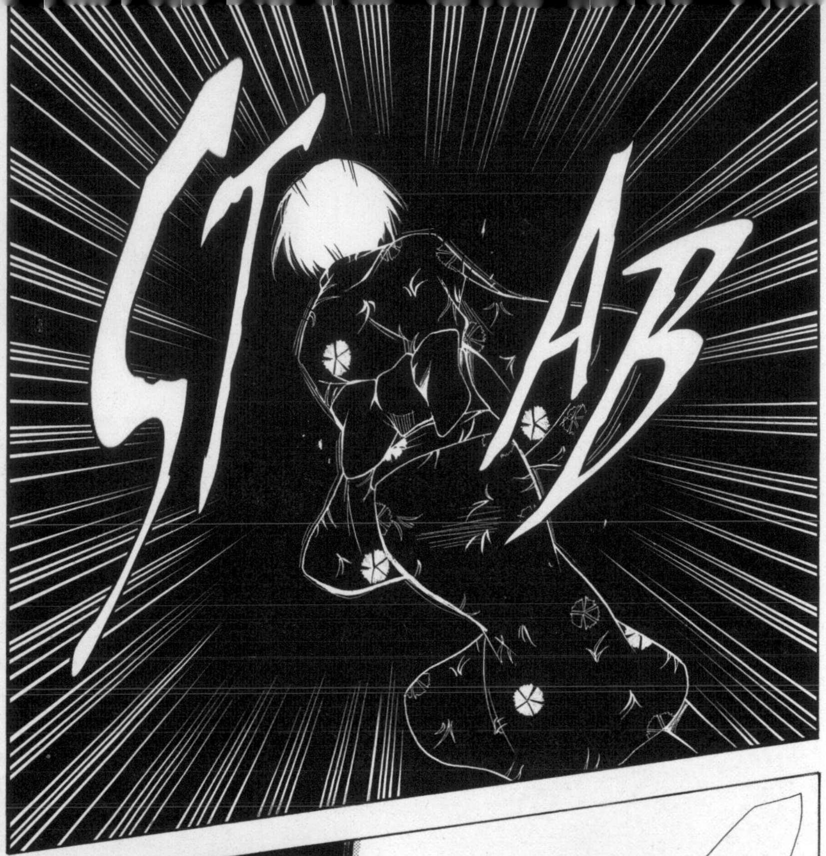
STAB
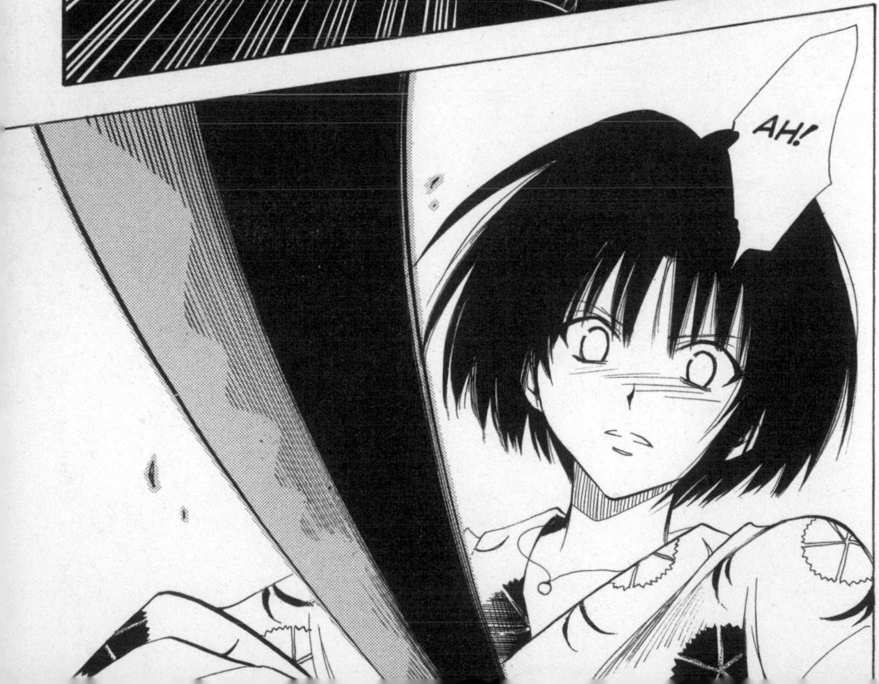
AH!

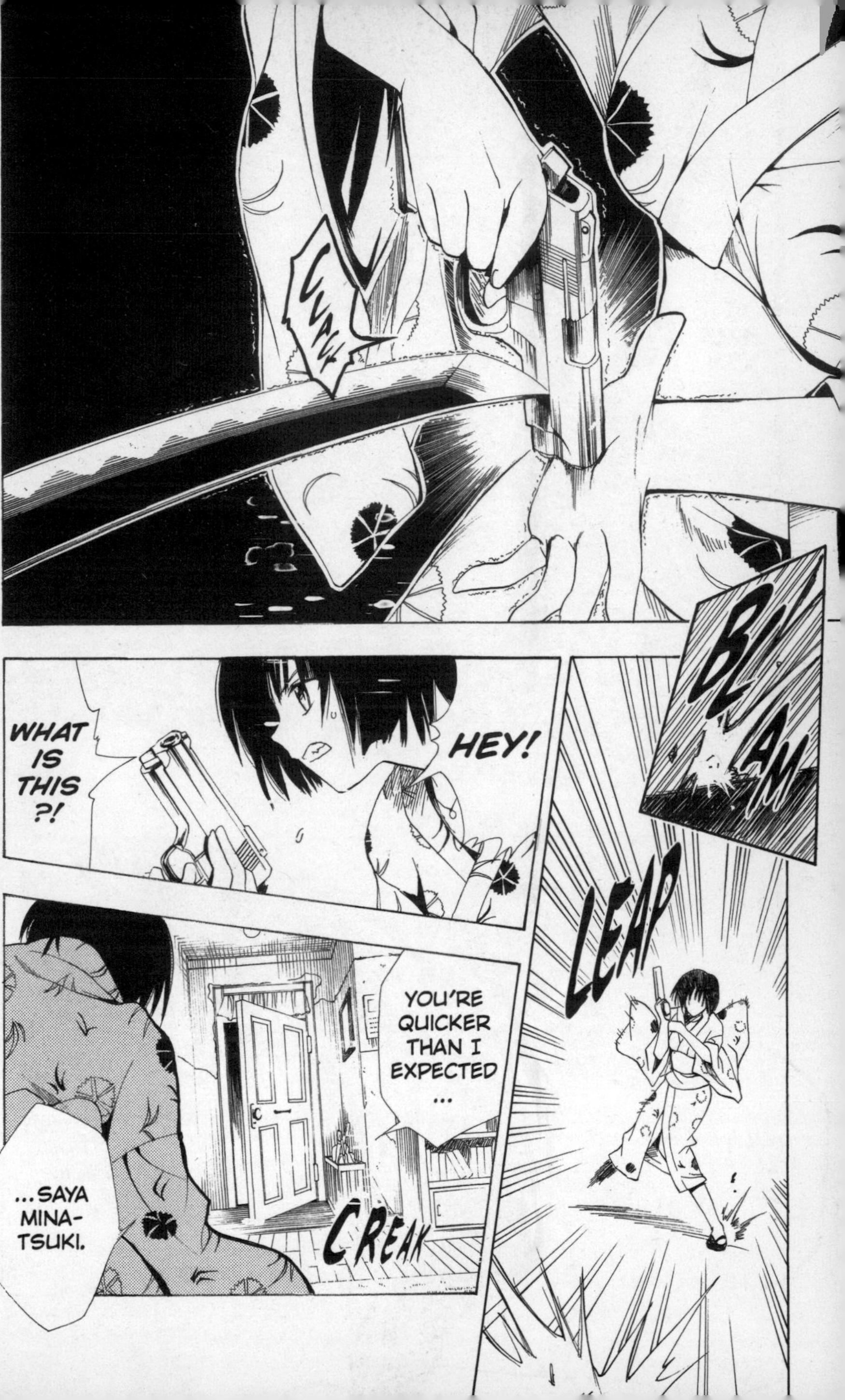
CLACK
BLAM
LEAP
HEY!
WHAT IS THIS ?!
YOU'RE QUICKER THAN I EXPECTED ...
CREAK
...SAYA MINA-TSUKI.

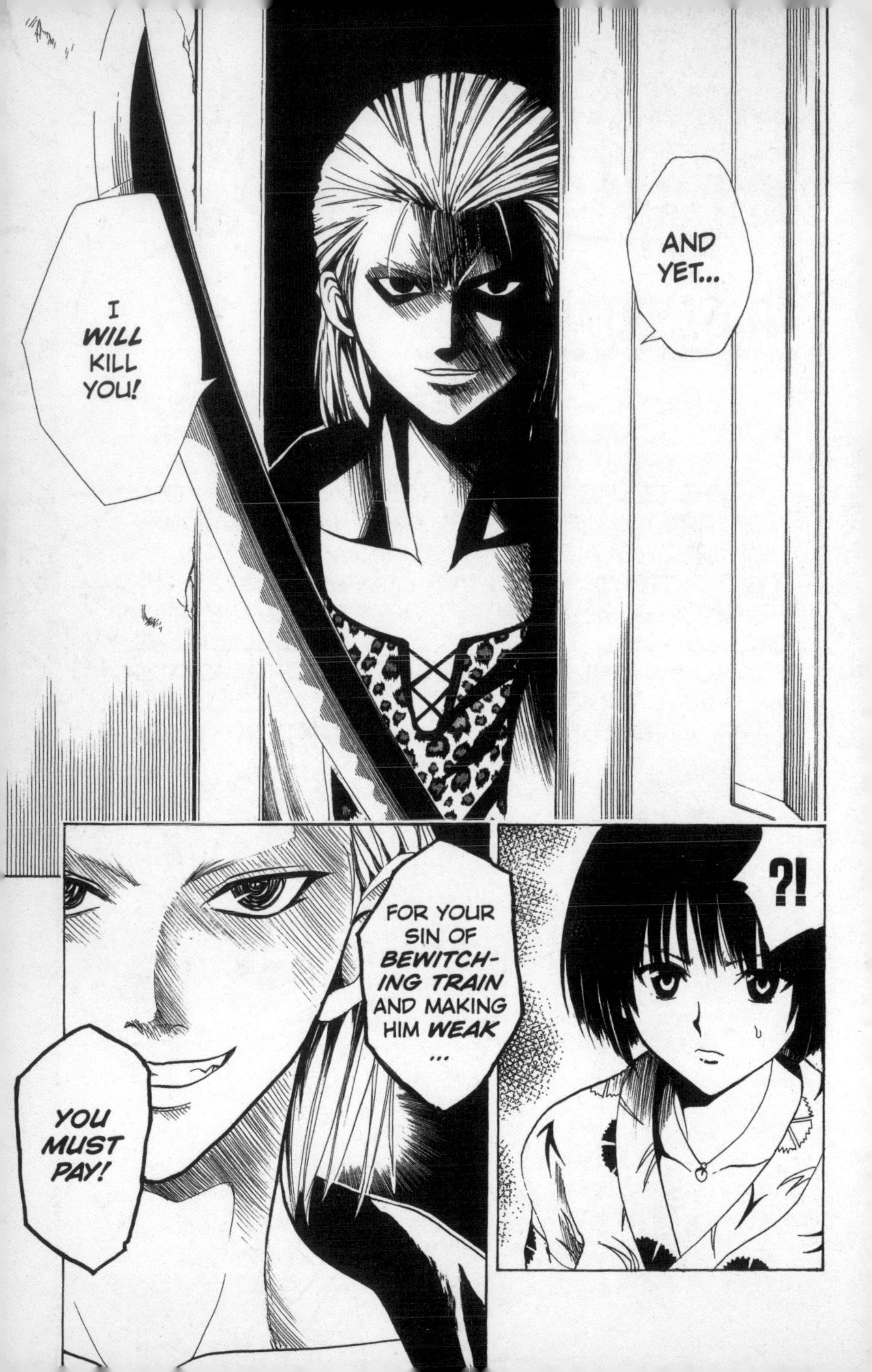
AND YET...
I WILL KILL YOU!
?!
FOR YOUR SIN OF BEWITCHING TRAIN AND MAKING HIM WEAK...
YOU MUST PAY!

THE ELDER COUNCIL

CHRONOS, THE INTERNATIONAL CRIME SYNDICATE, SAID TO CONTROL ONE THIRD OF THE WORLD'S ECONOMY, IS RUN BY THE COUNCIL OF ELDERS CONSISTING OF SUPREME LEADER WILZARK (ALSO KNOWN AS "SAICHOUROU, THE SUPREME ELDER") AND TWO OTHERS. THE TRIAD COMMUNICATES WITH THE ORGANIZATION THROUGH A PROJECTION SCREEN AND THEIR TRUE WHEREABOUTS ARE KNOWN ONLY TO A FEW, ONE OF WHOM IS SEPHIRIA. IT WAS THE COUNCIL OF ELDERS THAT APPOINTED TRAIN TO THE CHRONO NUMBERS.

The Elder, Supreme Leader of Chronos
Wilzark

READ THIS WAY

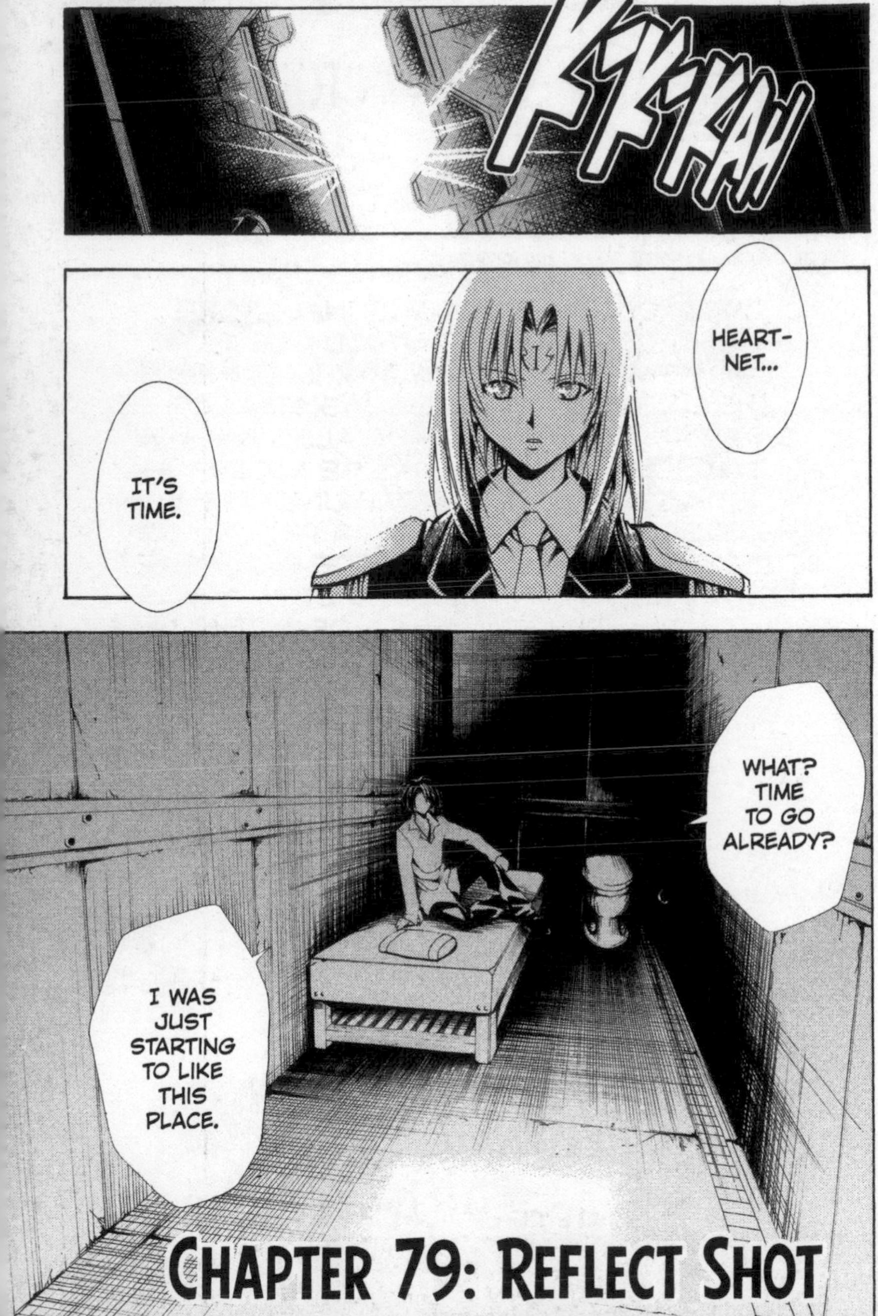
K-K-KAN
HEART-NET...
IT'S TIME.
WHAT? TIME TO GO ALREADY?
I WAS JUST STARTING TO LIKE THIS PLACE.

Chapter 79: Reflect Shot

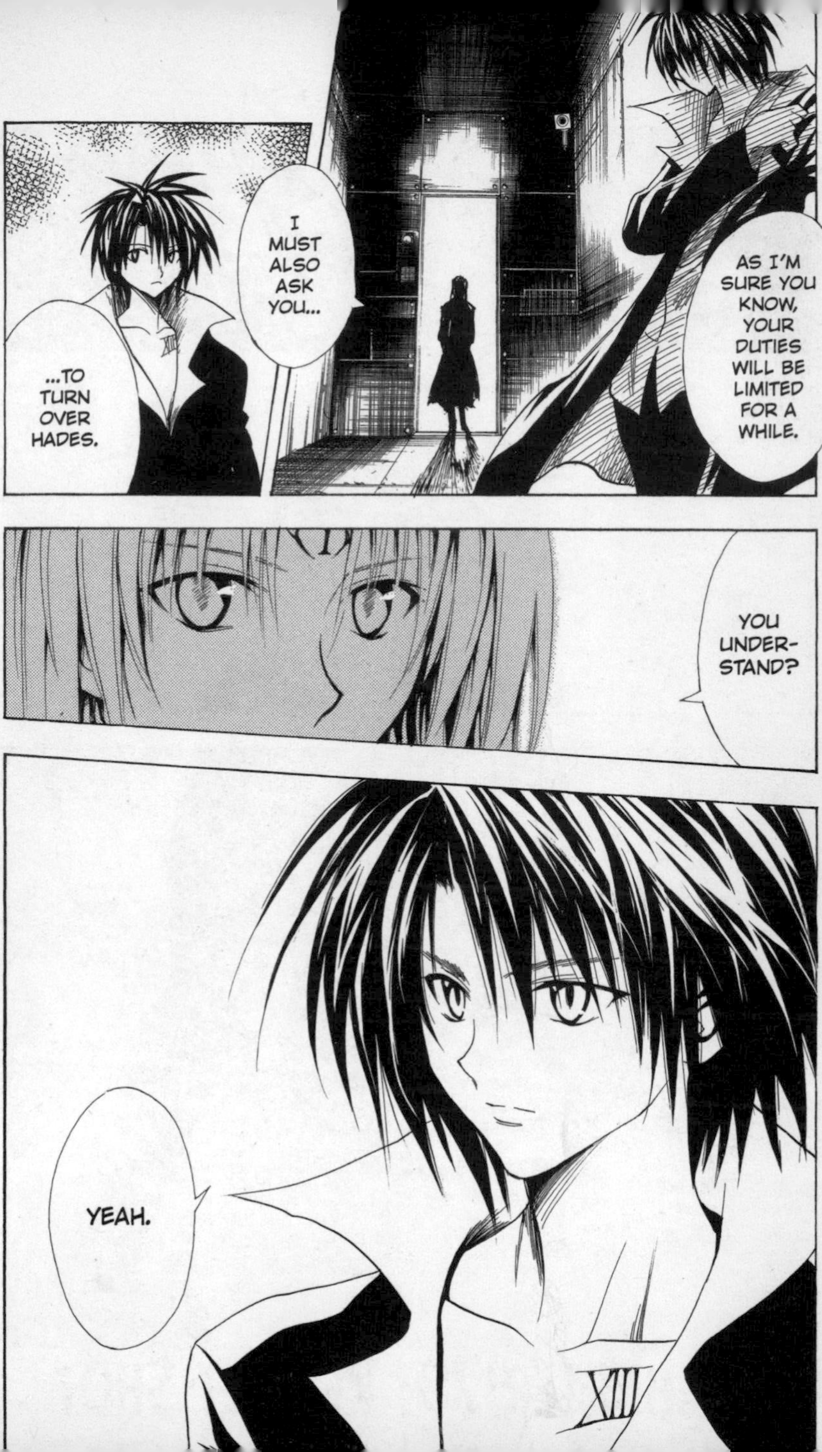
AS I'M SURE YOU KNOW, YOUR DUTIES WILL BE LIMITED FOR A WHILE.
I MUST ALSO ASK YOU...
...TO TURN OVER HADES.
YOU UNDER-STAND?
YEAH.

READ THIS WAY

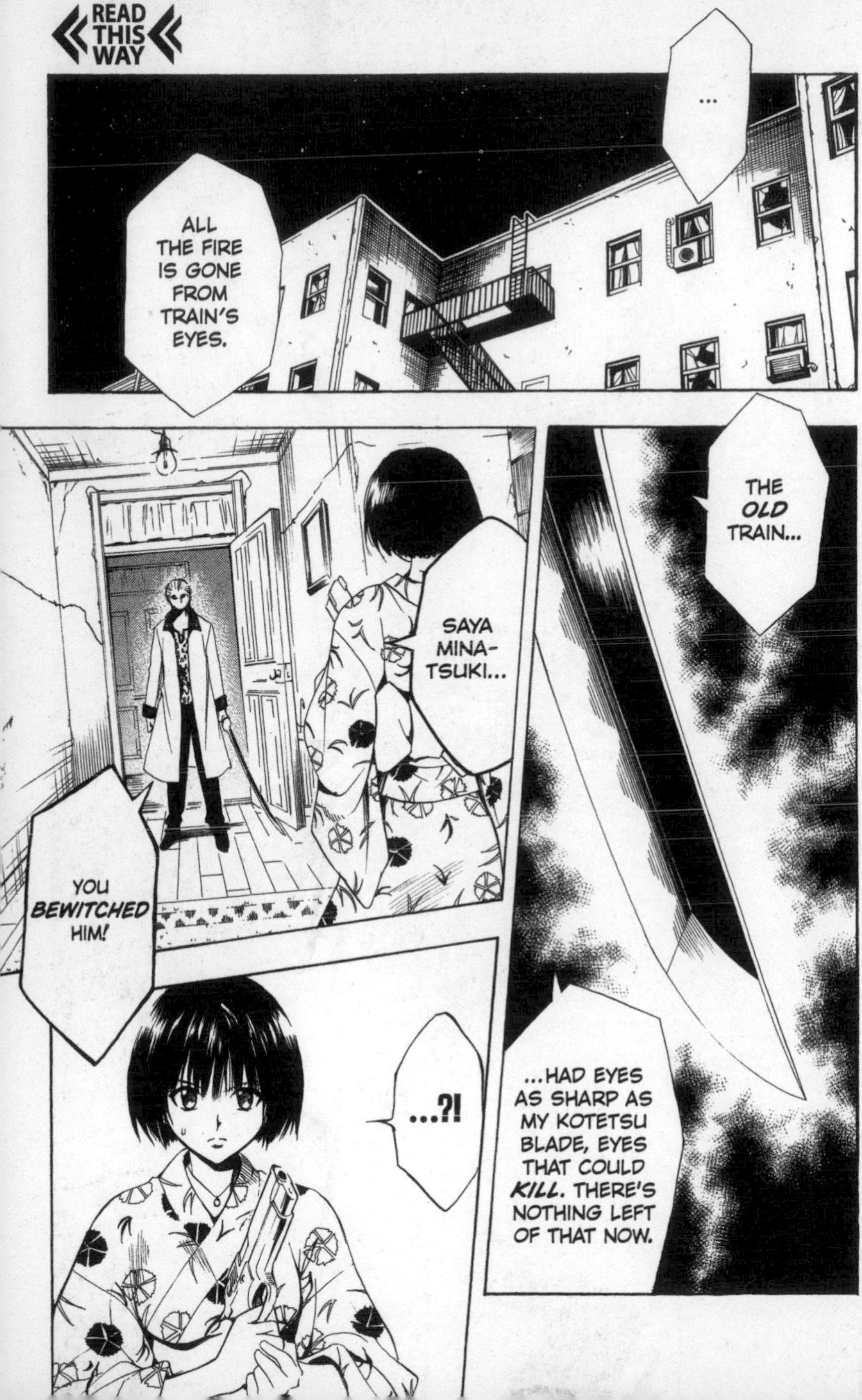
...
ALL THE FIRE IS GONE FROM TRAIN'S EYES.
THE *OLD* TRAIN...
...HAD EYES AS SHARP AS MY KOTETSU BLADE, EYES THAT COULD ***KILL***. THERE'S NOTHING LEFT OF THAT NOW.
SAYA MINA-TSUKI...
YOU ***BEWITCHED*** HIM!
...?!

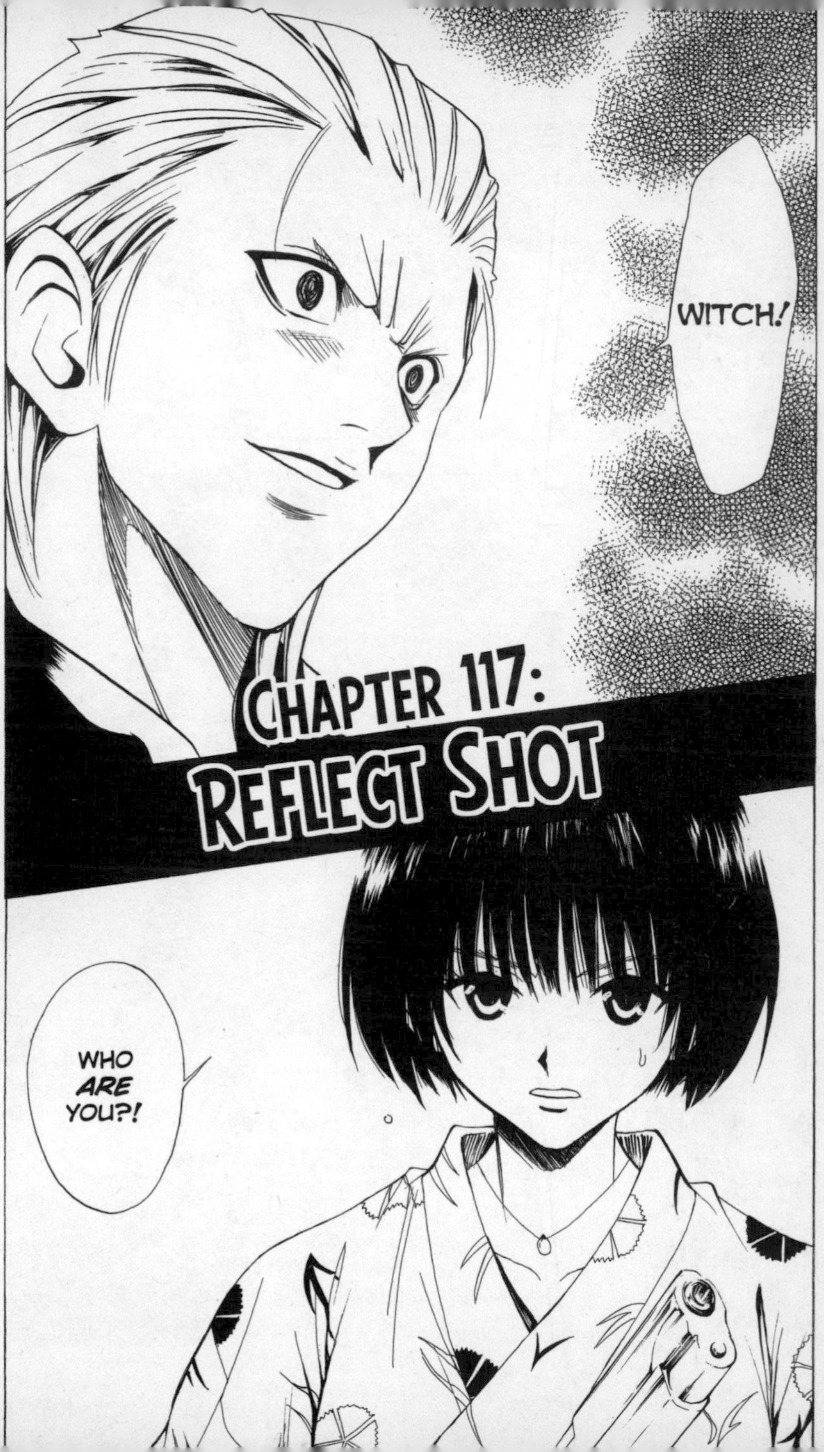
WITCH!
CHAPTER 117:
REFLECT SHOT
WHO *ARE* YOU?!

READ THIS WAY

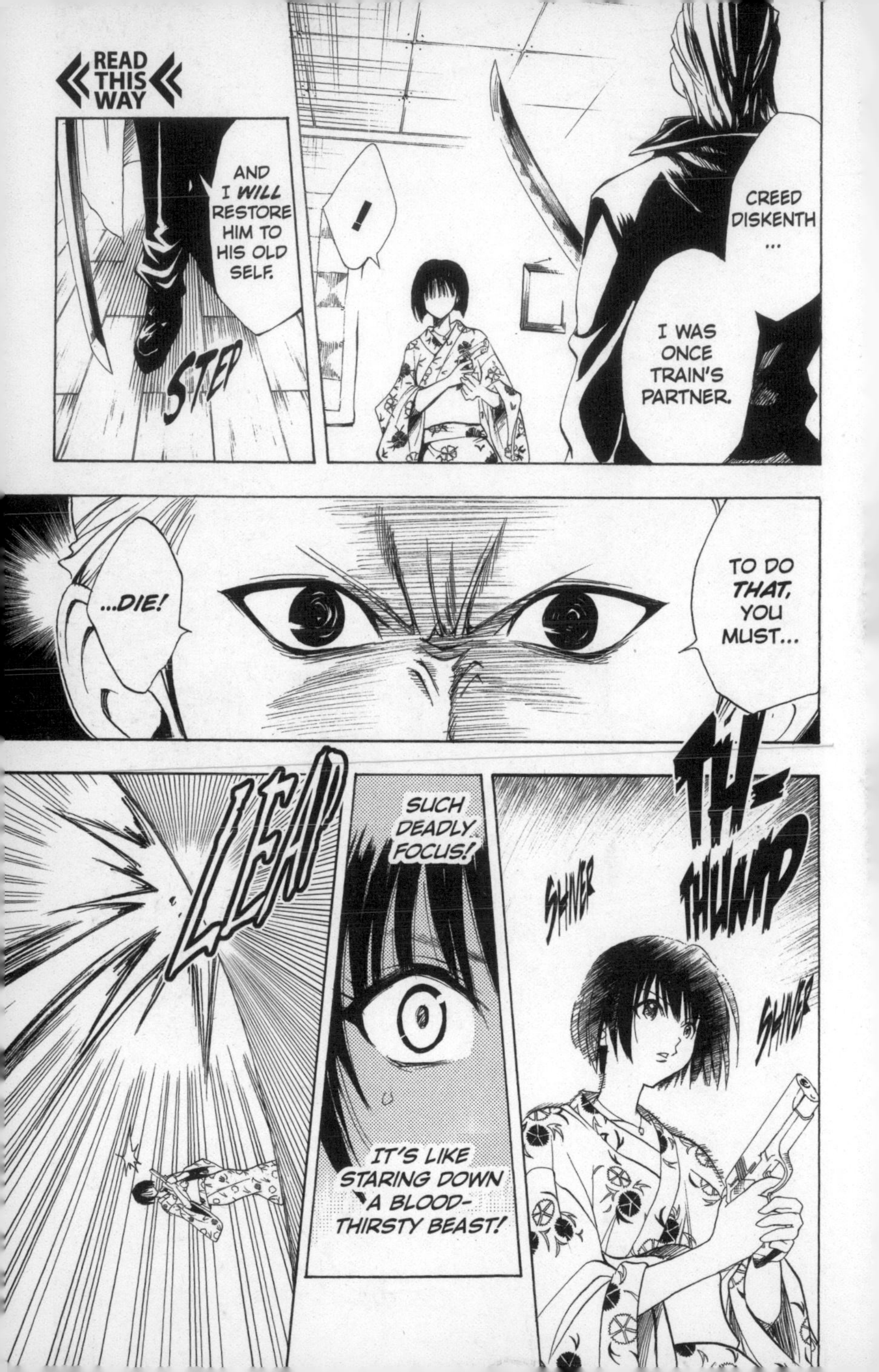
CREED DISKENTH ...
I WAS ONCE TRAIN'S PARTNER.
!
AND I *WILL* RESTORE HIM TO HIS OLD SELF.
STEP
TO DO *THAT,* YOU MUST...
...DIE!
TH-THUMP
SHIVER
SHIVER
SUCH DEADLY FOCUS!
IT'S LIKE STARING DOWN A BLOOD-THIRSTY BEAST!
LEAP

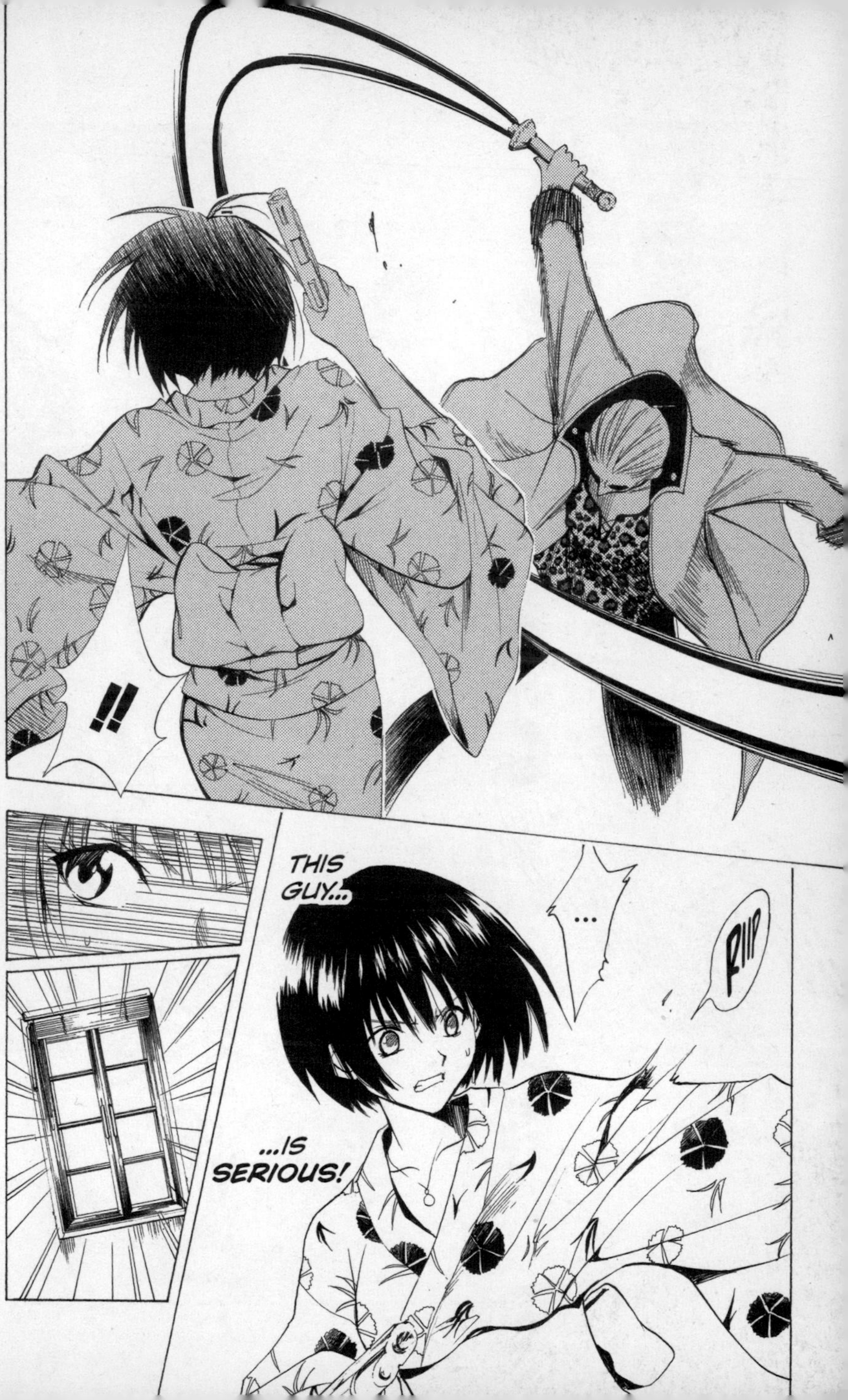
!!
RIIP
...
THIS GUY...
...IS SERIOUS!

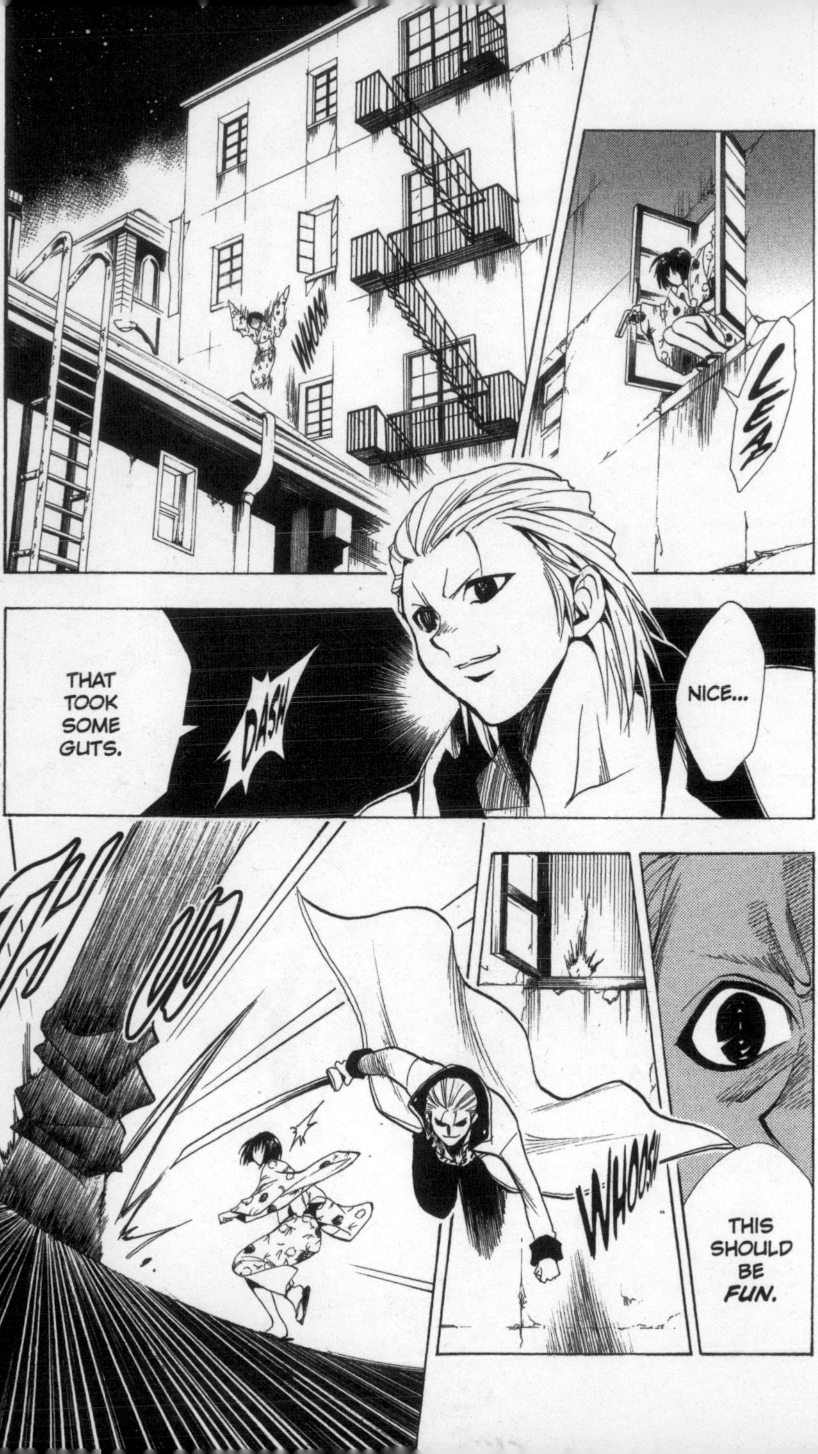
WHOOSH
NICE...
THAT TOOK SOME GUTS.
DASH
THIS SHOULD BE *FUN*.
WHOOSH

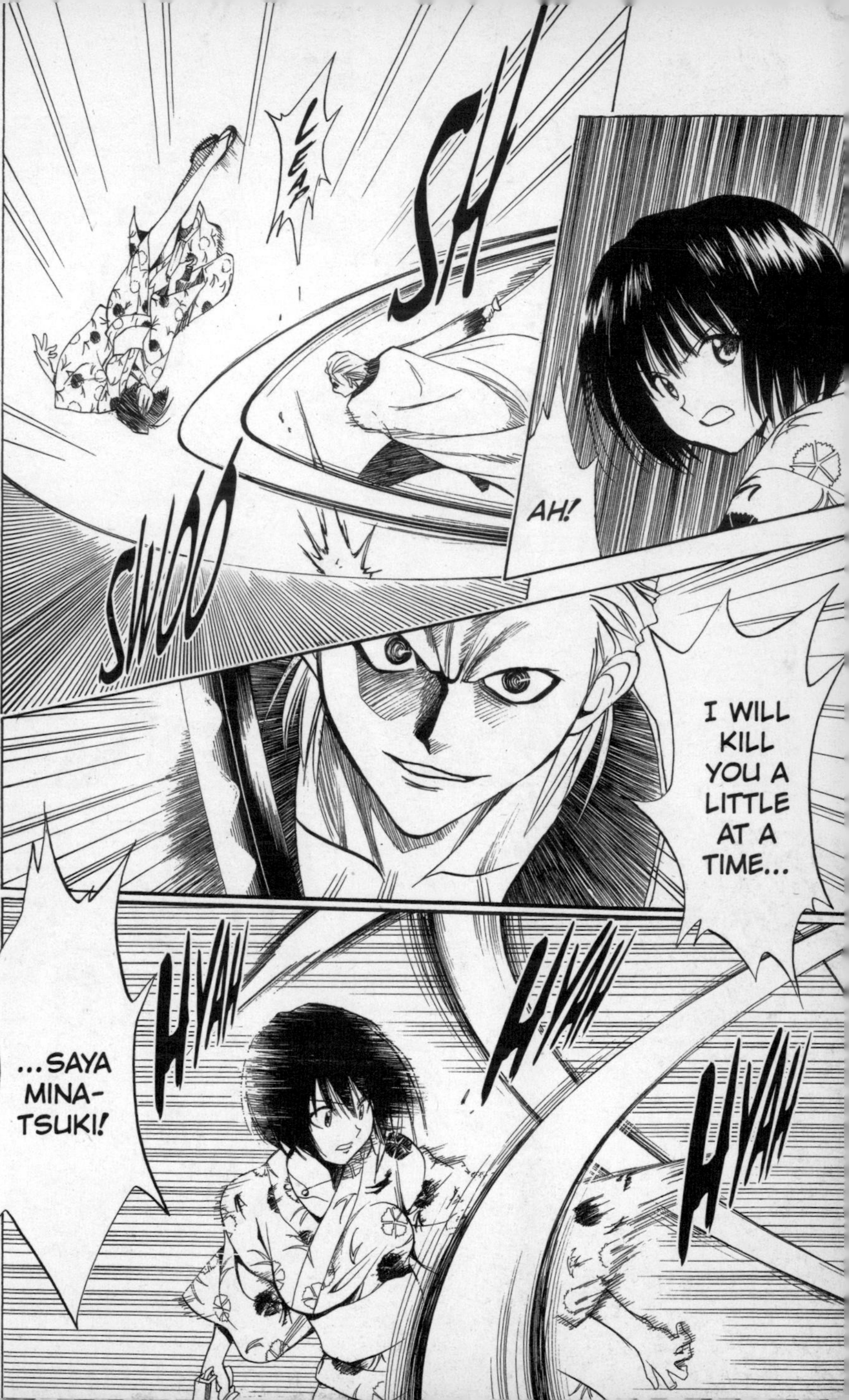
AH!
SH
LEAP
SWOO
I WILL KILL YOU A LITTLE AT A TIME...
HYAH
HYAH
HYAH
...SAYA MINA-TSUKI!

READ THIS WAY

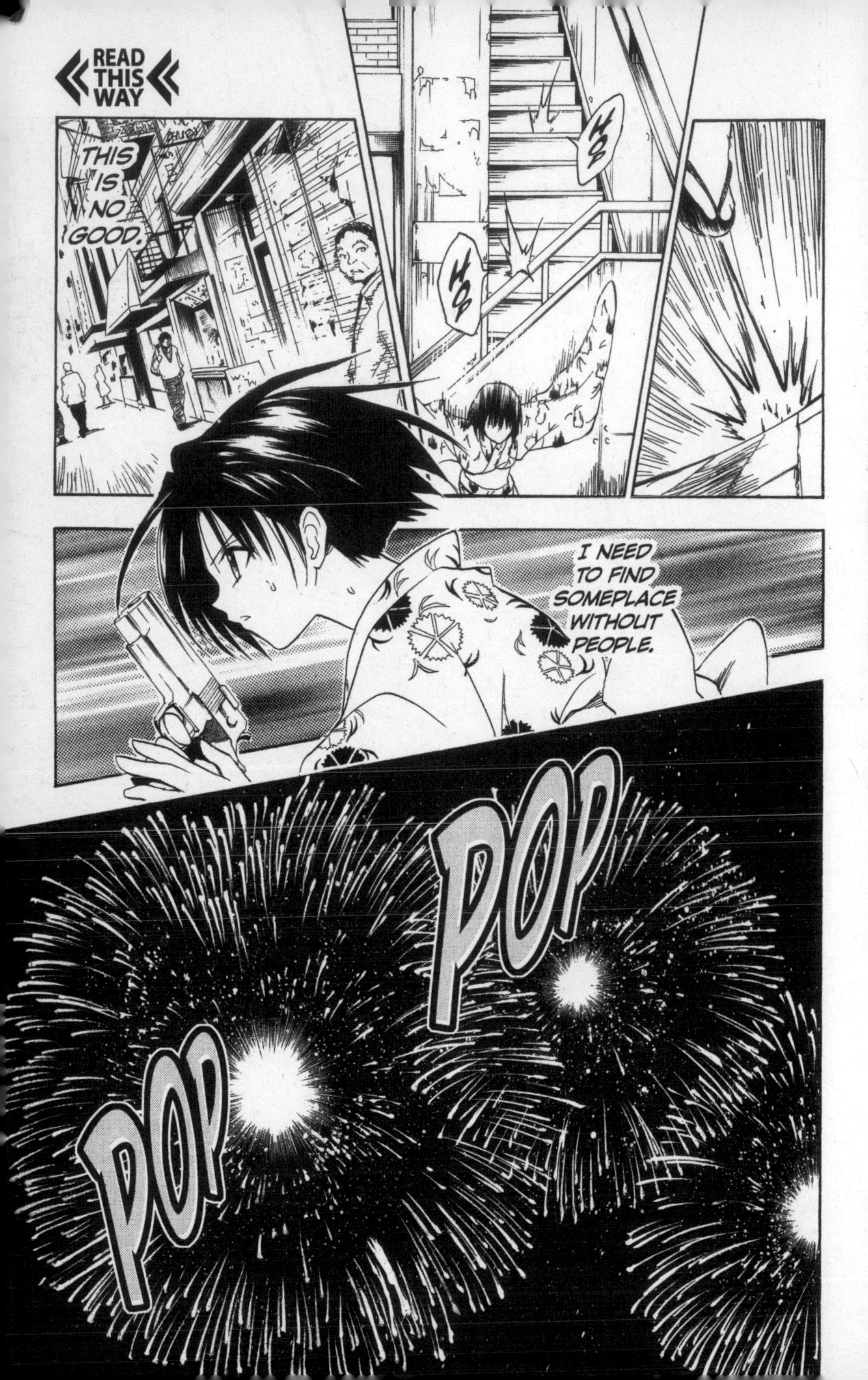
HOP
HOP
THIS IS NO GOOD.
I NEED TO FIND SOMEPLACE WITHOUT PEOPLE.
POP
POP

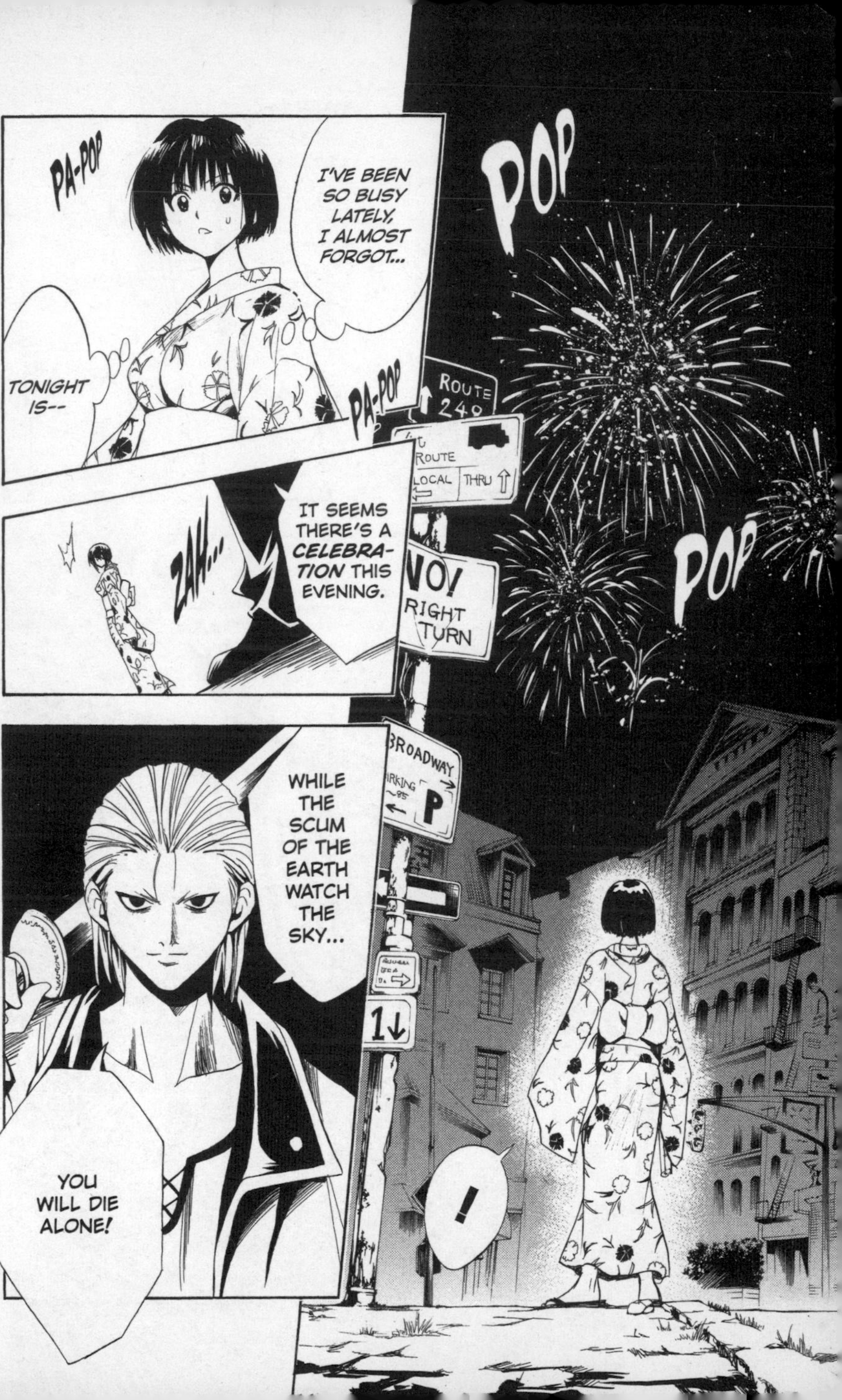
POP
POP
ROUTE 249
ROUTE
LOCAL
THRU
RIGHT TURN
BROADWAY
P
1
!
PA-POP
I'VE BEEN SO BUSY LATELY, I ALMOST FORGOT...
TONIGHT IS--
PA-POP
IT SEEMS THERE'S A CELEBRATION THIS EVENING.
ZAH...
WHILE THE SCUM OF THE EARTH WATCH THE SKY...
YOU WILL DIE ALONE!

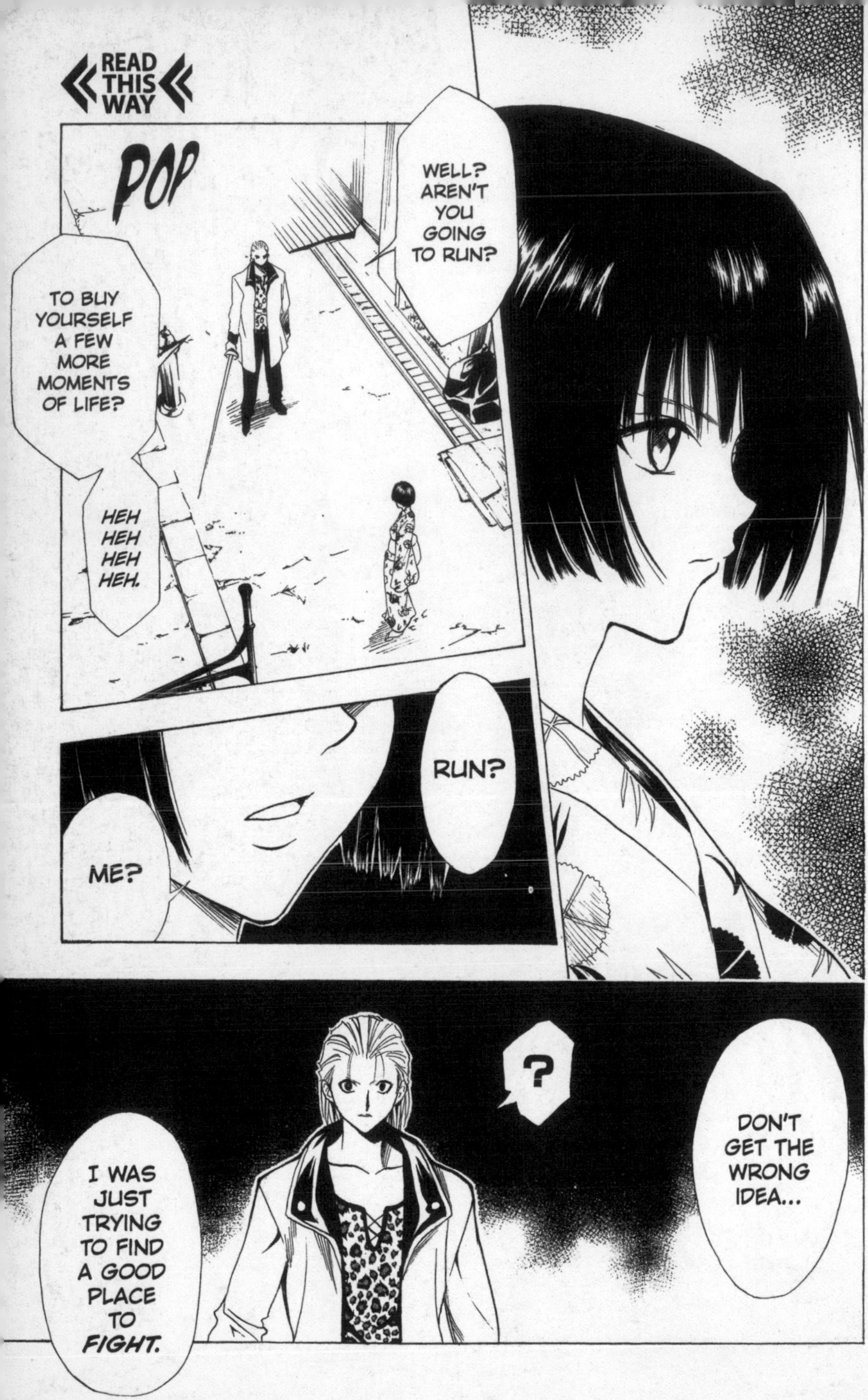
READ THIS WAY
WELL? AREN'T YOU GOING TO RUN?
POP
TO BUY YOURSELF A FEW MORE MOMENTS OF LIFE?
HEH HEH HEH HEH.
RUN?
ME?
DON'T GET THE WRONG IDEA...
?
I WAS JUST TRYING TO FIND A GOOD PLACE TO *FIGHT*.

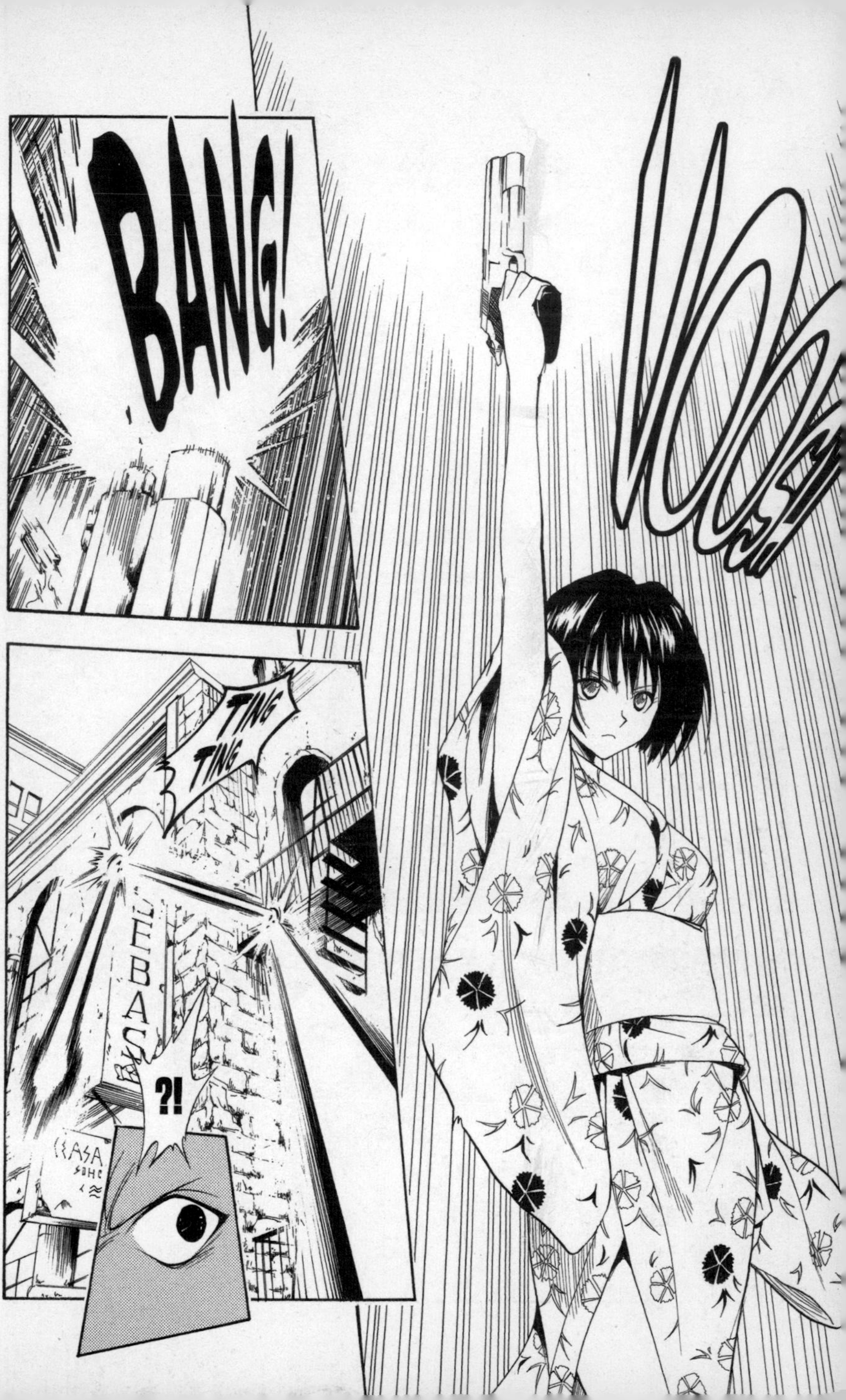
BANG!
TING TING
?!

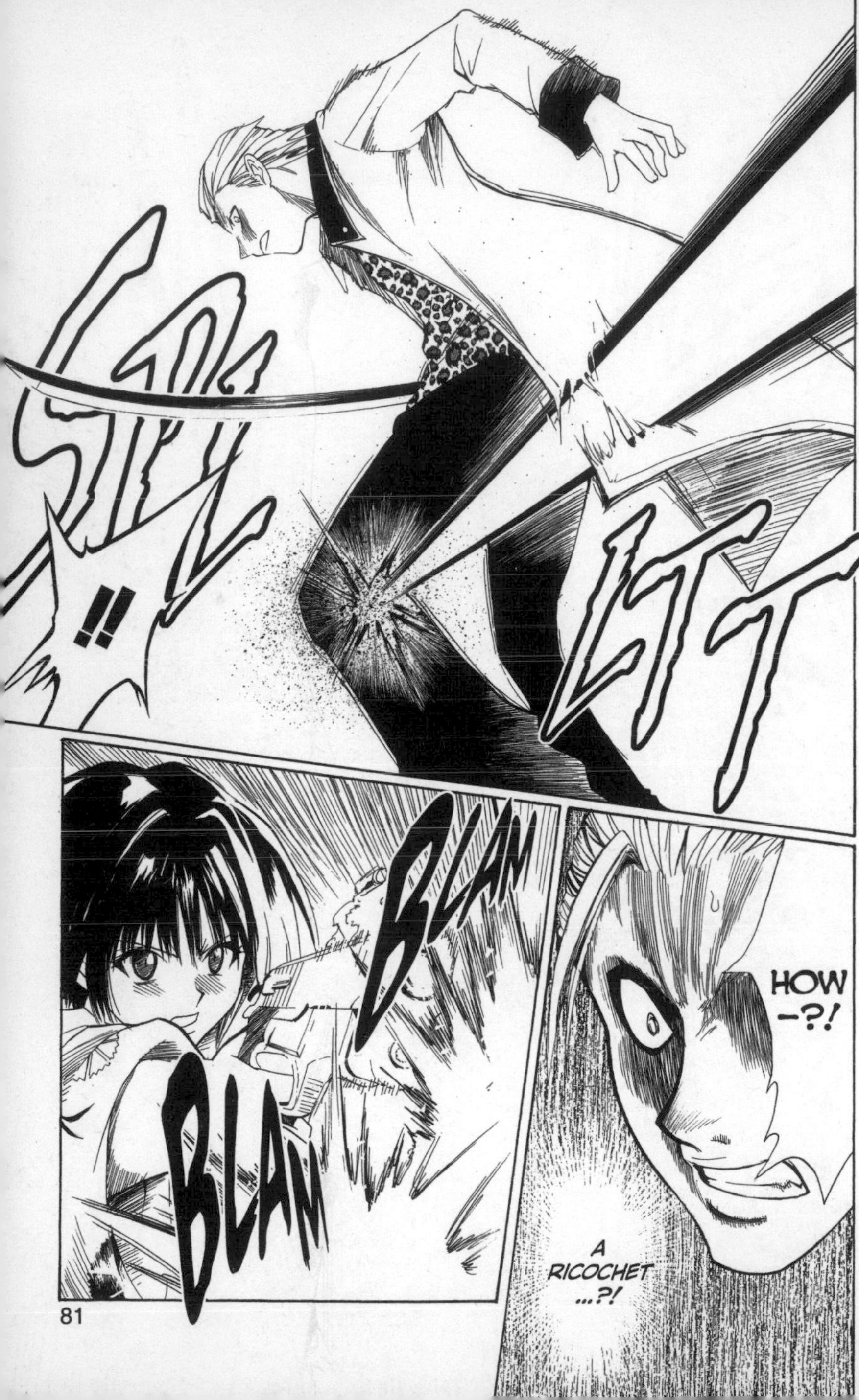
SPLITT!!
HOW—?!
A RICOCHET...?!
BLAM
BLAM

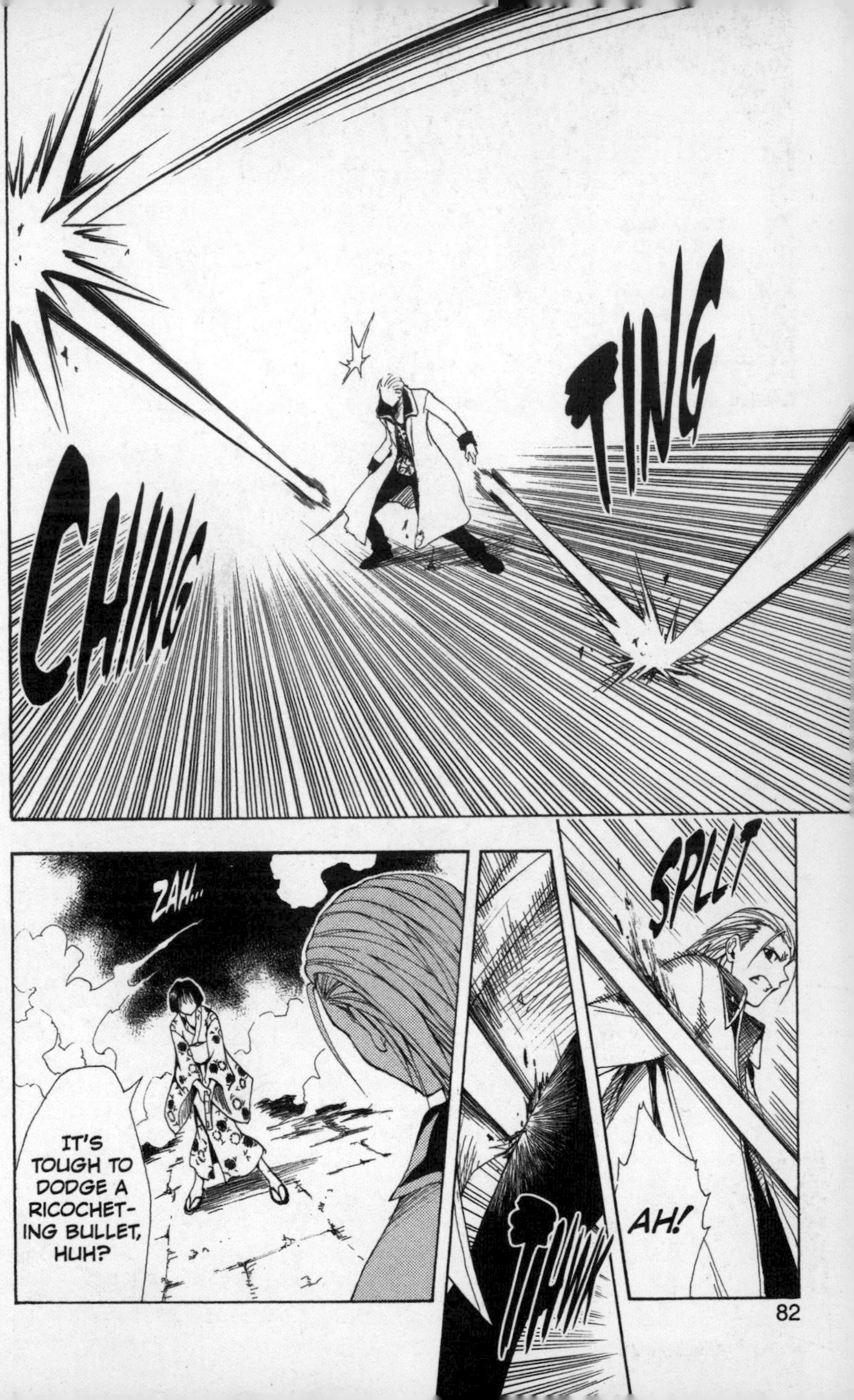
TING
CHING
SPLLT
AH!
ZAH...
IT'S TOUGH TO DODGE A RICOCHETING BULLET, HUH?

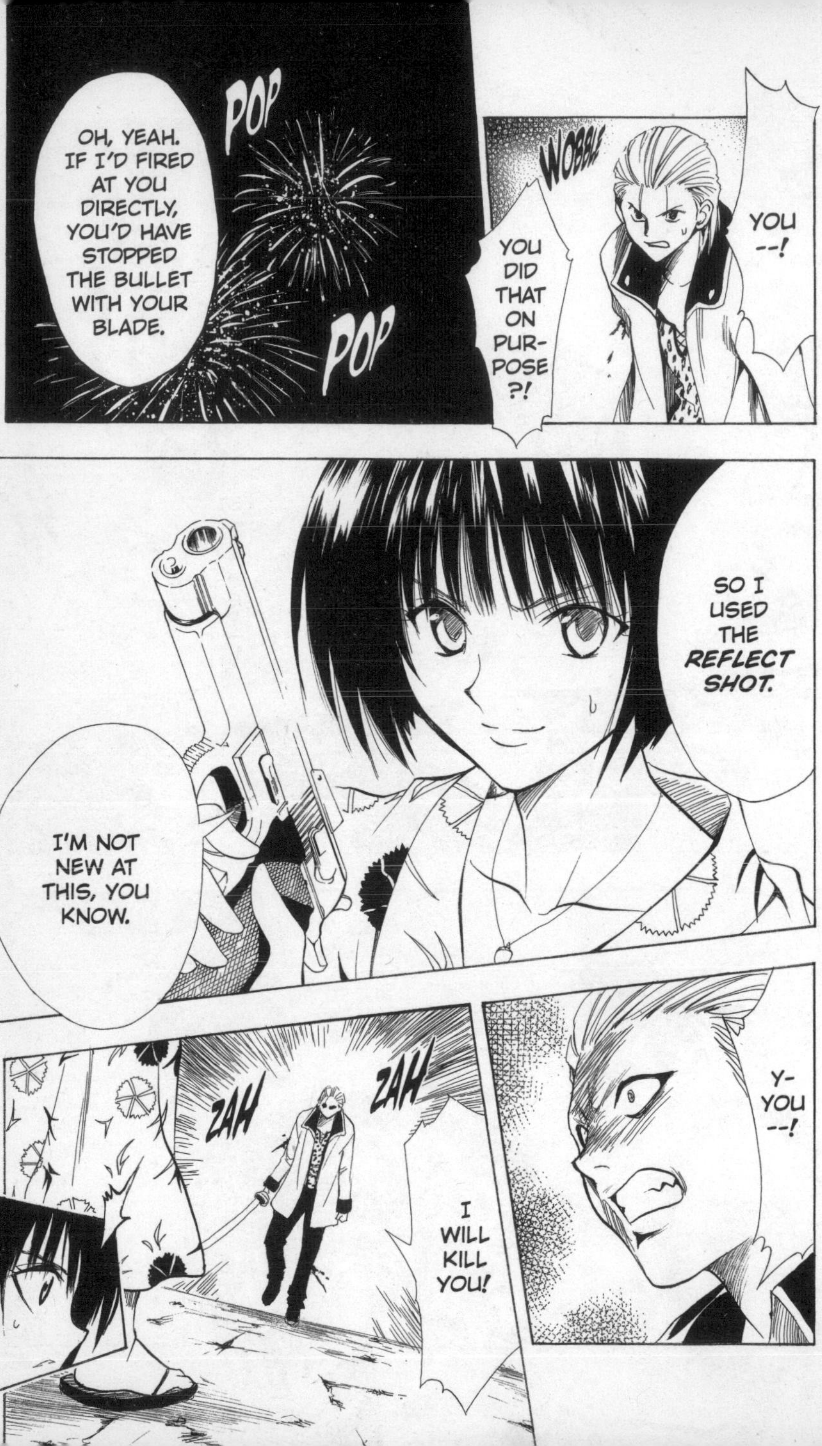
WOBBLE
YOU --!
YOU DID THAT ON PUR-POSE?!
POP
OH, YEAH. IF I'D FIRED AT YOU DIRECTLY, YOU'D HAVE STOPPED THE BULLET WITH YOUR BLADE.
POP
SO I USED THE *REFLECT SHOT.*
I'M NOT NEW AT THIS, YOU KNOW.
Y-YOU --!
ZAH
ZAH
I WILL KILL YOU!

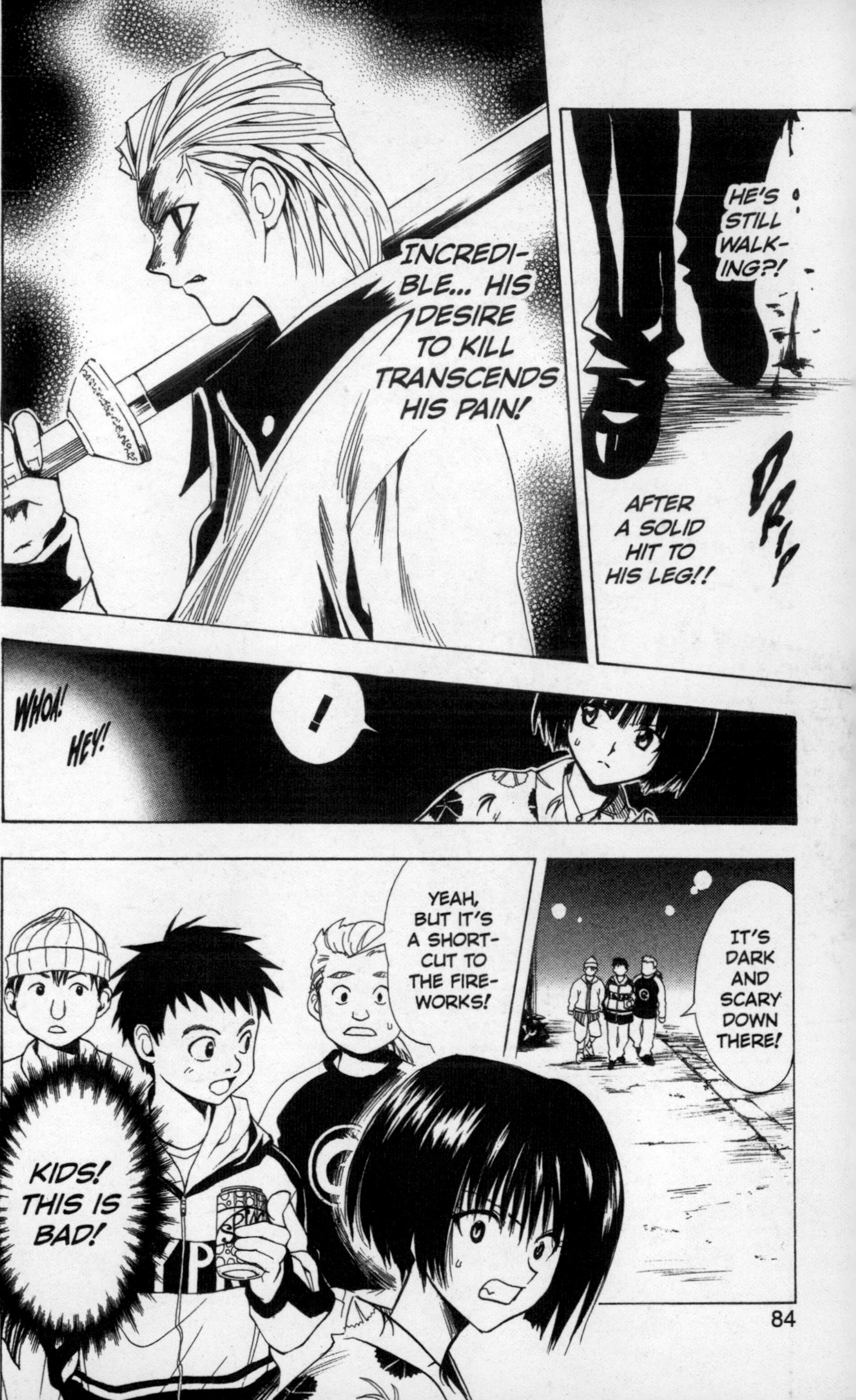
HE'S STILL WALKING?!
AFTER A SOLID HIT TO HIS LEG!!
INCREDIBLE... HIS DESIRE TO KILL TRANSCENDS HIS PAIN!
!
WHOA!
HEY!
IT'S DARK AND SCARY DOWN THERE!
YEAH, BUT IT'S A SHORTCUT TO THE FIREWORKS!
KIDS! THIS IS BAD!

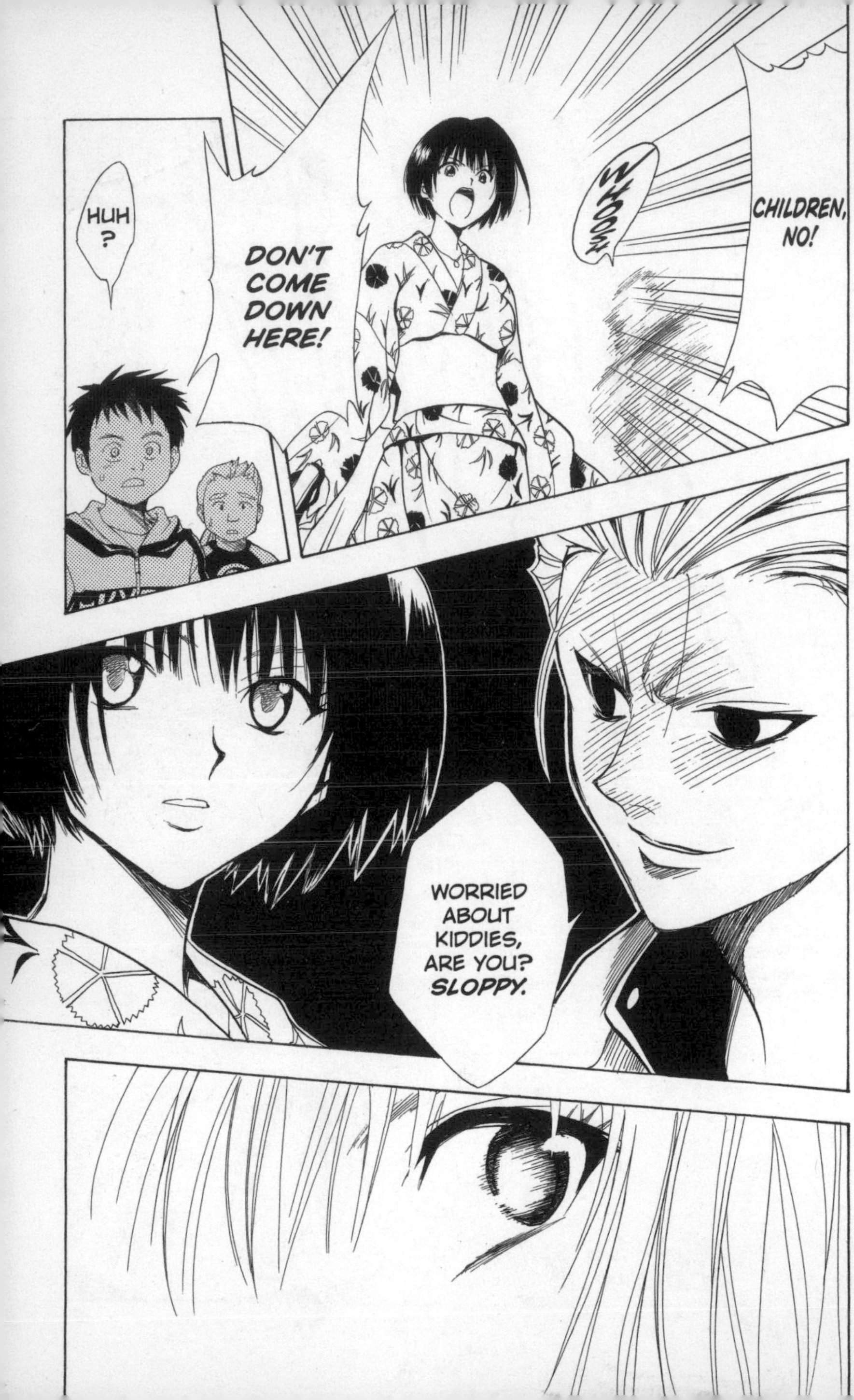
CHILDREN, NO!
WHOOSH
DON'T COME DOWN HERE!
HUH ?
WORRIED ABOUT KIDDIES, ARE YOU? *SLOPPY.*

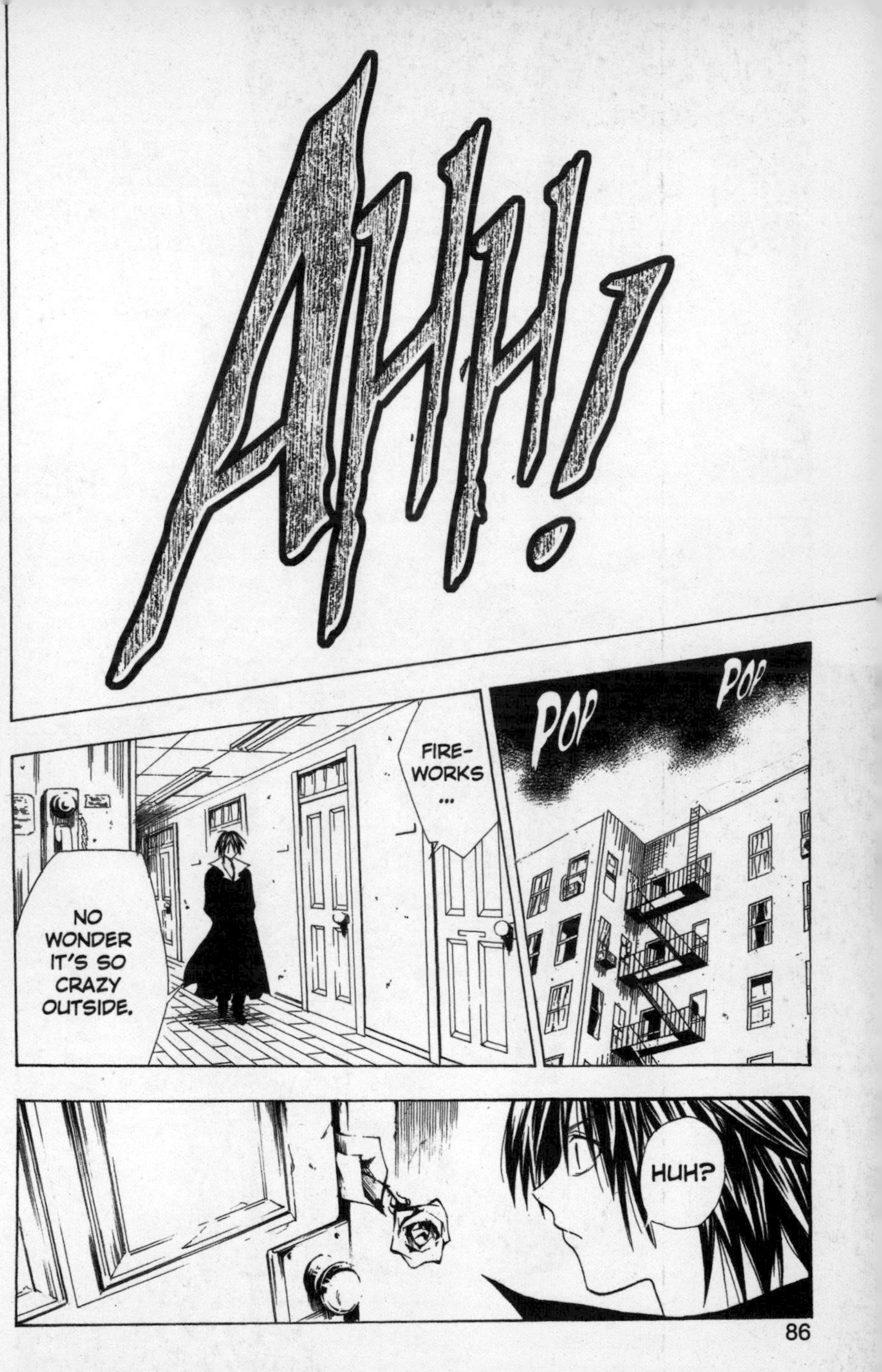
AHH!!
POP
POP
FIRE-WORKS ...
NO WONDER IT'S SO CRAZY OUTSIDE.
HUH?

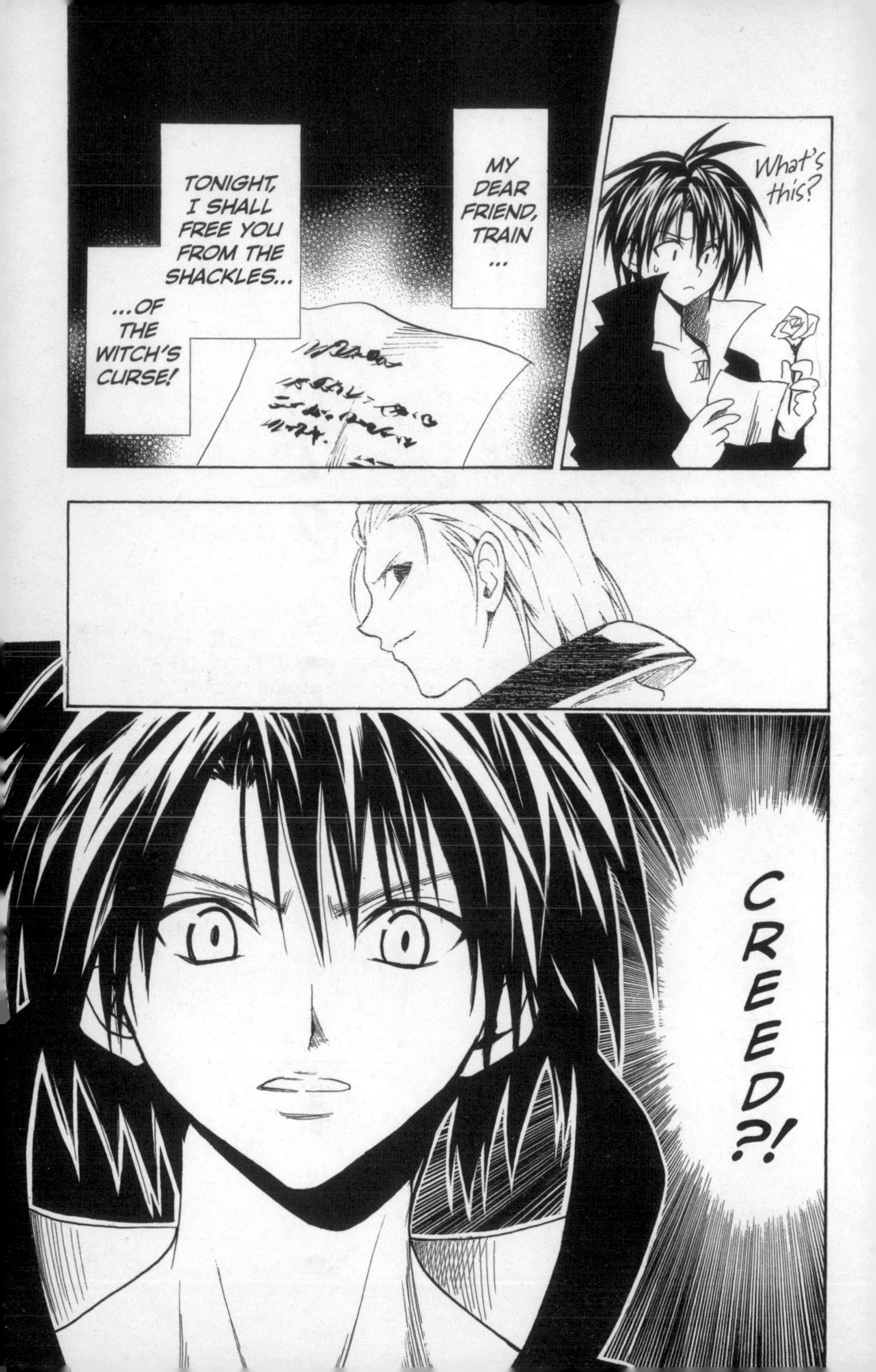
What's this?
MY DEAR FRIEND, TRAIN ...
TONIGHT, I SHALL FREE YOU FROM THE SHACKLES...
...OF THE WITCH'S CURSE!
CREED?!

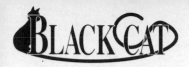

BLACK CAT **FACTOID**

REFLECT SHOT

FOR ALL ITS GOOD QUALITIES, A PISTOL FIRES IN A STRAIGHT LINE AND A CLEVER FOE CAN PREDICT AND EVADE ITS ATTACK. HOWEVER, A BULLET CAN BE MADE TO RICOCHET (LIKE A PINBALL) OFF OF ROCKS AND THE HARD CORNERS OF BILLBOARDS, ENABLING ATTACKS FROM VARIOUS ANGLES. THAT IS THE REFLECT SHOT.

THE DEGREE OF DIFFICULTY IS, OF COURSE, VERY HIGH. THIS SPECIALTY SHOT REQUIRES PERFECT ANGLE ASSESSMENT, AIM, AND EXPERIENCE. IT TOOK SAYA FIVE YEARS TO MASTER.

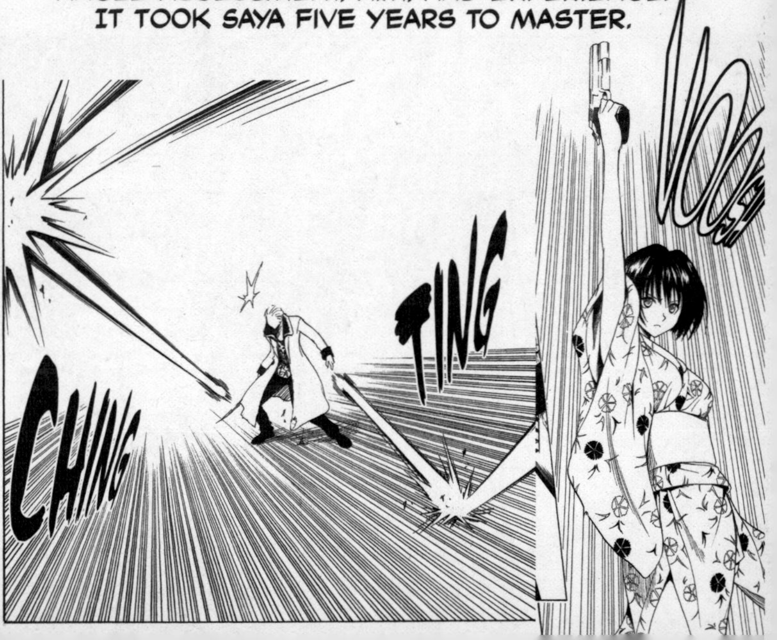
TING
CHING

Chapter 118: One Last Act of Courage

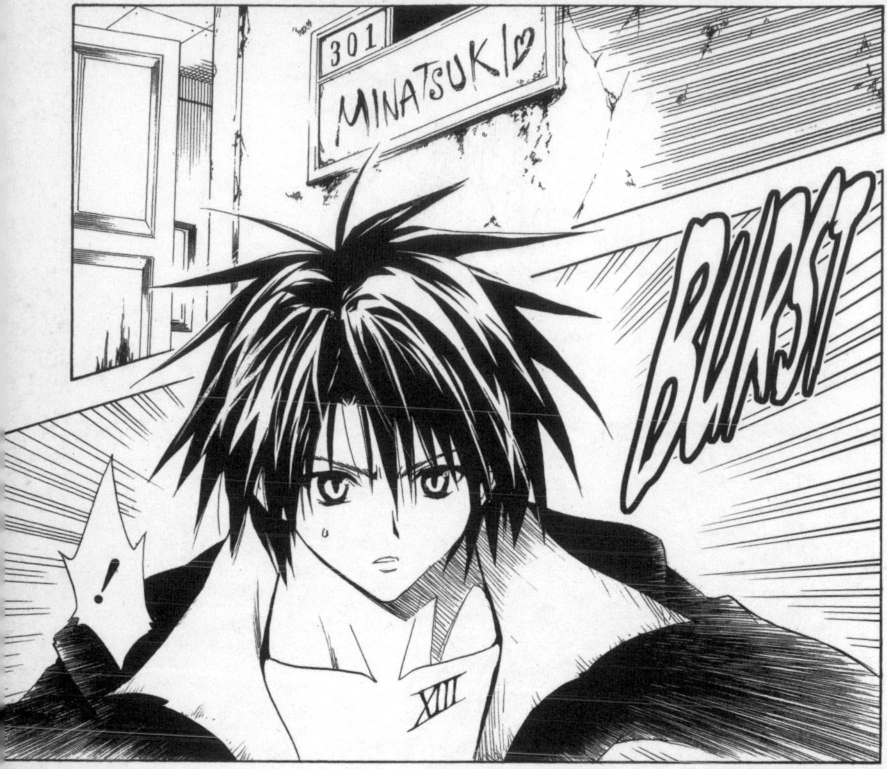
301
MINATSUKI
BURST
!

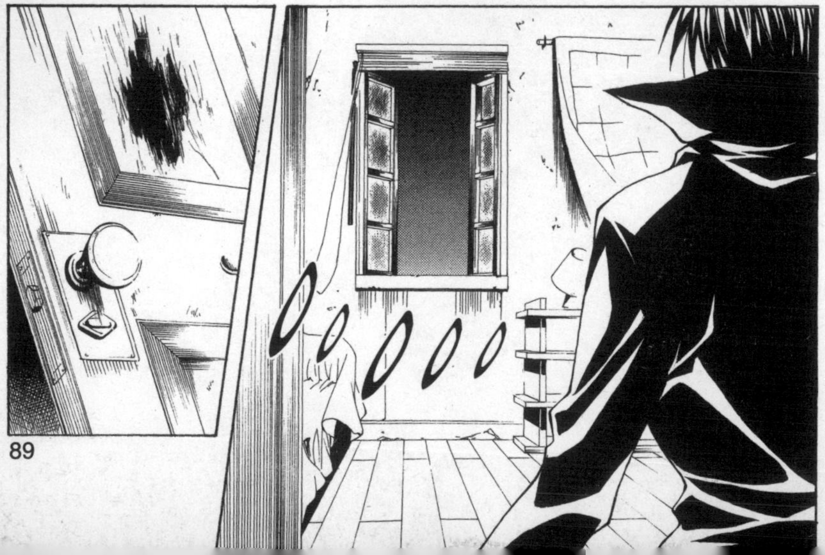

...

"...OF THE WITCH'S CURSE!"

"TONIGHT, I SHALL FREE YOU FROM THE SHACKLES...

CREED...

WHAT THE HELL ARE YOU DOING?!

CRUSH

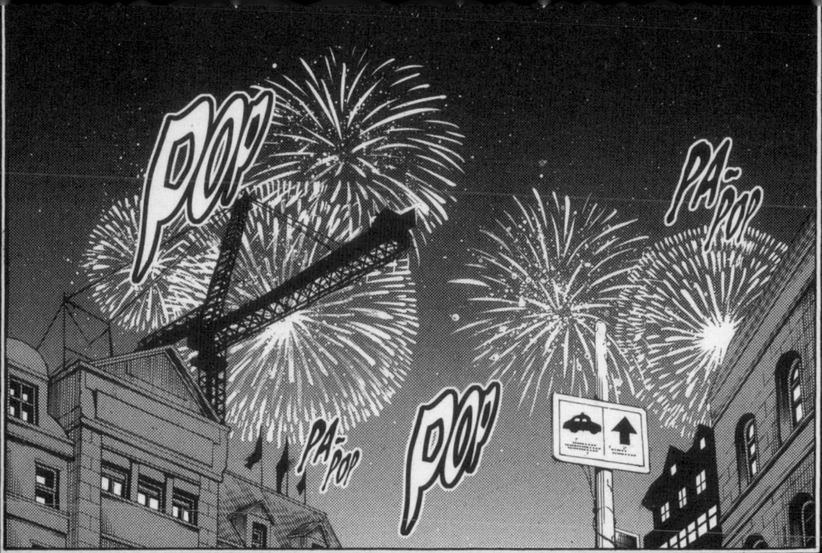
PA-POP
POP
POP
PA-POP

Chapter 118: One Last Act of Courage

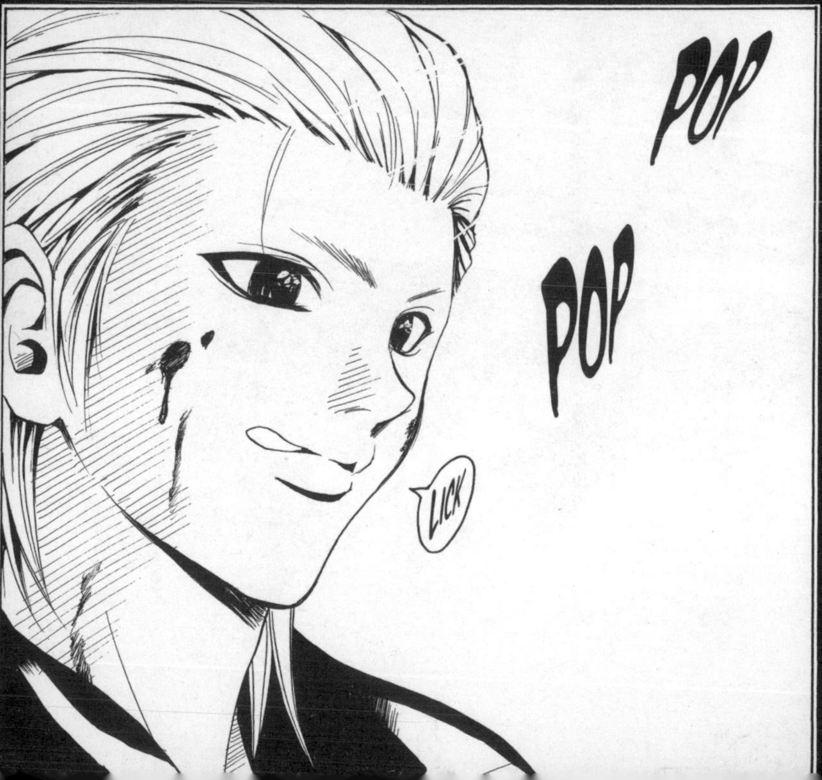
POP
POP
LICK

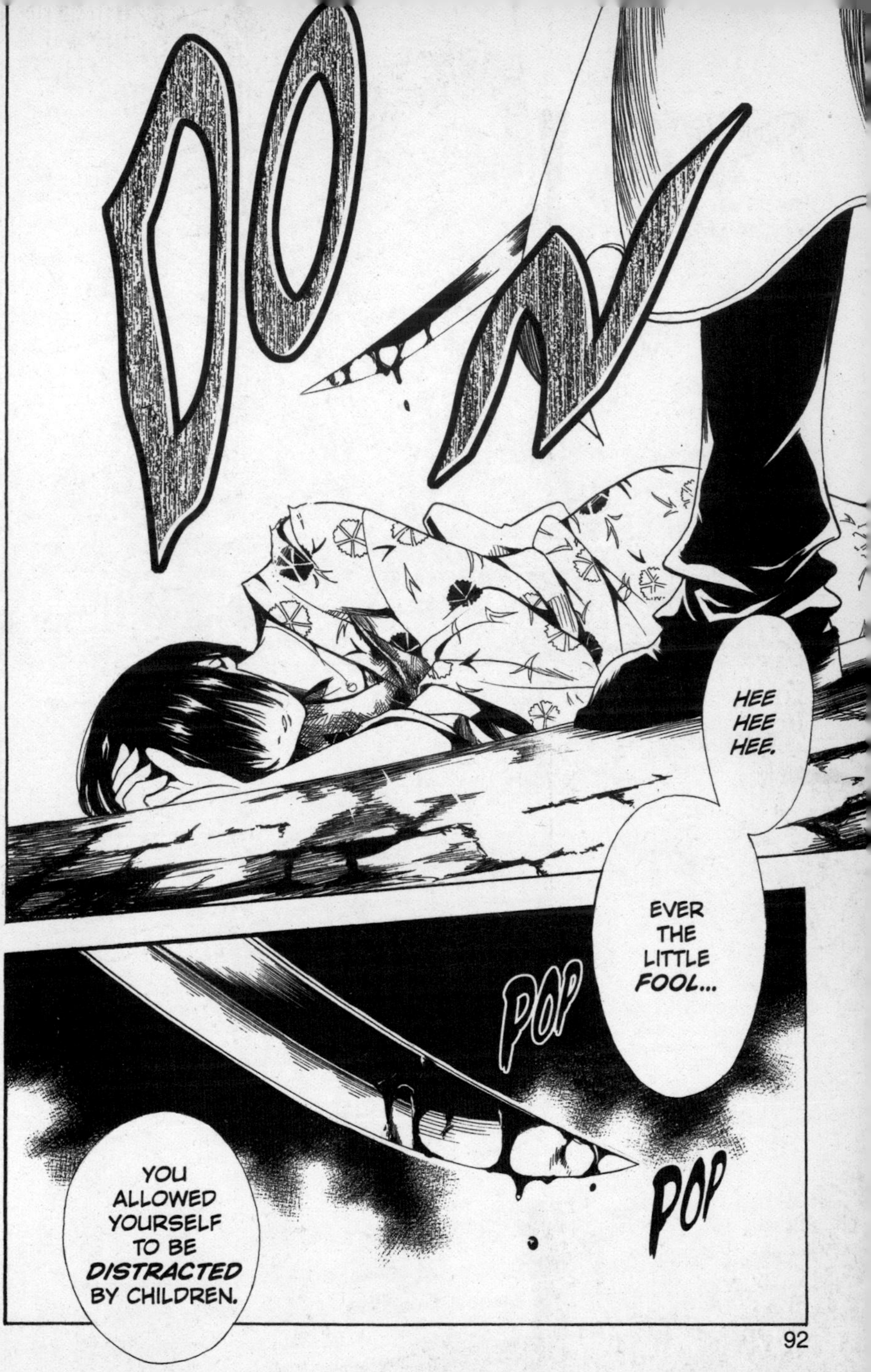
DON
HEE HEE HEE.
EVER THE LITTLE FOOL...
POP
POP
YOU ALLOWED YOURSELF TO BE DISTRACTED BY CHILDREN.

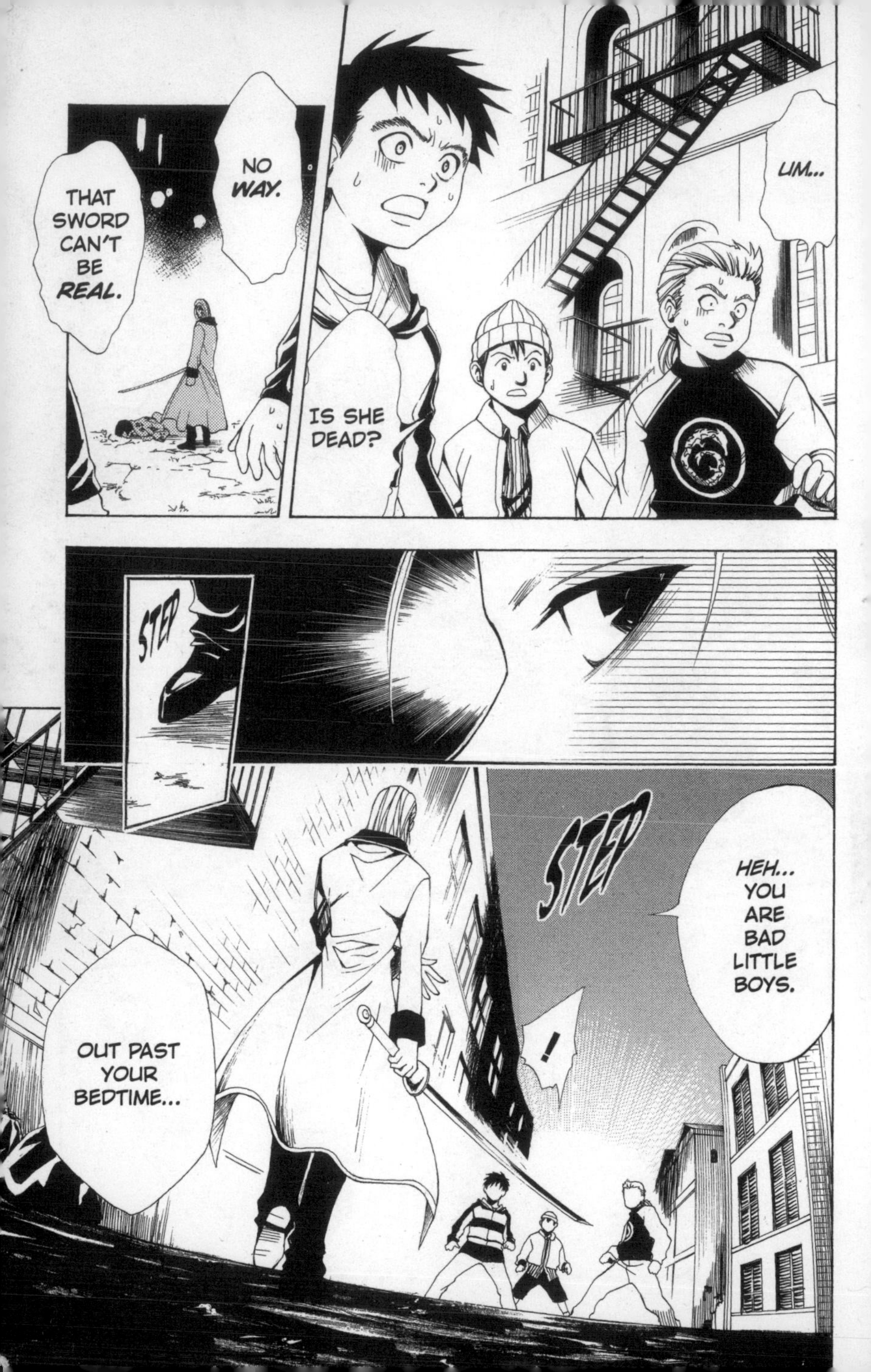
UM...
NO WAY.
IS SHE DEAD?
THAT SWORD CAN'T BE REAL.
STEP
STEP
HEH... YOU ARE BAD LITTLE BOYS.
!
OUT PAST YOUR BEDTIME...

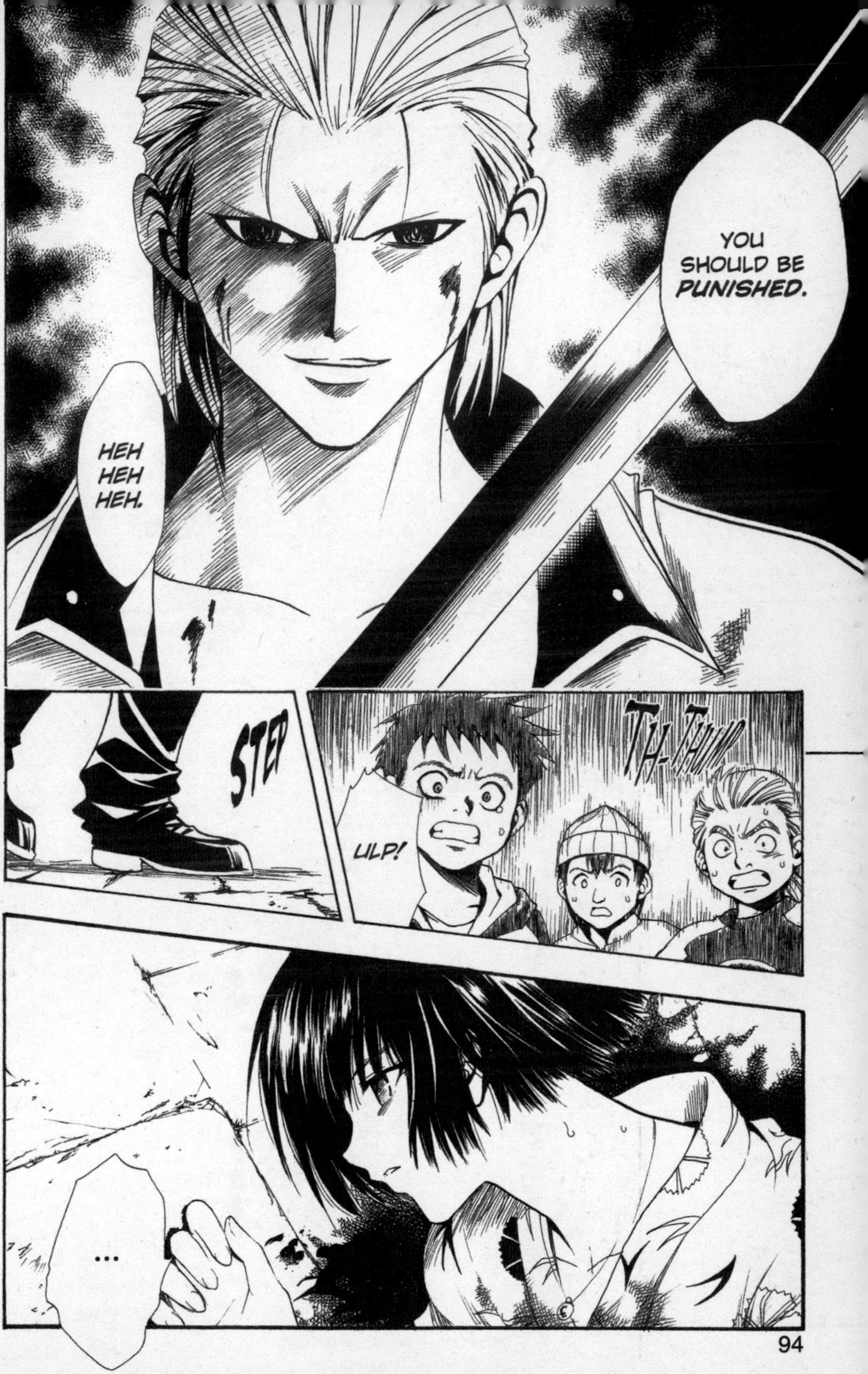
YOU SHOULD BE PUNISHED.
HEH HEH HEH.
TH-THUMP
ULP!
STEP
...

READ THIS WAY

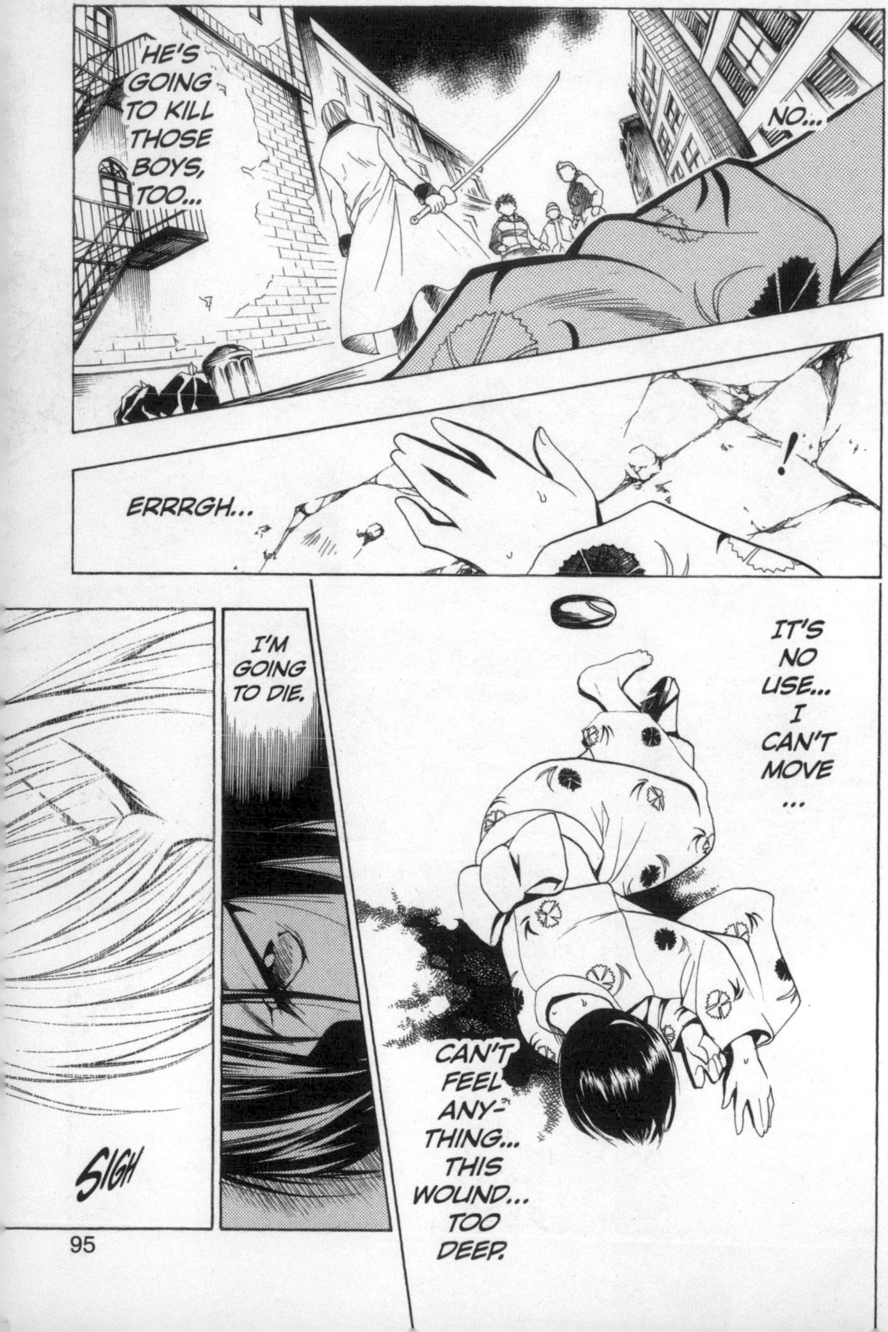

NO...
HE'S GOING TO KILL THOSE BOYS, TOO...
!
ERRRGH...
IT'S NO USE... I CAN'T MOVE...
CAN'T FEEL ANY-THING... THIS WOUND... TOO DEEP.
I'M GOING TO DIE.
SIGH

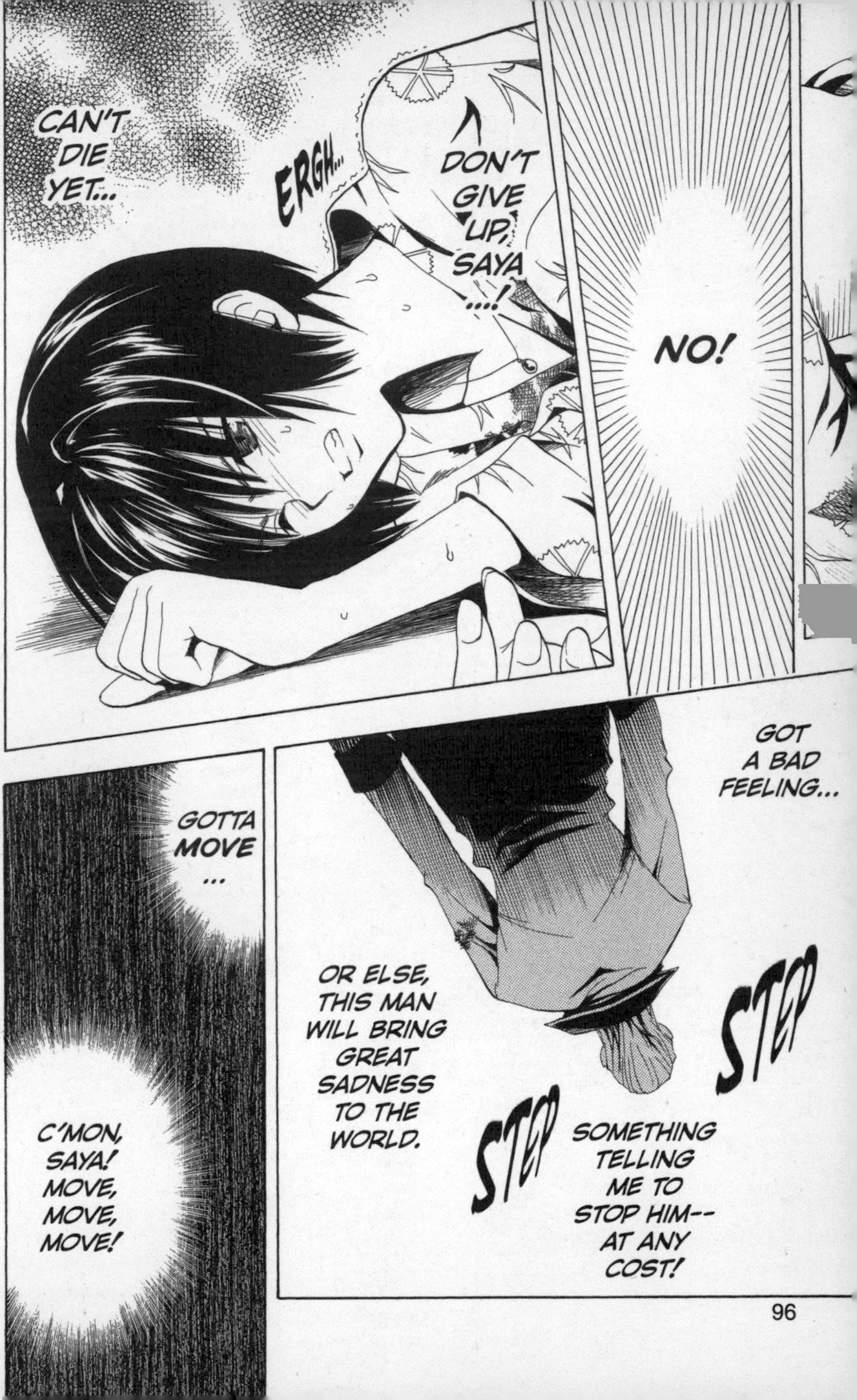
NO!
DON'T GIVE UP, SAYA ...!
ERGH...
CAN'T DIE YET...
GOT A BAD FEELING...
STEP
STEP
SOMETHING TELLING ME TO STOP HIM-- AT ANY COST!
OR ELSE, THIS MAN WILL BRING GREAT SADNESS TO THE WORLD.
GOTTA MOVE ...
C'MON, SAYA! MOVE, MOVE, MOVE!

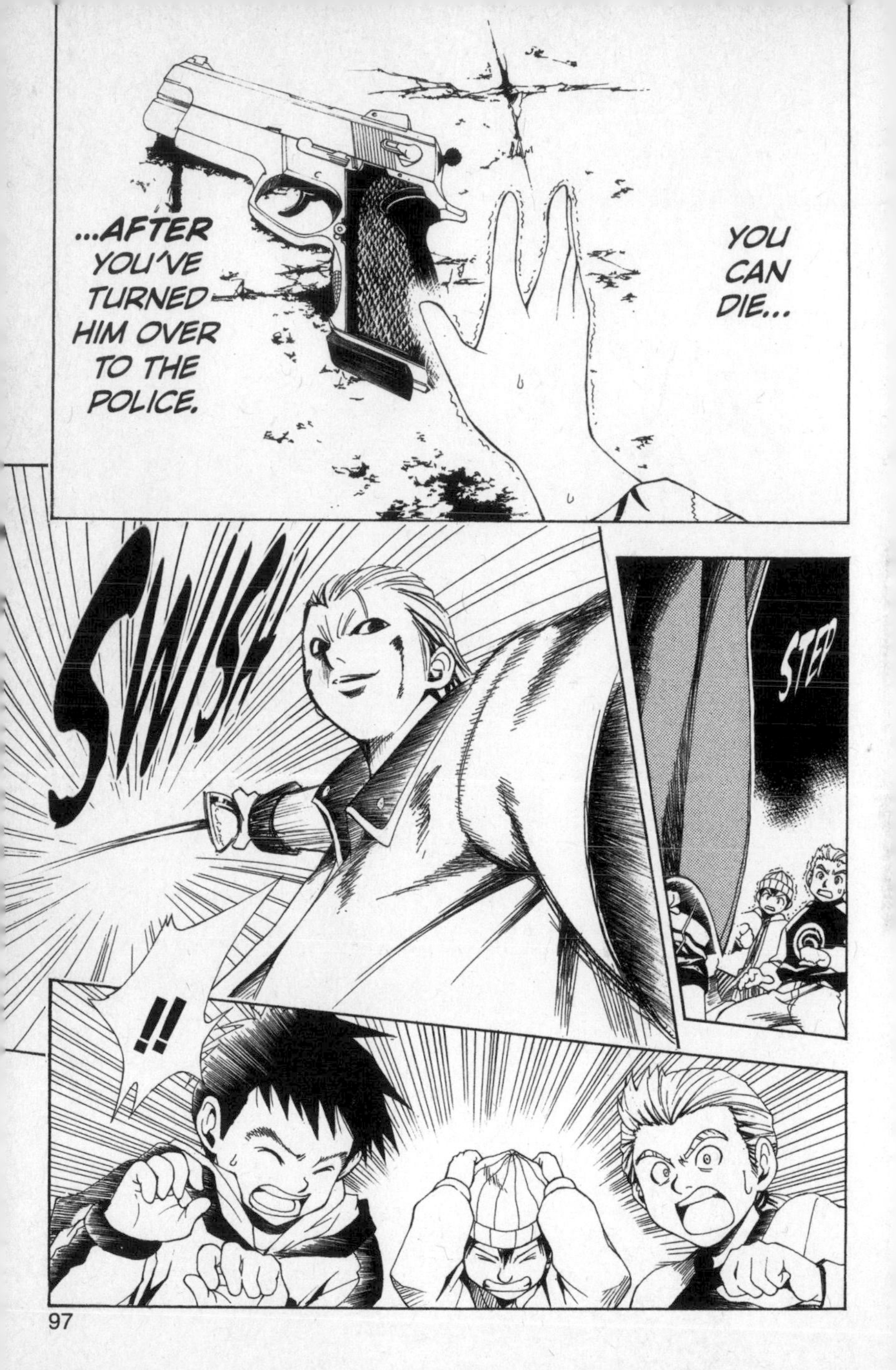
YOU CAN DIE...
...AFTER YOU'VE TURNED HIM OVER TO THE POLICE.
STEP
SWISH
!!

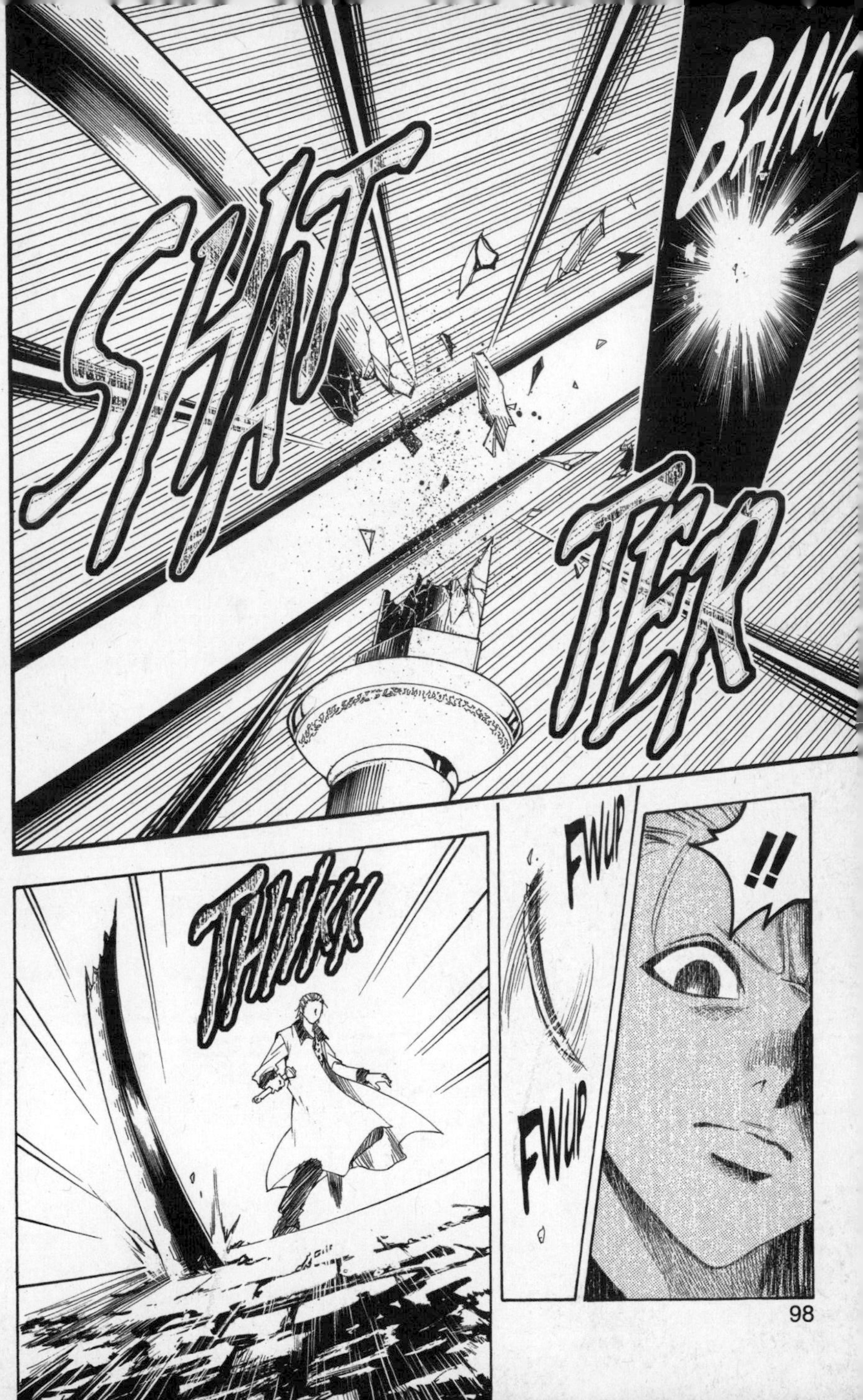
BANG
SHAT
TER
!!
FWUP
FWUP
THUNK

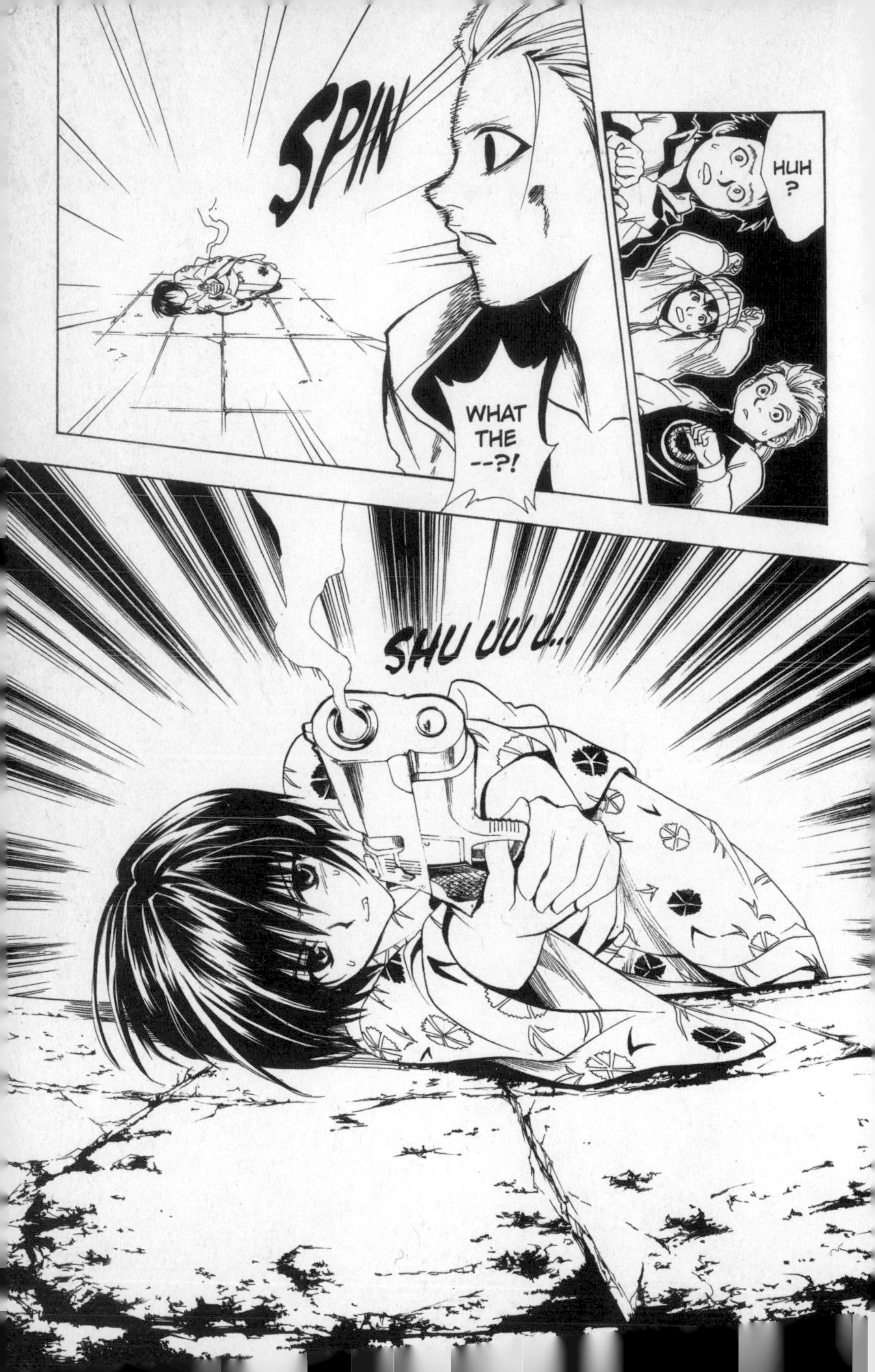
HUH ?
SPIN
WHAT THE --?!
SHU UU U...

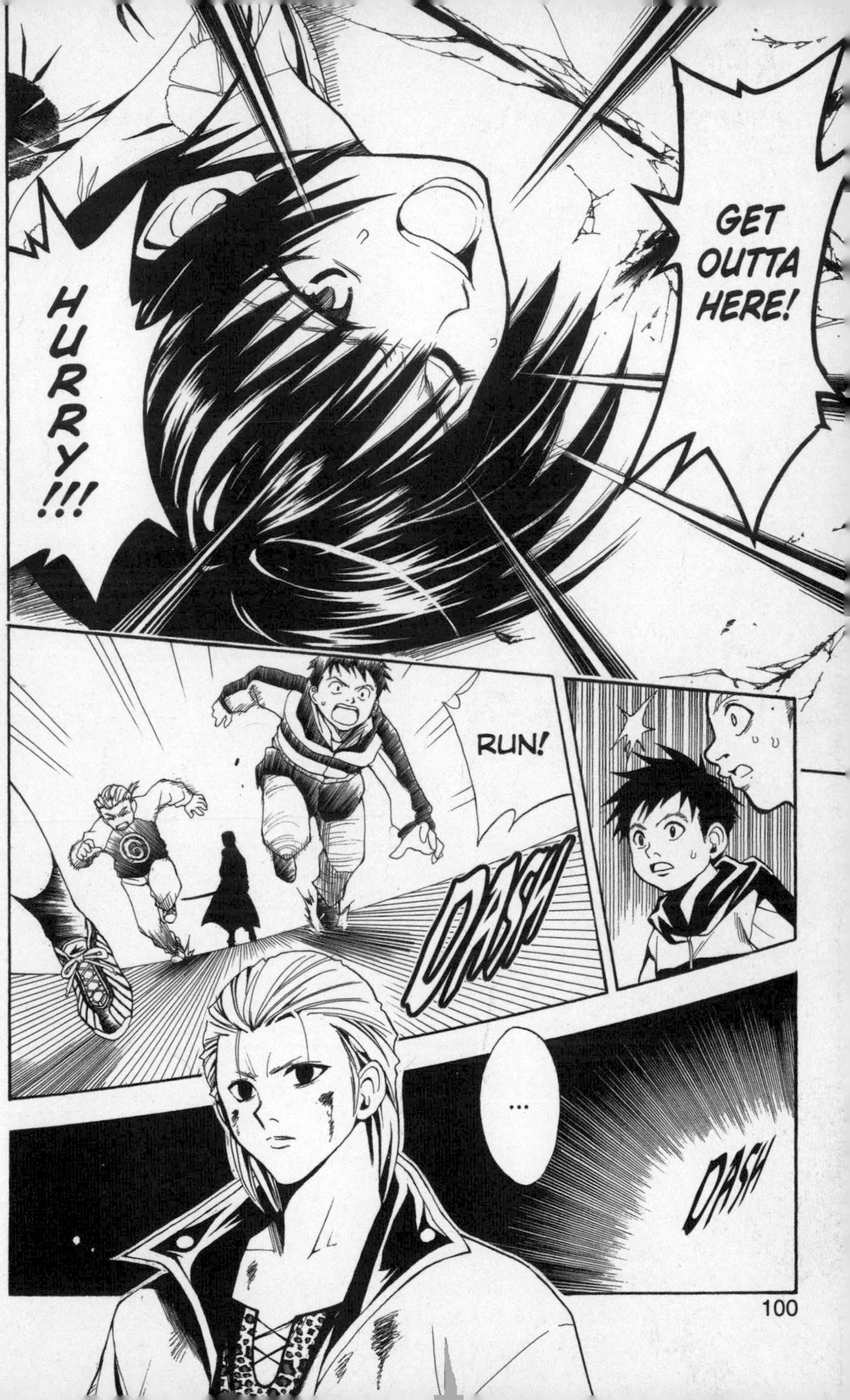
GET OUTTA HERE!
HURRY!!!
RUN!
DASH
...
DASH

READ THIS WAY

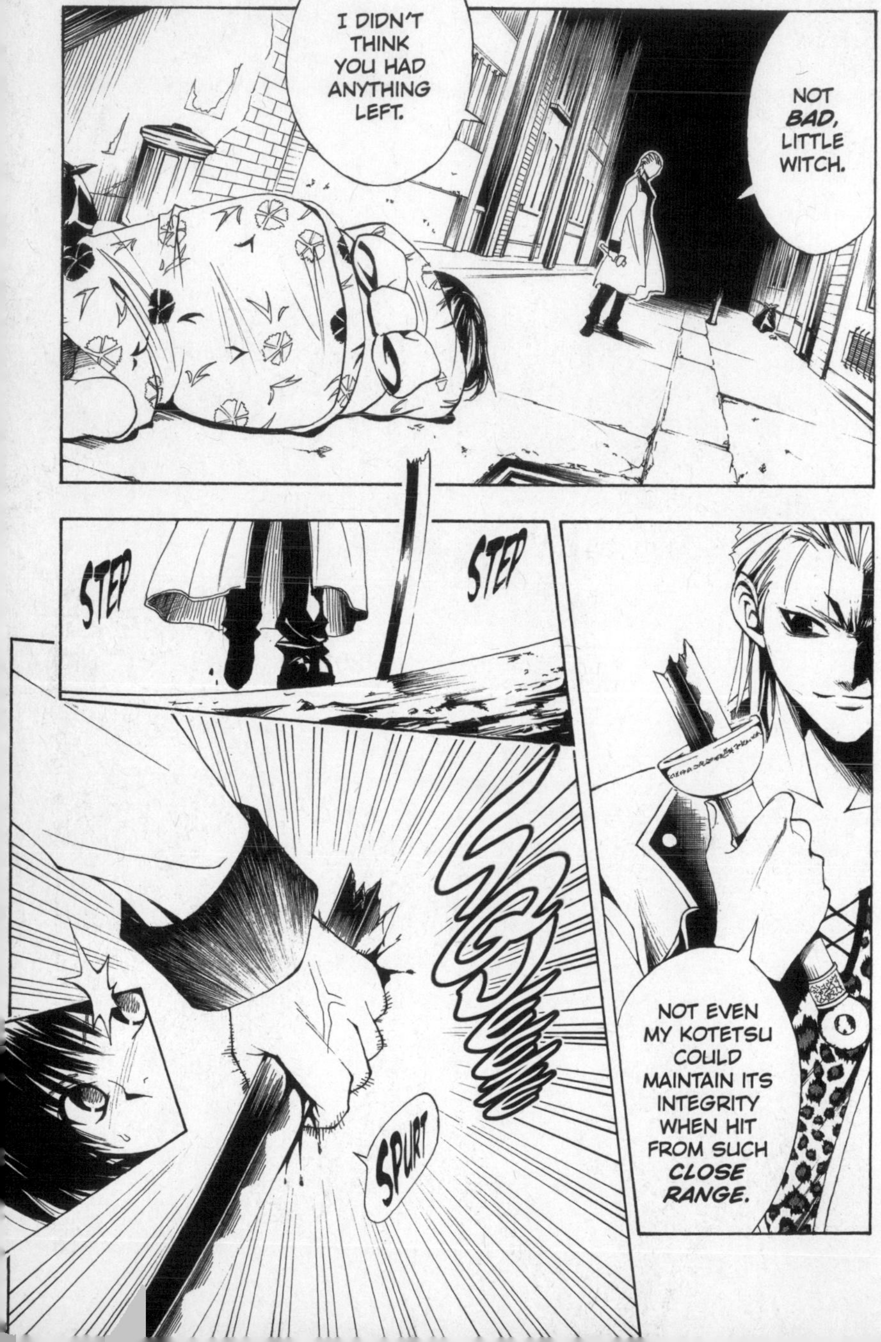
NOT BAD, LITTLE WITCH.
I DIDN'T THINK YOU HAD ANYTHING LEFT.
NOT EVEN MY KOTETSU COULD MAINTAIN ITS INTEGRITY WHEN HIT FROM SUCH CLOSE RANGE.
STEP
STEP
SPURT

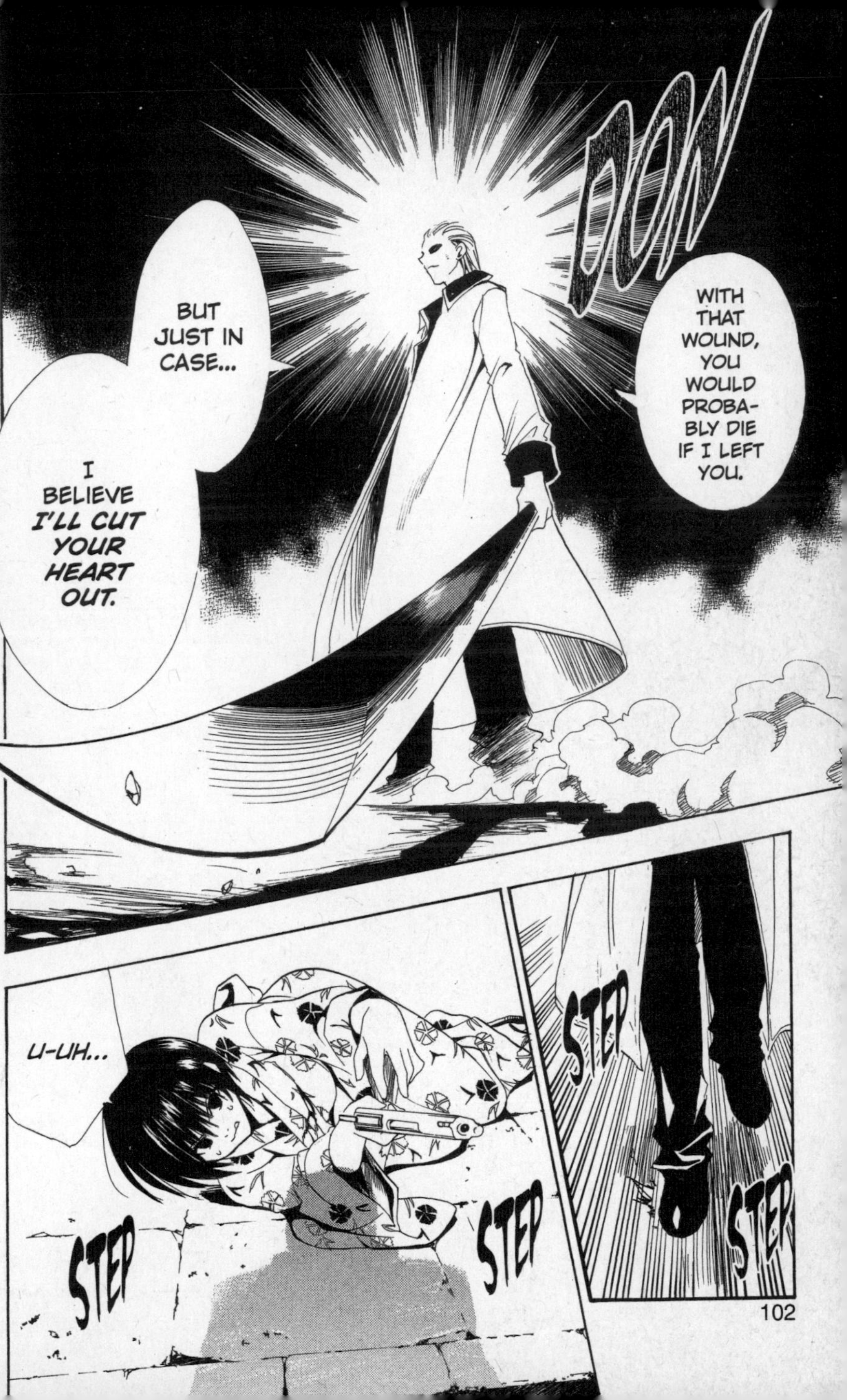
WITH THAT WOUND, YOU WOULD PROBABLY DIE IF I LEFT YOU.
BUT JUST IN CASE...
I BELIEVE *I'LL CUT YOUR HEART OUT.*
STEP
STEP
U-UH...
STEP
STEP

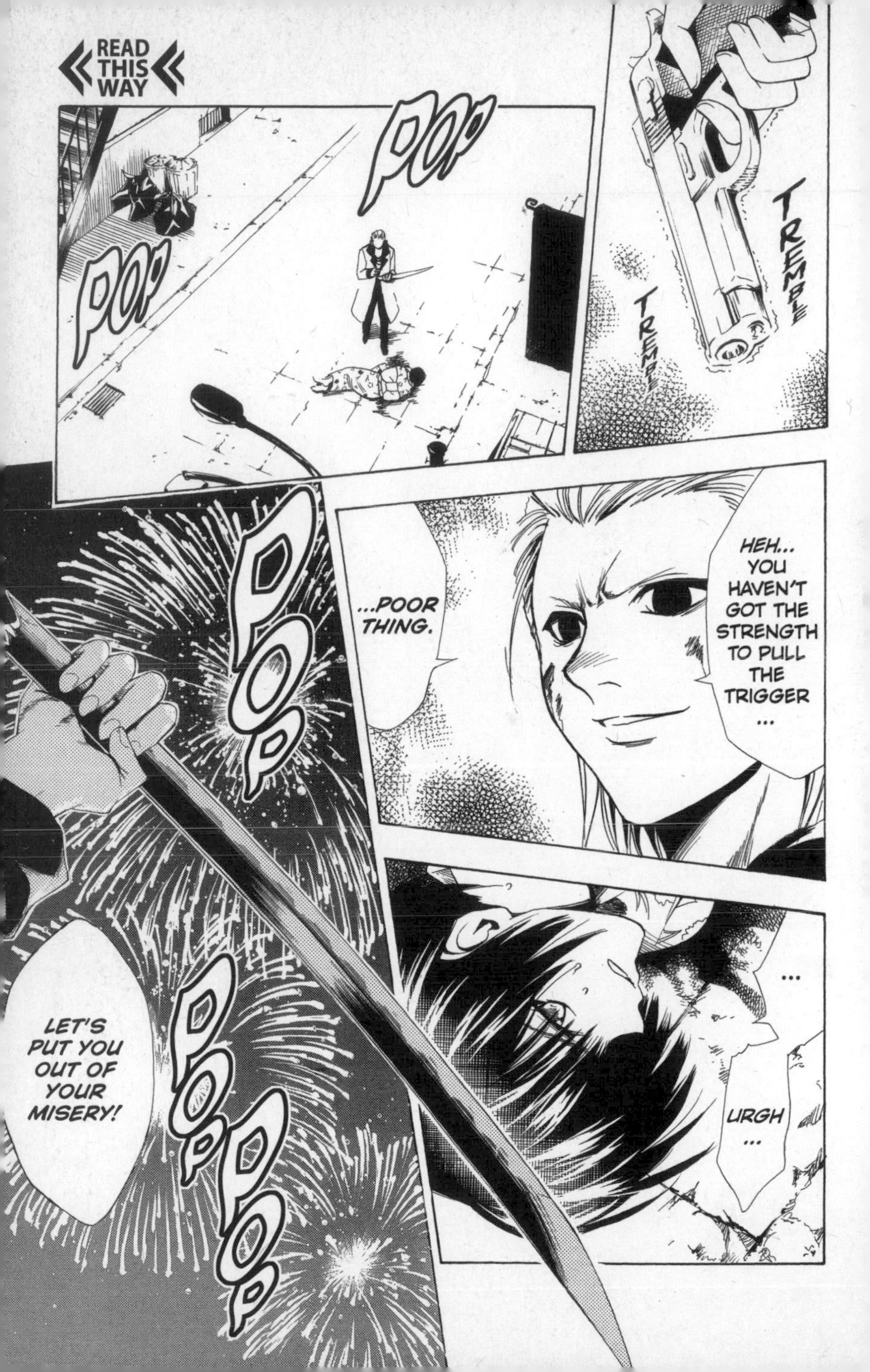
READ THIS WAY
TREMBLE
TREMBLE
POP
POP
HEH... YOU HAVEN'T GOT THE STRENGTH TO PULL THE TRIGGER ...
...POOR THING.
...
URGH ...
POP POP
POP POP POP
LET'S PUT YOU OUT OF YOUR MISERY!

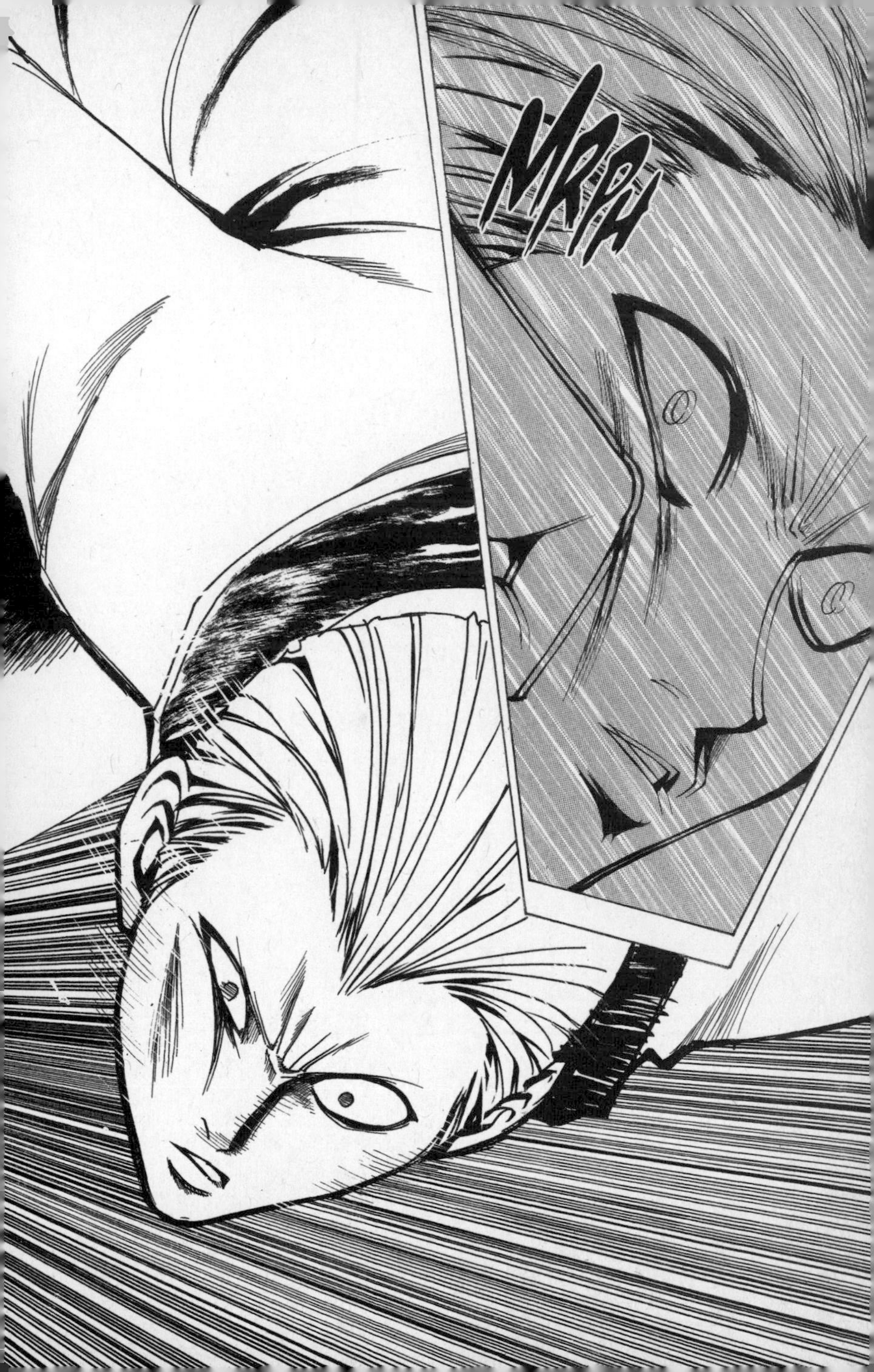
MRPH

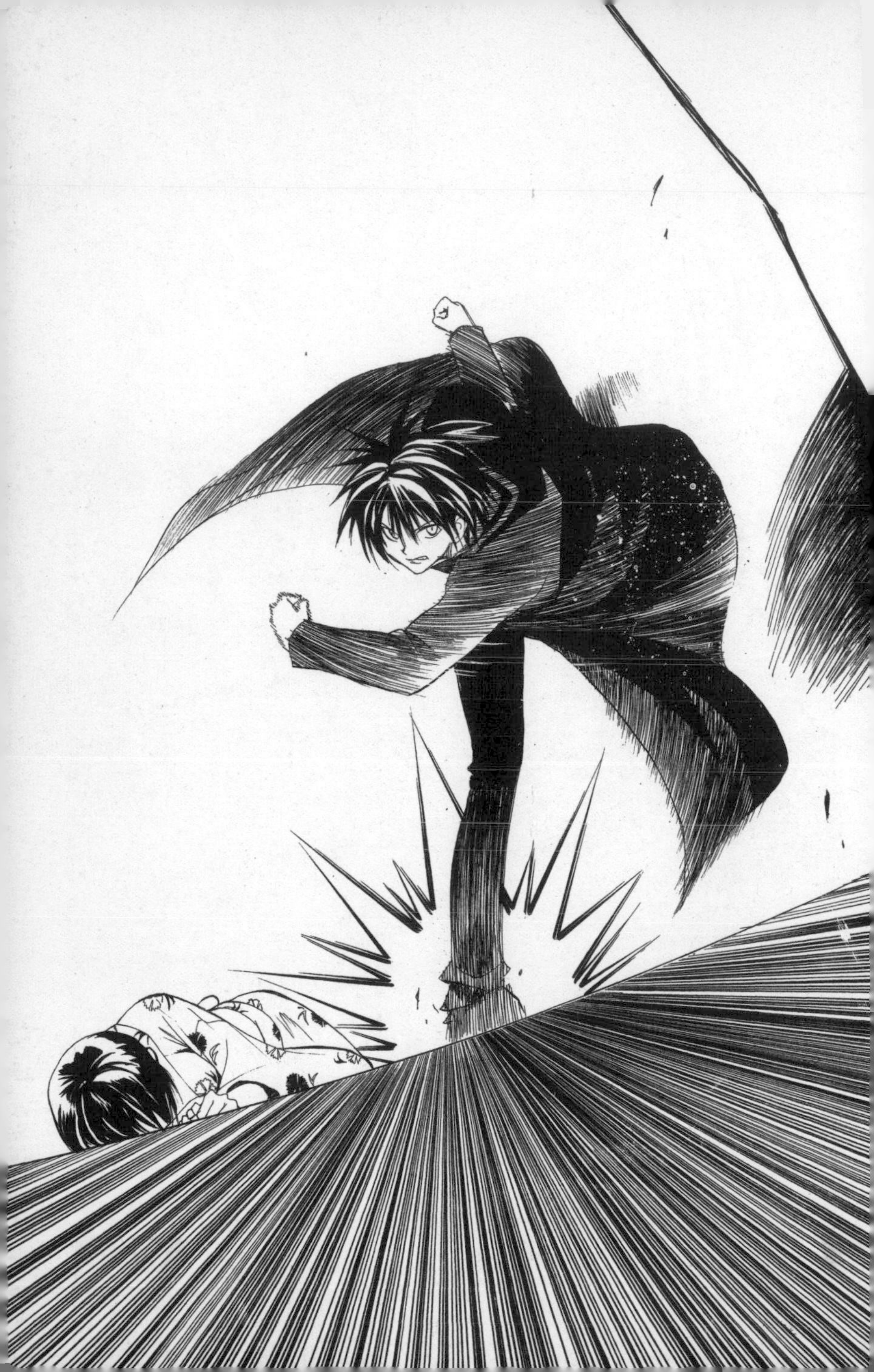

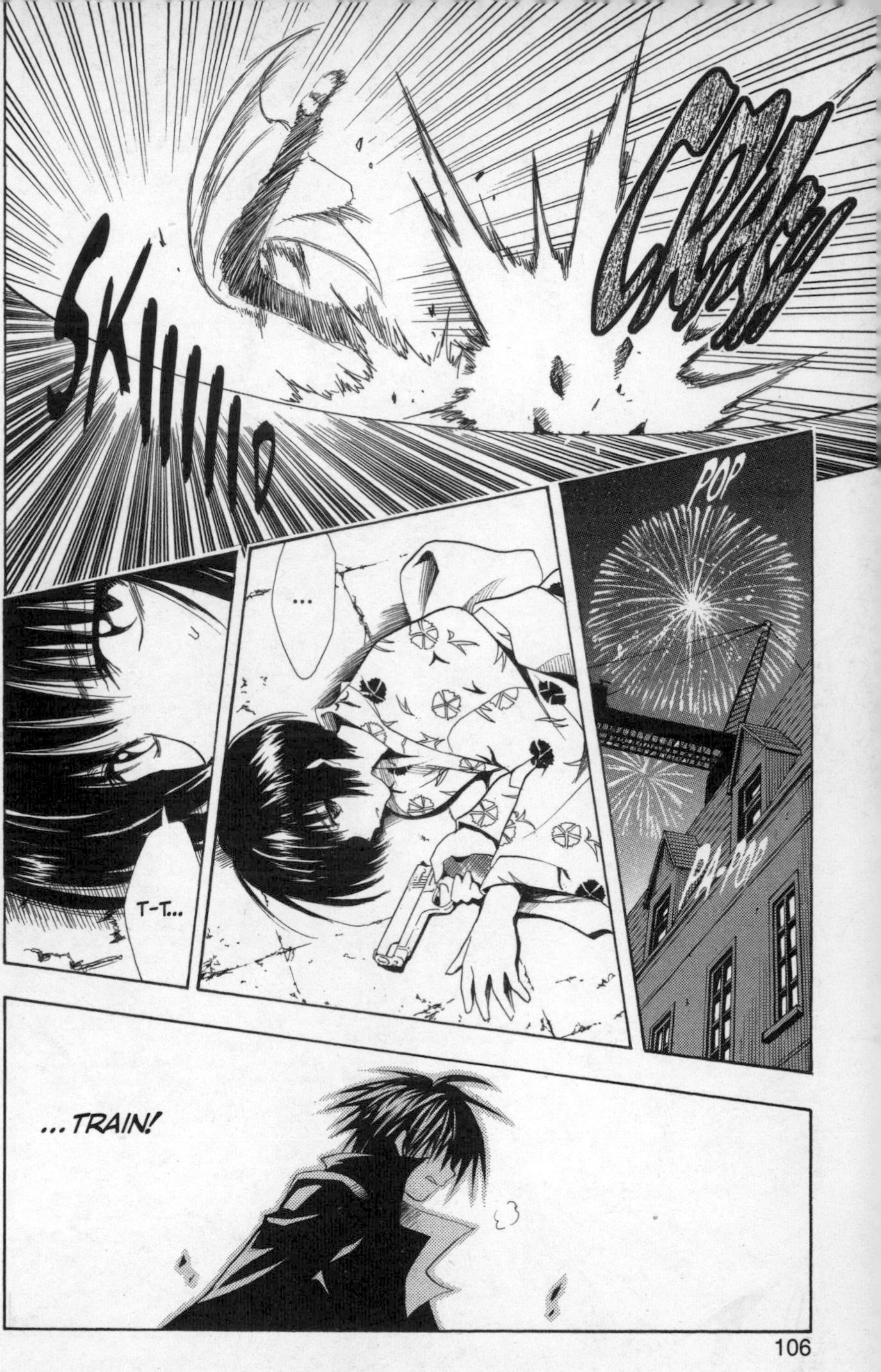
SKIIIID
POP
PA-POP
...
T-T...
...TRAIN!

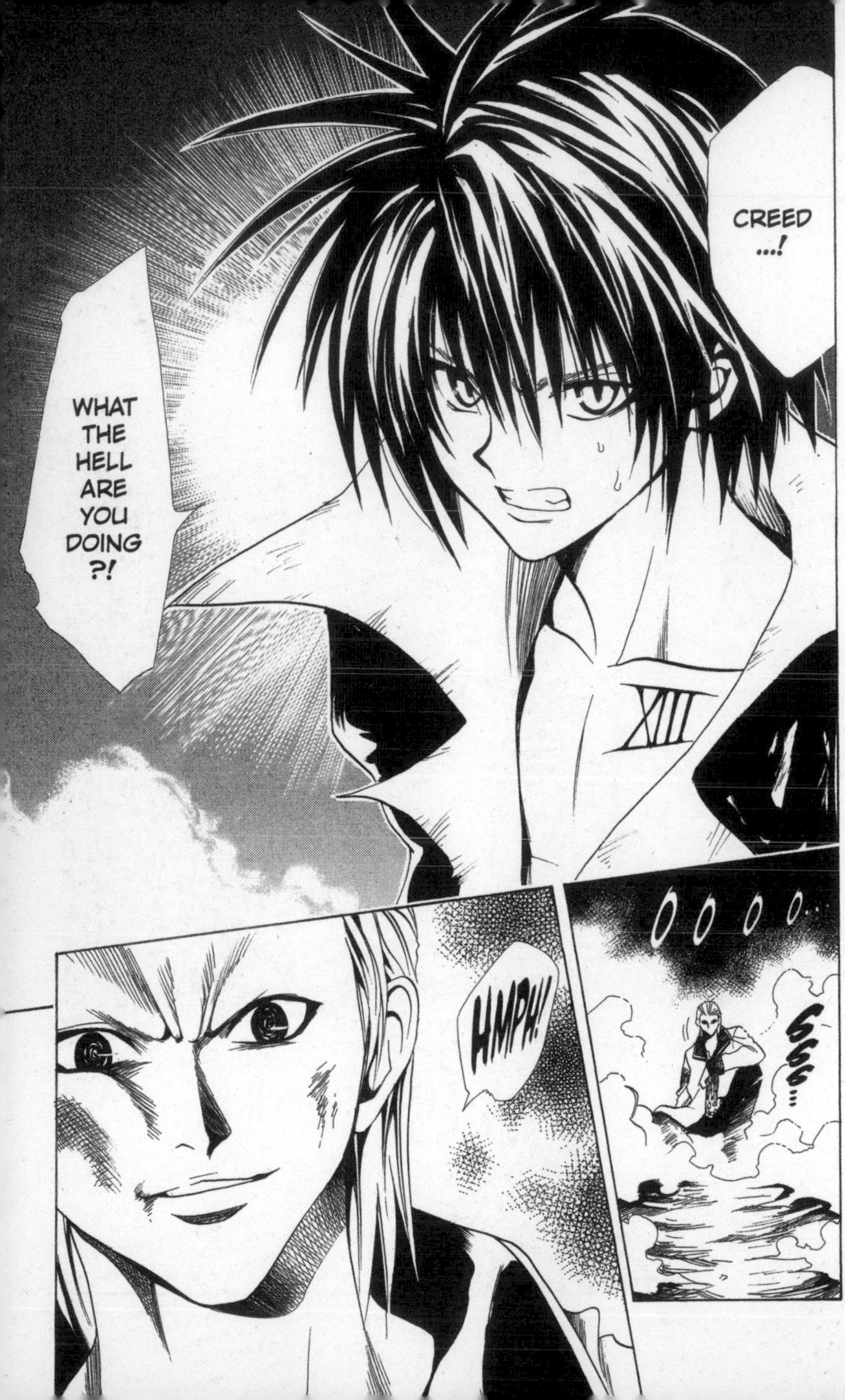
CREED ...!
WHAT THE HELL ARE YOU DOING ?!
OOOO...
GGG...
HMPH!

Chapter 119: Dear Friend

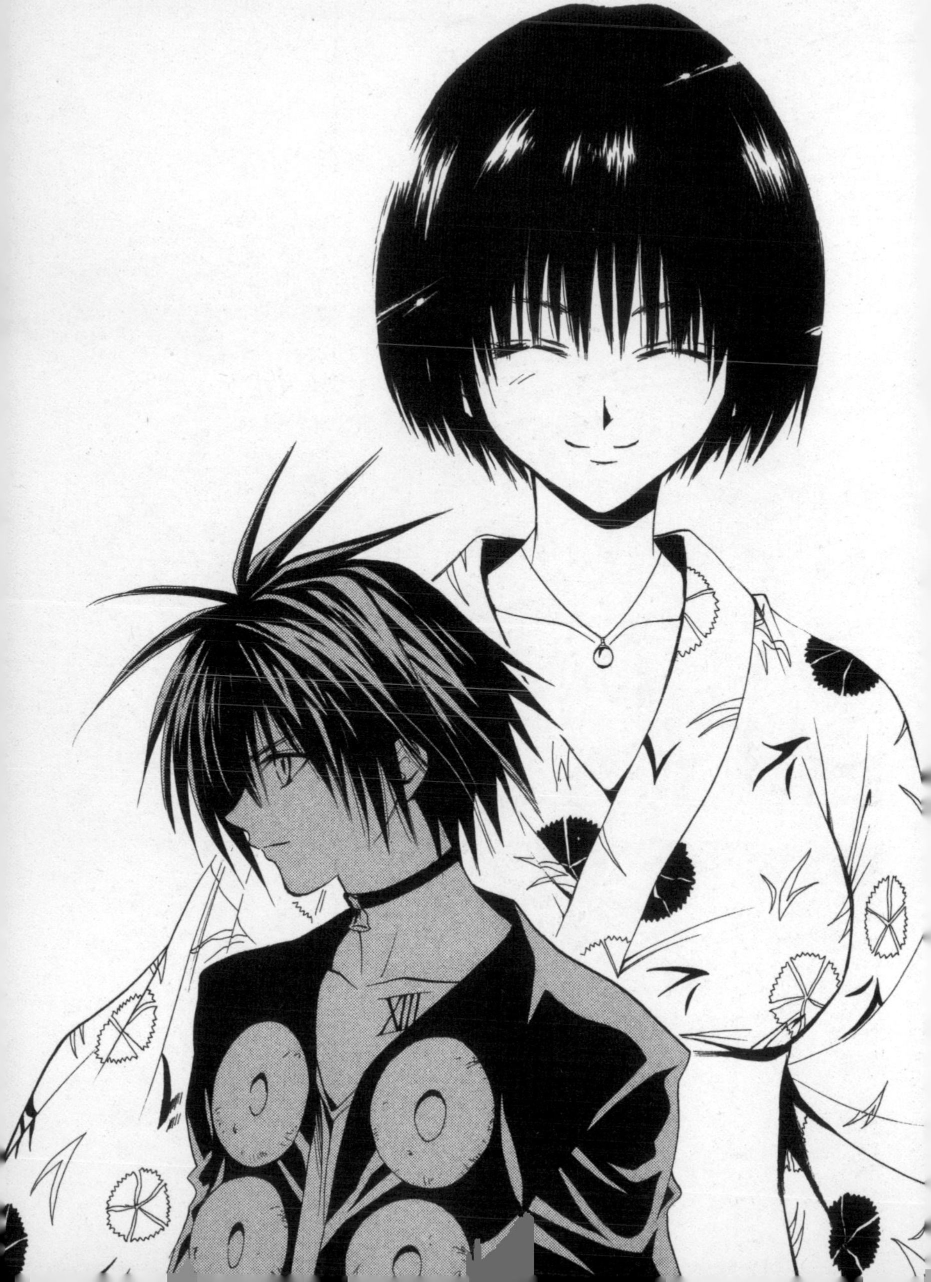

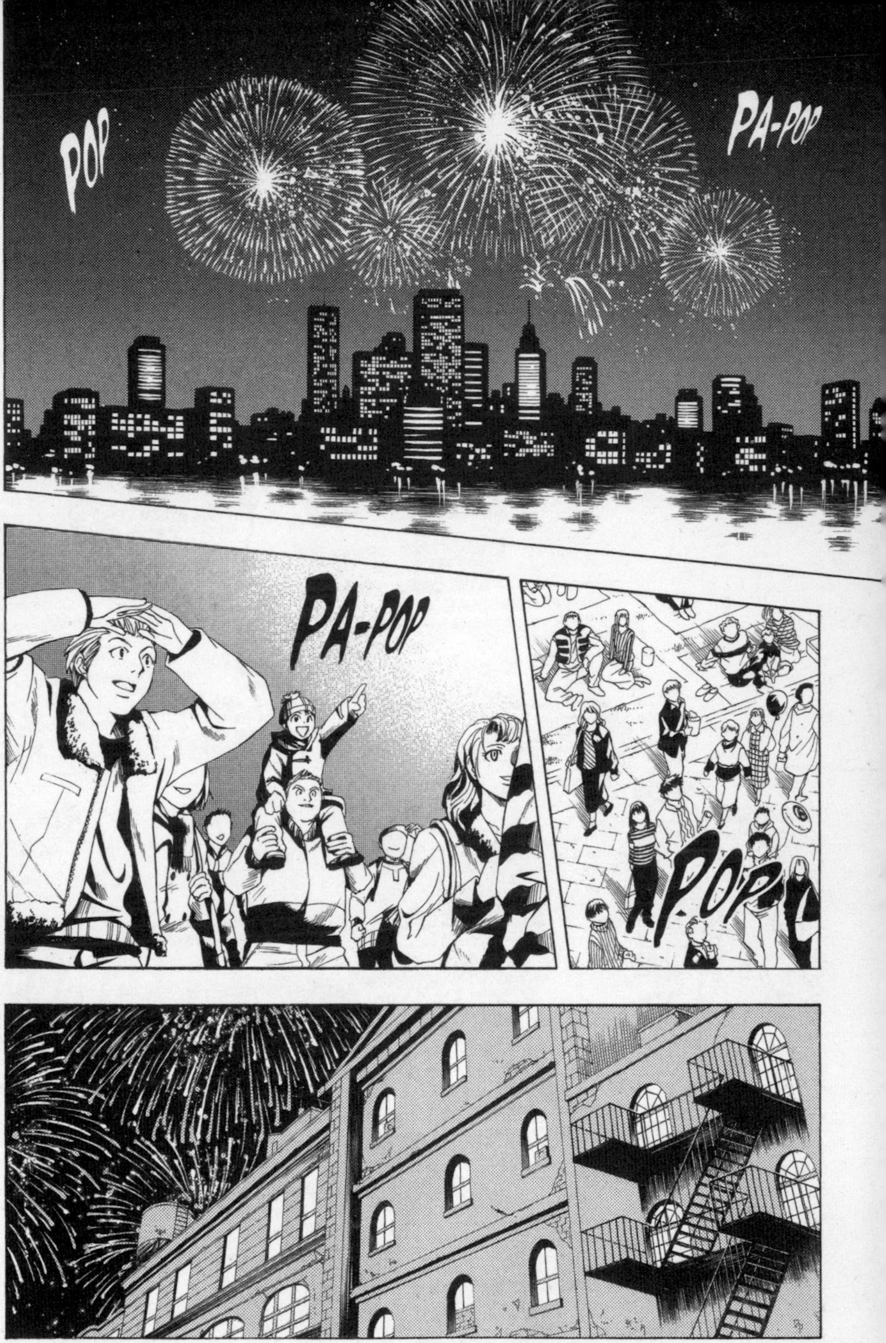
PA-POP
POP
POP
PA-POP

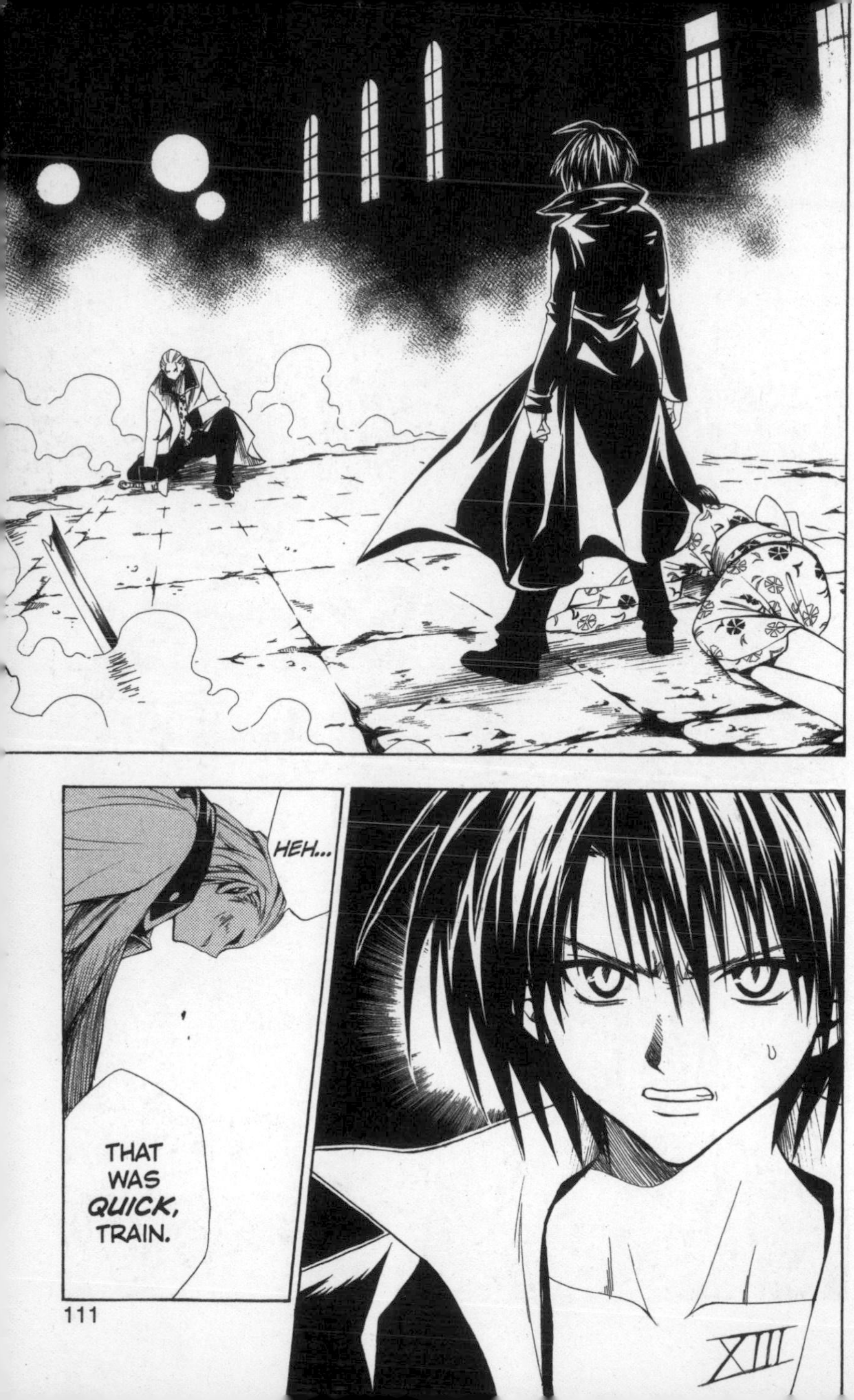
XIII
HEH...
THAT WAS *QUICK*, TRAIN.

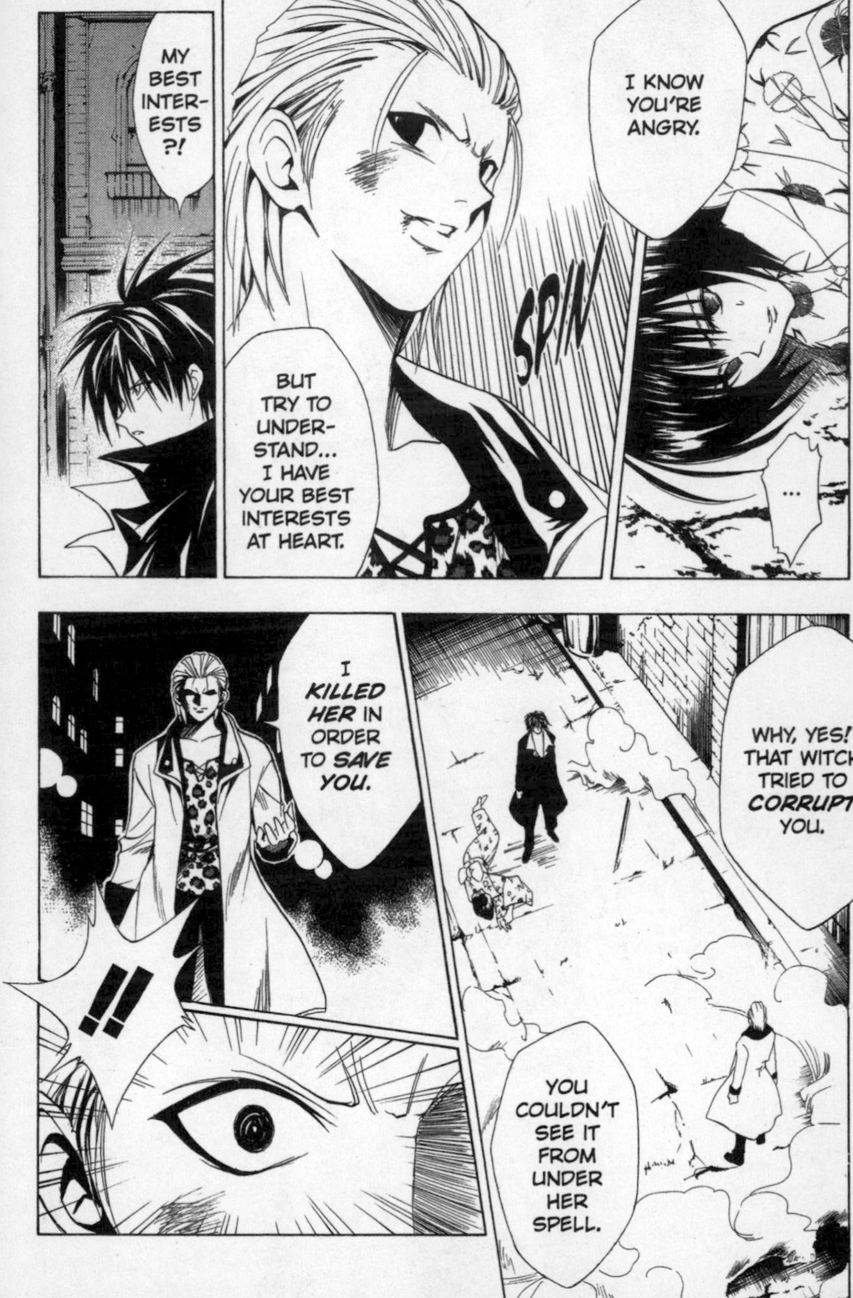
I KNOW YOU'RE ANGRY.
SPIN
...
BUT TRY TO UNDERSTAND... I HAVE YOUR BEST INTERESTS AT HEART.
MY BEST INTERESTS ?!
WHY, YES! THAT WITCH TRIED TO *CORRUPT* YOU.
YOU COULDN'T SEE IT FROM UNDER HER SPELL.
I *KILLED HER* IN ORDER TO *SAVE YOU.*
!!

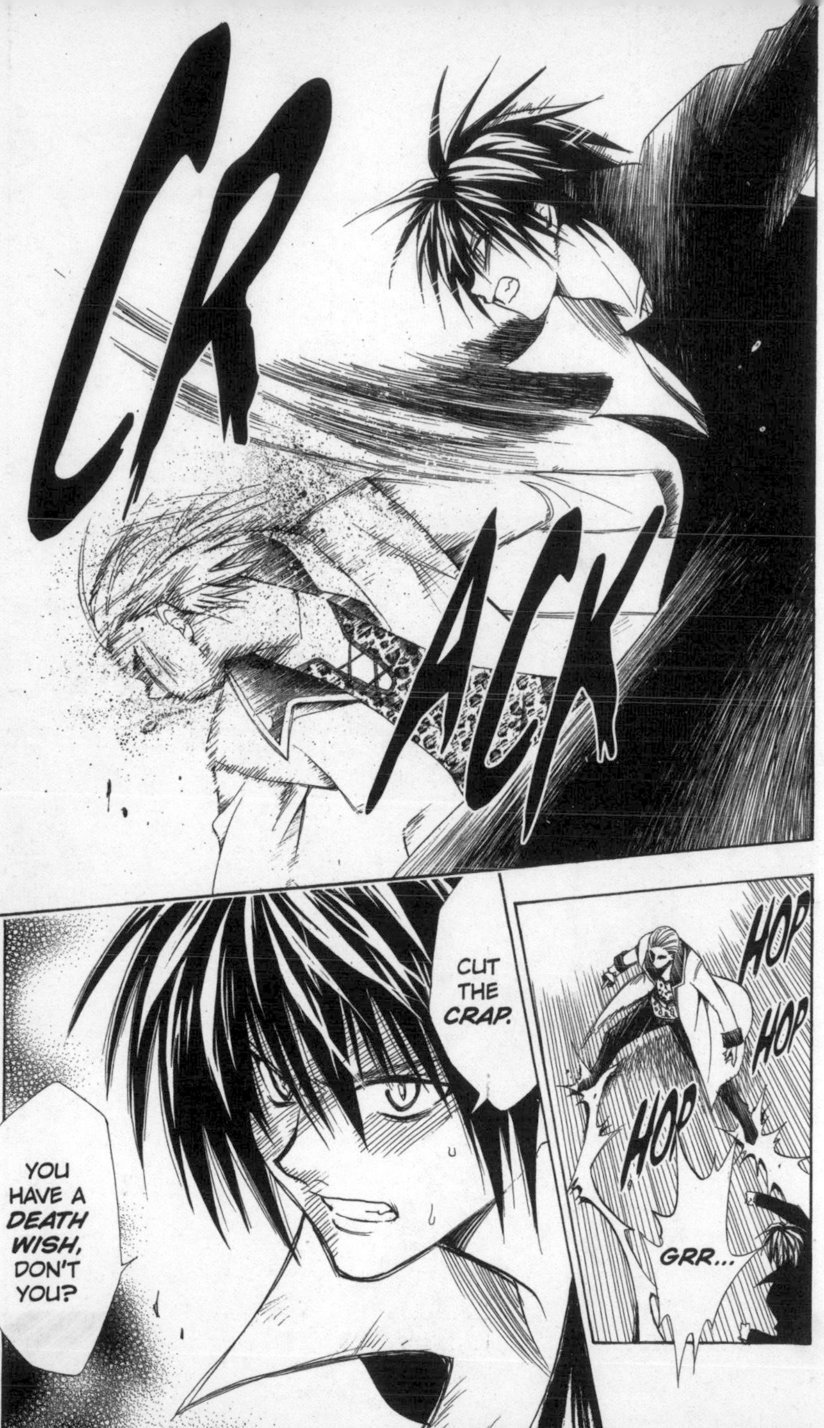
CRACK
HOP HOP HOP
GRR...
CUT THE CRAP.
YOU HAVE A DEATH WISH, DON'T YOU?

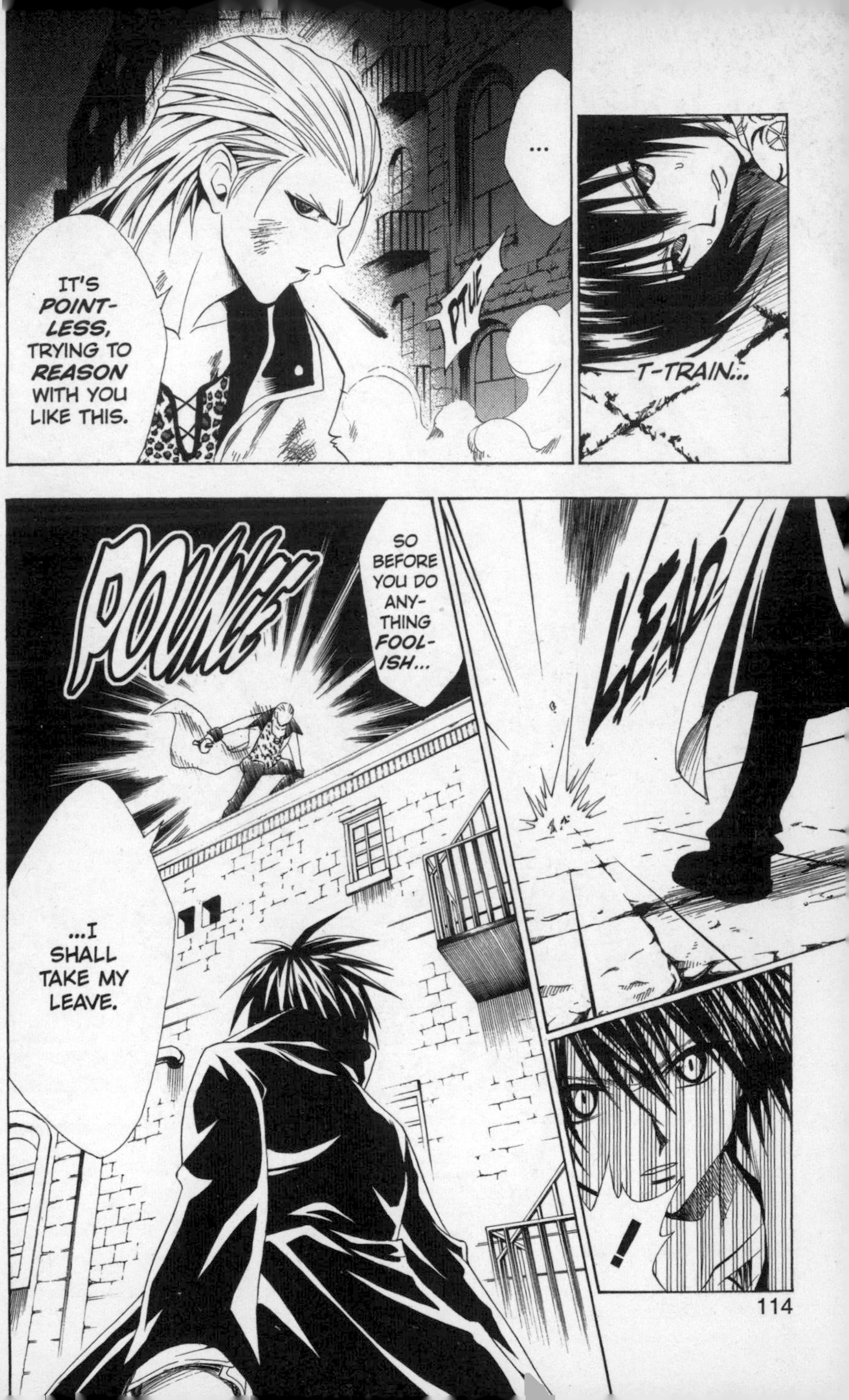
T-TRAIN...
...
PTUE
IT'S POINTLESS, TRYING TO REASON WITH YOU LIKE THIS.
LEAP
!
SO BEFORE YOU DO ANYTHING FOOLISH...
POUNCE
...I SHALL TAKE MY LEAVE.

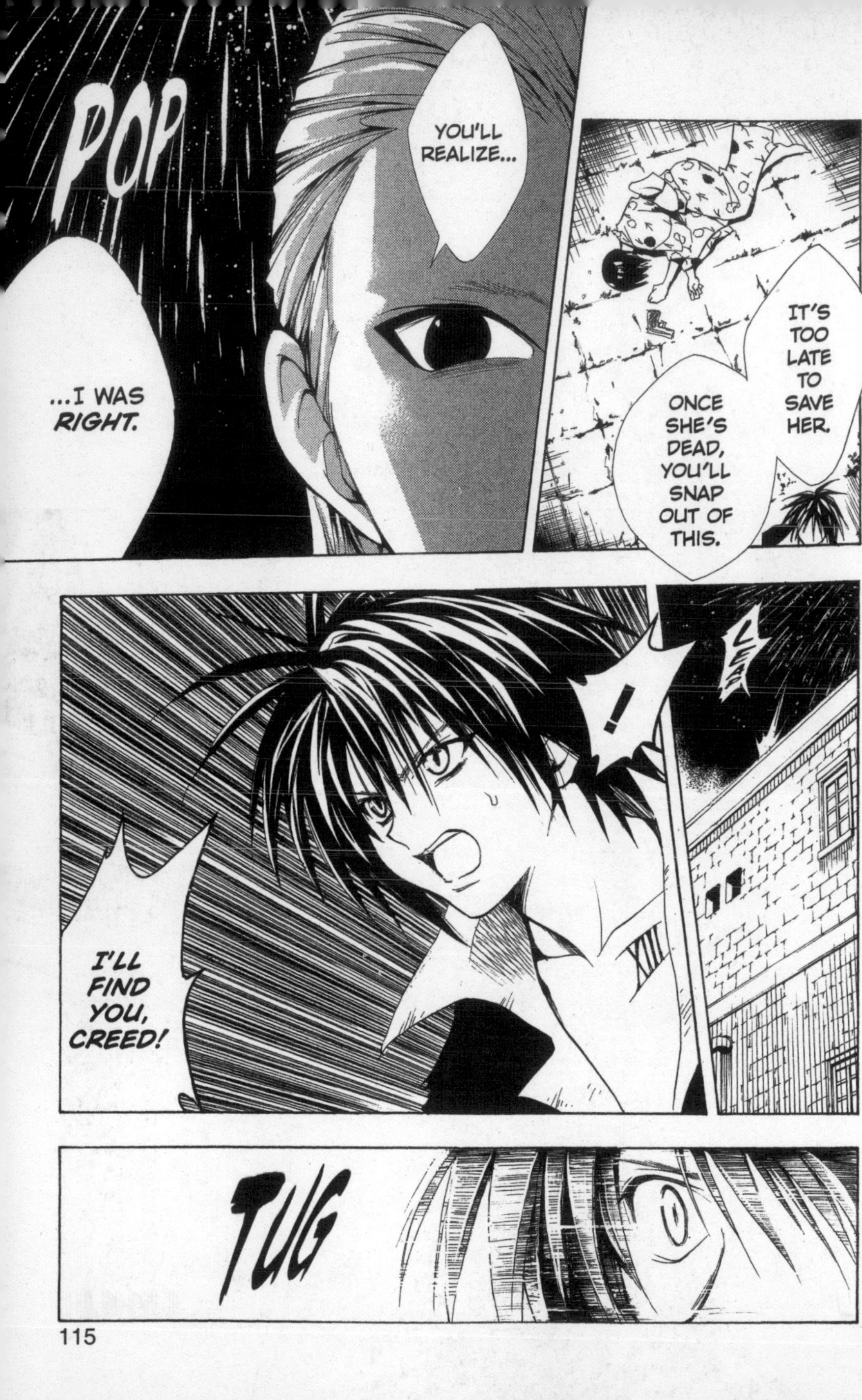
IT'S TOO LATE TO SAVE HER.
ONCE SHE'S DEAD, YOU'LL SNAP OUT OF THIS.
YOU'LL REALIZE...
POP
...I WAS RIGHT.
!
I'LL FIND YOU, CREED!
TUG

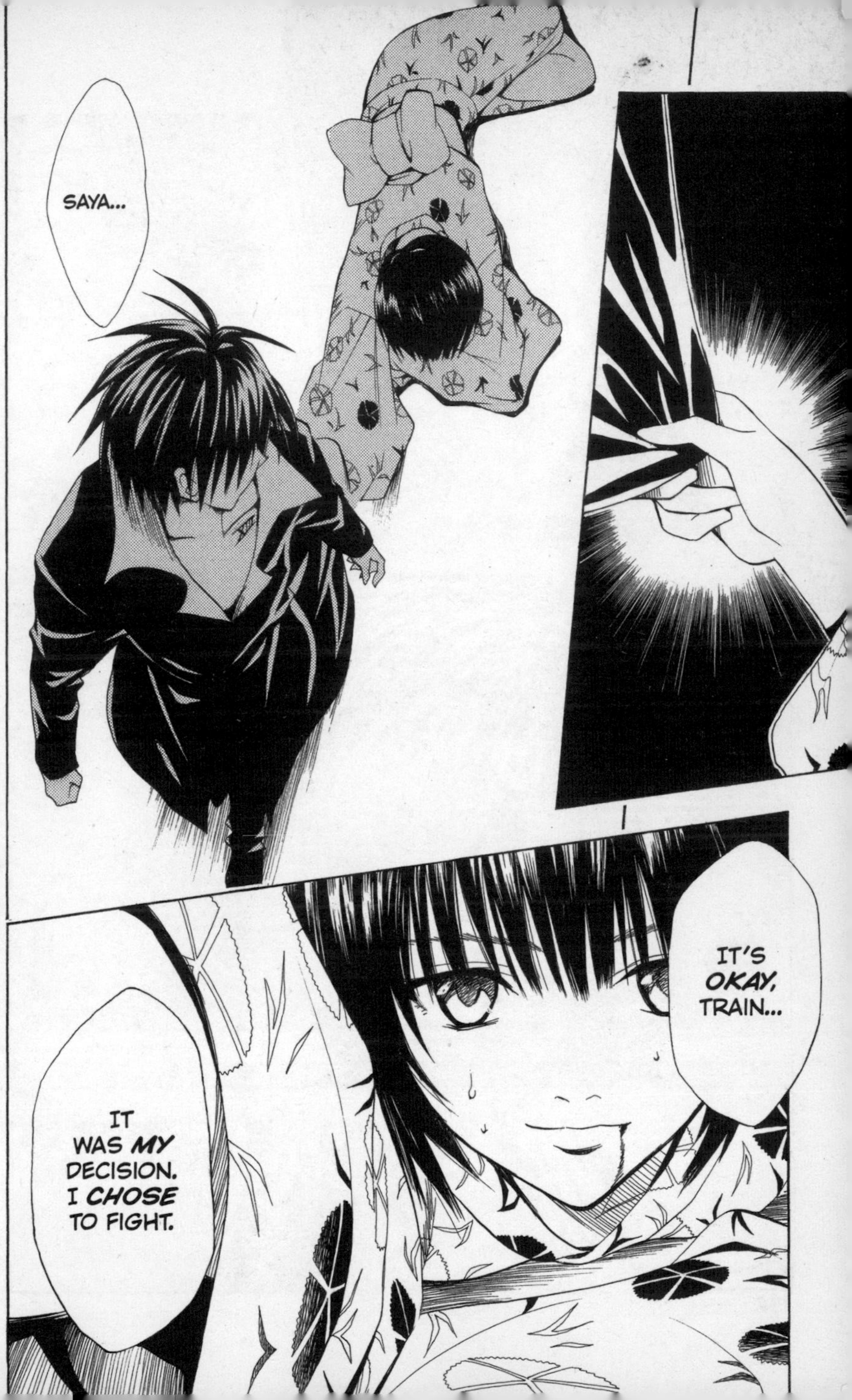
SAYA...
IT'S *OKAY,* TRAIN...
IT WAS *MY* DECISION. I *CHOSE* TO FIGHT.

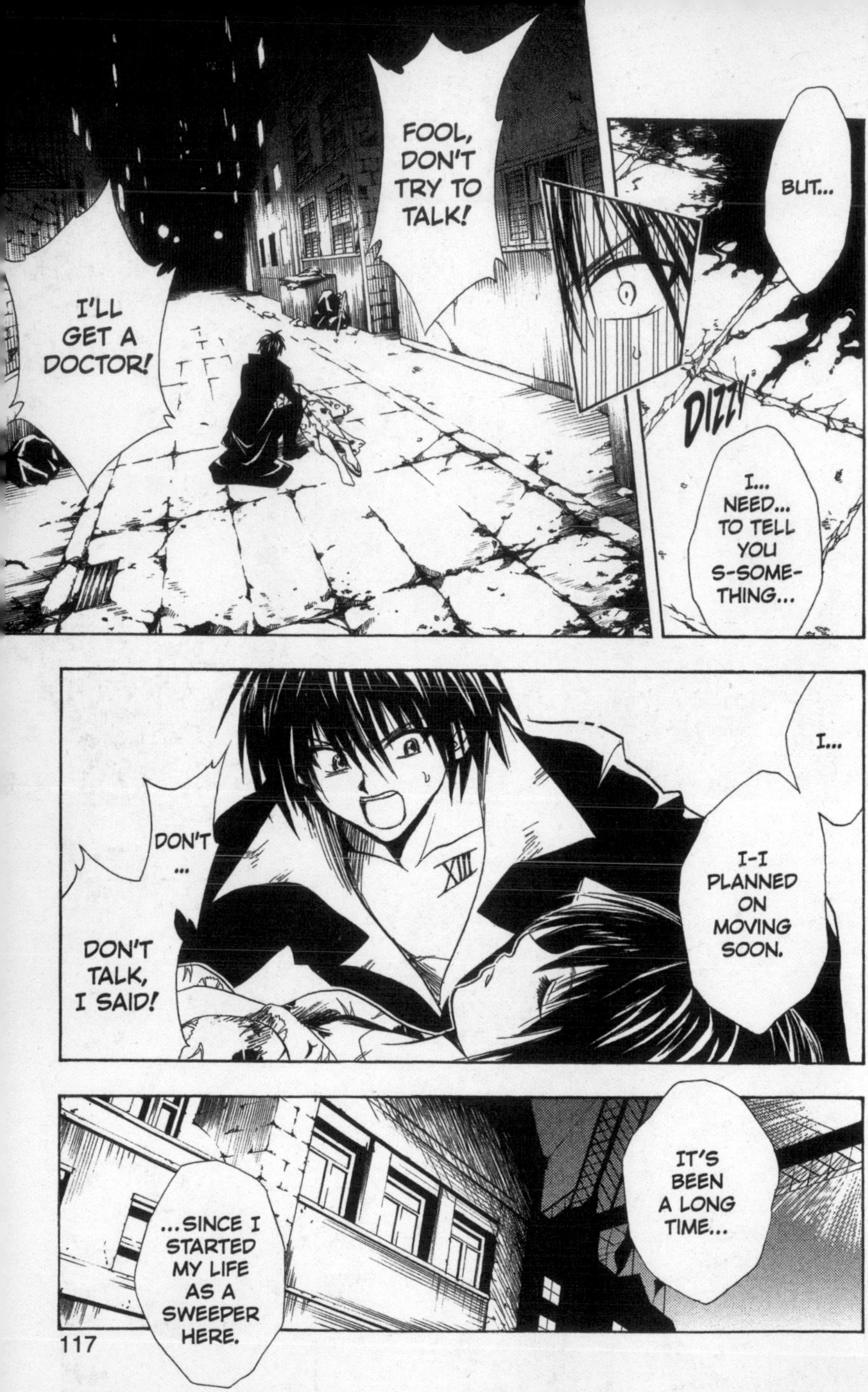
BUT...
DIZZY
I... NEED... TO TELL YOU S-SOME-THING...
FOOL, DON'T TRY TO TALK!
I'LL GET A DOCTOR!
I...
I-I PLANNED ON MOVING SOON.
DON'T ...
DON'T TALK, I SAID!
IT'S BEEN A LONG TIME...
...SINCE I STARTED MY LIFE AS A SWEEPER HERE.

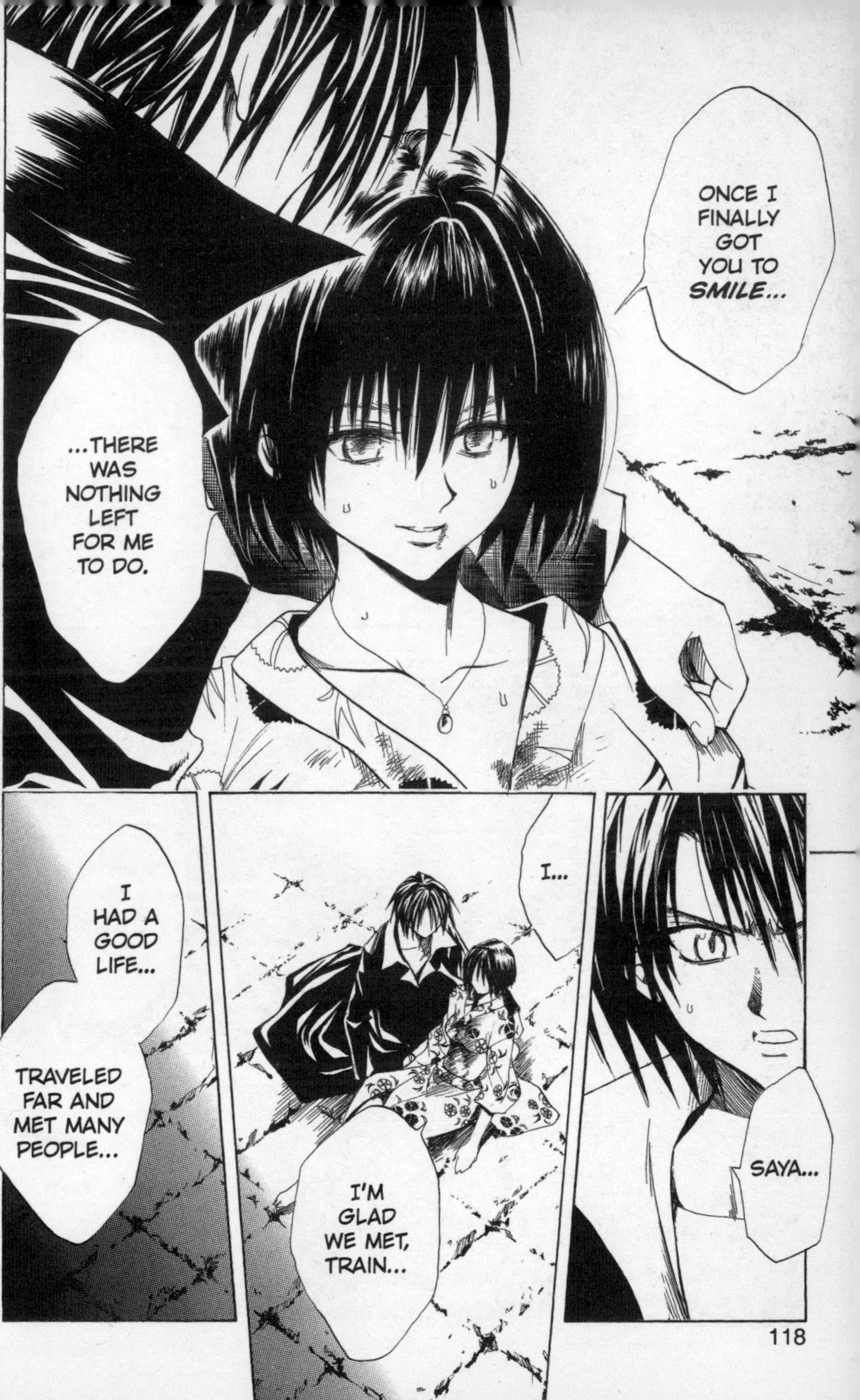
ONCE I FINALLY GOT YOU TO **SMILE...**
...THERE WAS NOTHING LEFT FOR ME TO DO.
SAYA...
I...
I'M GLAD WE MET, TRAIN...
I HAD A GOOD LIFE...
TRAVELED FAR AND MET MANY PEOPLE...

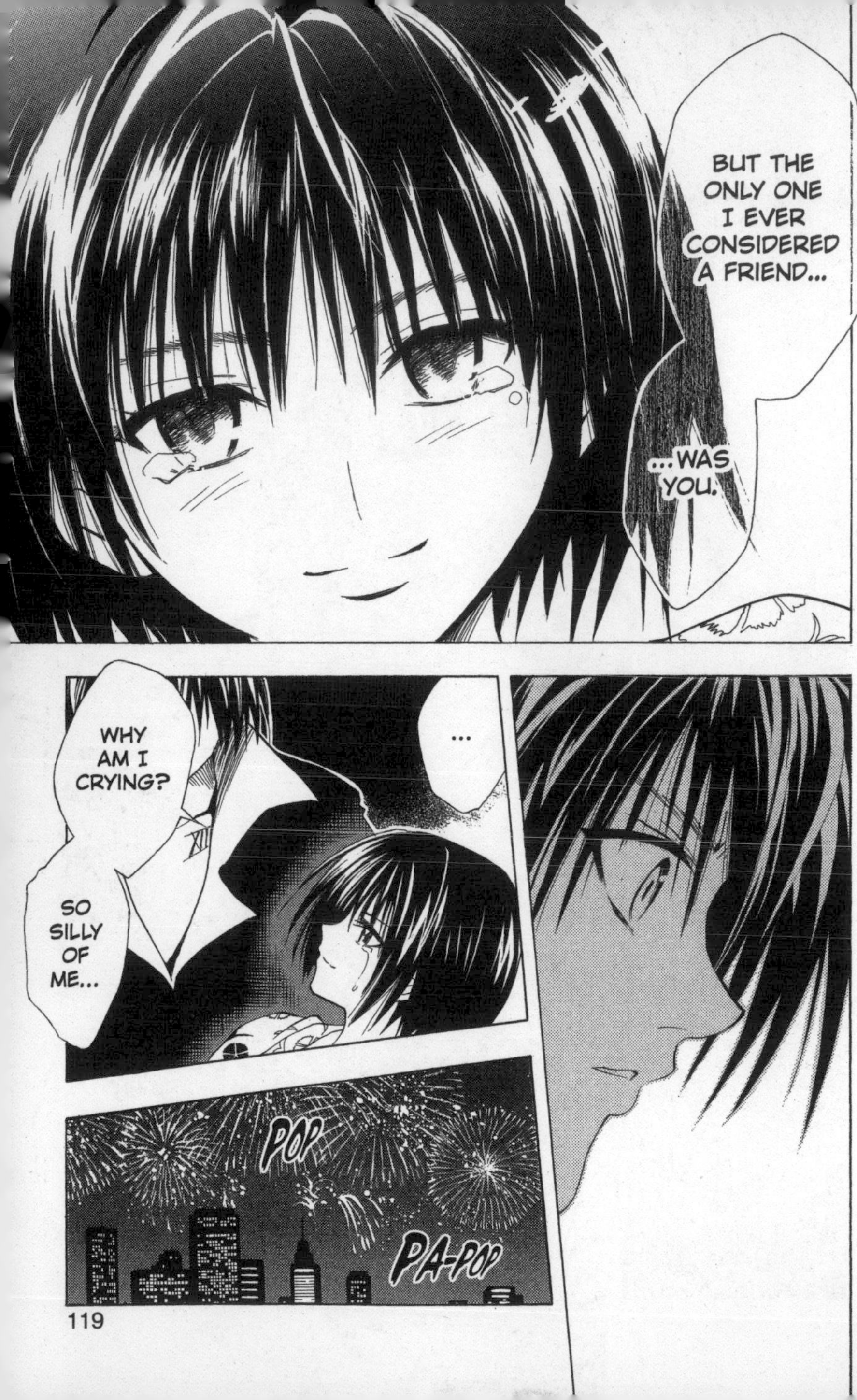
BUT THE ONLY ONE I EVER CONSIDERED A FRIEND...
...WAS YOU.
...
WHY AM I CRYING?
SO SILLY OF ME...
POP
PA-POP

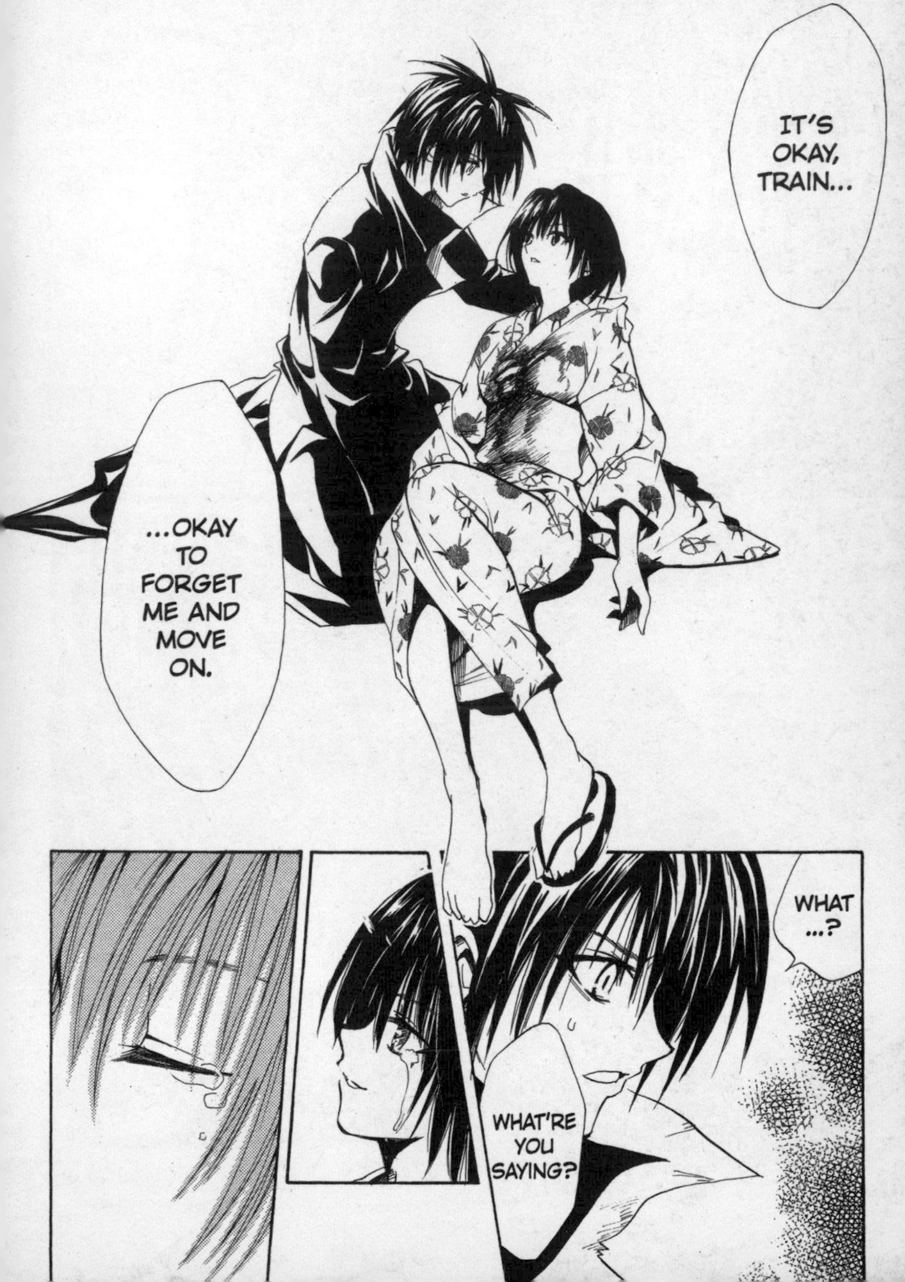
IT'S OKAY, TRAIN...
...OKAY TO FORGET ME AND MOVE ON.
WHAT ...?
WHAT'RE YOU SAYING?

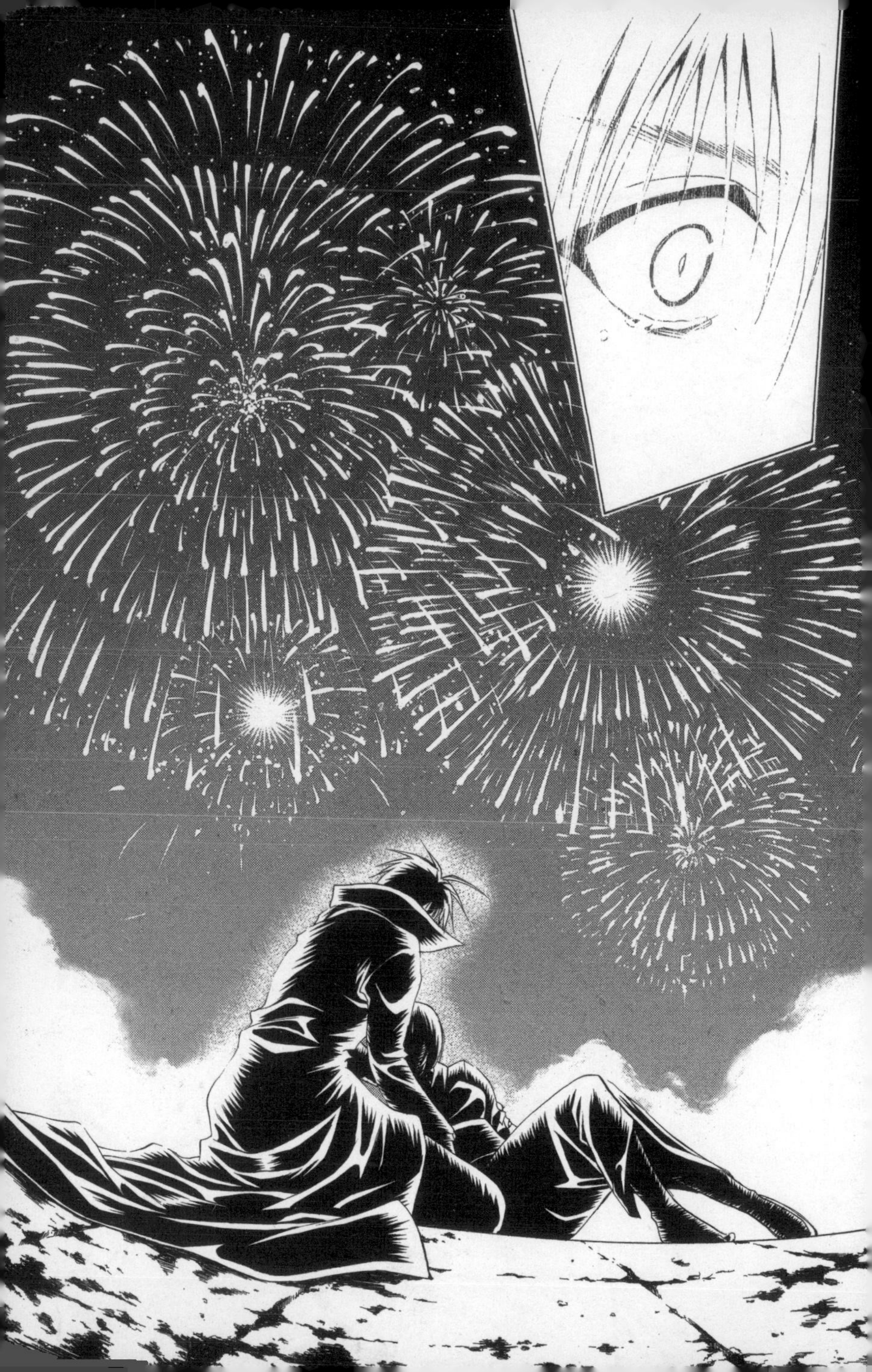

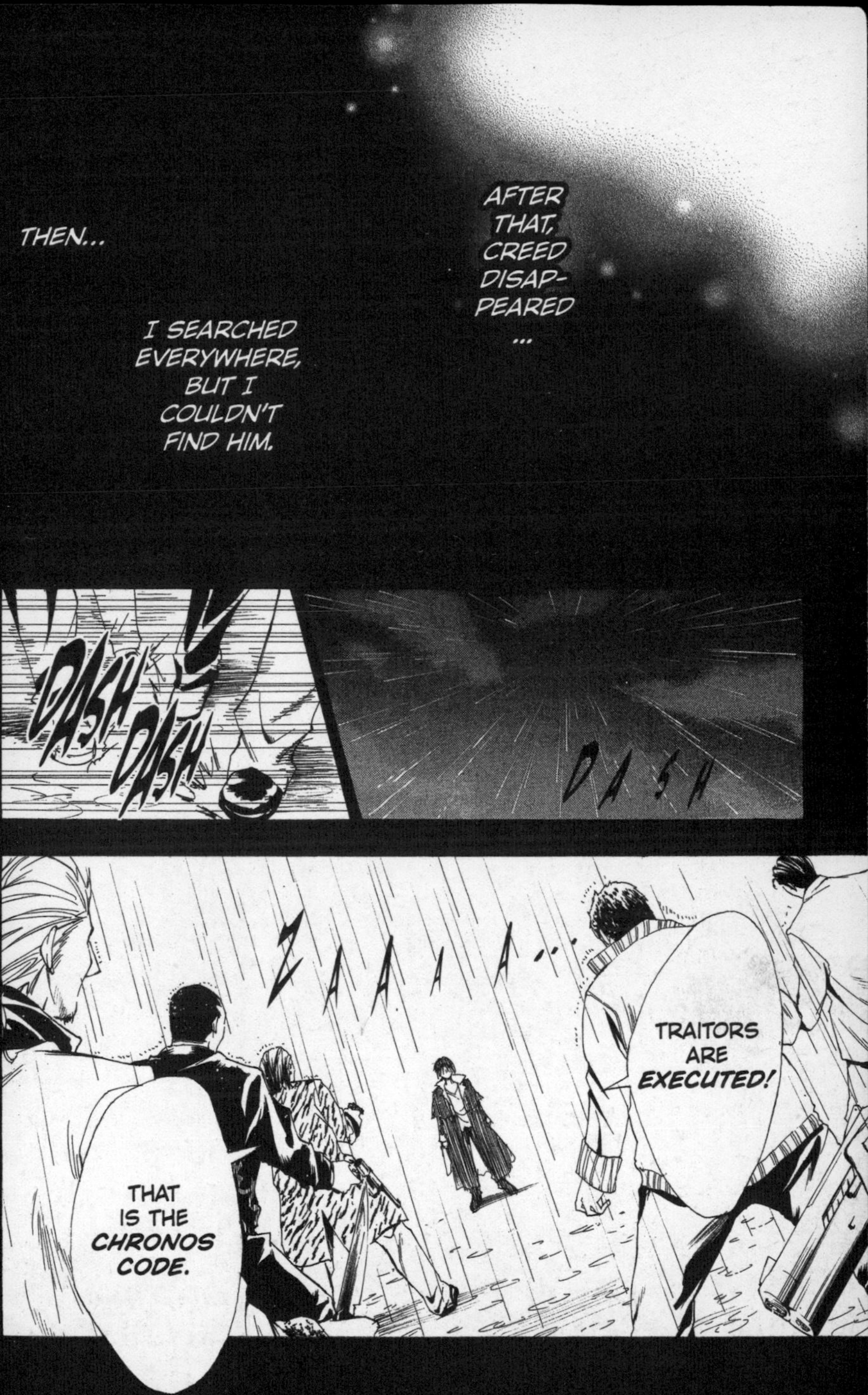
AFTER THAT, CREED DISAPPEARED...
THEN...
I SEARCHED EVERYWHERE, BUT I COULDN'T FIND HIM.
DASH
DASH
DASH
ZAAAA...
TRAITORS ARE EXECUTED!
THAT IS THE CHRONOS CODE.

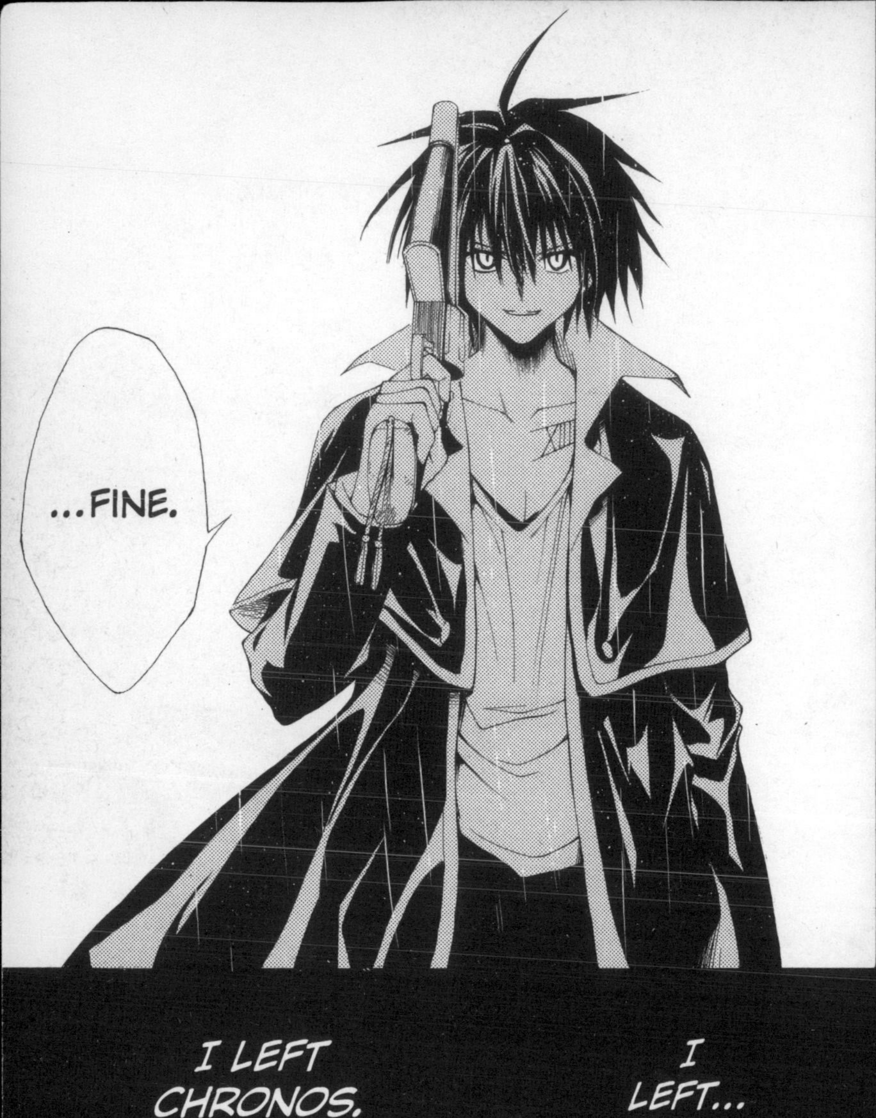
...FINE.
I LEFT...
I LEFT CHRONOS.

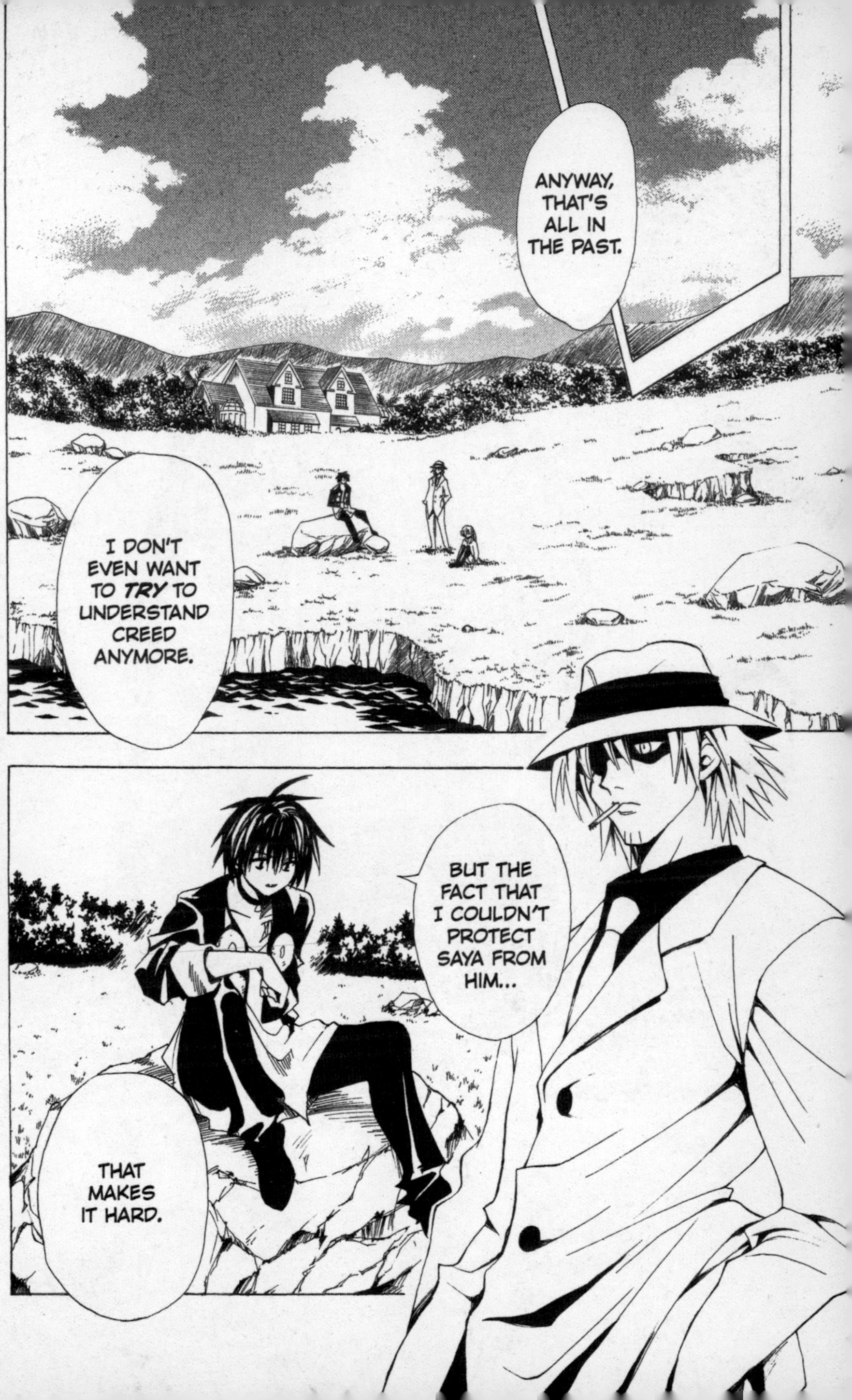
ANYWAY, THAT'S ALL IN THE PAST.
I DON'T EVEN WANT TO **TRY** TO UNDERSTAND CREED ANYMORE.
BUT THE FACT THAT I COULDN'T PROTECT SAYA FROM HIM...
THAT MAKES IT HARD.

READ THIS WAY

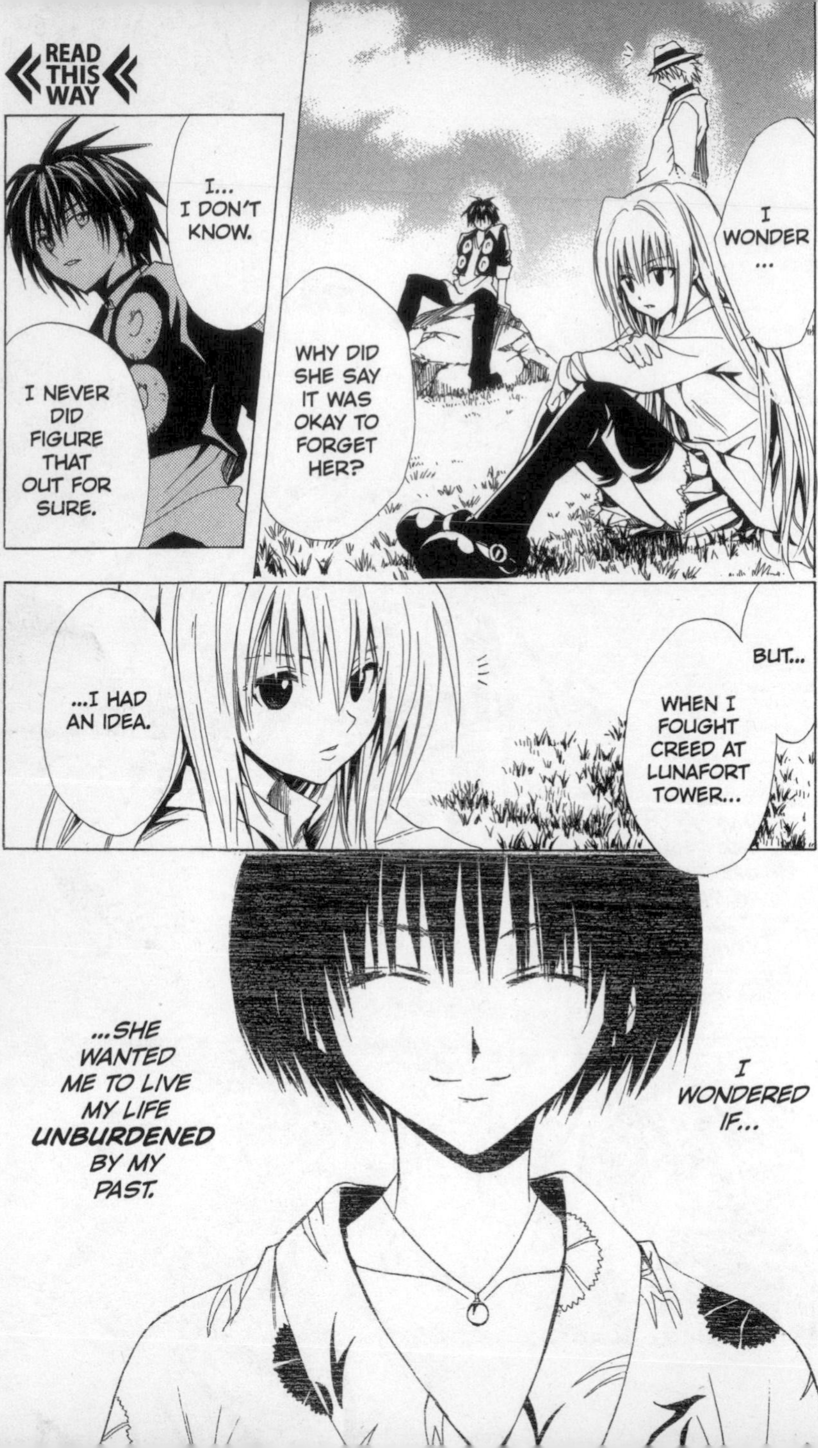

I WONDER...
WHY DID SHE SAY IT WAS OKAY TO FORGET HER?
I... I DON'T KNOW.
I NEVER DID FIGURE THAT OUT FOR SURE.
BUT...
WHEN I FOUGHT CREED AT LUNAFORT TOWER...
...I HAD AN IDEA.
I WONDERED IF...
...SHE WANTED ME TO LIVE MY LIFE UNBURDENED BY MY PAST.

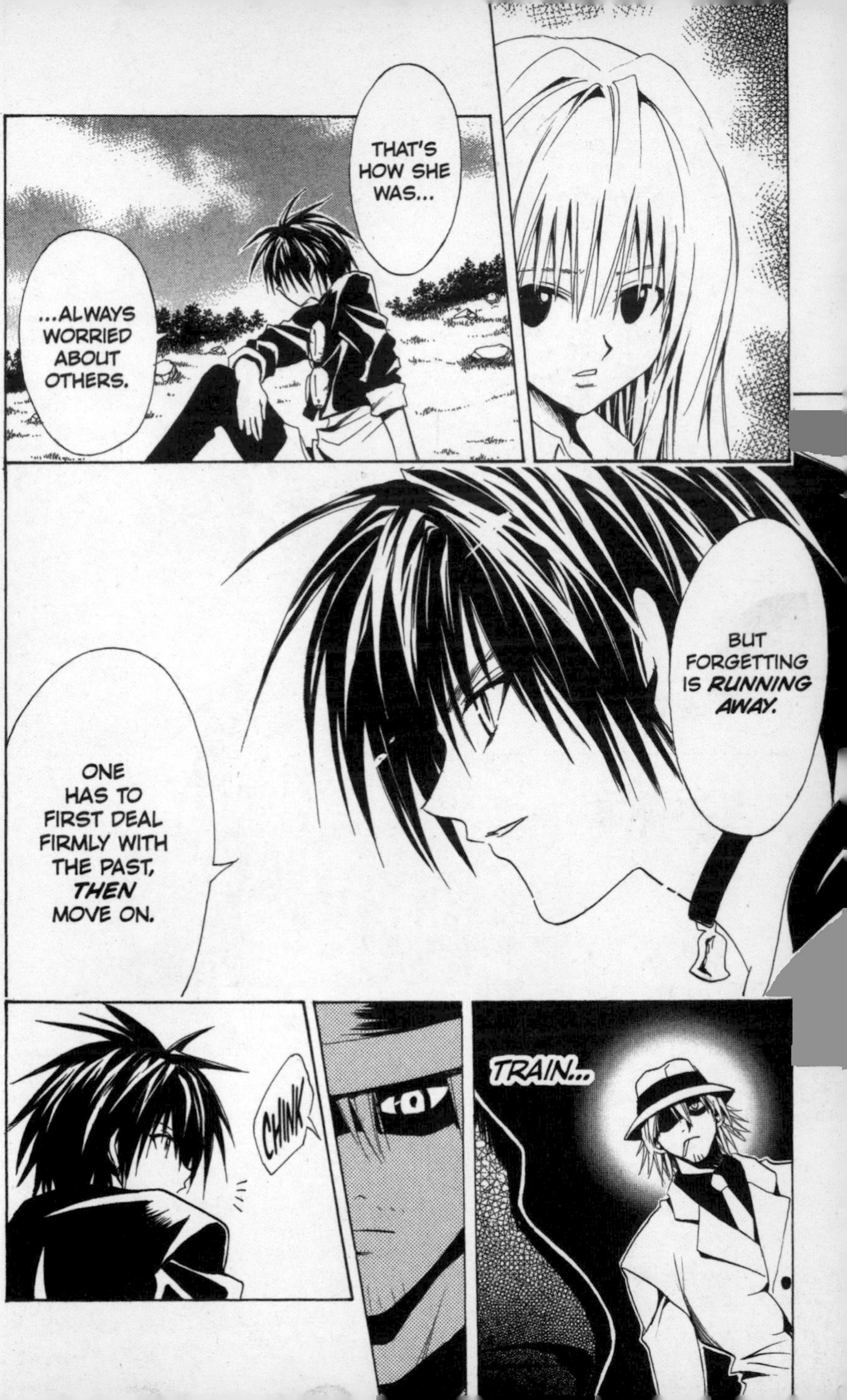
THAT'S HOW SHE WAS...
...ALWAYS WORRIED ABOUT OTHERS.
BUT FORGETTING IS *RUNNING AWAY.*
ONE HAS TO FIRST DEAL FIRMLY WITH THE PAST, *THEN* MOVE ON.
TRAIN...
CHINK

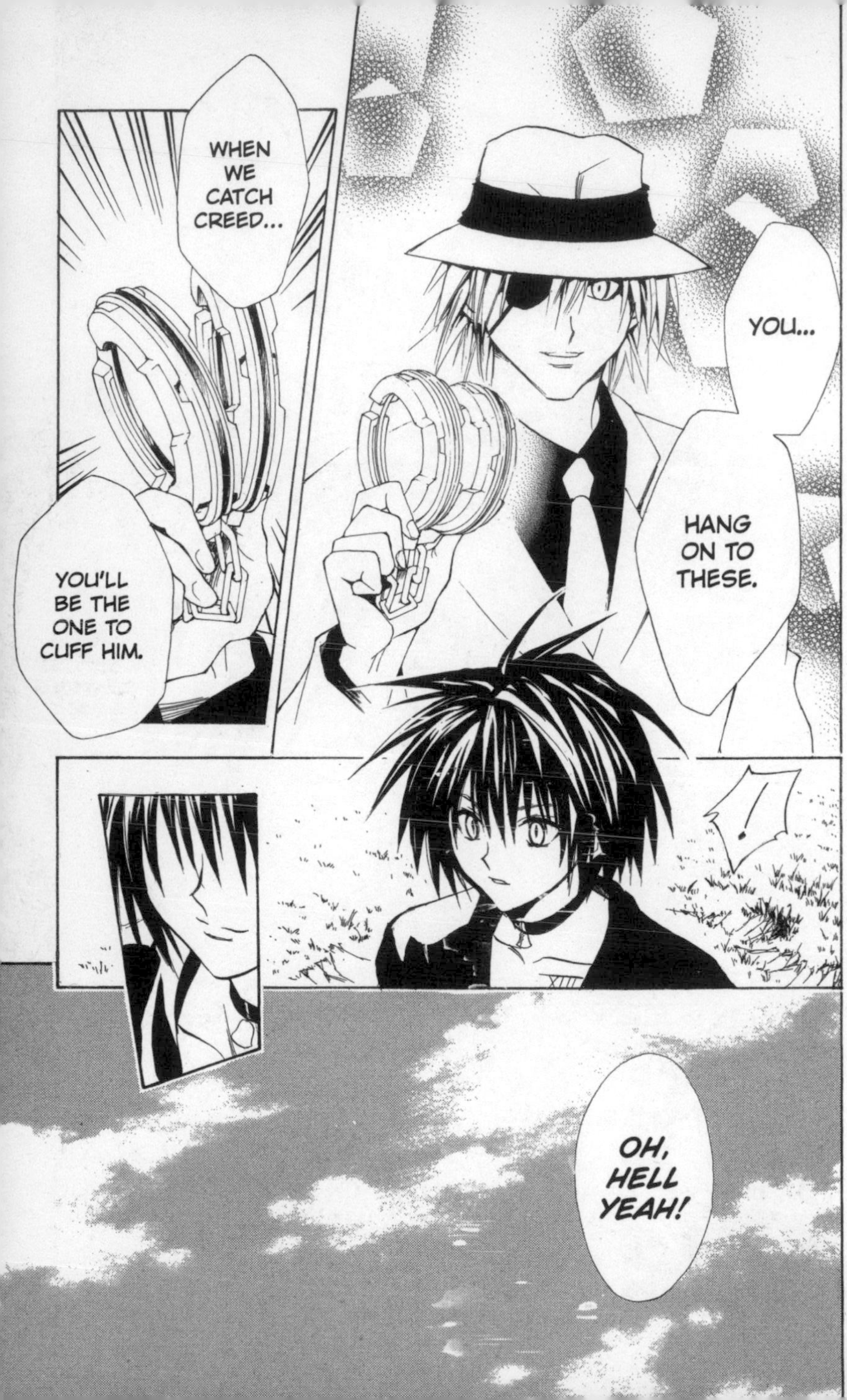
YOU...
HANG ON TO THESE.
WHEN WE CATCH CREED...
YOU'LL BE THE ONE TO CUFF HIM.
!
OH, HELL YEAH!

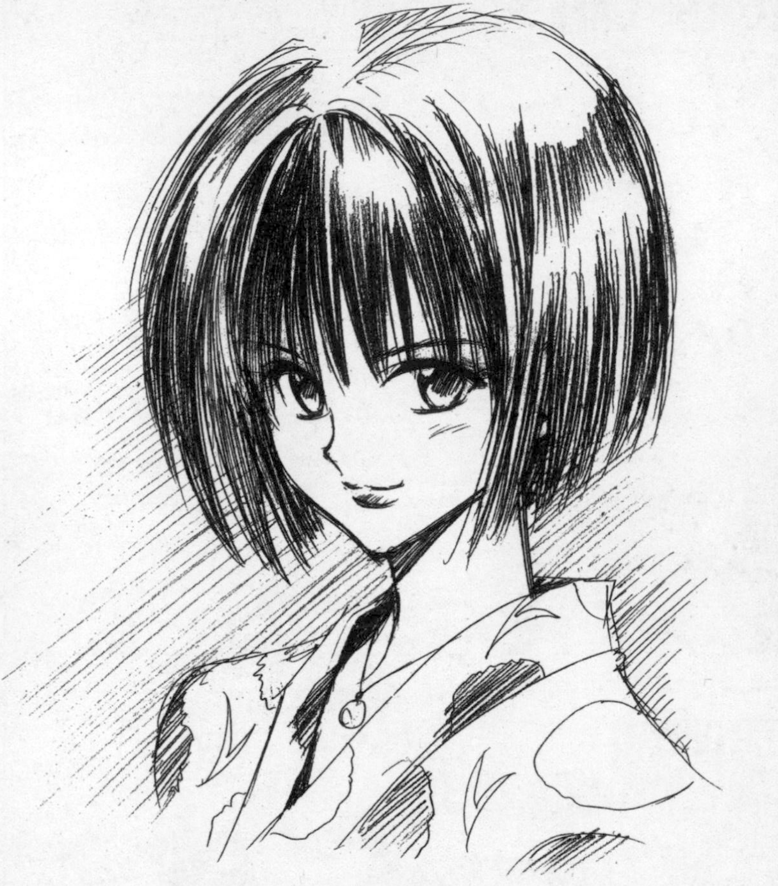

CHAPTER 119 WAS TOUGH, BUT SINCE SAYA'S DEATH WAS CRUCIAL TO THE DEVELOPMENT OF TRAIN'S CHARACTER, THERE WAS NO WAY TO AVOID IT. AFTER SOME CONSIDERATION I DECIDED THAT RATHER THAN HAVE TRAIN ***TELL*** THE STORY, I'D TURN BACK THE CLOCK TWO AND A HALF YEARS AND ***SHOW*** WHAT HAPPENED. HENCE, SOME OF WHAT'S IN THIS CHAPTER, TRAIN ISN'T PRIVY TO. THE STORY TRAIN TOLD SVEN AND EVE INCLUDES SOME CONJECTURE.

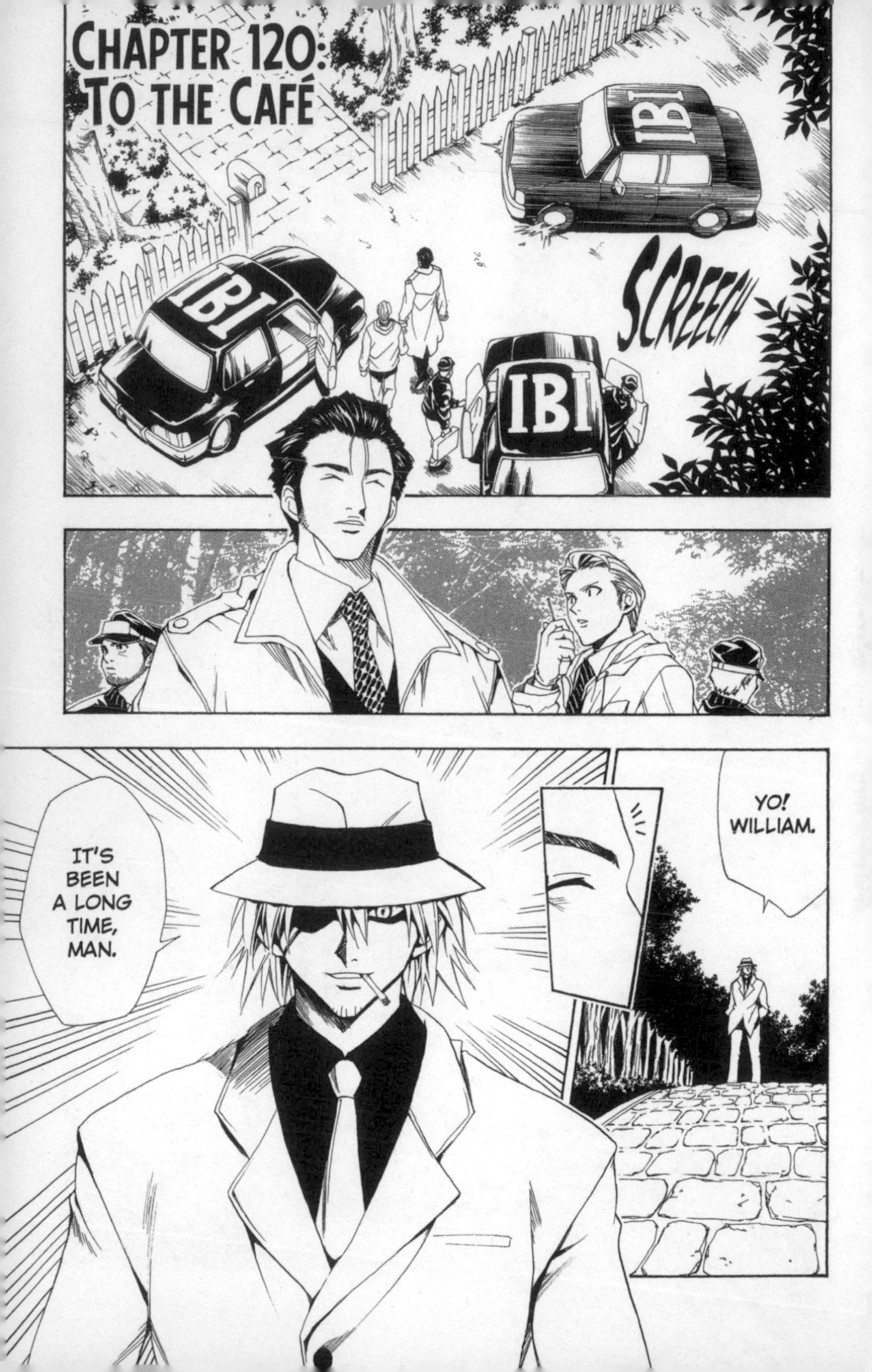
CHAPTER 120:
TO THE CAFÉ
IBI
IBI
IBI
SCREECH
YO! WILLIAM.
IT'S BEEN A LONG TIME, MAN.

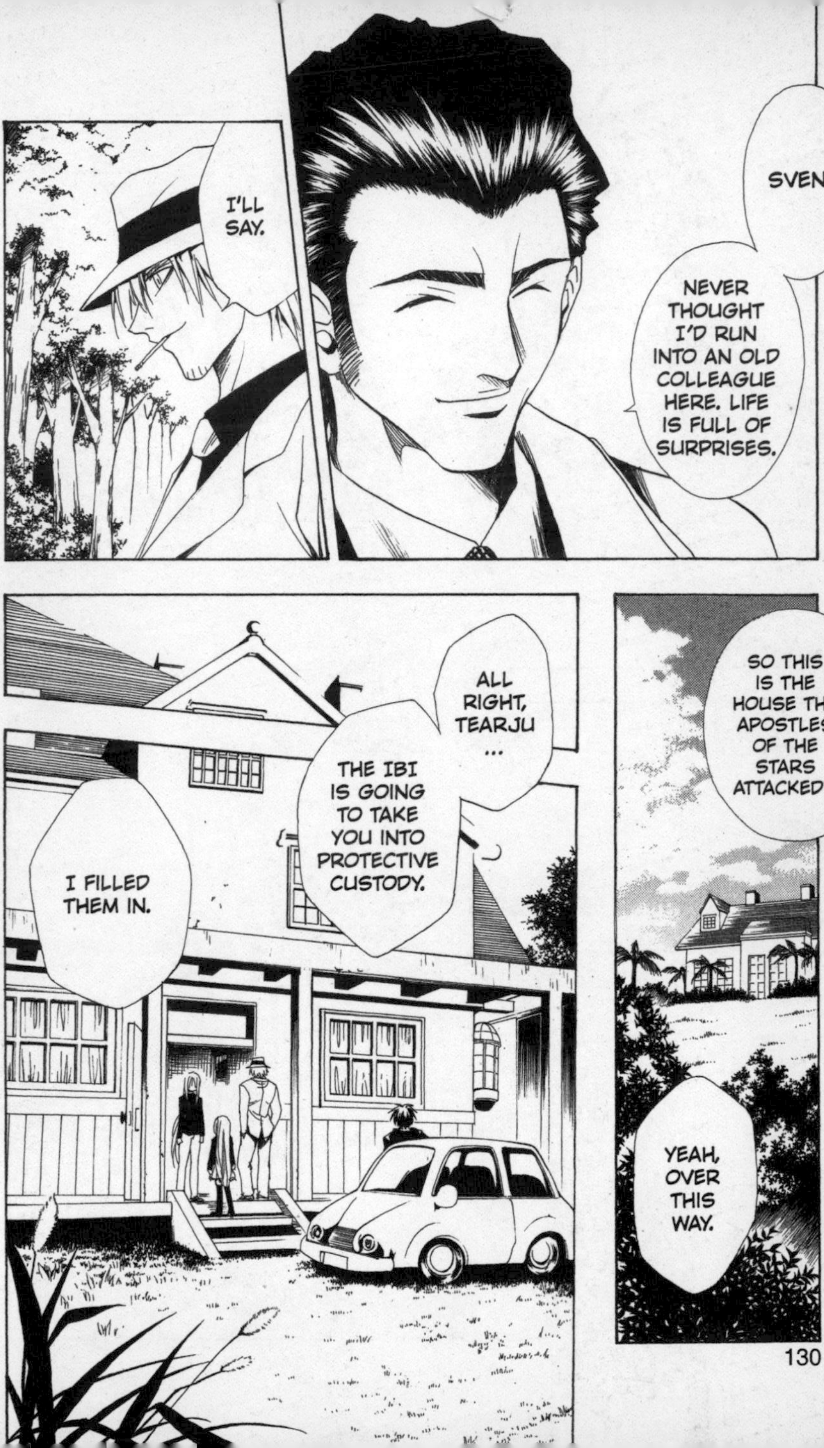
SVEN!
NEVER THOUGHT I'D RUN INTO AN OLD COLLEAGUE HERE. LIFE IS FULL OF SURPRISES.
I'LL SAY.
SO THIS IS THE HOUSE THE APOSTLES OF THE STARS ATTACKED?
YEAH, OVER THIS WAY.
ALL RIGHT, TEARJU...
THE IBI IS GOING TO TAKE YOU INTO PROTECTIVE CUSTODY.
I FILLED THEM IN.

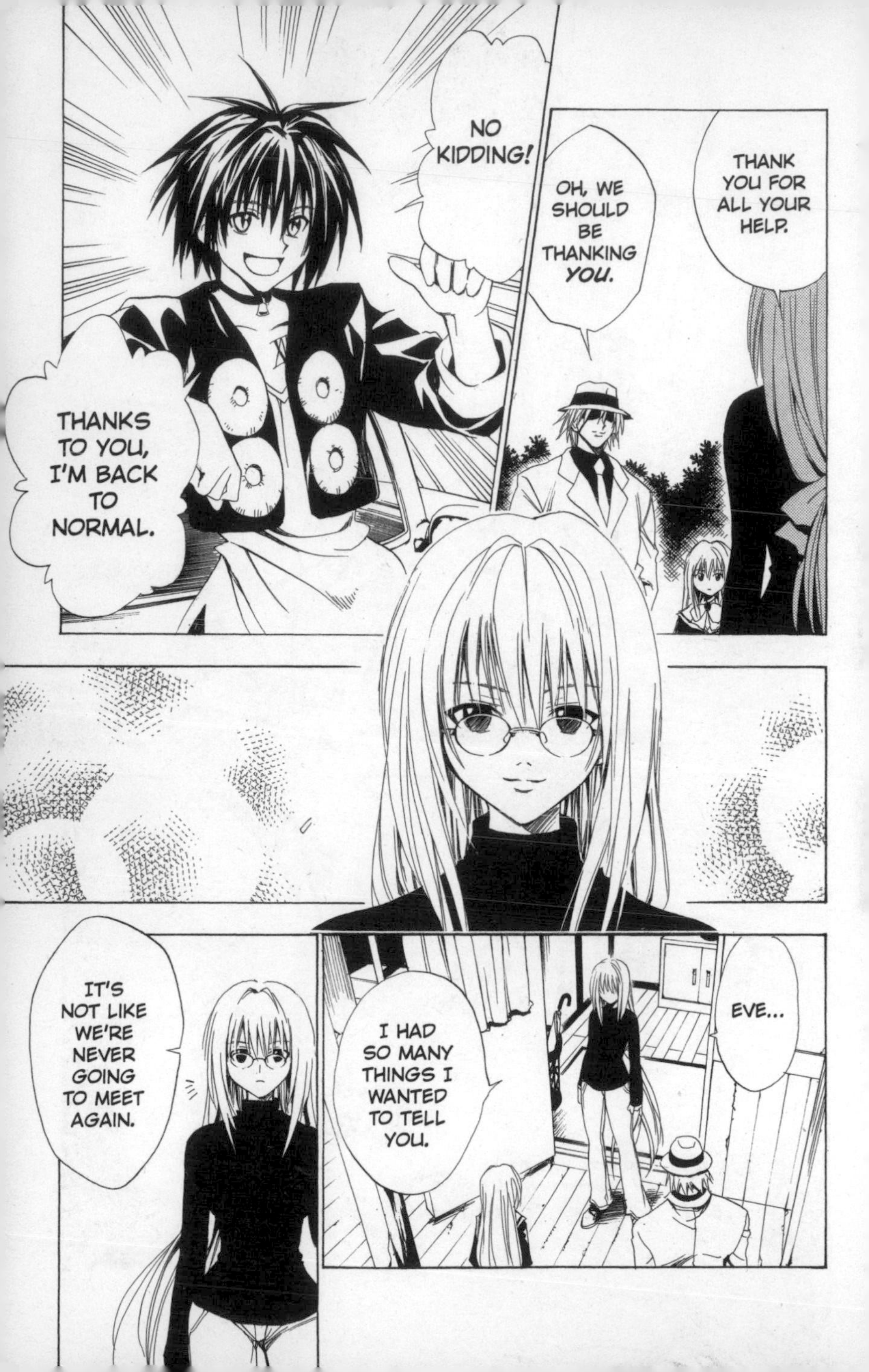
THANK YOU FOR ALL YOUR HELP.
OH, WE SHOULD BE THANKING YOU.
NO KIDDING!
THANKS TO YOU, I'M BACK TO NORMAL.
EVE...
I HAD SO MANY THINGS I WANTED TO TELL YOU.
IT'S NOT LIKE WE'RE NEVER GOING TO MEET AGAIN.

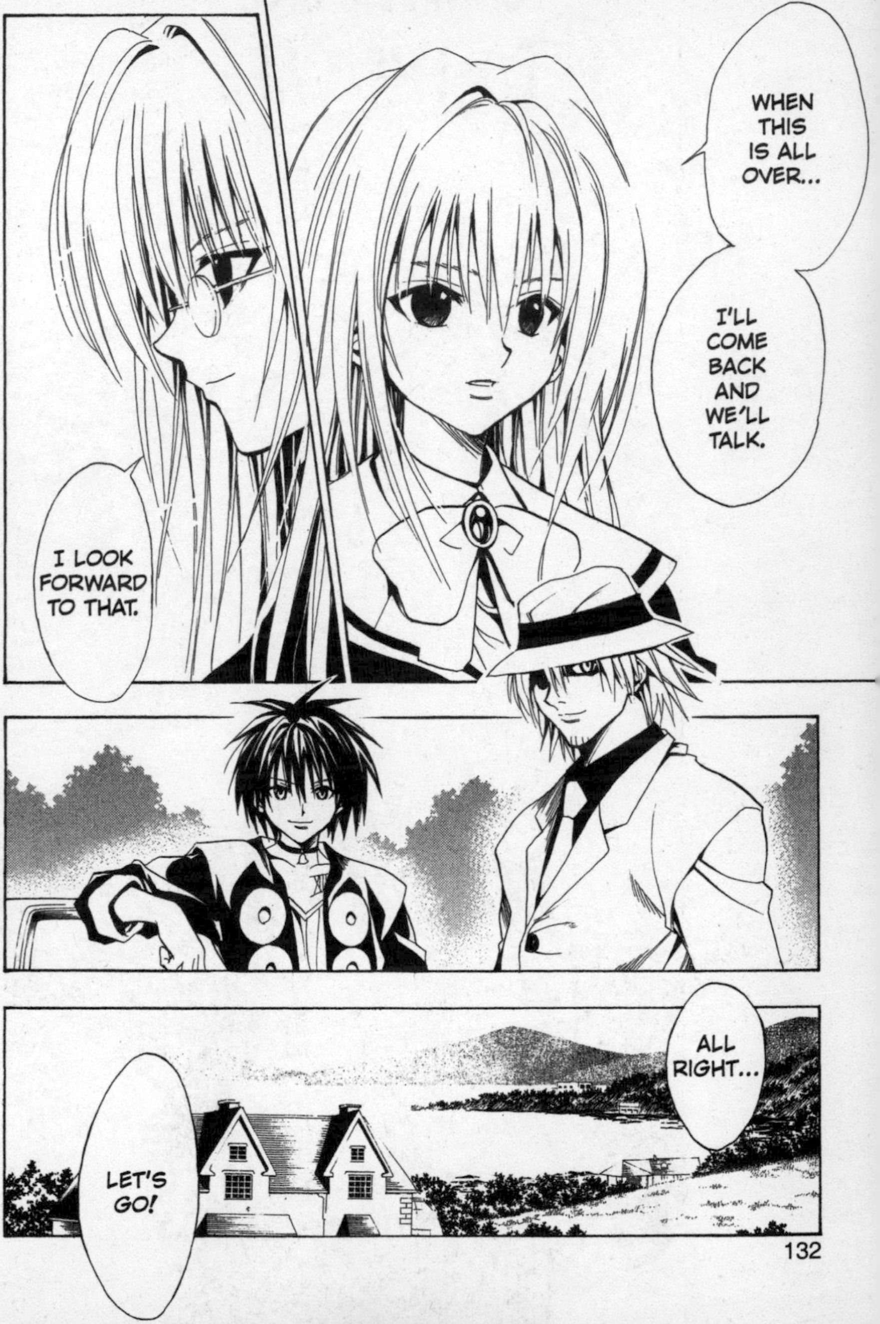
WHEN THIS IS ALL OVER...
I'LL COME BACK AND WE'LL TALK.
I LOOK FORWARD TO THAT.
ALL RIGHT...
LET'S GO!

Chapter 120: To the Café

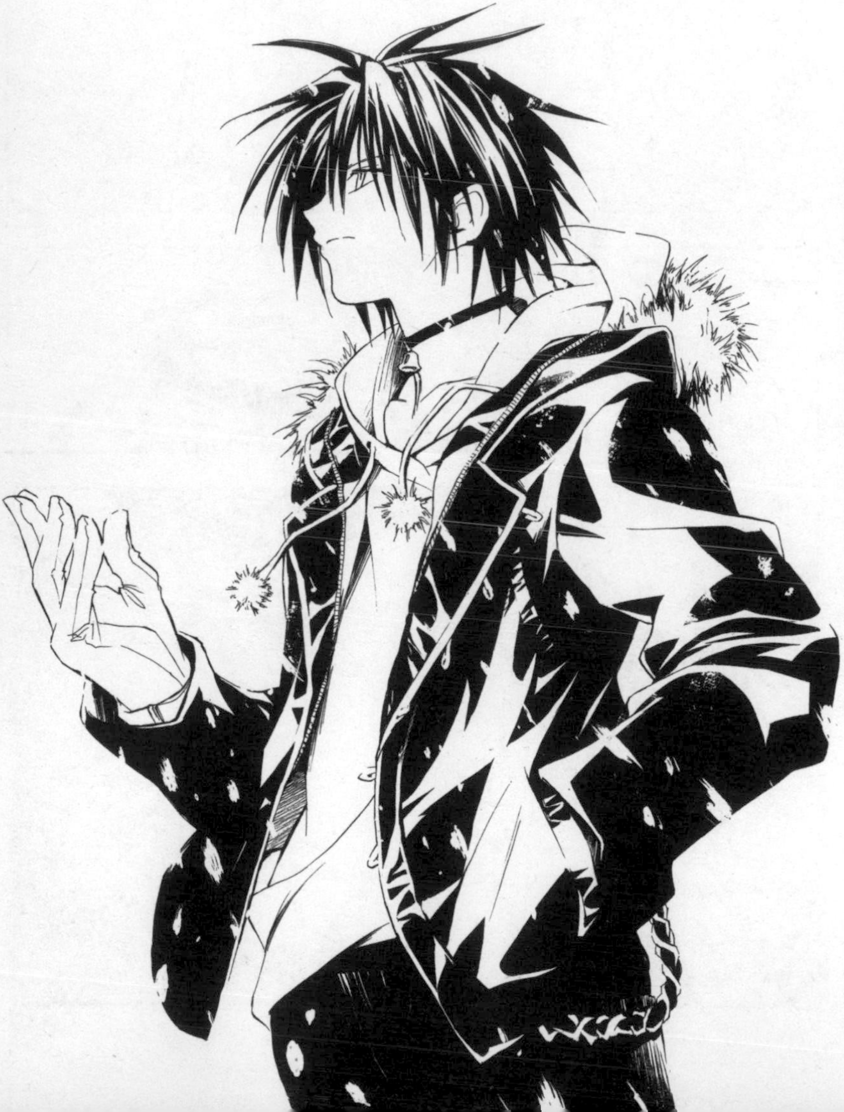

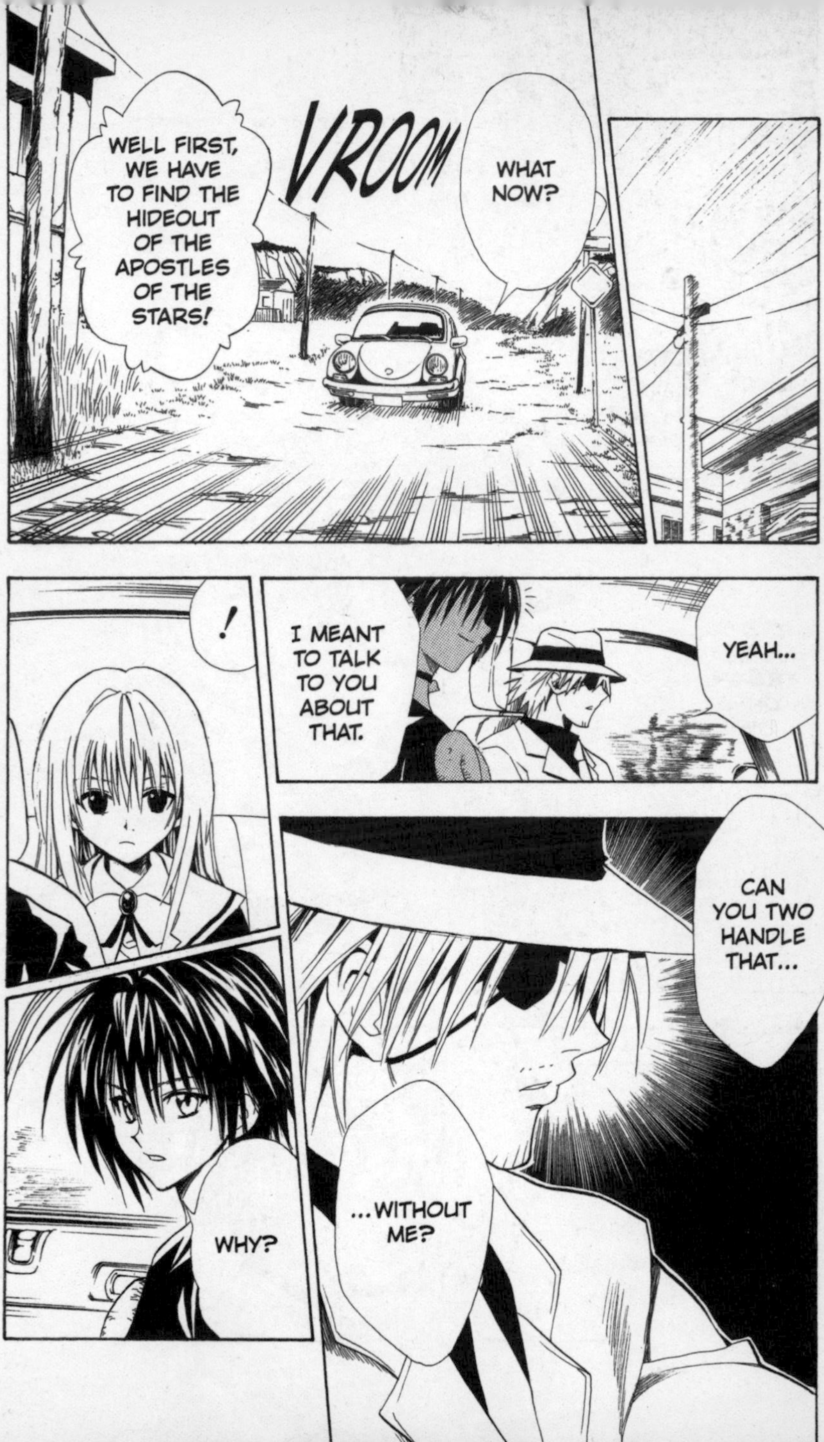
WHAT NOW?
VROOM
WELL FIRST, WE HAVE TO FIND THE HIDEOUT OF THE APOSTLES OF THE STARS!
YEAH...
I MEANT TO TALK TO YOU ABOUT THAT.
CAN YOU TWO HANDLE THAT...
...WITHOUT ME?
!
WHY?

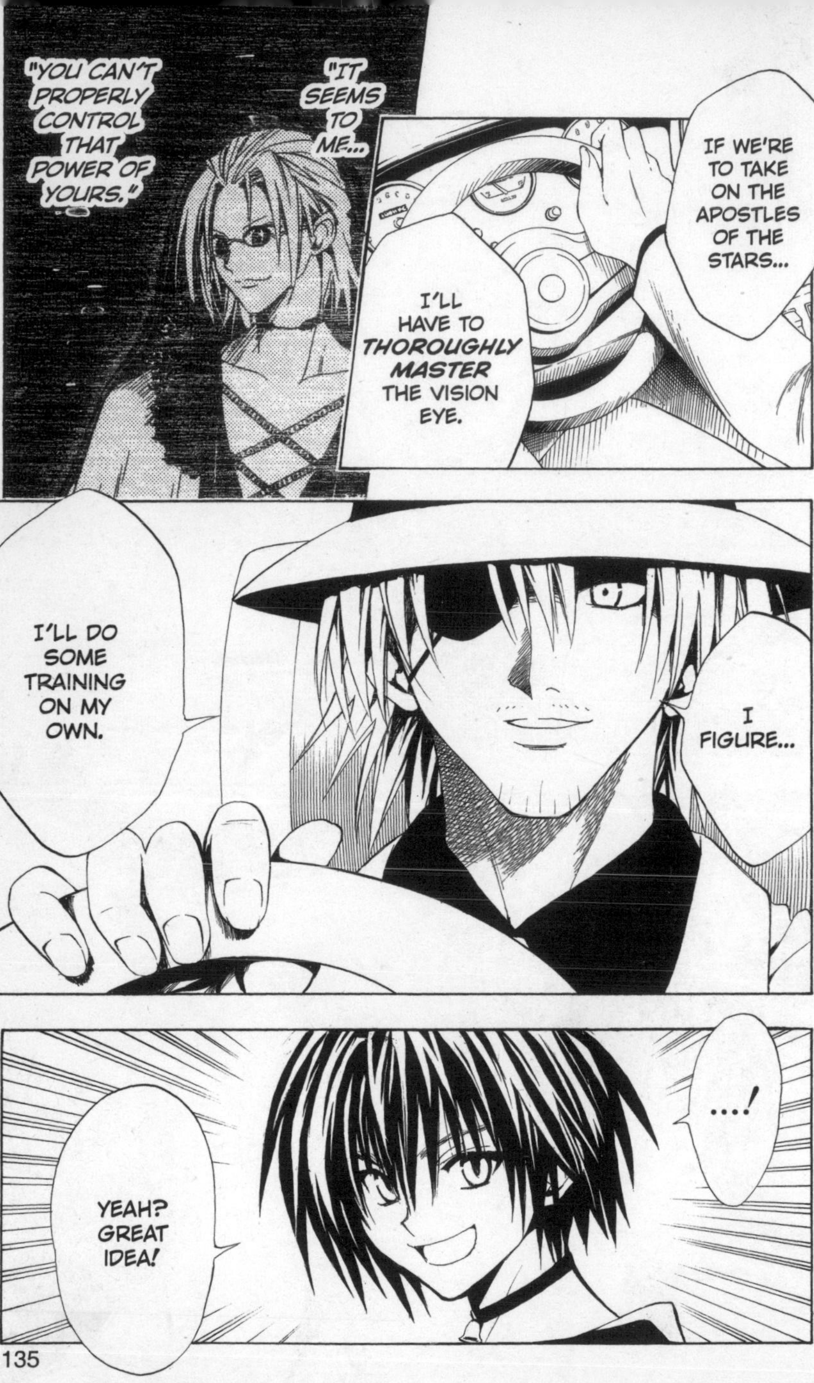
IF WE'RE TO TAKE ON THE APOSTLES OF THE STARS...
I'LL HAVE TO *THOROUGHLY MASTER* THE VISION EYE.
"IT SEEMS TO ME...
"YOU CAN'T PROPERLY CONTROL THAT POWER OF YOURS."
I FIGURE...
I'LL DO SOME TRAINING ON MY OWN.
...!
YEAH? GREAT IDEA!

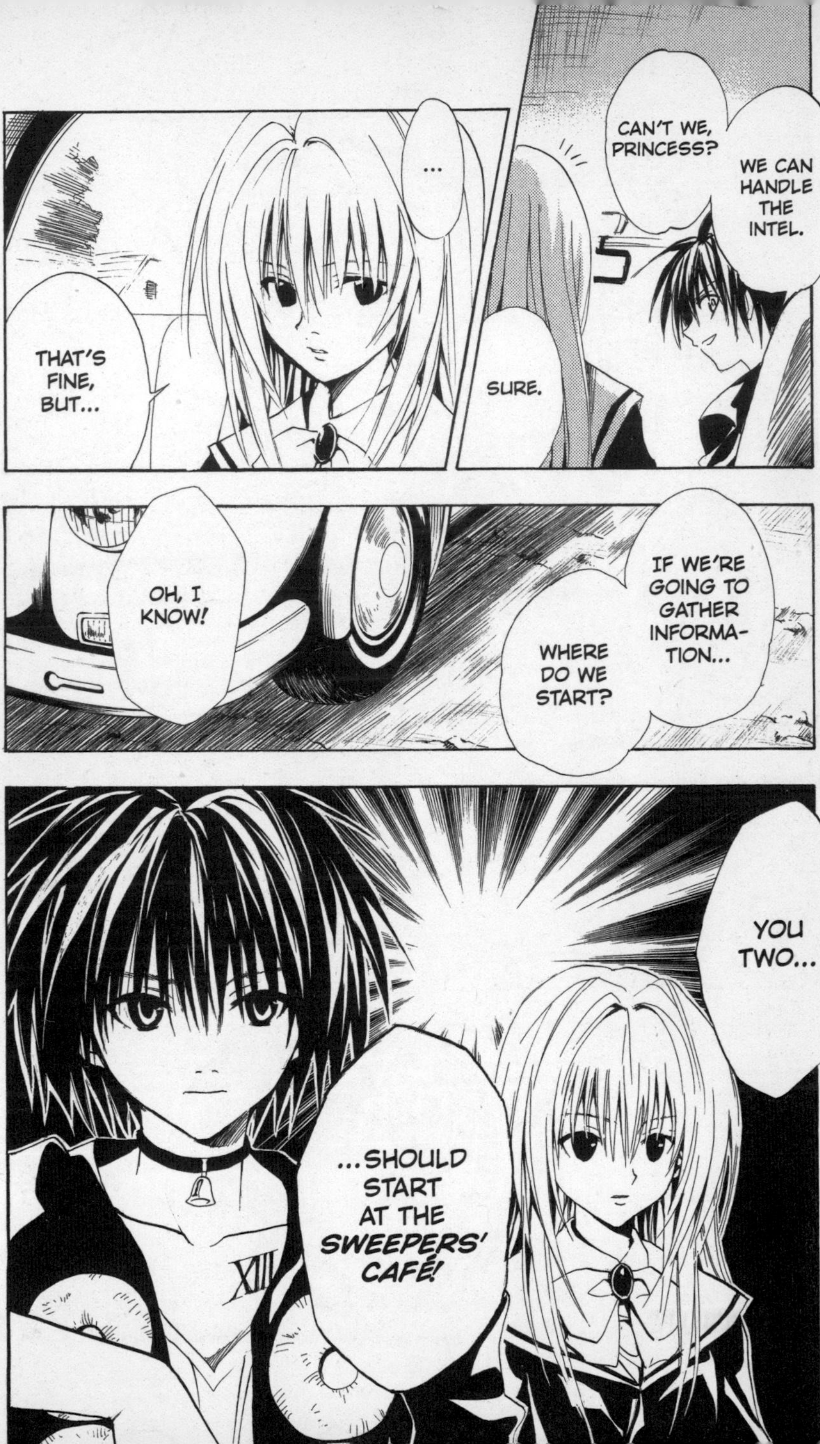
WE CAN HANDLE THE INTEL.
CAN'T WE, PRINCESS?
SURE.
...
THAT'S FINE, BUT...
IF WE'RE GOING TO GATHER INFORMATION...
WHERE DO WE START?
OH, I KNOW!
YOU TWO...
...SHOULD START AT THE *SWEEPERS' CAFÉ!*

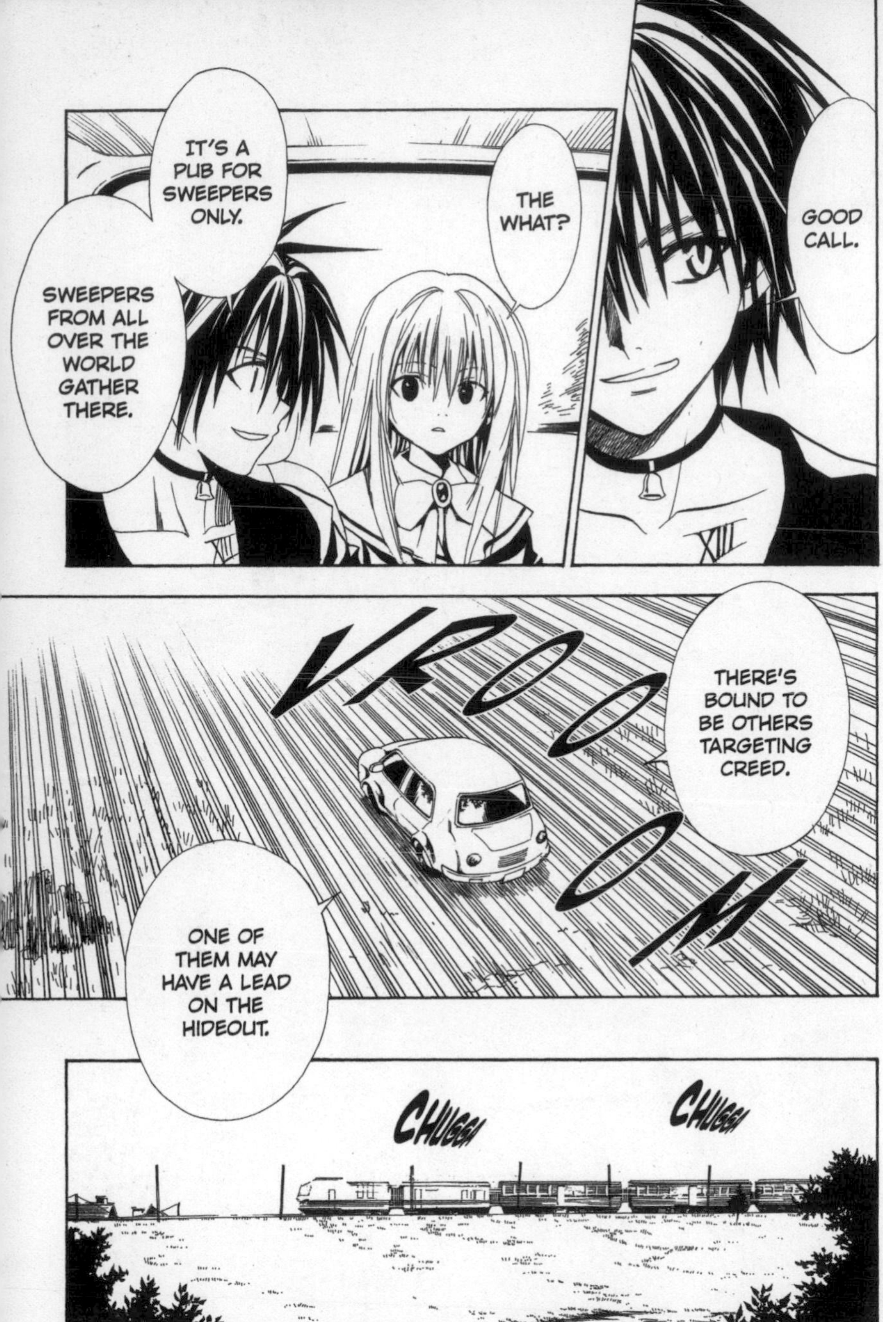
GOOD CALL.
THE WHAT?
IT'S A PUB FOR SWEEPERS ONLY.
SWEEPERS FROM ALL OVER THE WORLD GATHER THERE.
VROOOOM
THERE'S BOUND TO BE OTHERS TARGETING CREED.
ONE OF THEM MAY HAVE A LEAD ON THE HIDEOUT.
CHUGGA
CHUGGA

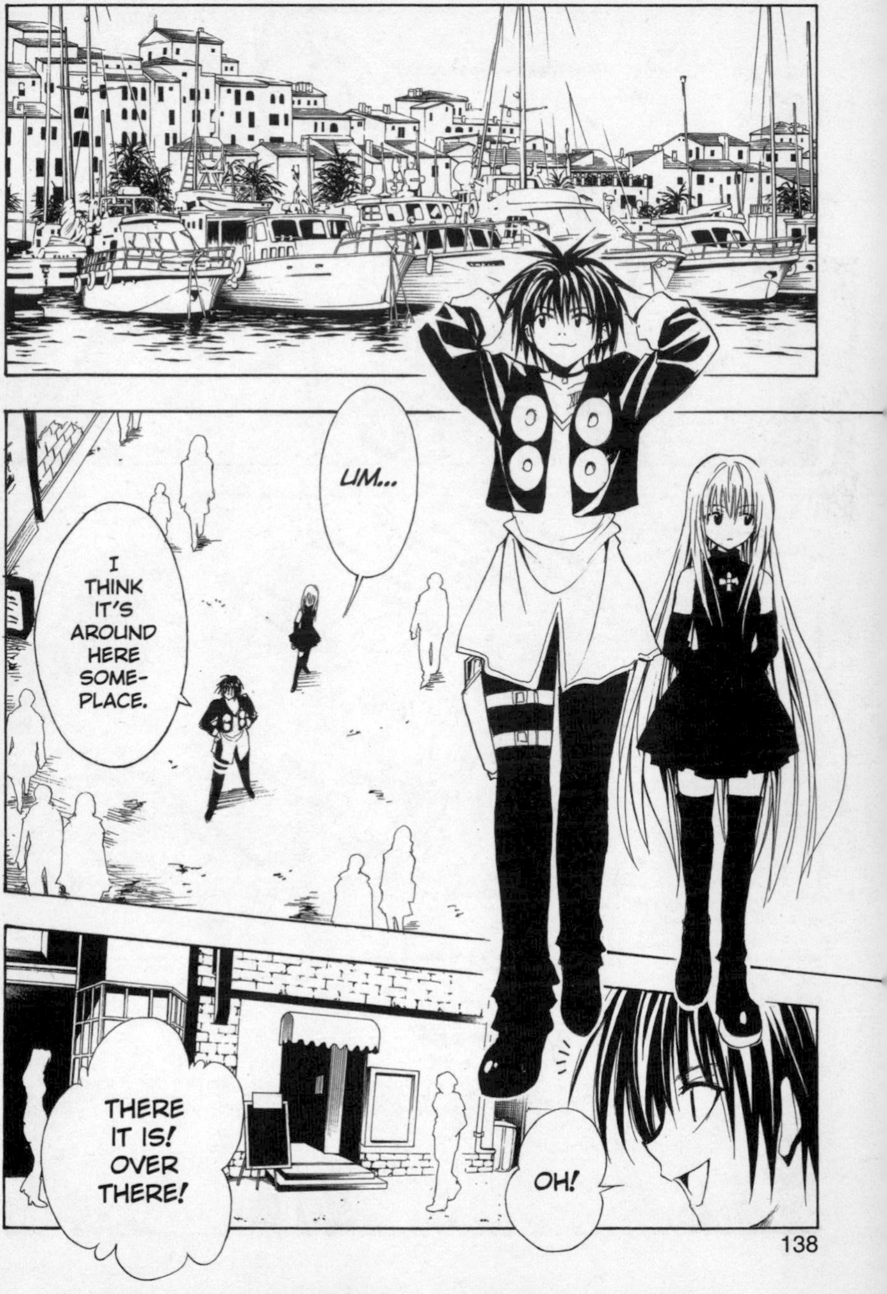
UM...
I THINK IT'S AROUND HERE SOME-PLACE.
OH!
THERE IT IS! OVER THERE!

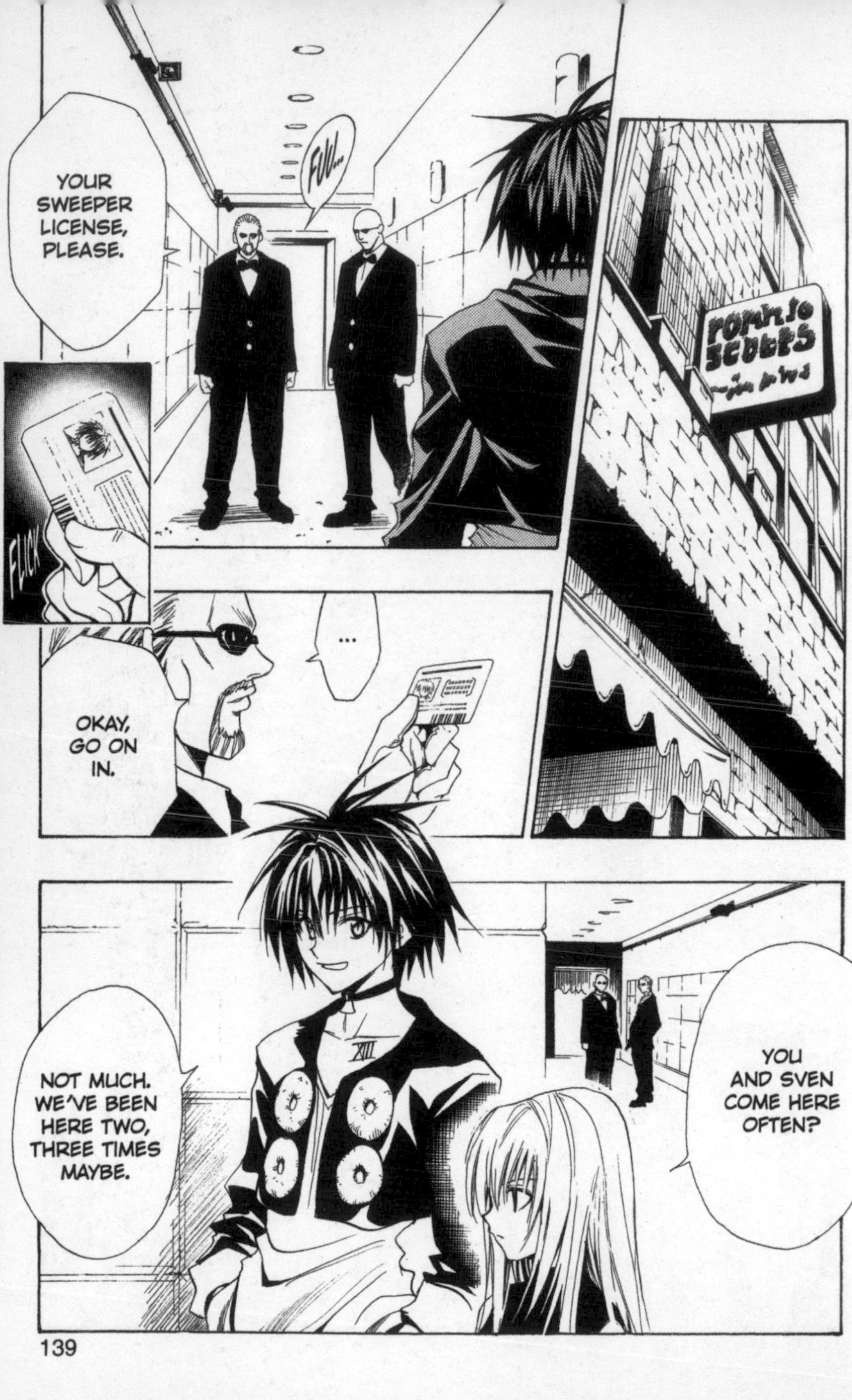
FUU...
YOUR SWEEPER LICENSE, PLEASE.
FLICK
...
OKAY, GO ON IN.
YOU AND SVEN COME HERE OFTEN?
NOT MUCH. WE'VE BEEN HERE TWO, THREE TIMES MAYBE.

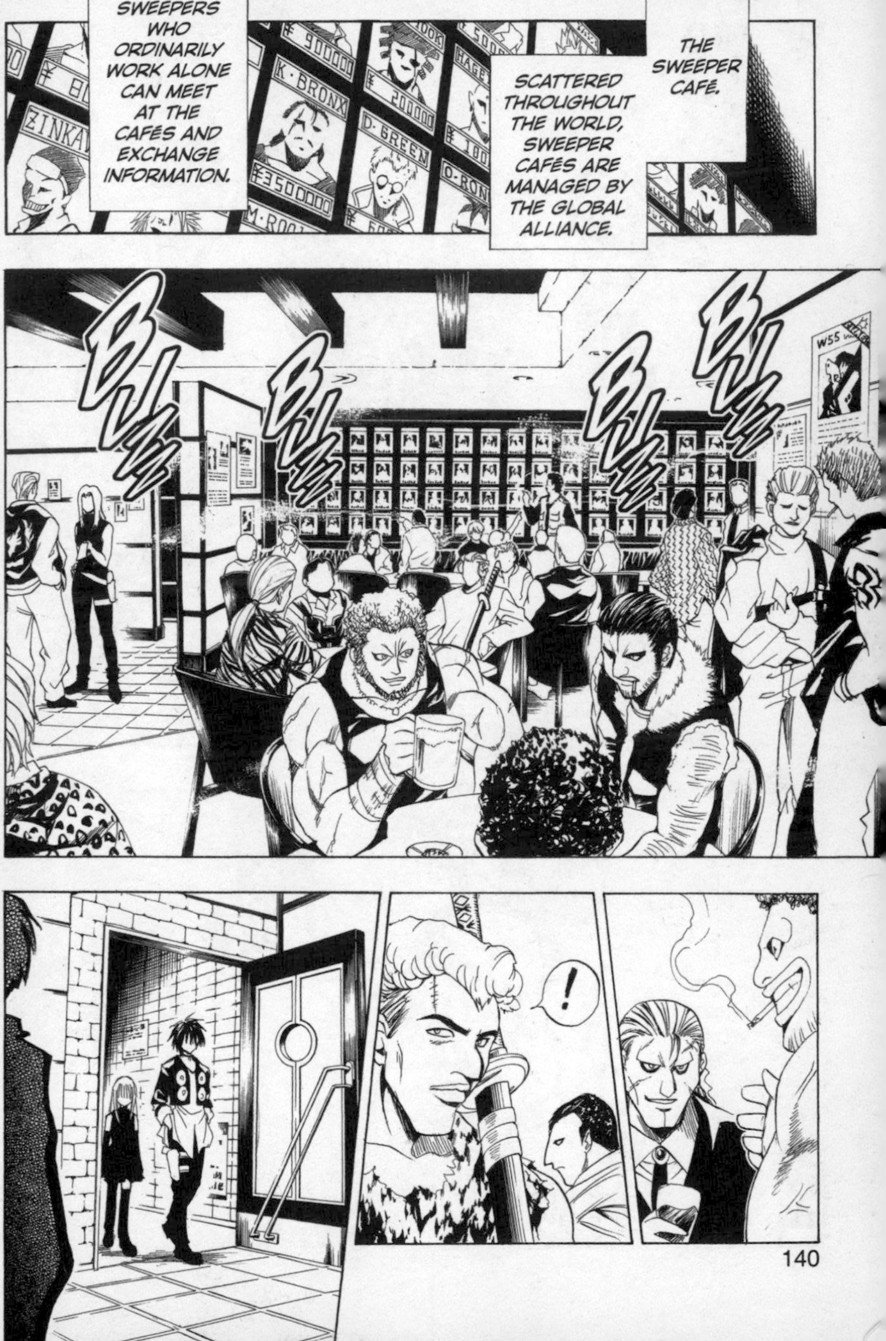
THE SWEEPER CAFÉ.
SCATTERED THROUGHOUT THE WORLD, SWEEPER CAFÉS ARE MANAGED BY THE GLOBAL ALLIANCE.
SWEEPERS WHO ORDINARILY WORK ALONE CAN MEET AT THE CAFÉS AND EXCHANGE INFORMATION.
BLAM
BLAM
BLAM
BLAM
!

READ THIS WAY

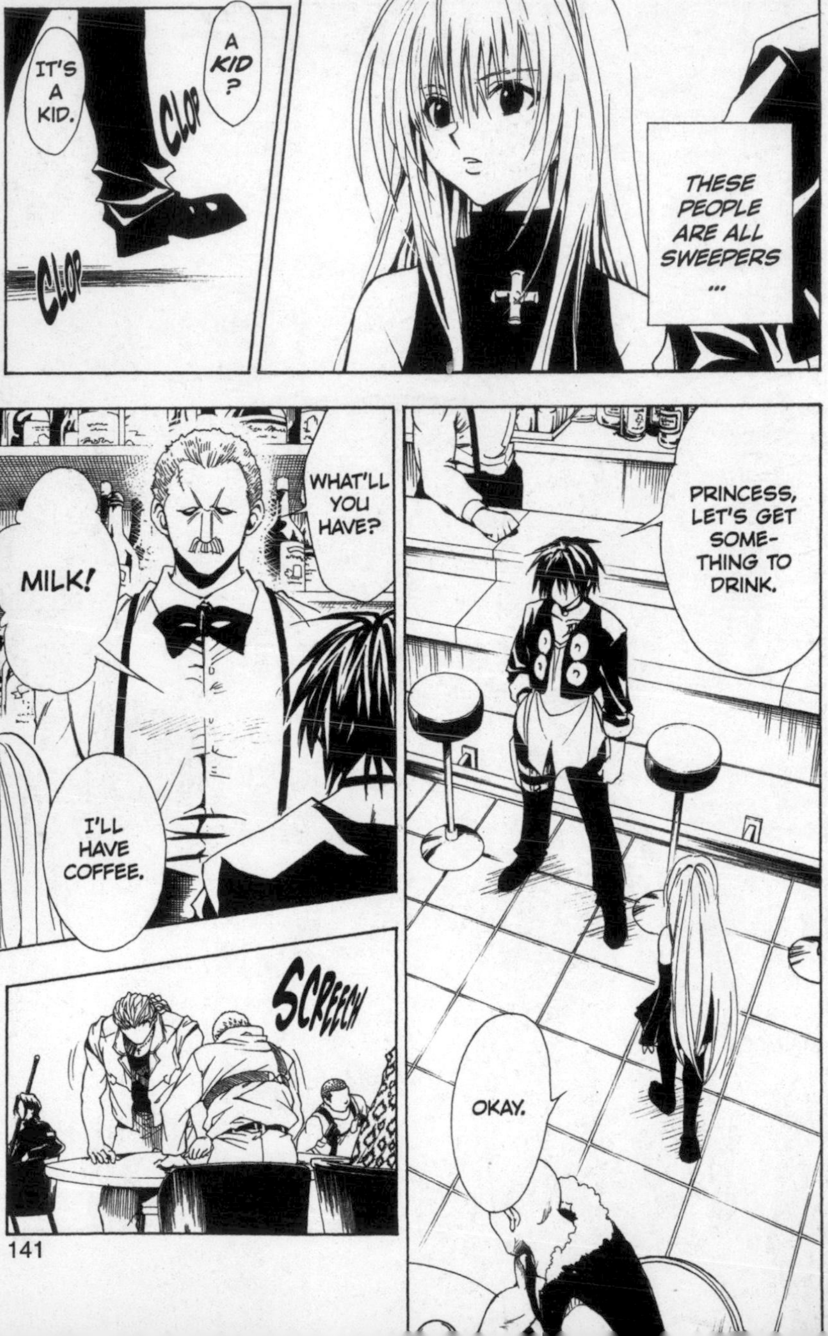
THESE PEOPLE ARE ALL SWEEPERS ...
A KID?
IT'S A KID.
CLOP
CLOP
PRINCESS, LET'S GET SOME-THING TO DRINK.
OKAY.
WHAT'LL YOU HAVE?
MILK!
I'LL HAVE COFFEE.
SCREECH

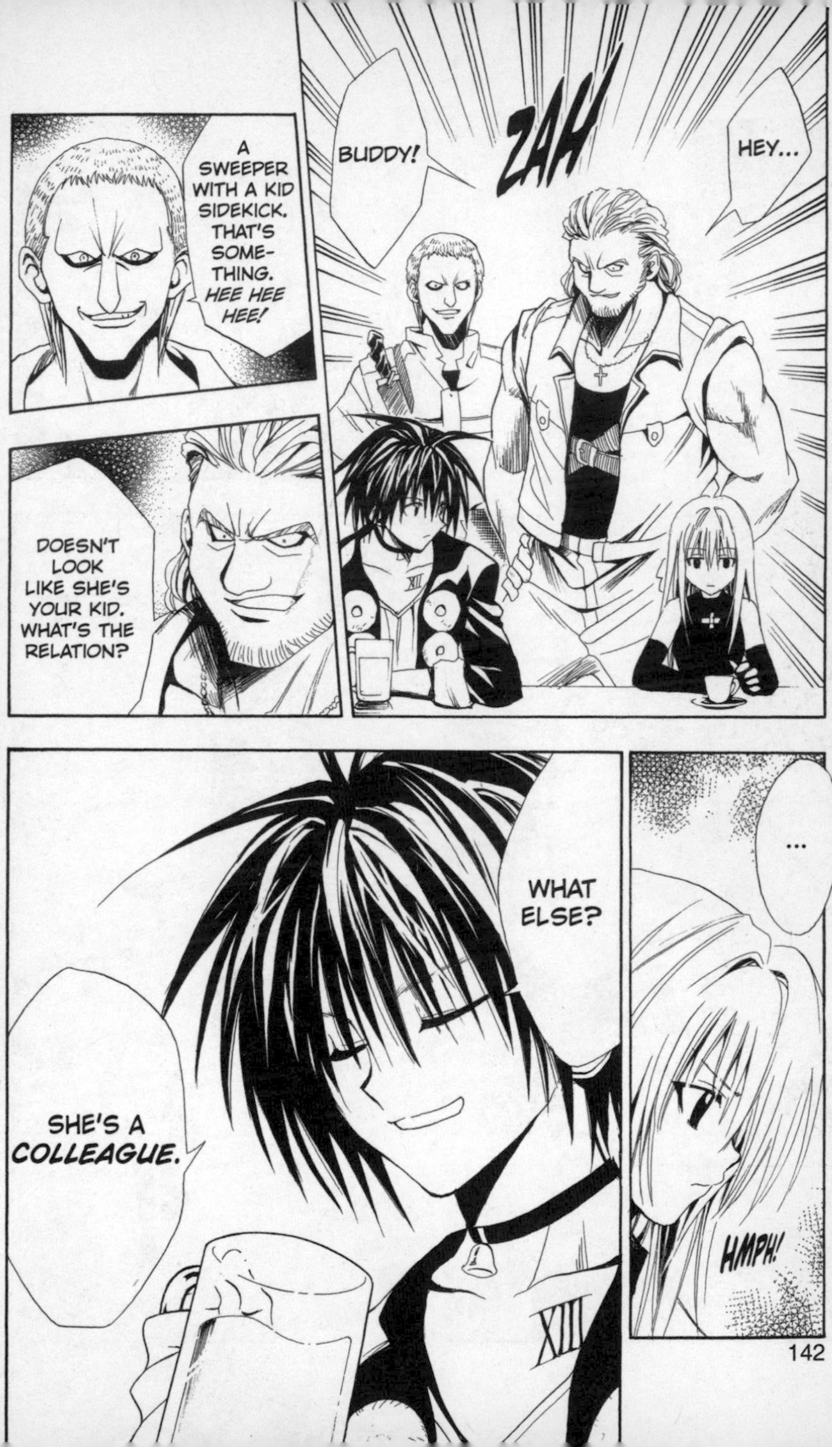
HEY...
ZAH
BUDDY!
A SWEEPER WITH A KID SIDEKICK. THAT'S SOME-THING. *HEE HEE HEE!*
DOESN'T LOOK LIKE SHE'S YOUR KID. WHAT'S THE RELATION?
...
HMPH!
WHAT ELSE?
SHE'S A **COLLEAGUE.**
XIII

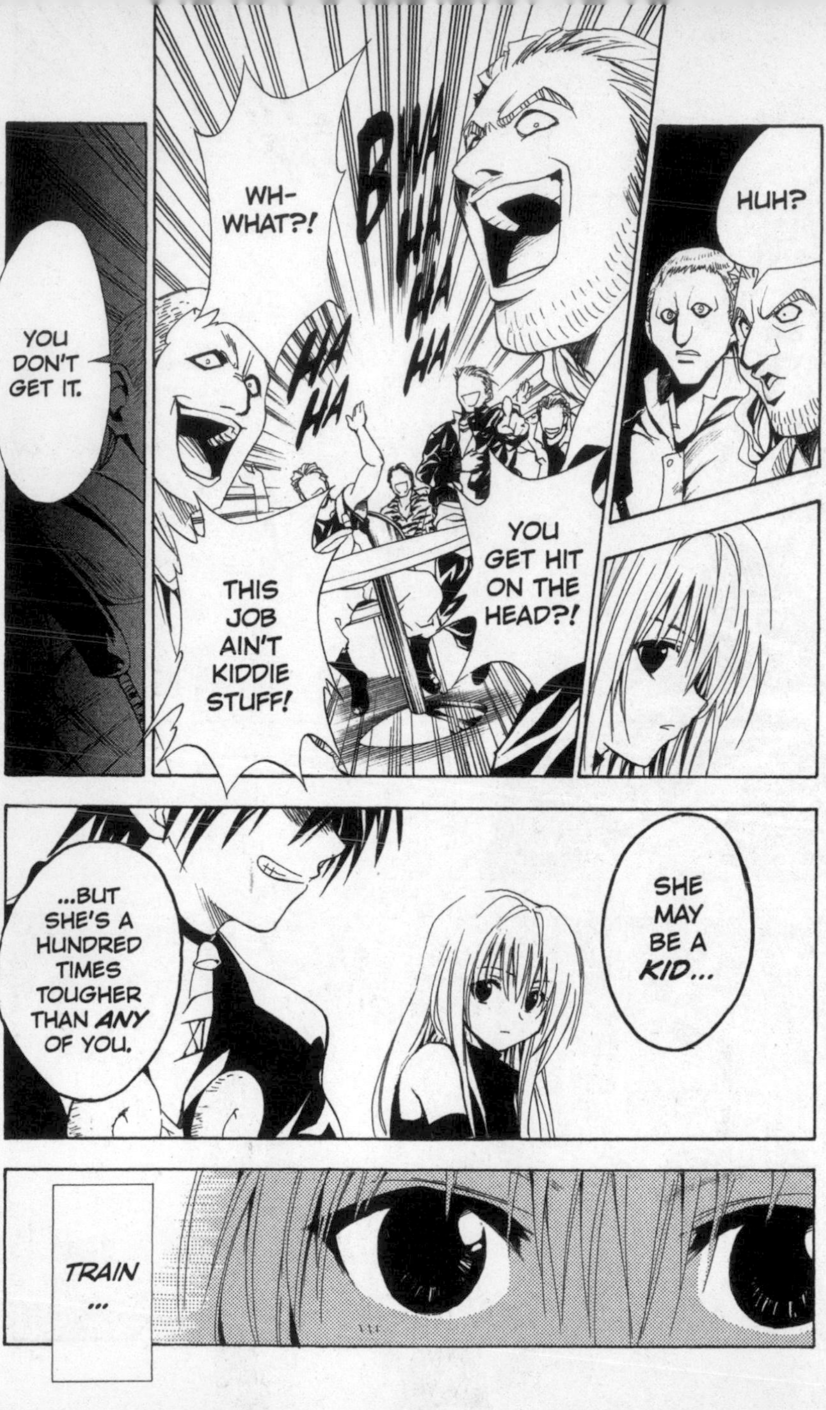
HUH?
WH- WHAT?!
BWAHAHAHA
HAHA
YOU GET HIT ON THE HEAD?!
THIS JOB AIN'T KIDDIE STUFF!
YOU DON'T GET IT.
SHE MAY BE A *KID*...
...BUT SHE'S A HUNDRED TIMES TOUGHER THAN *ANY* OF YOU.
TRAIN ...

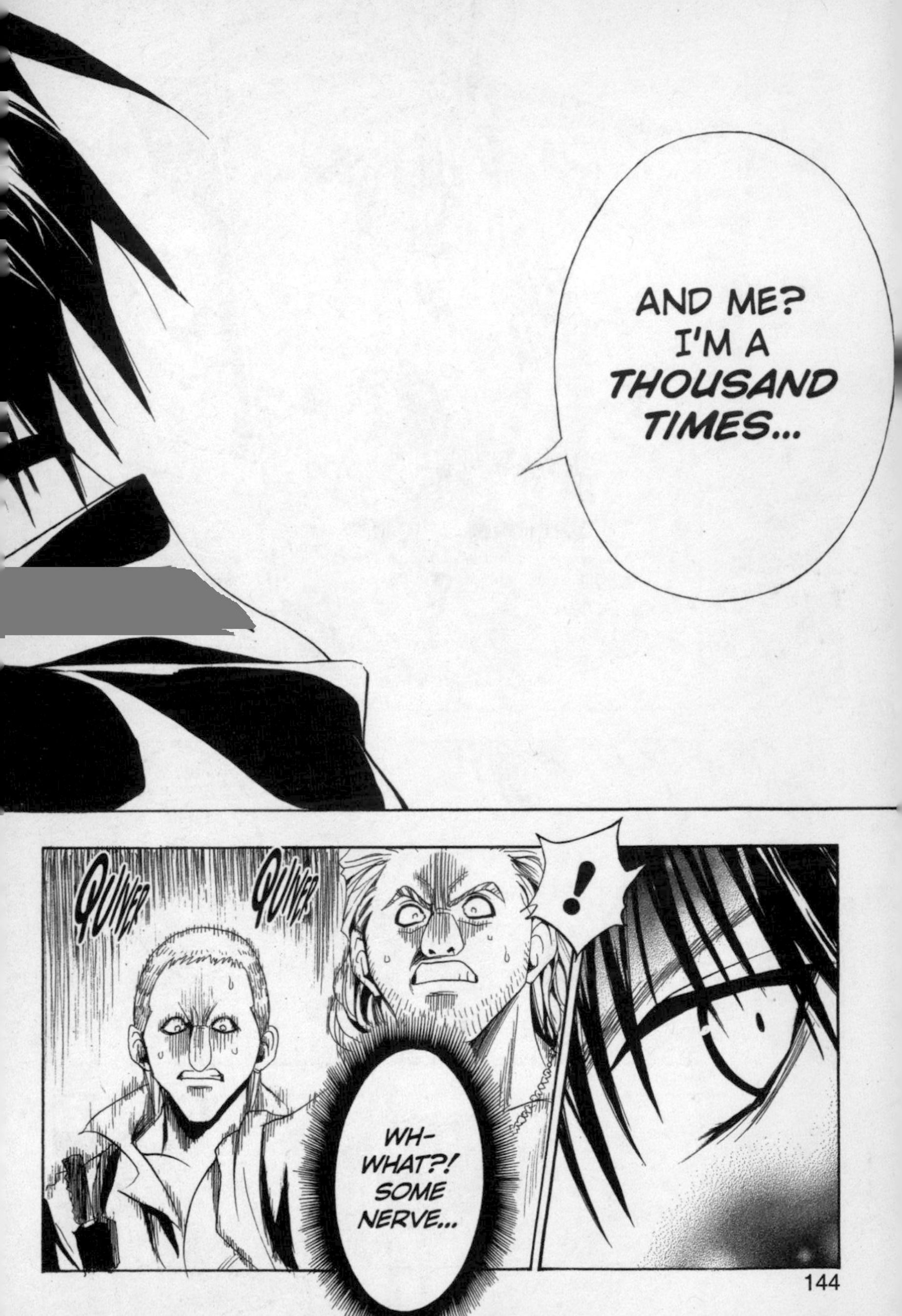
AND ME? I'M A *THOUSAND TIMES...*
!
QUIVER
QUIVER
WH-WHAT?! SOME NERVE...

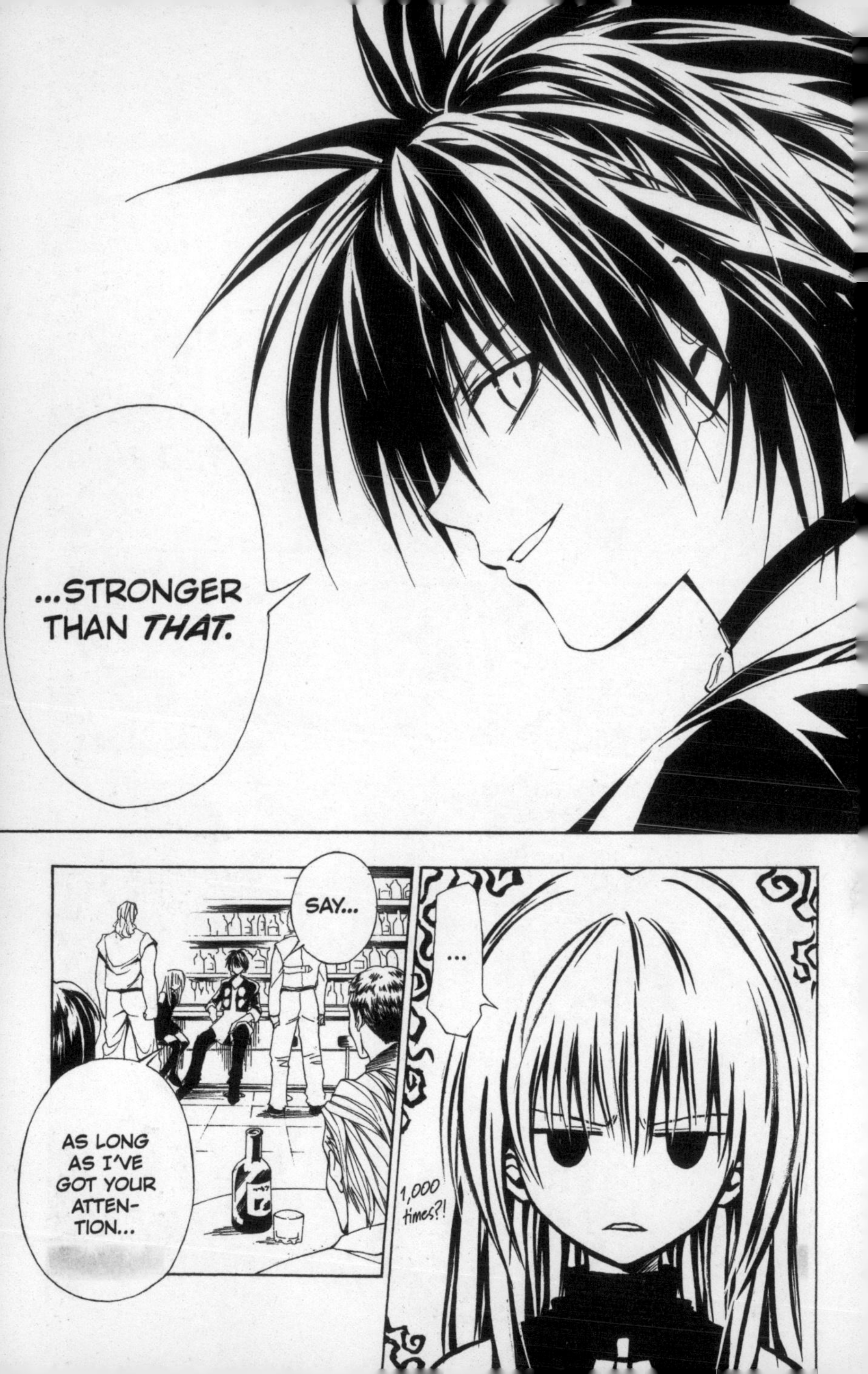
...STRONGER THAN *THAT.*
...
1,000 times?!
SAY...
AS LONG AS I'VE GOT YOUR ATTENTION...

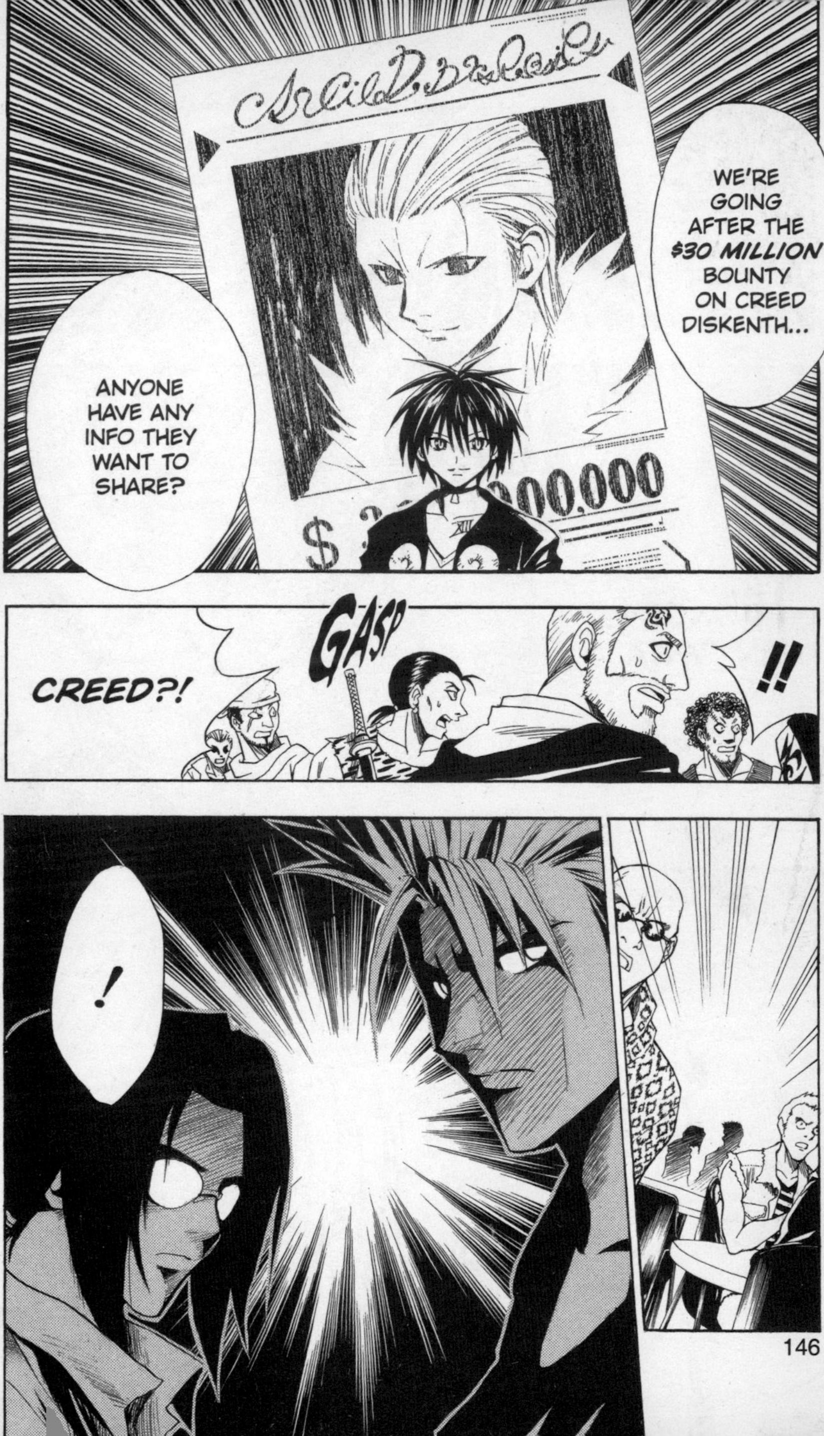
WE'RE GOING AFTER THE $30 MILLION BOUNTY ON CREED DISKENTH...
ANYONE HAVE ANY INFO THEY WANT TO SHARE?
!!
GASP
CREED?!
!

READ THIS WAY

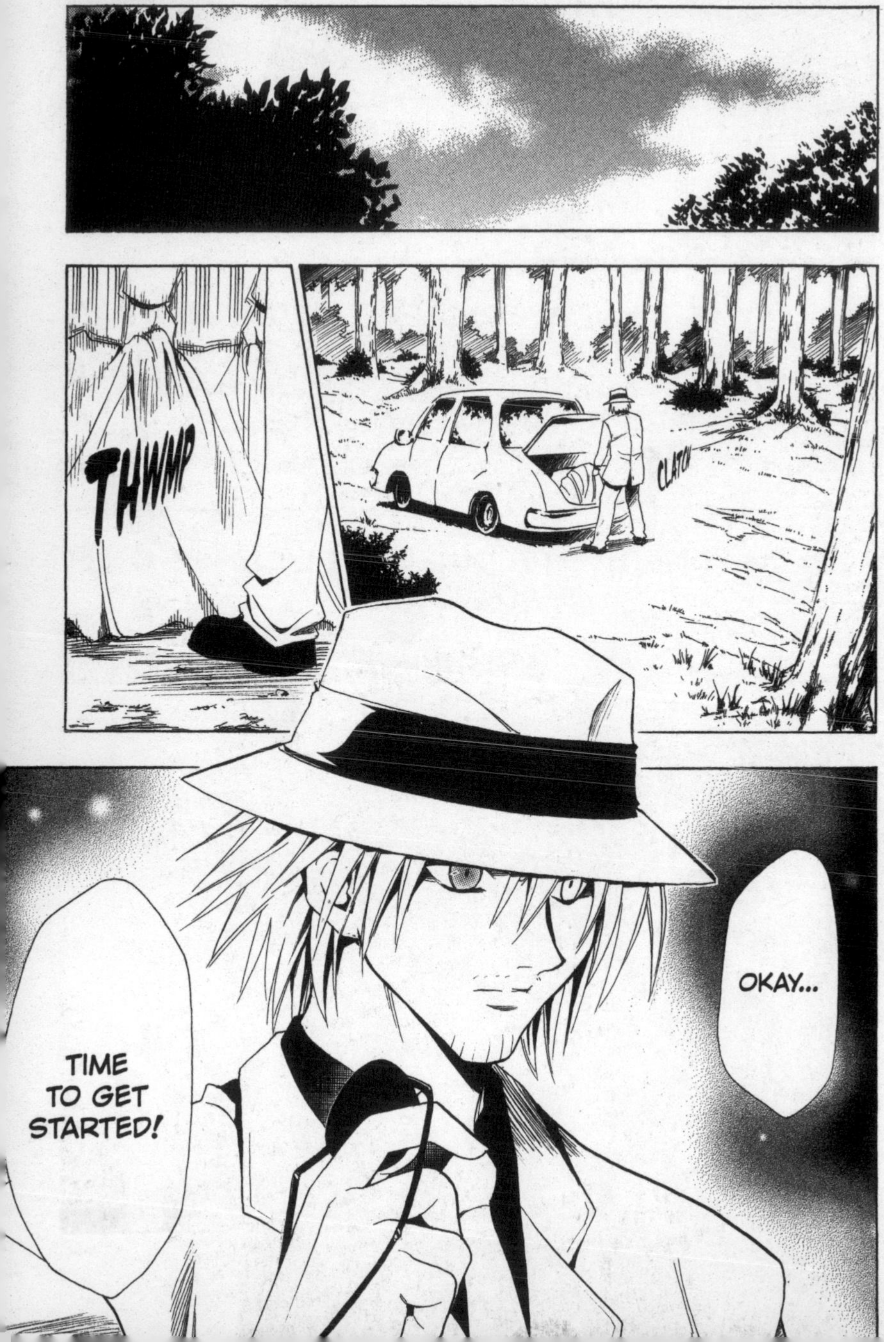
CLATCH
THWMP
OKAY...
TIME TO GET STARTED!

SWEEPERS' CAFÉ

WHILE SWEEPER CAFÉS DO EXIST
THROUGHOUT THE WORLD, MOST OF
THEM ARE SMALL AND TUCKED AWAY
IN HARD-TO-FIND PLACES. HENCE,
SWEEPER SKILLS ARE REQUIRED
JUST TO FIND THEM.

ANYONE WITH A SWEEPER LICENSE
IS ADMITTED.

(CIVILIANS MAY ENTER IF ACCOMPANIED
BY A LICENSED SWEEPER.)

CHAPTER 121: MAN OF FISTS

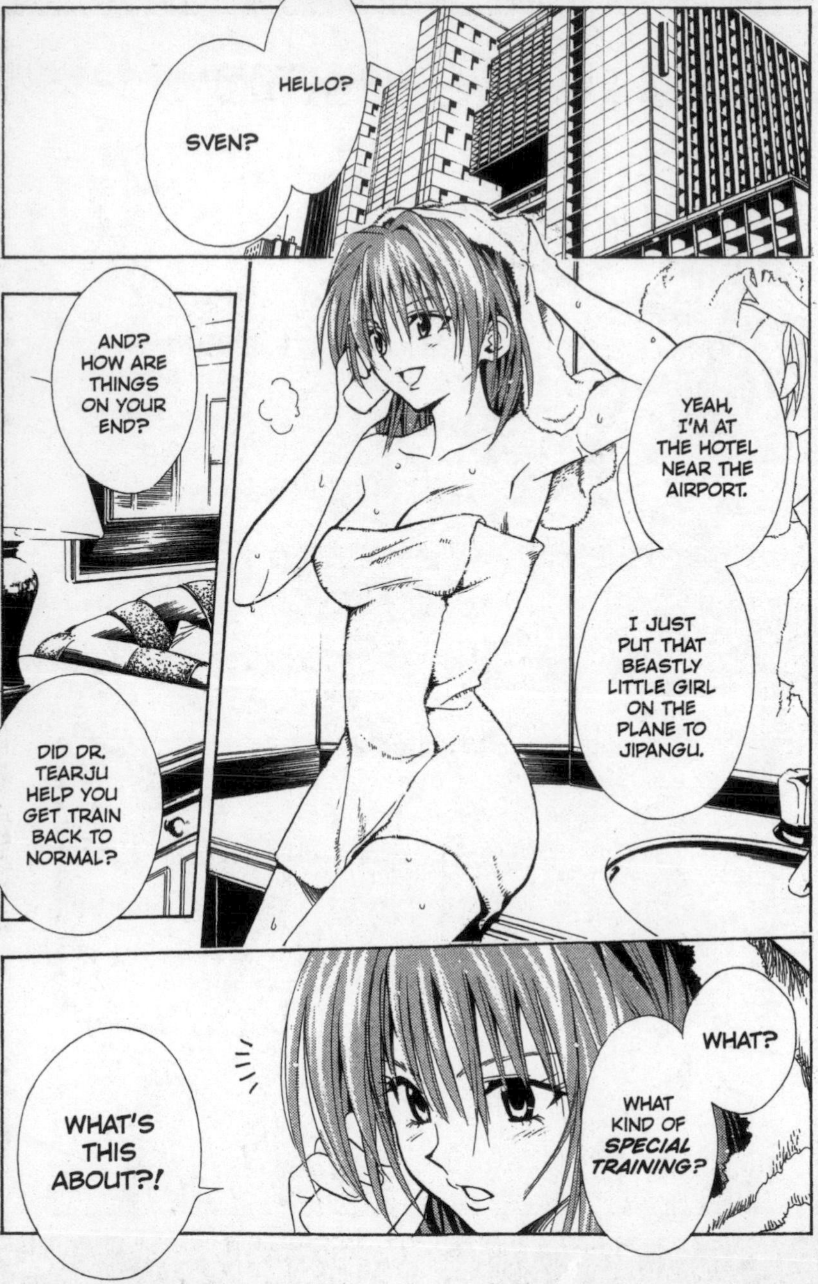
HELLO?
SVEN?
YEAH, I'M AT THE HOTEL NEAR THE AIRPORT.
I JUST PUT THAT BEASTLY LITTLE GIRL ON THE PLANE TO JIPANGU.
AND? HOW ARE THINGS ON YOUR END?
DID DR. TEARJU HELP YOU GET TRAIN BACK TO NORMAL?
WHAT?
WHAT KIND OF *SPECIAL TRAINING*?
WHAT'S THIS ABOUT?!

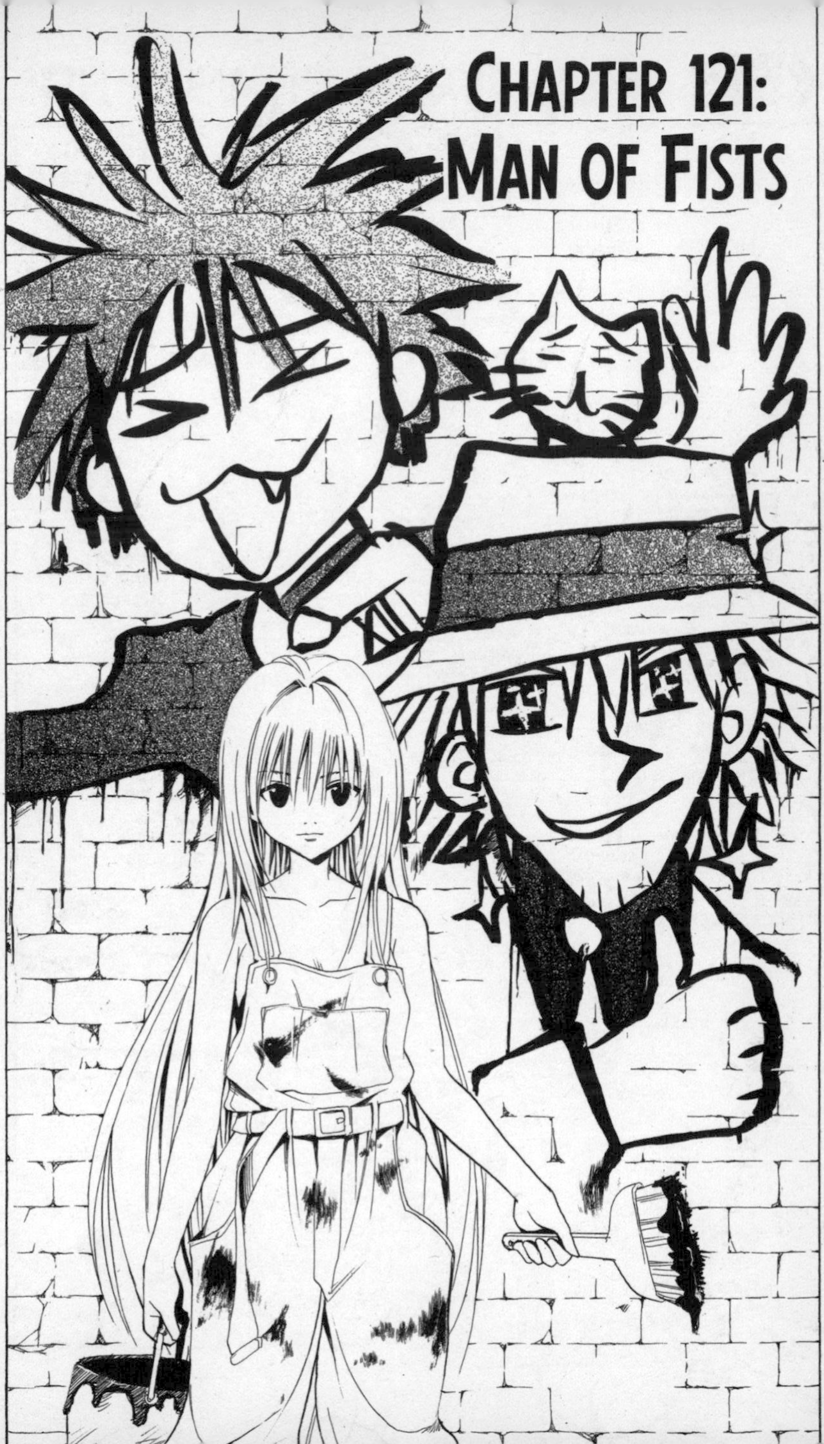
CHAPTER 121:
MAN OF FISTS

READ THIS WAY

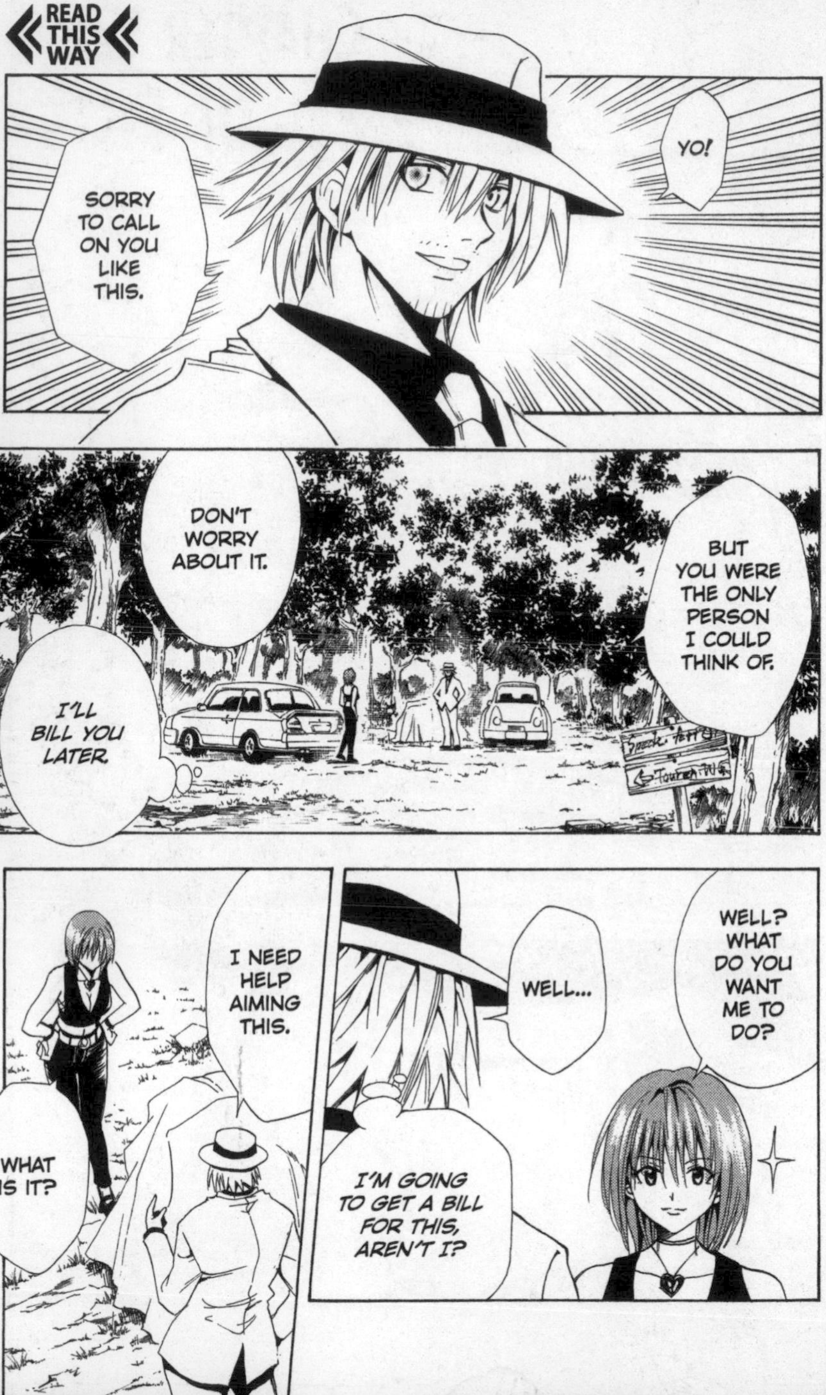
YO!
SORRY TO CALL ON YOU LIKE THIS.
BUT YOU WERE THE ONLY PERSON I COULD THINK OF.
DON'T WORRY ABOUT IT.
I'LL BILL YOU LATER.
WELL? WHAT DO YOU WANT ME TO DO?
WELL...
I'M GOING TO GET A BILL FOR THIS, AREN'T I?
I NEED HELP AIMING THIS.
WHAT IS IT?

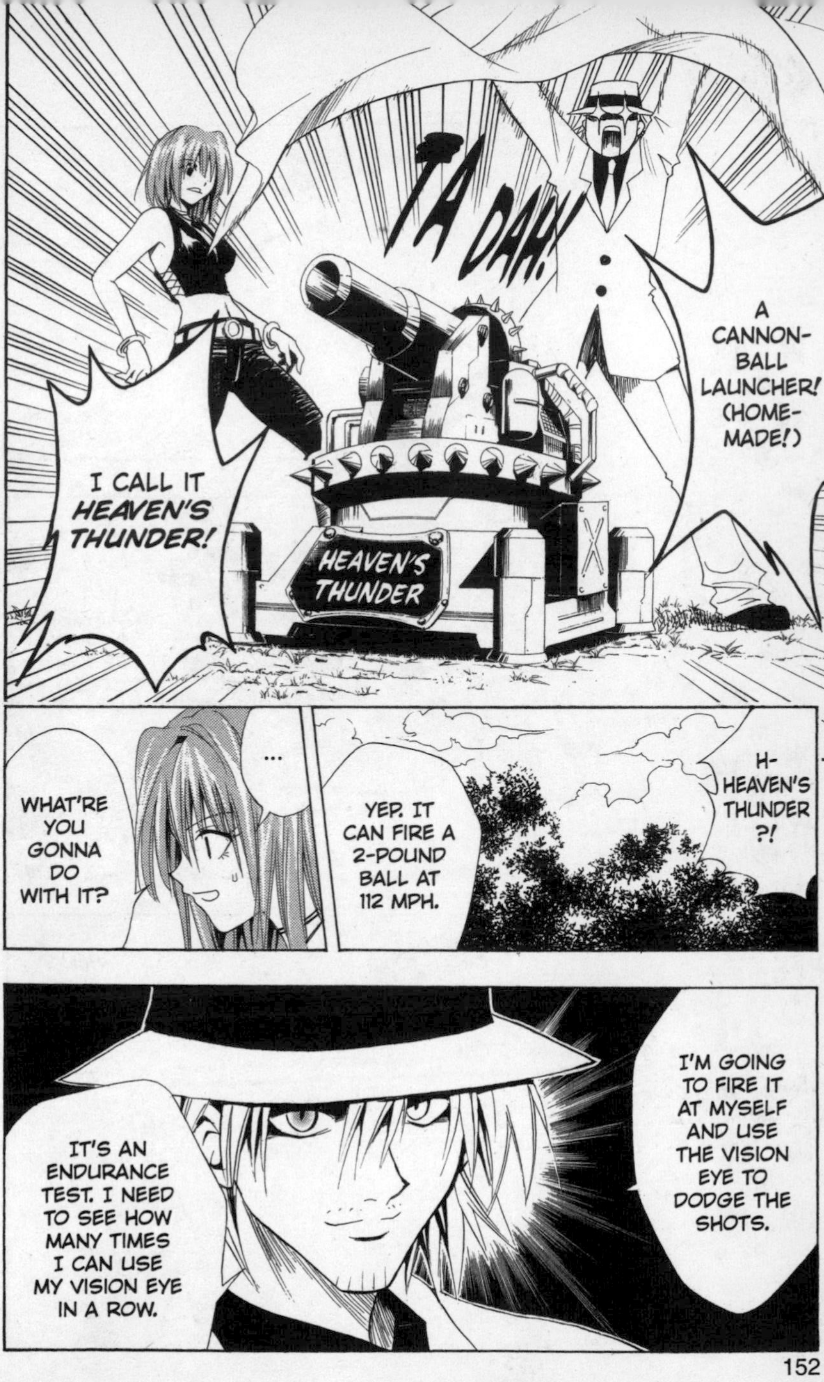
TA DAH!
A CANNON-BALL LAUNCHER! (HOME-MADE!)
HEAVEN'S THUNDER
I CALL IT *HEAVEN'S THUNDER!*
H-HEAVEN'S THUNDER?!
YEP. IT CAN FIRE A 2-POUND BALL AT 112 MPH.
...
WHAT'RE YOU GONNA DO WITH IT?
I'M GOING TO FIRE IT AT MYSELF AND USE THE VISION EYE TO DODGE THE SHOTS.
IT'S AN ENDURANCE TEST. I NEED TO SEE HOW MANY TIMES I CAN USE MY VISION EYE IN A ROW.

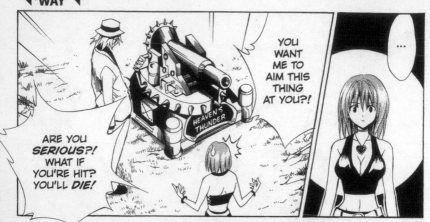

...

YOU WANT ME TO AIM THIS THING AT YOU?!

HEAVEN'S THUNDER

ARE YOU *SERIOUS*?! WHAT IF YOU'RE HIT? YOU'LL *DIE*!

IF I INTEND TO MEET THE APOSTLES OF THE STARS...

ON A LEVEL PLAYING FIELD...

...I HAVE TO DO THIS.

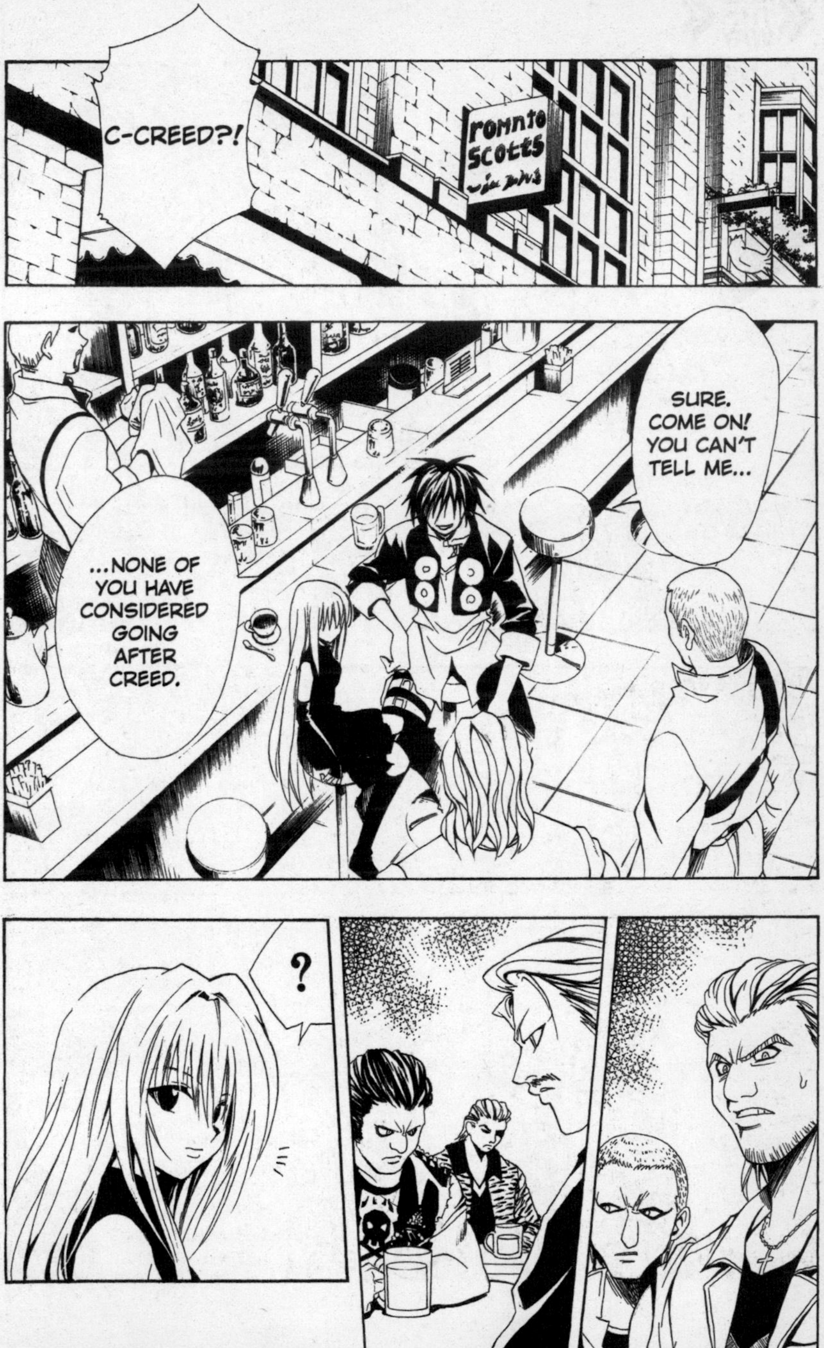
C-CREED?!
SURE. COME ON! YOU CAN'T TELL ME...
...NONE OF YOU HAVE CONSIDERED GOING AFTER CREED.
?

READ THIS WAY

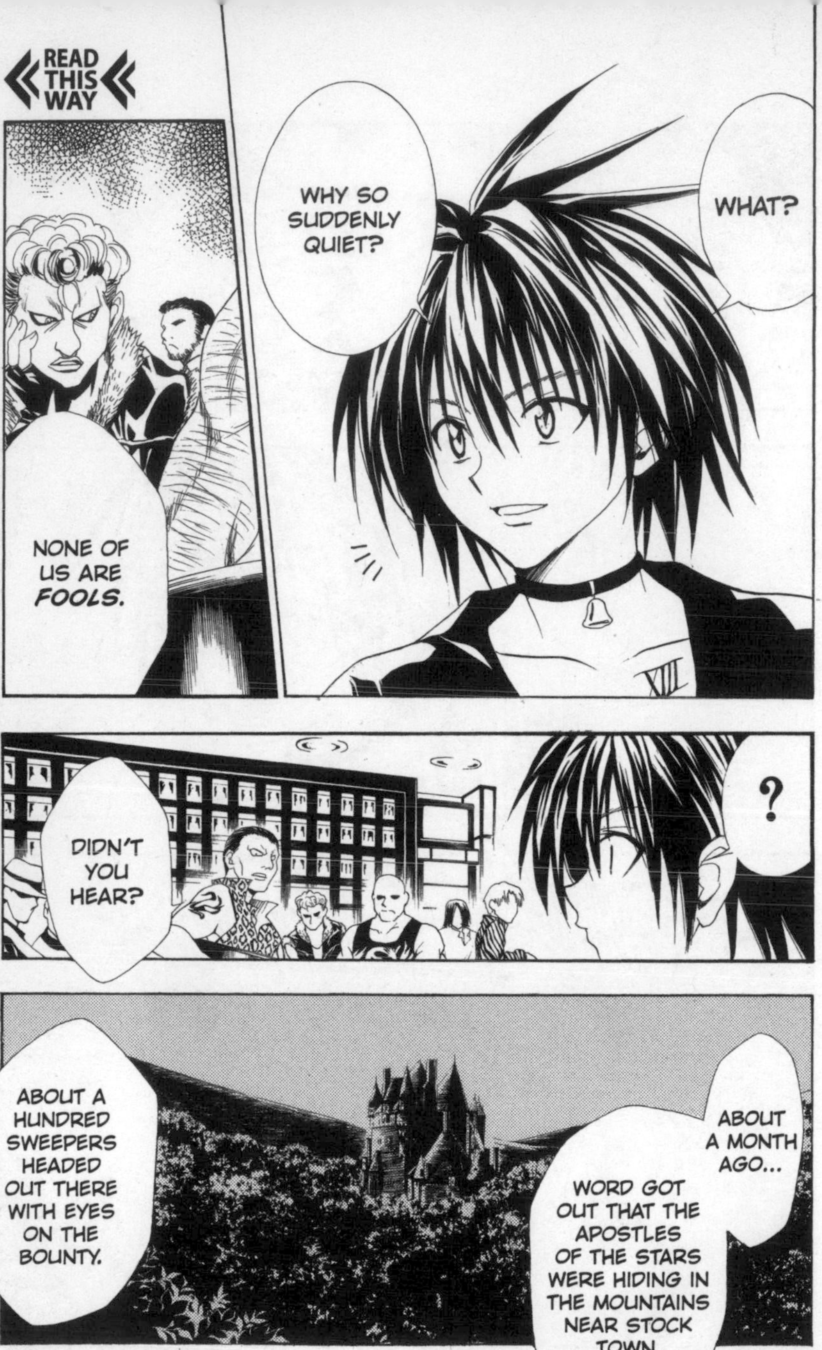
WHAT?
WHY SO SUDDENLY QUIET?
NONE OF US ARE *FOOLS.*
?
DIDN'T YOU HEAR?
ABOUT A MONTH AGO...
WORD GOT OUT THAT THE APOSTLES OF THE STARS WERE HIDING IN THE MOUNTAINS NEAR STOCK TOWN.
ABOUT A HUNDRED SWEEPERS HEADED OUT THERE WITH EYES ON THE BOUNTY.

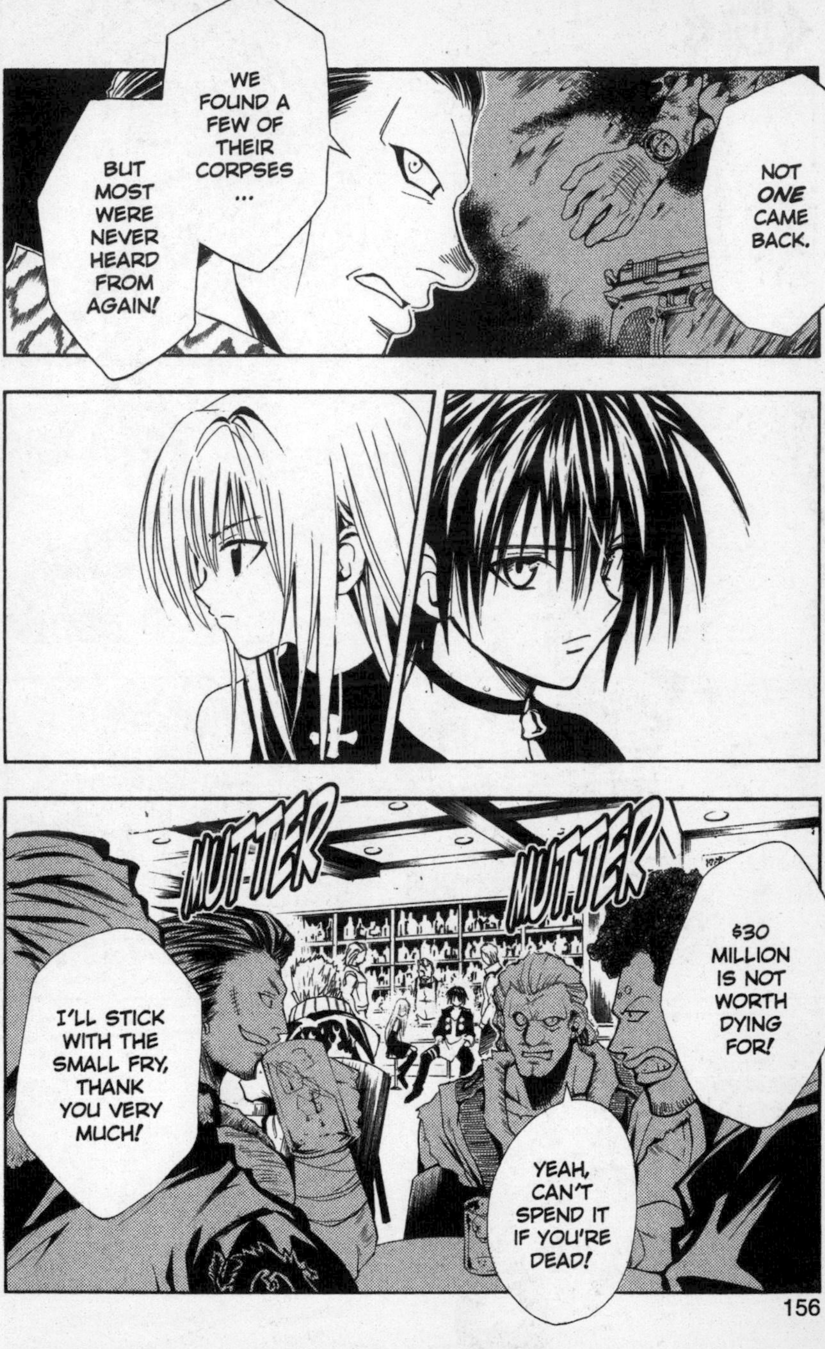
NOT ONE CAME BACK.
WE FOUND A FEW OF THEIR CORPSES ...
BUT MOST WERE NEVER HEARD FROM AGAIN!
MUTTER
MUTTER
$30 MILLION IS NOT WORTH DYING FOR!
YEAH, CAN'T SPEND IT IF YOU'RE DEAD!
I'LL STICK WITH THE SMALL FRY, THANK YOU VERY MUCH!

READ THIS WAY

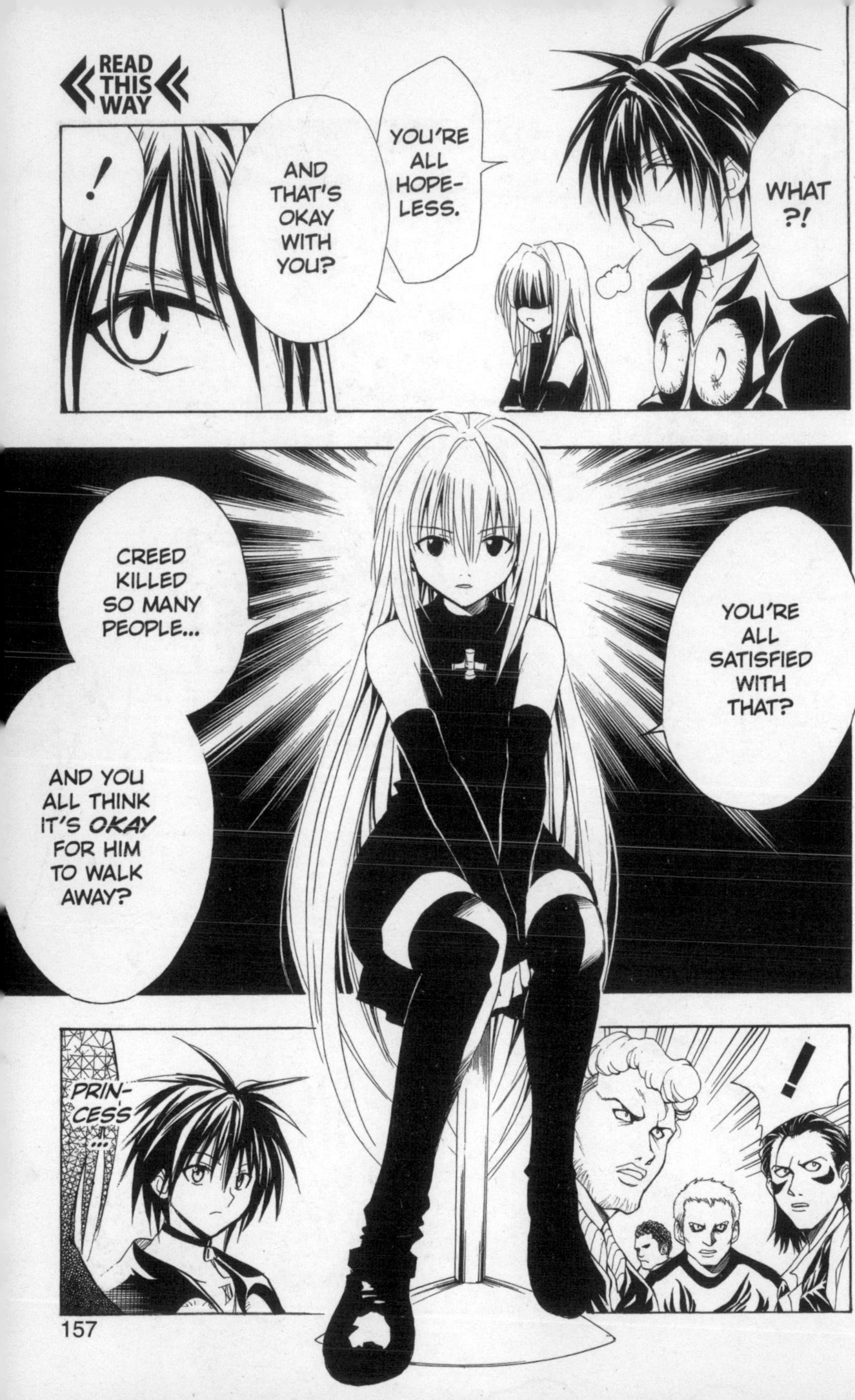
WHAT?!
YOU'RE ALL HOPE-LESS.
AND THAT'S OKAY WITH YOU?
!
YOU'RE ALL SATISFIED WITH THAT?
CREED KILLED SO MANY PEOPLE...
AND YOU ALL THINK IT'S *OKAY* FOR HIM TO WALK AWAY?
!
PRIN-CESS...

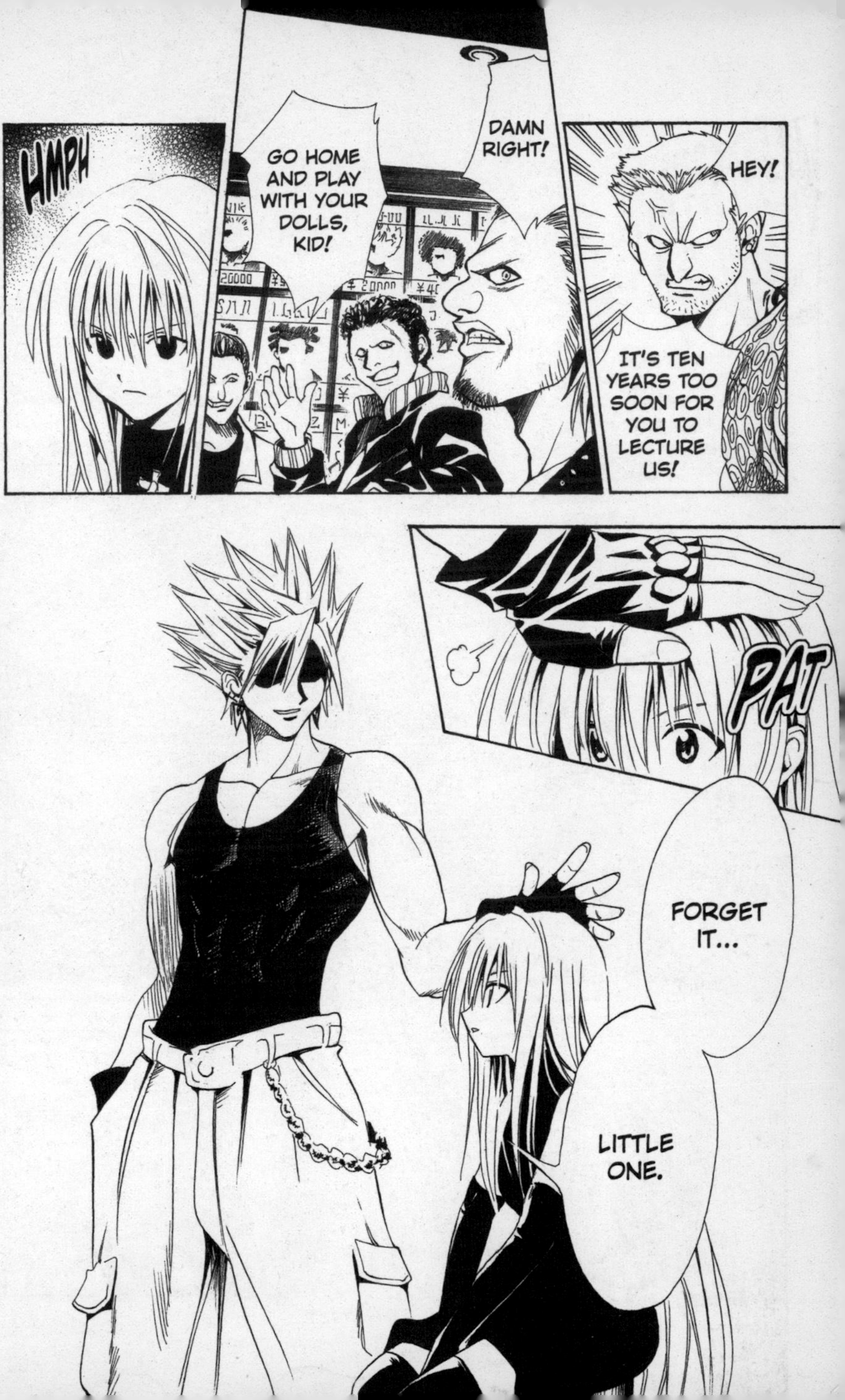
HEY!
IT'S TEN YEARS TOO SOON FOR YOU TO LECTURE US!
DAMN RIGHT!
GO HOME AND PLAY WITH YOUR DOLLS, KID!
HMPH
PAT
FORGET IT...
LITTLE ONE.

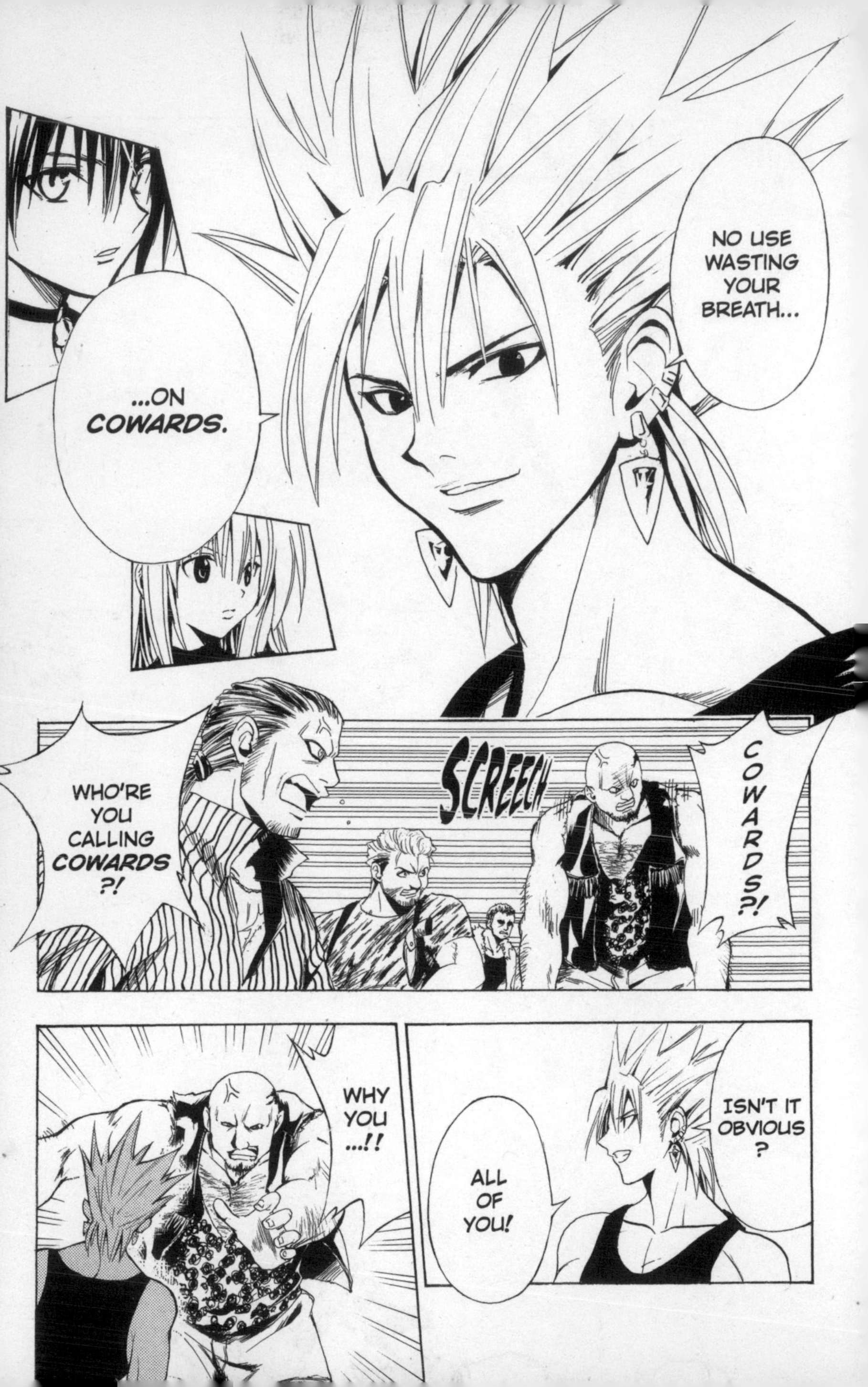
NO USE WASTING YOUR BREATH...
...ON COWARDS.
COWARDS?!
SCREECH
WHO'RE YOU CALLING COWARDS?!
ISN'T IT OBVIOUS?
ALL OF YOU!
WHY YOU...!!

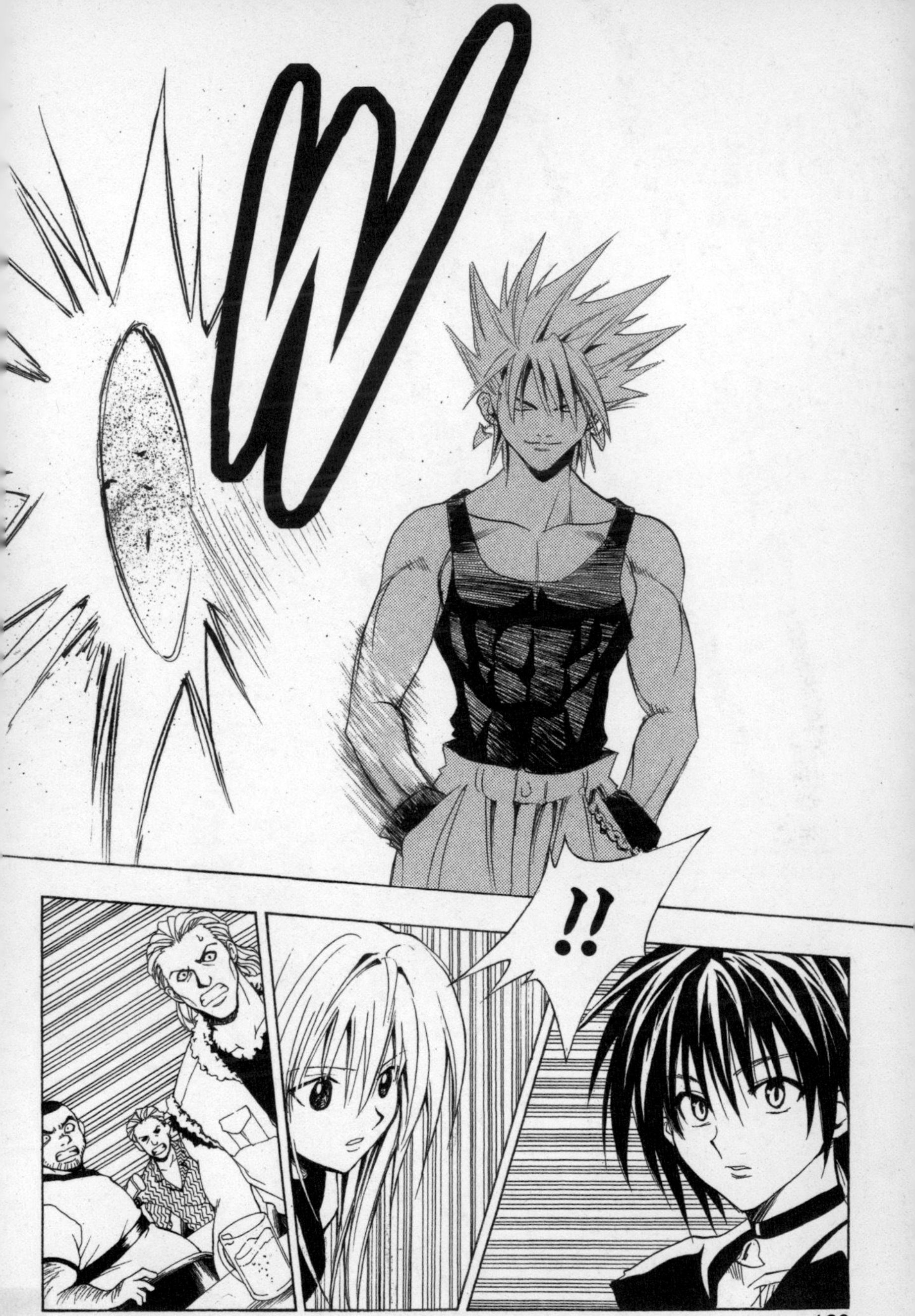
!!

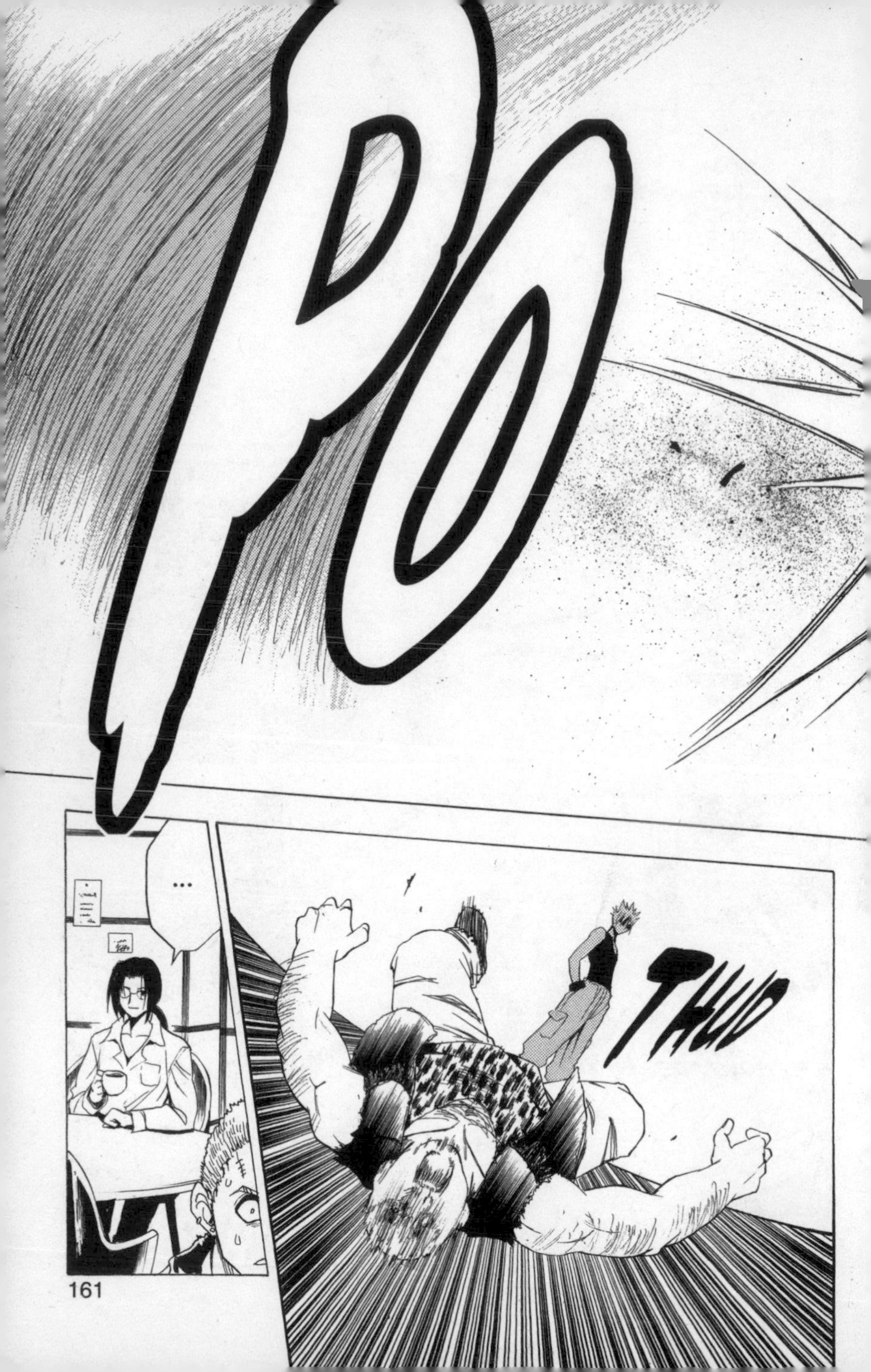
THUD
...

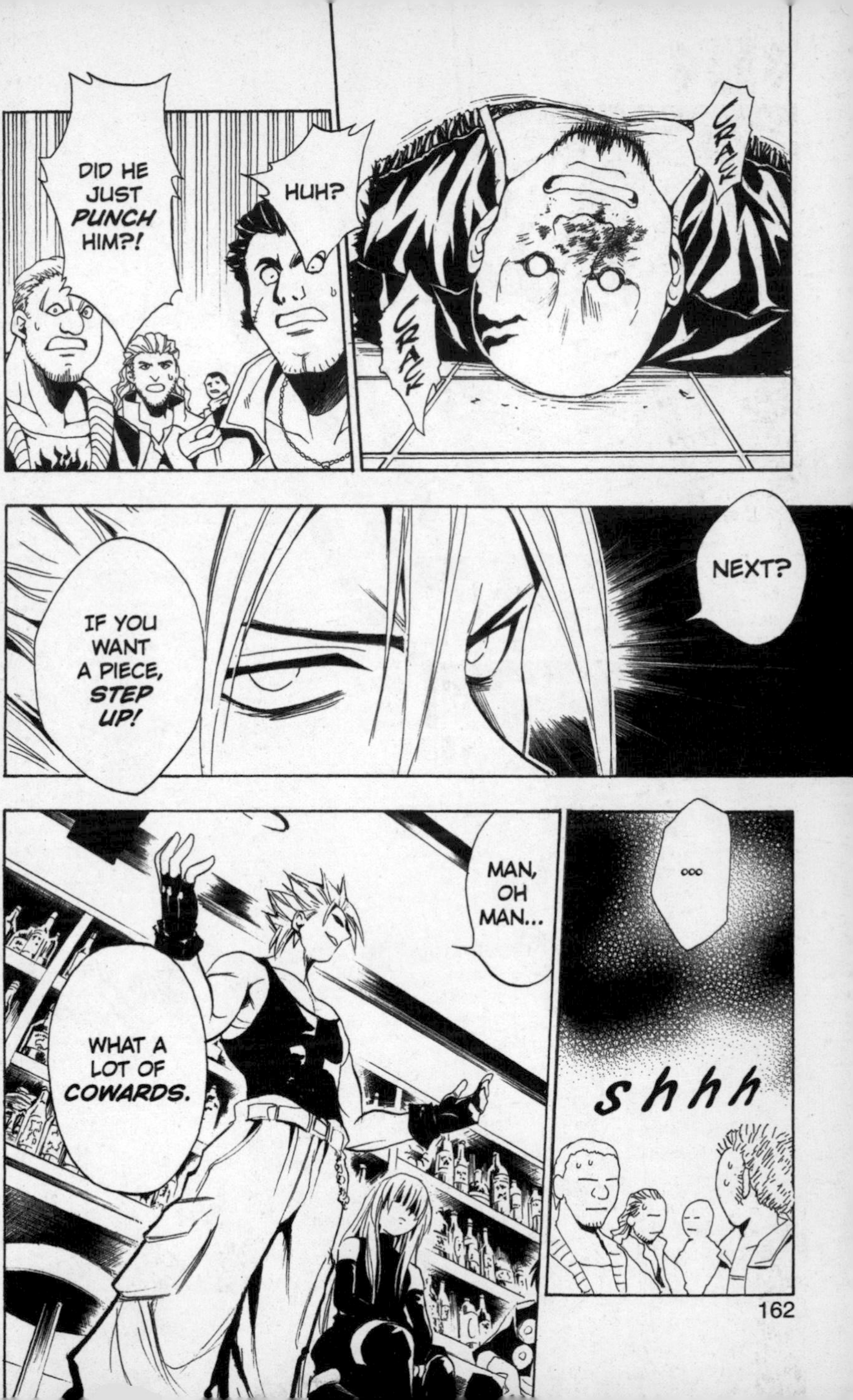
CRACK
CRACK
HUH?
DID HE JUST PUNCH HIM?!
NEXT?
IF YOU WANT A PIECE, STEP UP!
...
shhh
MAN, OH MAN...
WHAT A LOT OF COWARDS.

READ THIS WAY

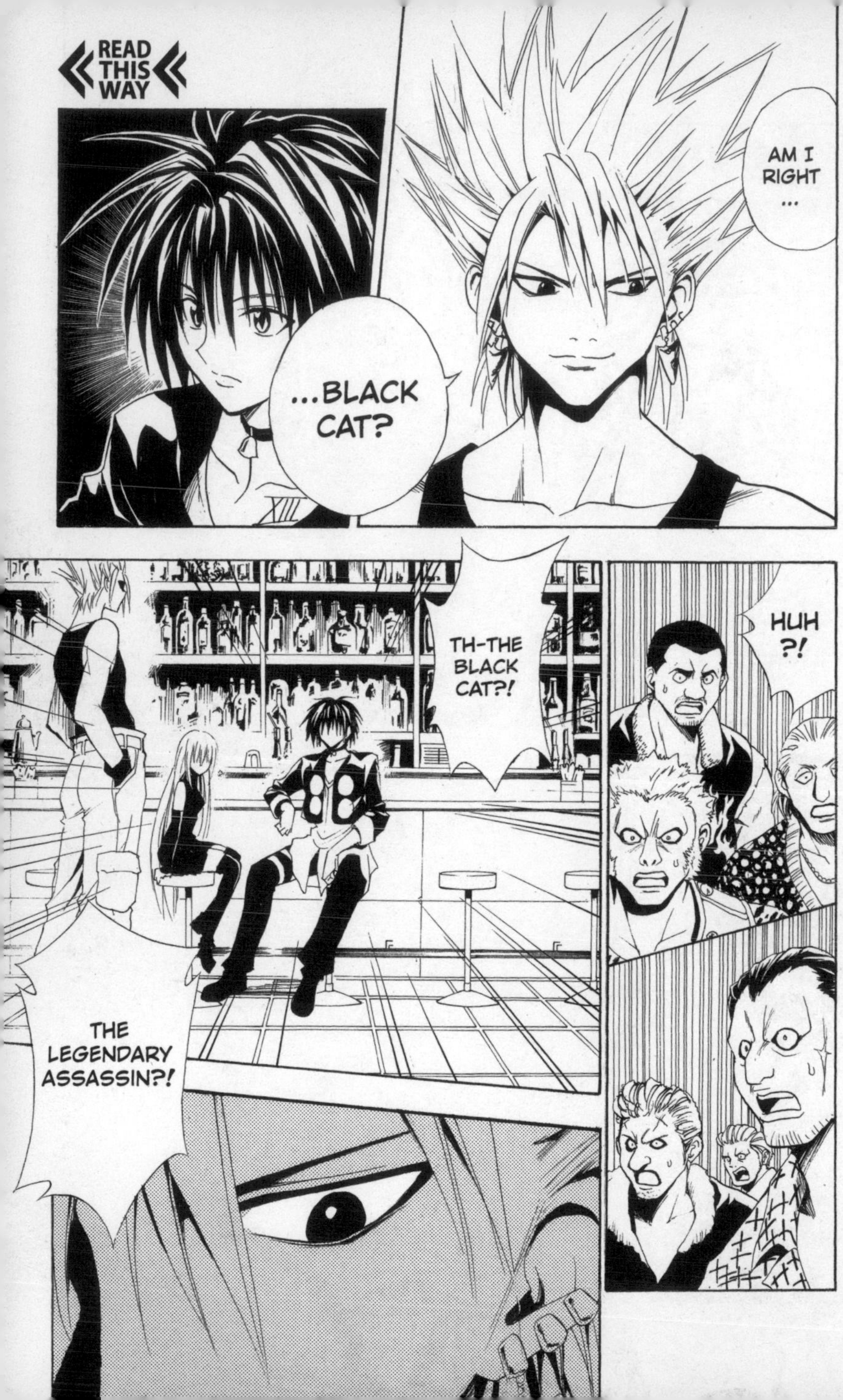
AM I RIGHT ...
...BLACK CAT?
HUH ?!
TH-THE BLACK CAT?!
THE LEGENDARY ASSASSIN?!

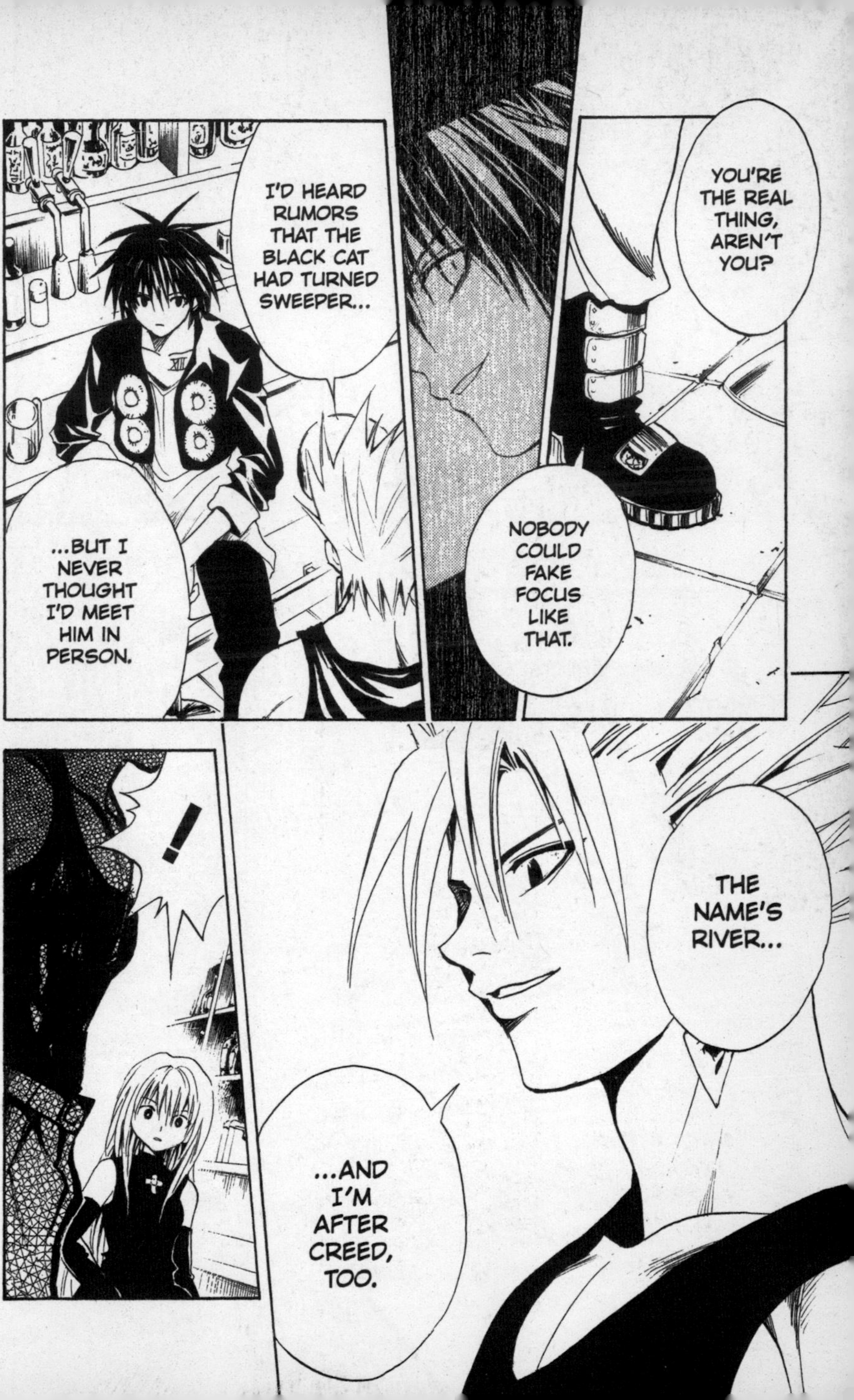
YOU'RE THE REAL THING, AREN'T YOU?
NOBODY COULD FAKE FOCUS LIKE THAT.
I'D HEARD RUMORS THAT THE BLACK CAT HAD TURNED SWEEPER...
...BUT I NEVER THOUGHT I'D MEET HIM IN PERSON.
THE NAME'S RIVER...
...AND I'M AFTER CREED, TOO.
!

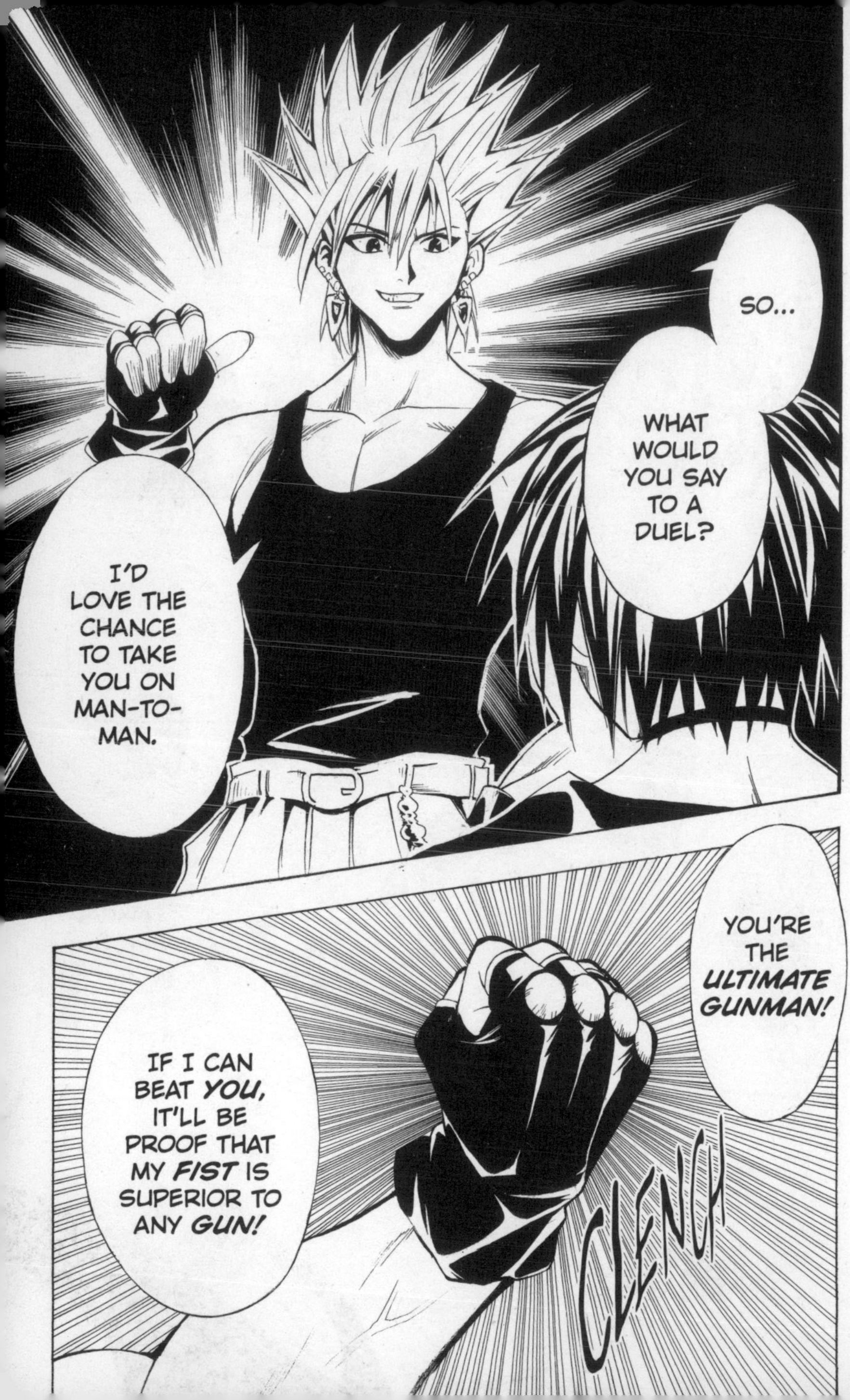
SO...
WHAT WOULD YOU SAY TO A DUEL?
I'D LOVE THE CHANCE TO TAKE YOU ON MAN-TO-MAN.
YOU'RE THE *ULTIMATE GUNMAN!*
IF I CAN BEAT *YOU,* IT'LL BE PROOF THAT MY *FIST* IS SUPERIOR TO ANY *GUN!*
CLENCH

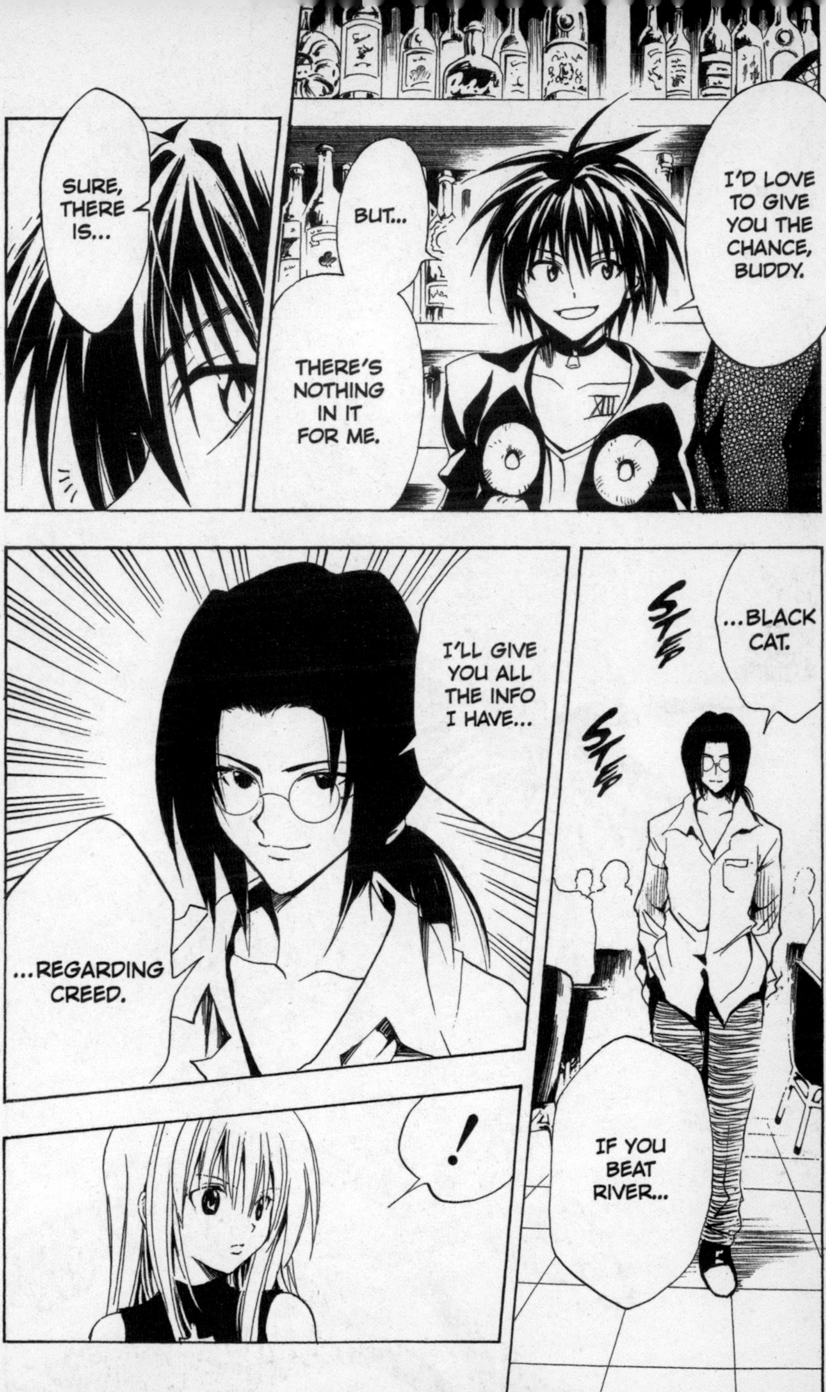
I'D LOVE TO GIVE YOU THE CHANCE, BUDDY.
BUT...
THERE'S NOTHING IN IT FOR ME.
SURE, THERE IS...
...BLACK CAT.
IF YOU BEAT RIVER...
I'LL GIVE YOU ALL THE INFO I HAVE...
...REGARDING CREED.
!

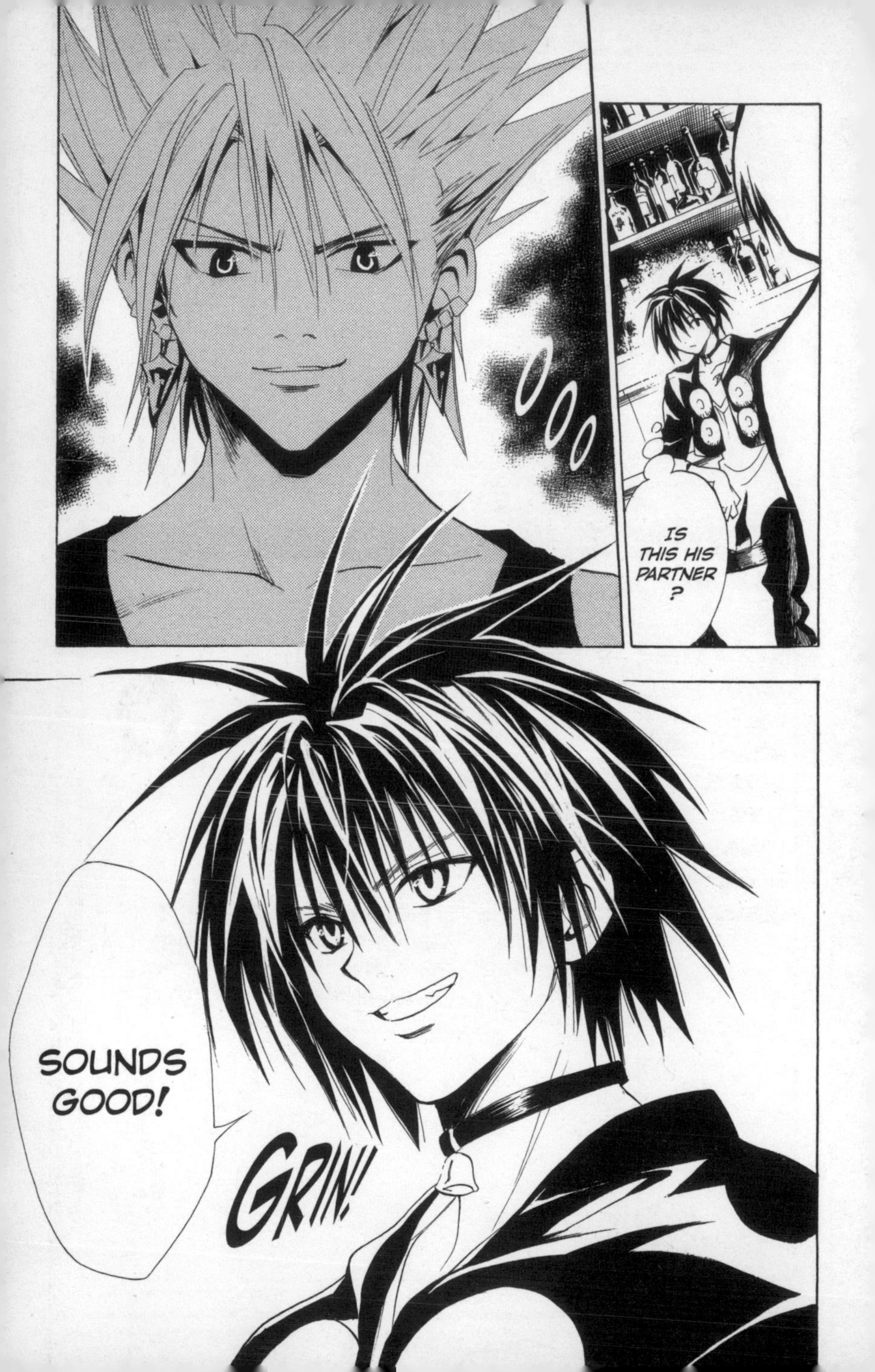
IS THIS HIS PARTNER ?
SOUNDS GOOD!
GRIN!

BLACKCAT

profile

RIVER ZASTORY

DATA	
BIRTHDATE:	MAY 19
AGE:	19
BLOOD TYPE:	A
HEIGHT:	179 CM
WEIGHT:	66 KG
ATTACK SPECIALTY:	GARBELL COMMANDO
HOBBY:	WORKING OUT
DISLIKES:	FROGS
LIKES:	HOTCAKES
COMMENTS:	RIVER IS THE RELENTLESS TYPE AND HE OFTEN GETS OVERLY PASSIONATE ABOUT HIS SWEEPER MISSIONS. THE PERSON HE RESPECTS MOST IN THE WORLD IS HIS GRANDFATHER, WHO TAUGHT HIM HOW TO FIGHT.

Chapter 122: Flash Fist

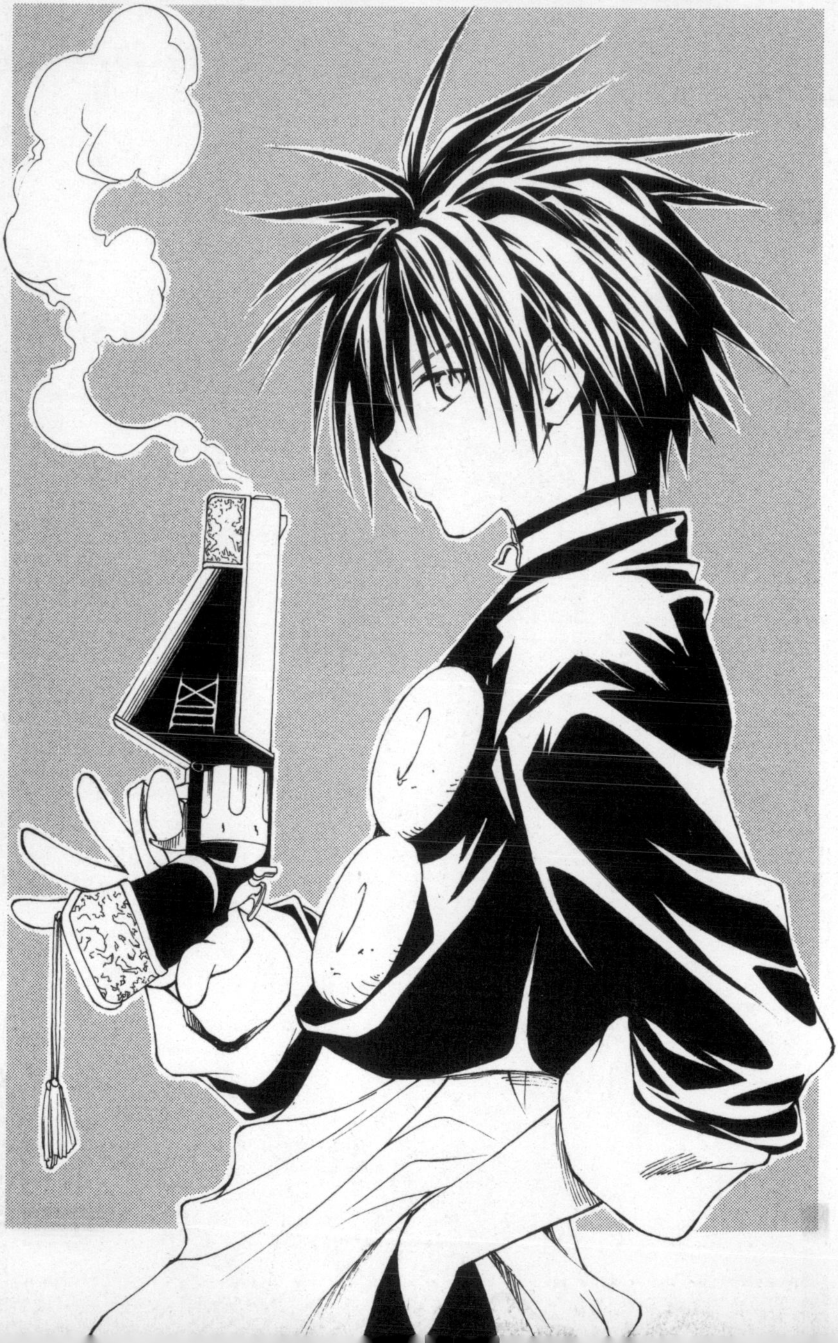

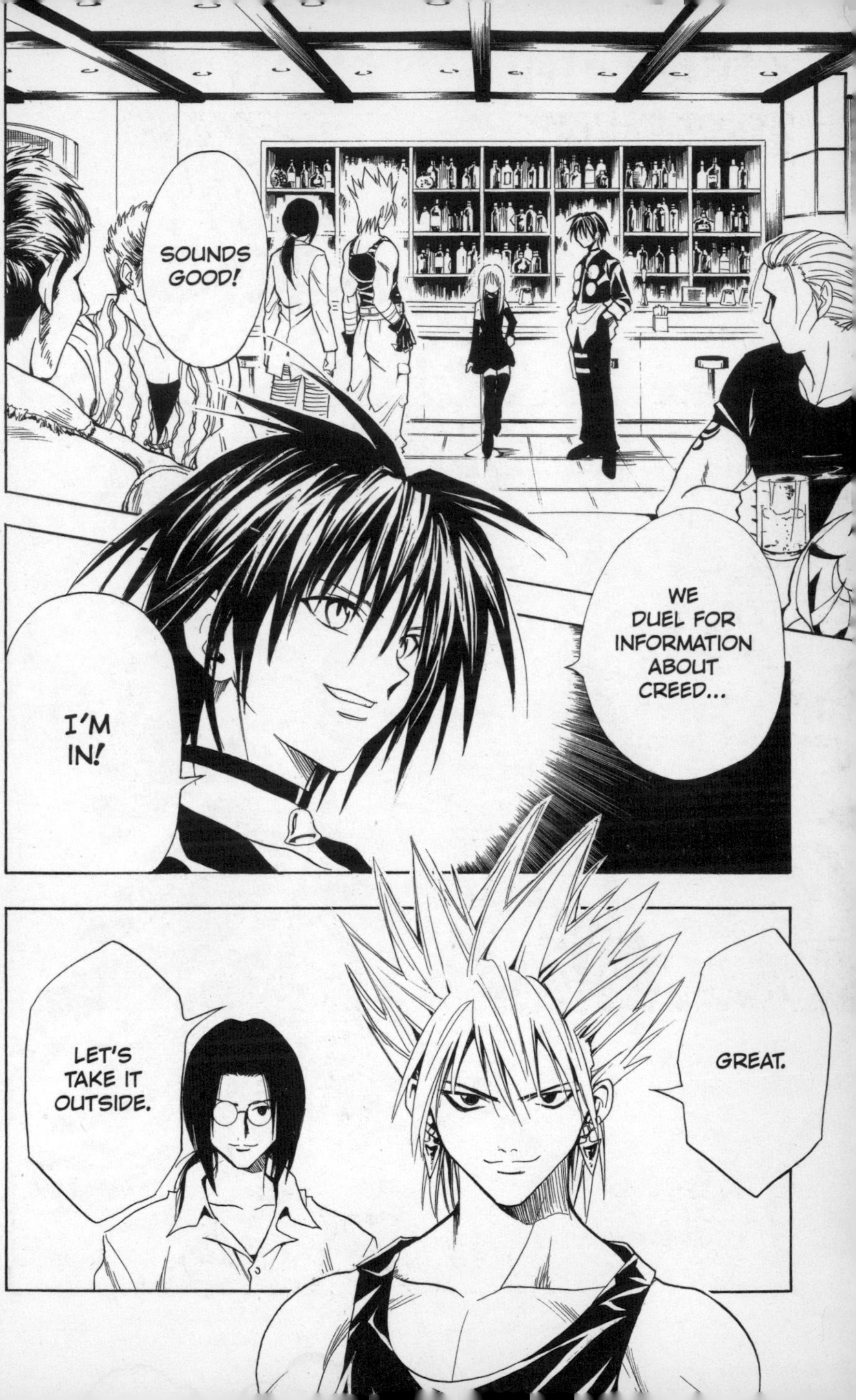
SOUNDS GOOD!
WE DUEL FOR INFORMATION ABOUT CREED...
I'M IN!
GREAT.
LET'S TAKE IT OUTSIDE.

READ THIS WAY

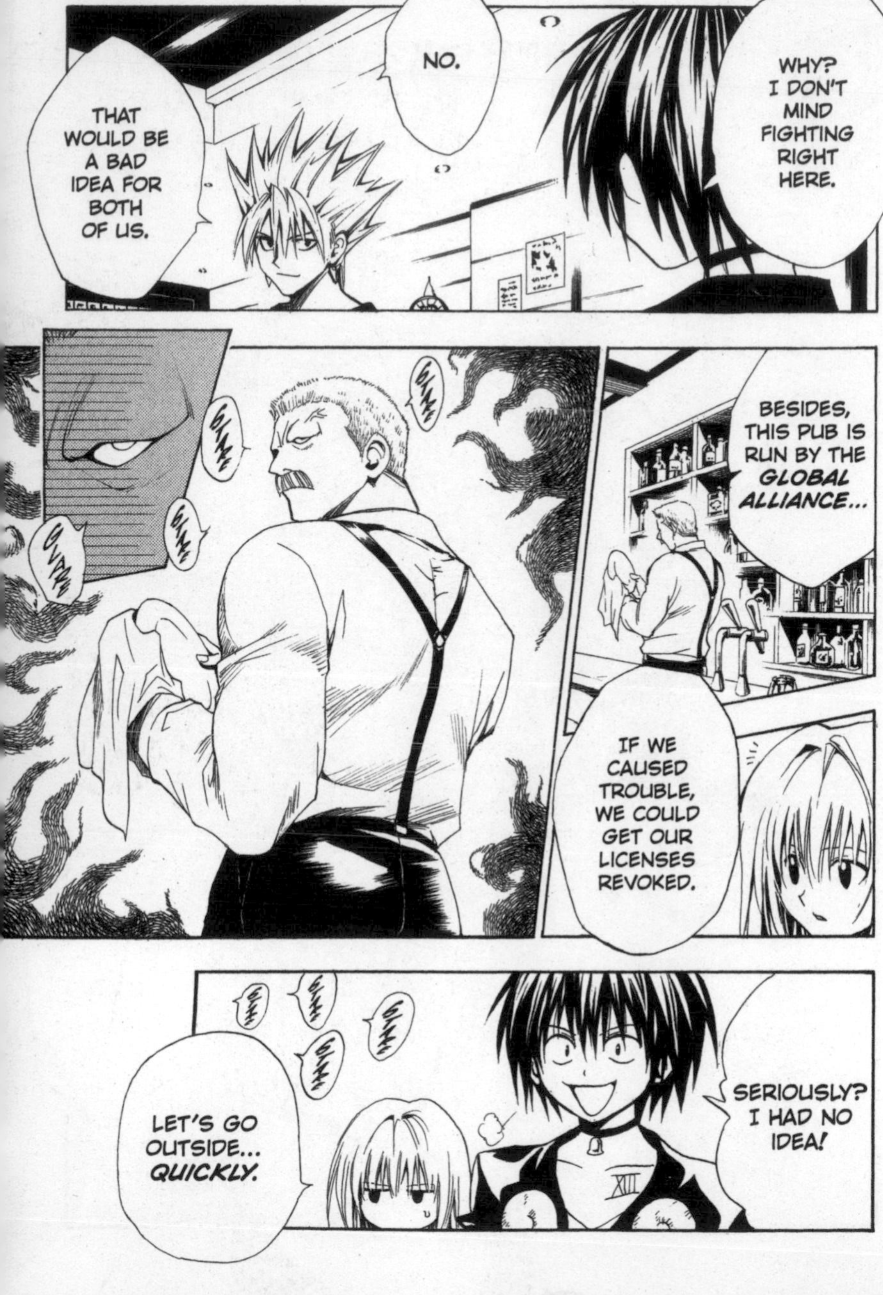
WHY? I DON'T MIND FIGHTING RIGHT HERE.
NO.
THAT WOULD BE A BAD IDEA FOR BOTH OF US.
BESIDES, THIS PUB IS RUN BY THE *GLOBAL ALLIANCE...*
IF WE CAUSED TROUBLE, WE COULD GET OUR LICENSES REVOKED.
GLARE
SERIOUSLY? I HAD NO IDEA!
LET'S GO OUTSIDE... *QUICKLY.*

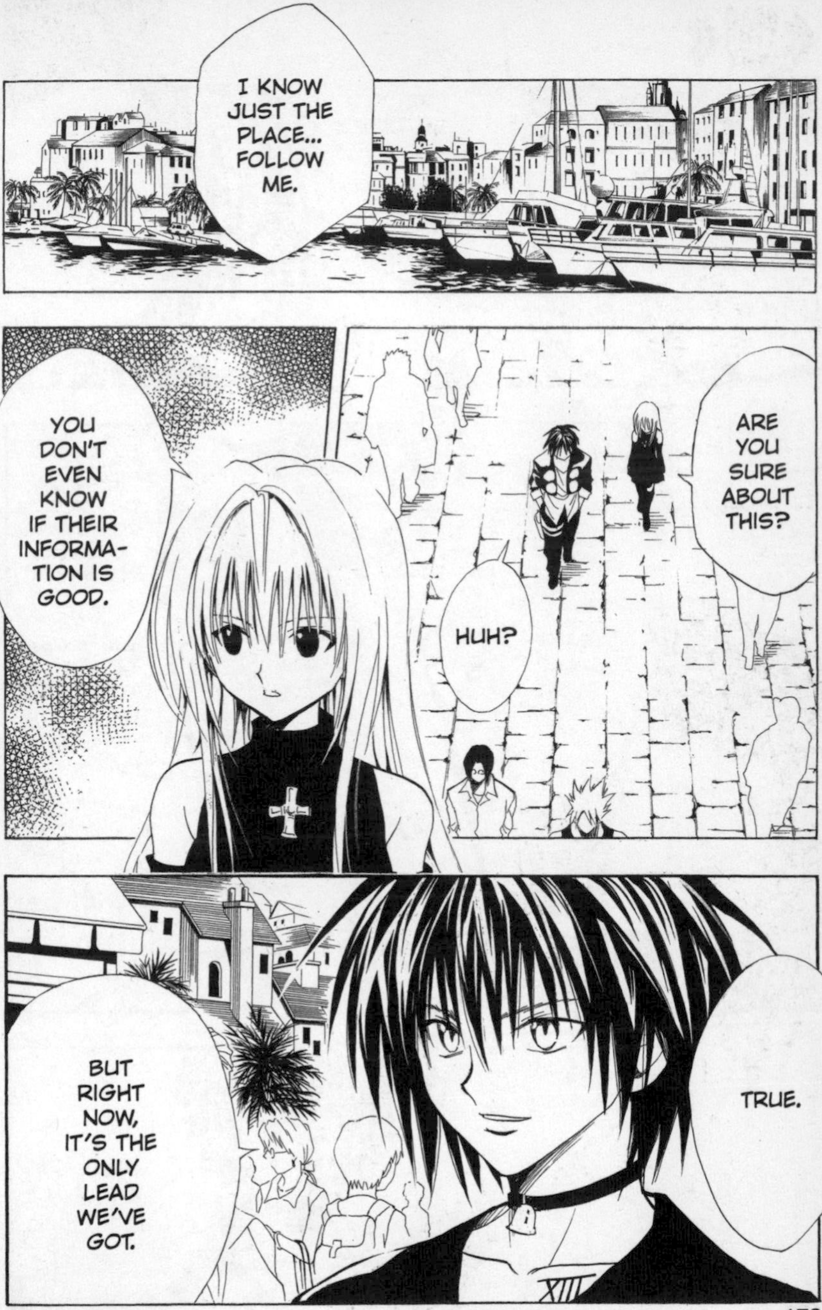
I KNOW JUST THE PLACE... FOLLOW ME.
ARE YOU SURE ABOUT THIS?
HUH?
YOU DON'T EVEN KNOW IF THEIR INFORMATION IS GOOD.
TRUE.
BUT RIGHT NOW, IT'S THE ONLY LEAD WE'VE GOT.

READ THIS WAY

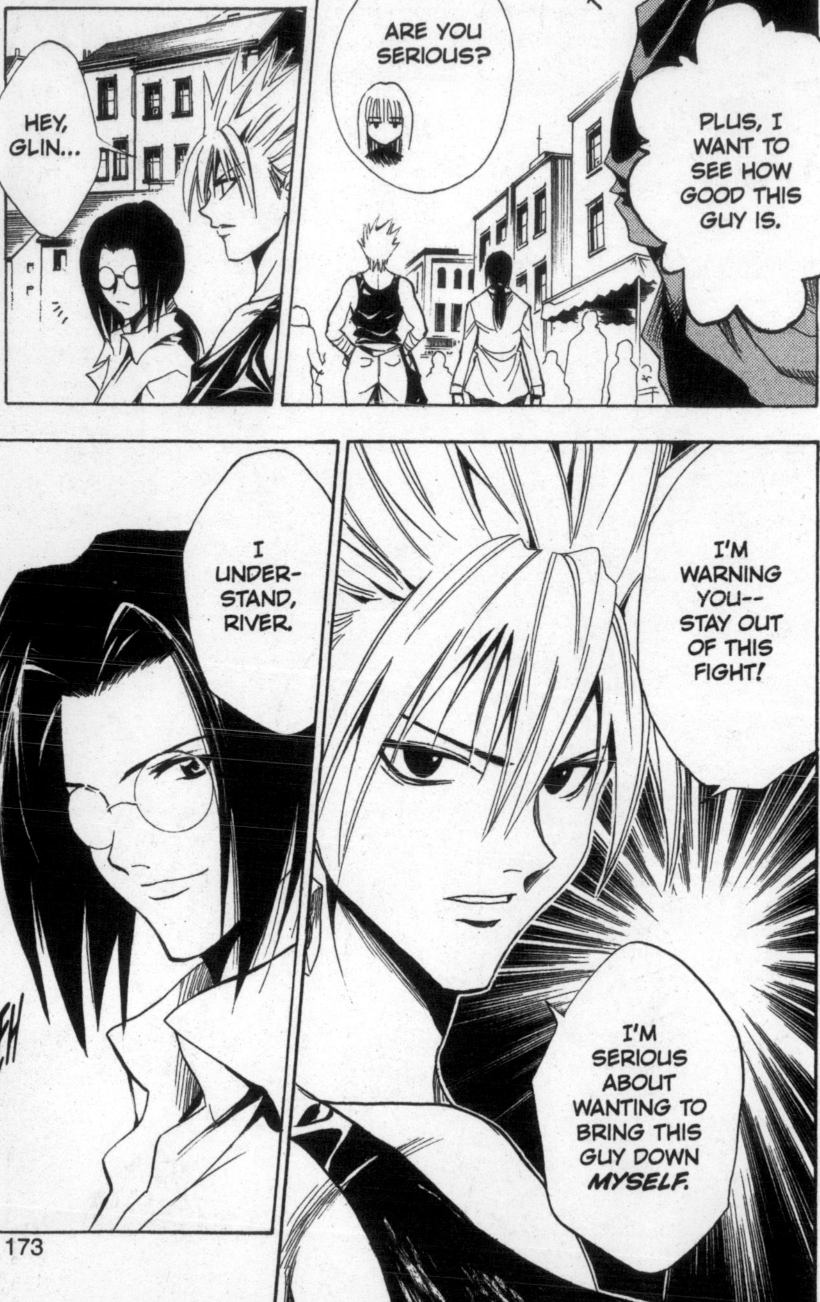
ARE YOU SERIOUS?
PLUS, I WANT TO SEE HOW GOOD THIS GUY IS.
HEY, GLIN...
I'M WARNING YOU-- STAY OUT OF THIS FIGHT!
I'M SERIOUS ABOUT WANTING TO BRING THIS GUY DOWN *MYSELF.*
I UNDER-STAND, RIVER.
HEH

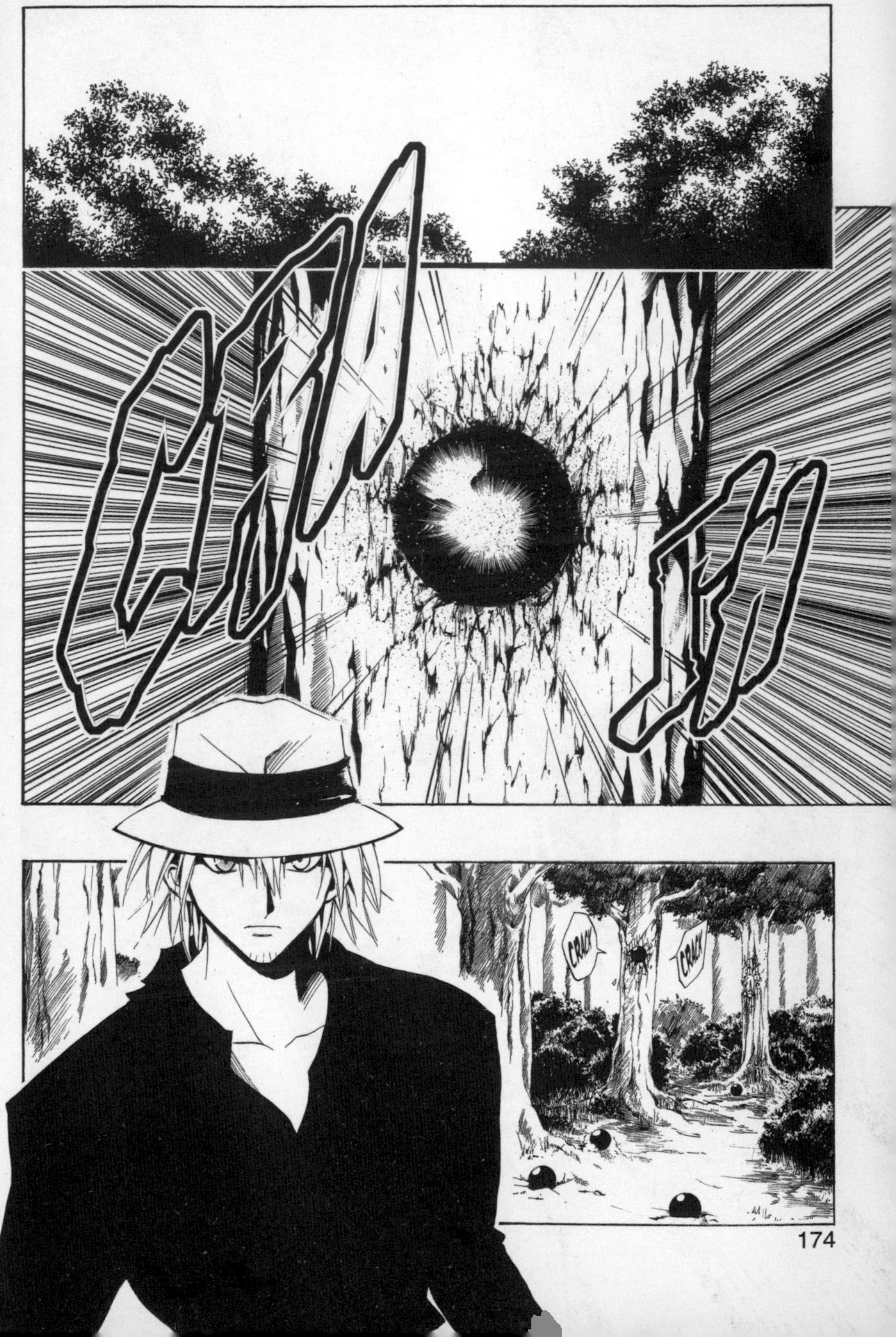
CRACK
CRACK

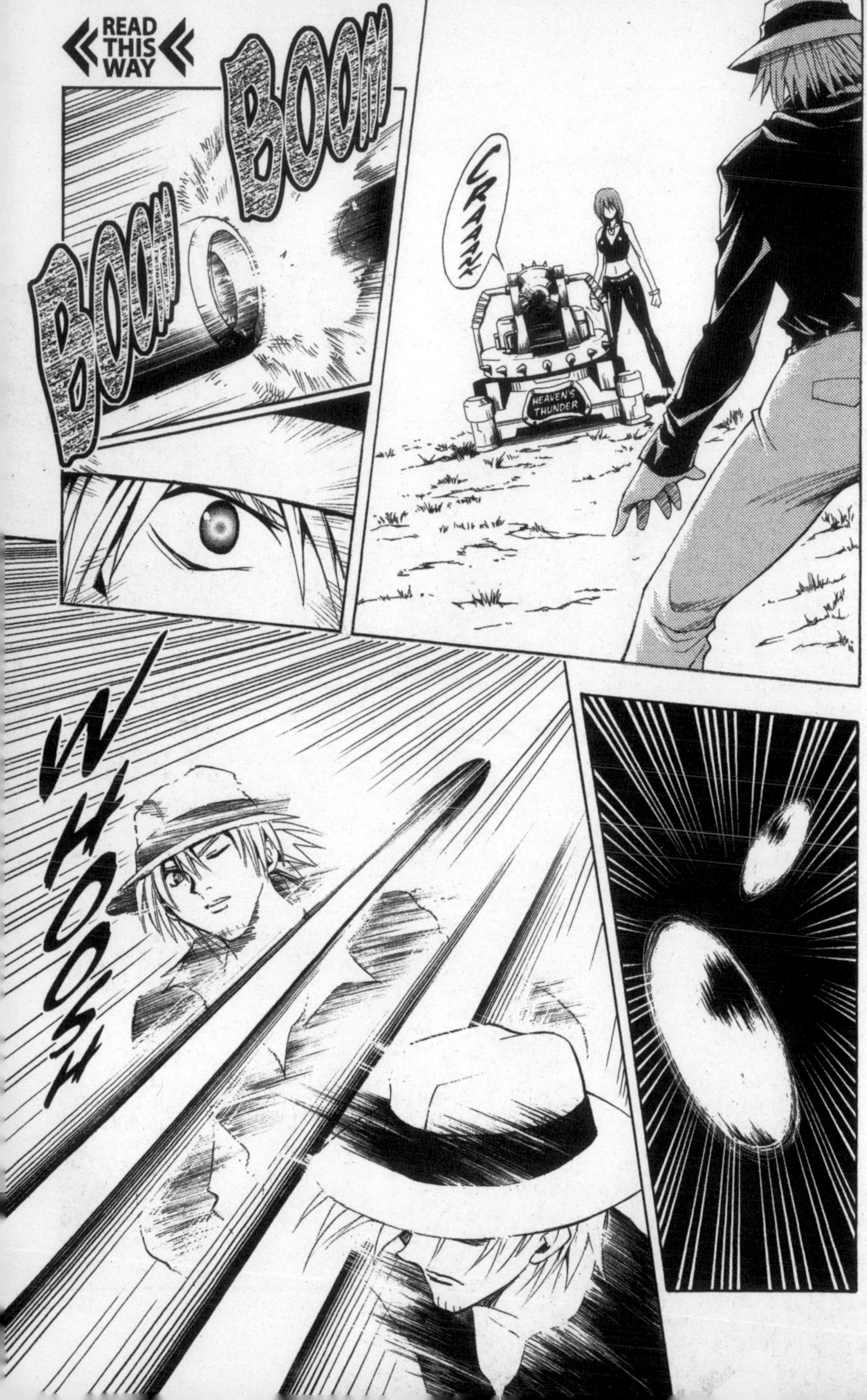
READ THIS WAY
CRAAANK
HEAVEN'S THUNDER
BOOM
BOOM
WHOOSH

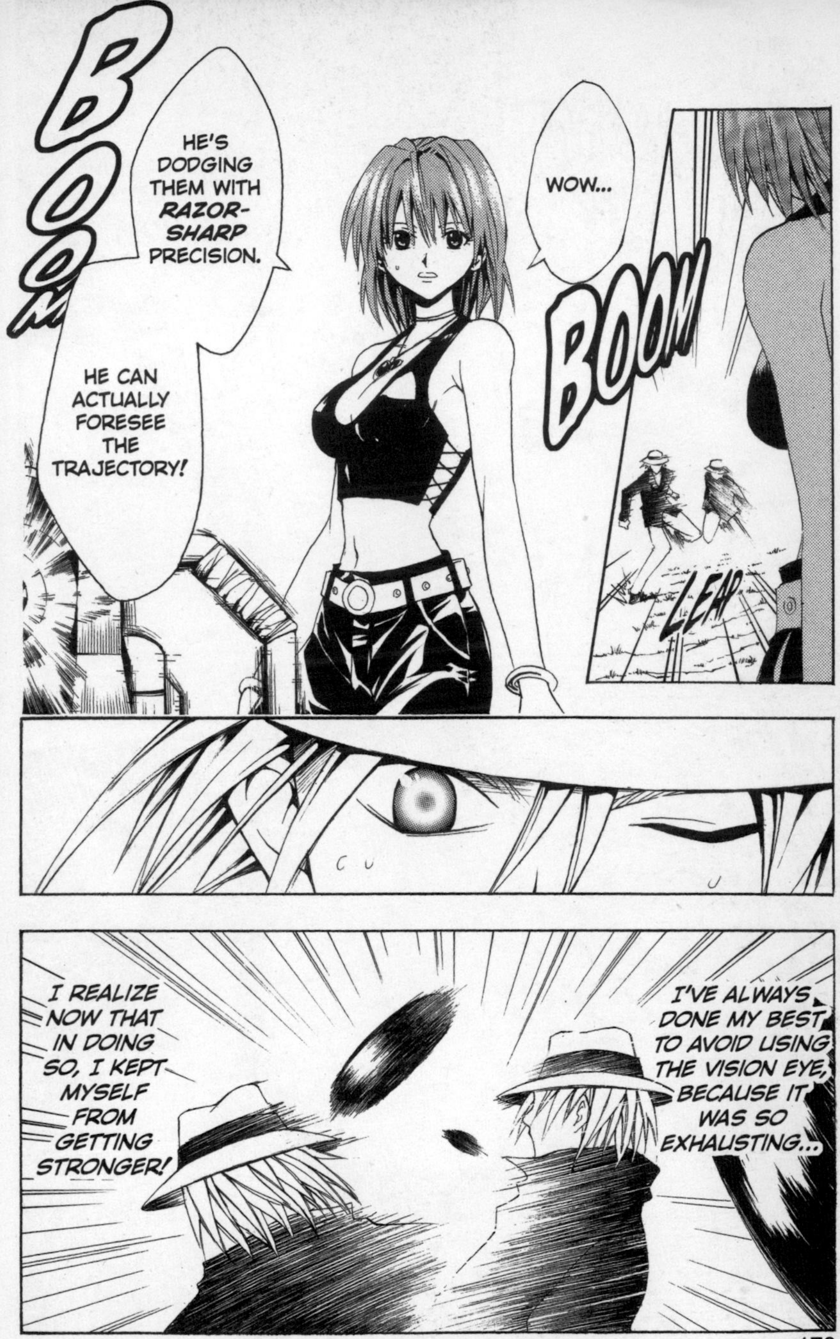
BOOM
LEAP
WOW...
HE'S DODGING THEM WITH RAZOR-SHARP PRECISION.
HE CAN ACTUALLY FORESEE THE TRAJECTORY!
BOOOM
I'VE ALWAYS DONE MY BEST TO AVOID USING THE VISION EYE, BECAUSE IT WAS SO EXHAUSTING...
I REALIZE NOW THAT IN DOING SO, I KEPT MYSELF FROM GETTING STRONGER!

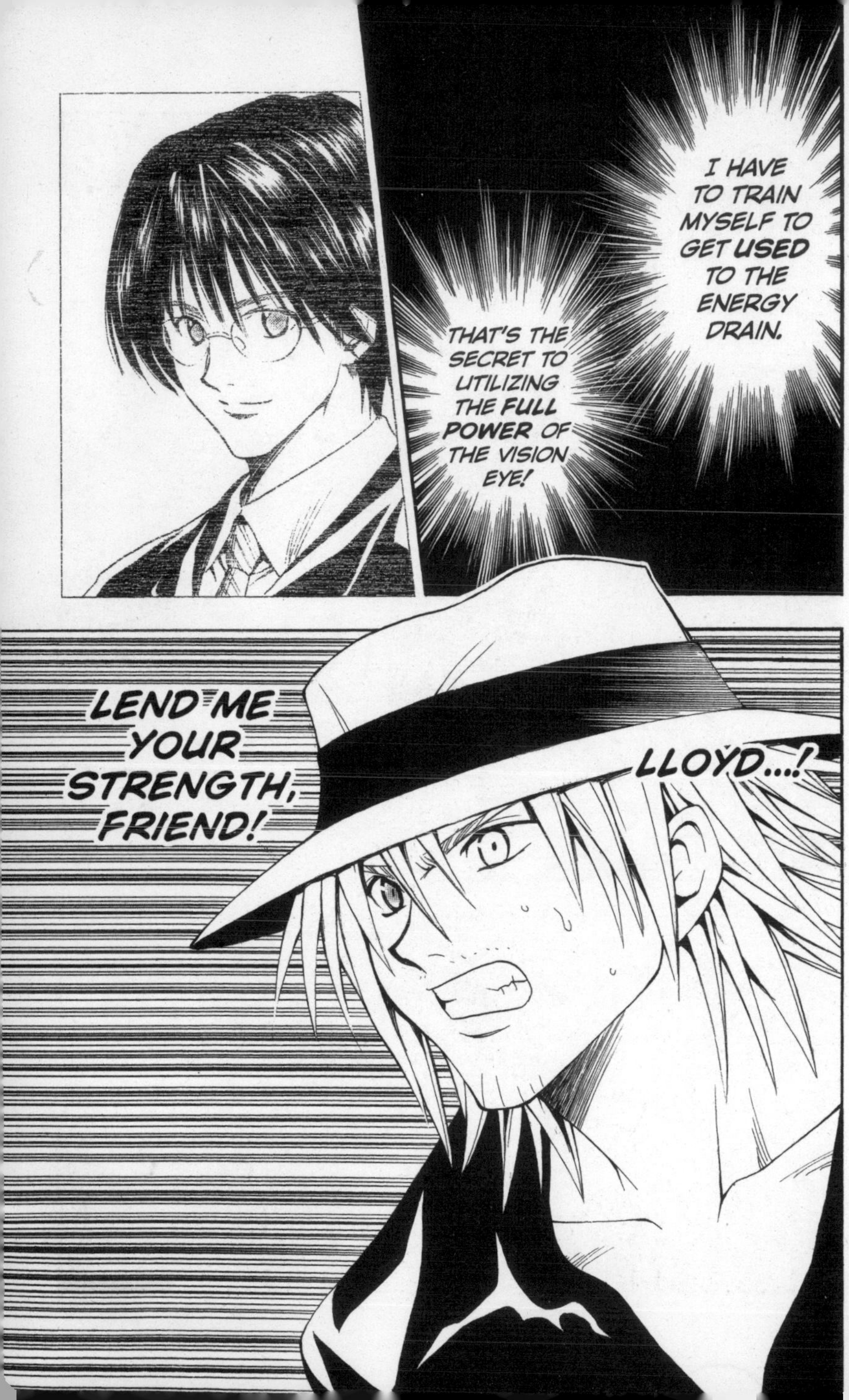
I HAVE TO TRAIN MYSELF TO GET USED TO THE ENERGY DRAIN.
THAT'S THE SECRET TO UTILIZING THE FULL POWER OF THE VISION EYE!
LEND ME YOUR STRENGTH, FRIEND!
LLOYD...!

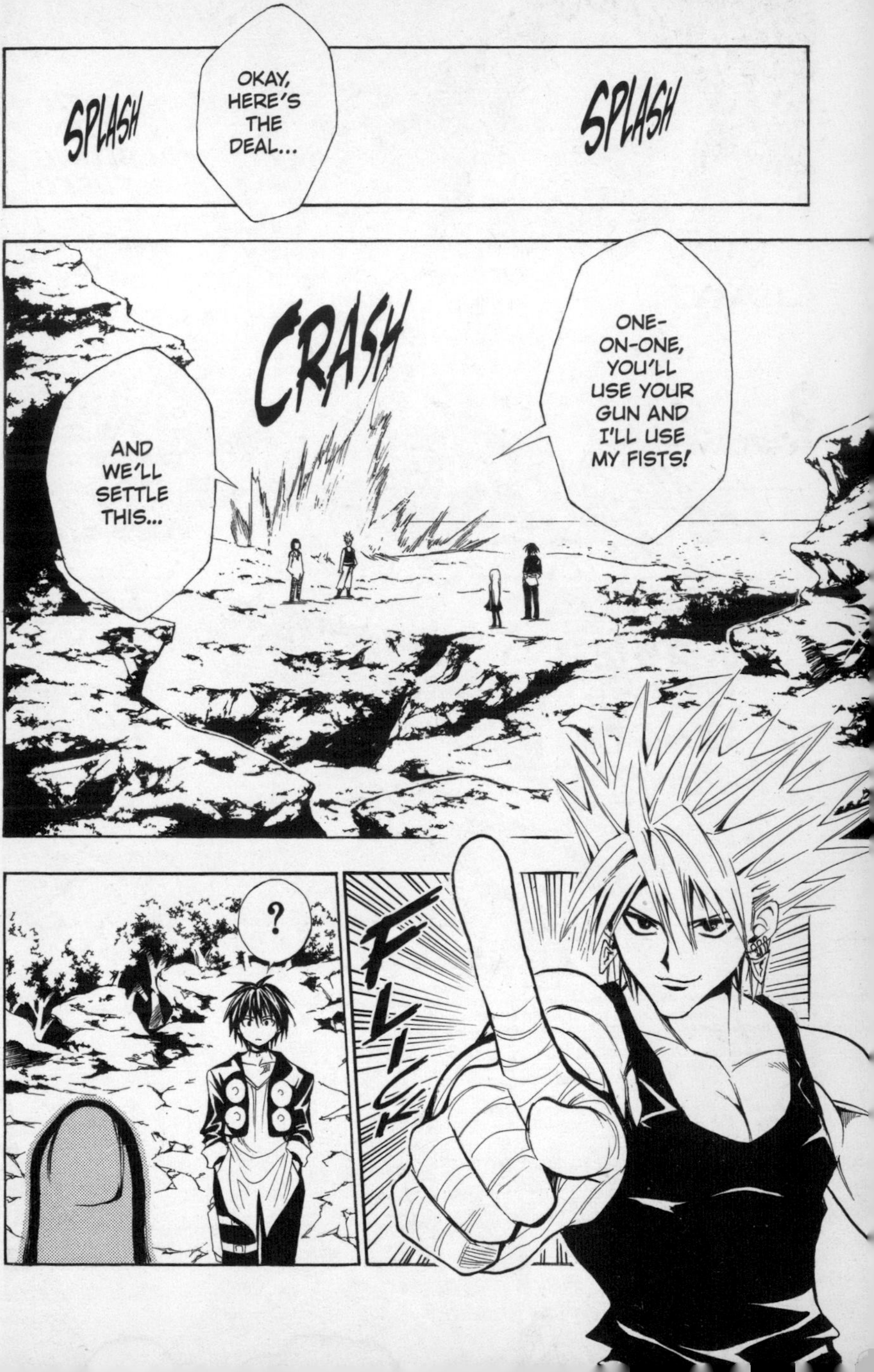
SPLASH
OKAY, HERE'S THE DEAL...
SPLASH
ONE-ON-ONE, YOU'LL USE YOUR GUN AND I'LL USE MY FISTS!
CRASH
AND WE'LL SETTLE THIS...
FLICK
?

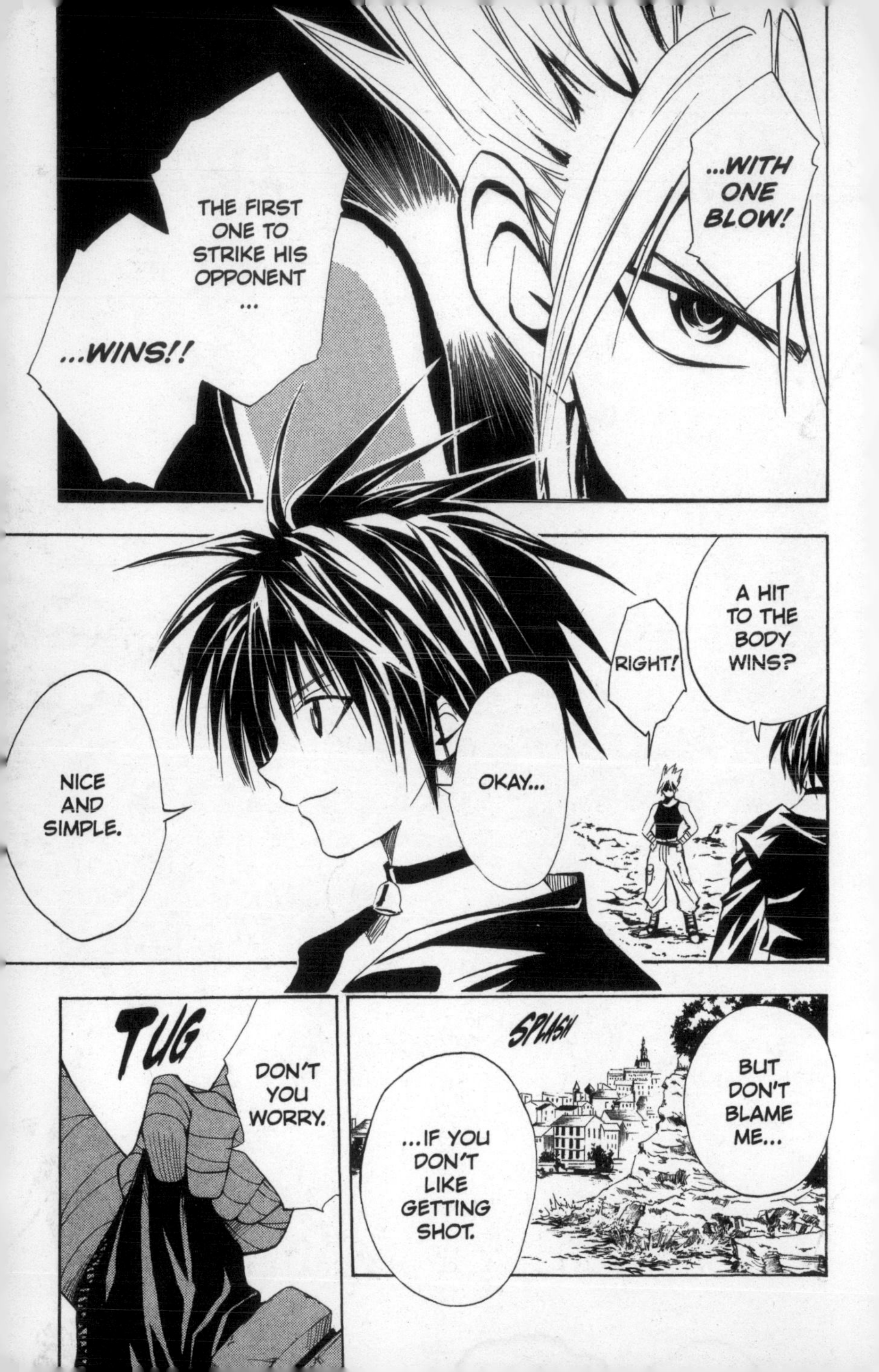
...WITH ONE BLOW!
THE FIRST ONE TO STRIKE HIS OPPONENT ...
...WINS!!
A HIT TO THE BODY WINS?
RIGHT!
OKAY...
NICE AND SIMPLE.
SPLASH
BUT DON'T BLAME ME...
...IF YOU DON'T LIKE GETTING SHOT.
TUG
DON'T YOU WORRY.

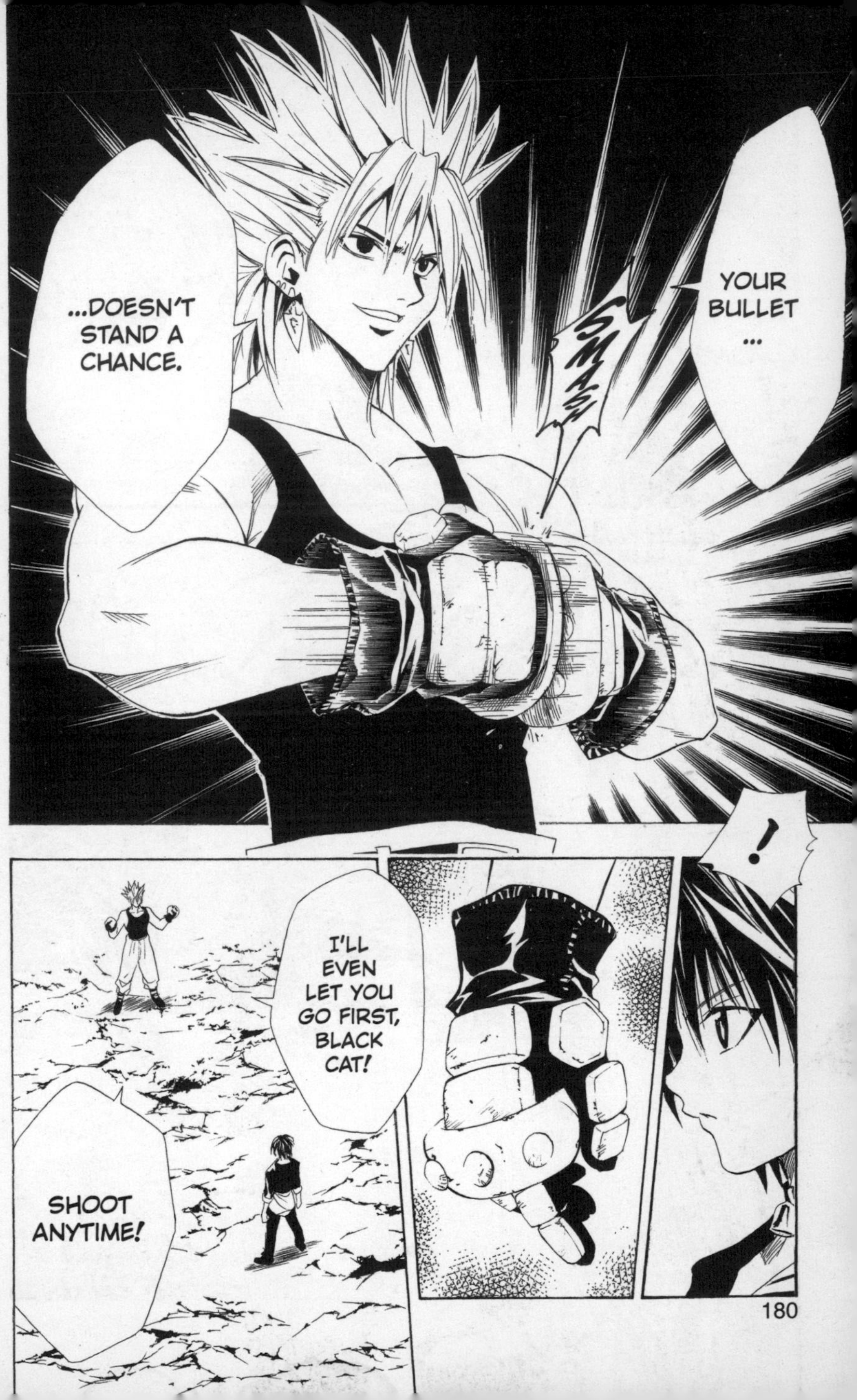
YOUR BULLET ...
SMASH
...DOESN'T STAND A CHANCE.
!
I'LL EVEN LET YOU GO FIRST, BLACK CAT!
SHOOT ANYTIME!

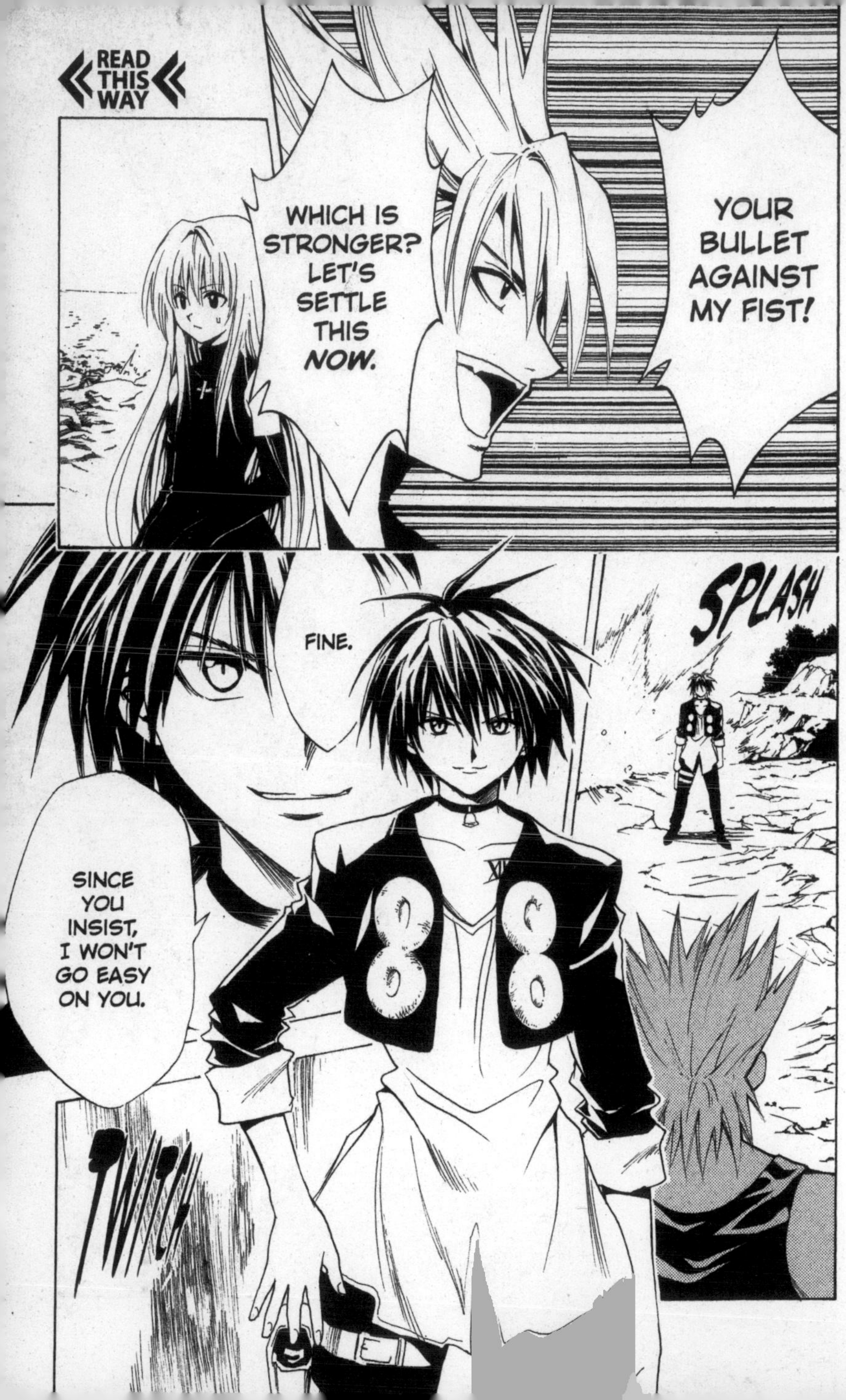
READ THIS WAY
YOUR BULLET AGAINST MY FIST!
WHICH IS STRONGER? LET'S SETTLE THIS *NOW.*
SPLASH
FINE.
SINCE YOU INSIST, I WON'T GO EASY ON YOU.
TWITCH

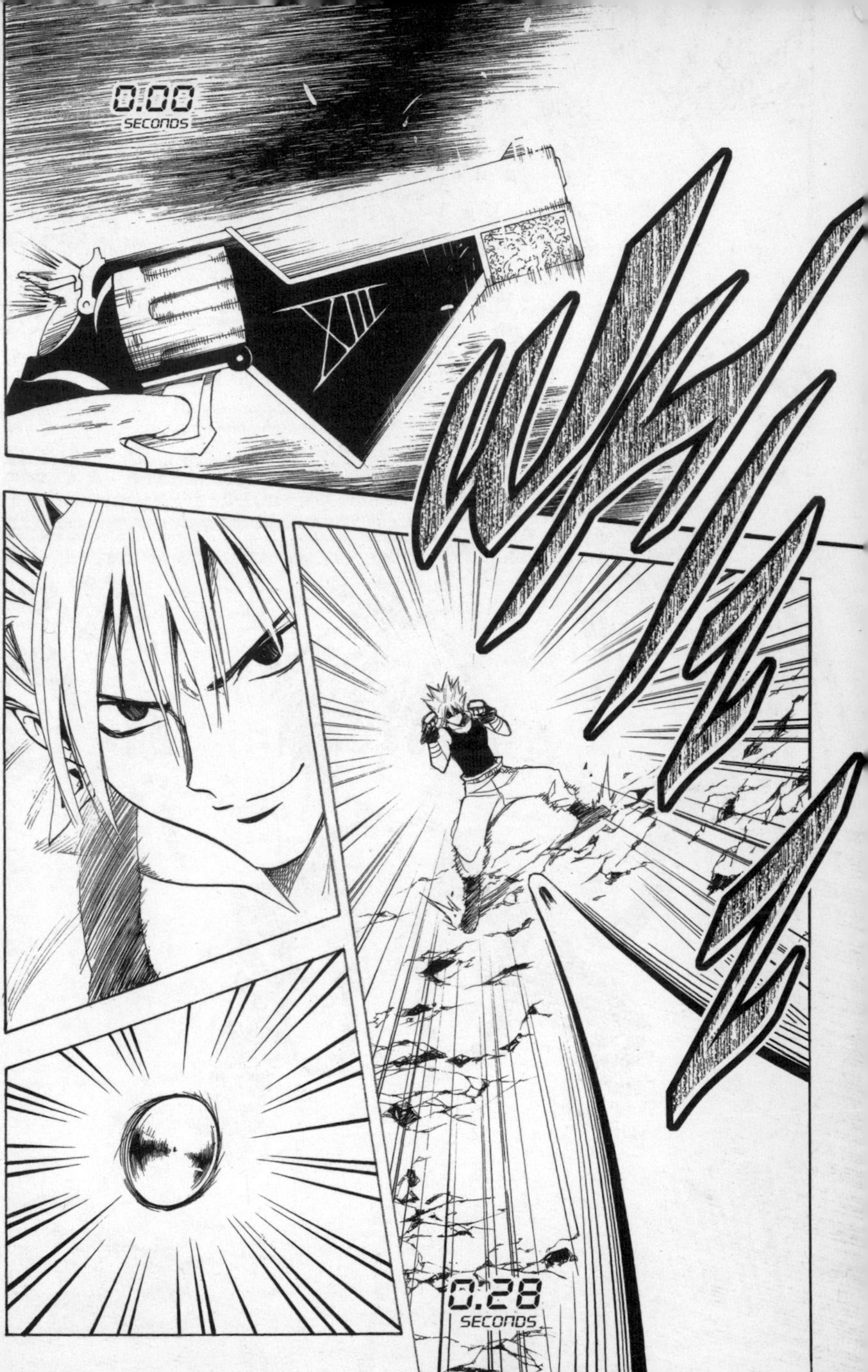
0:00
SECONDS
0.28
SECONDS

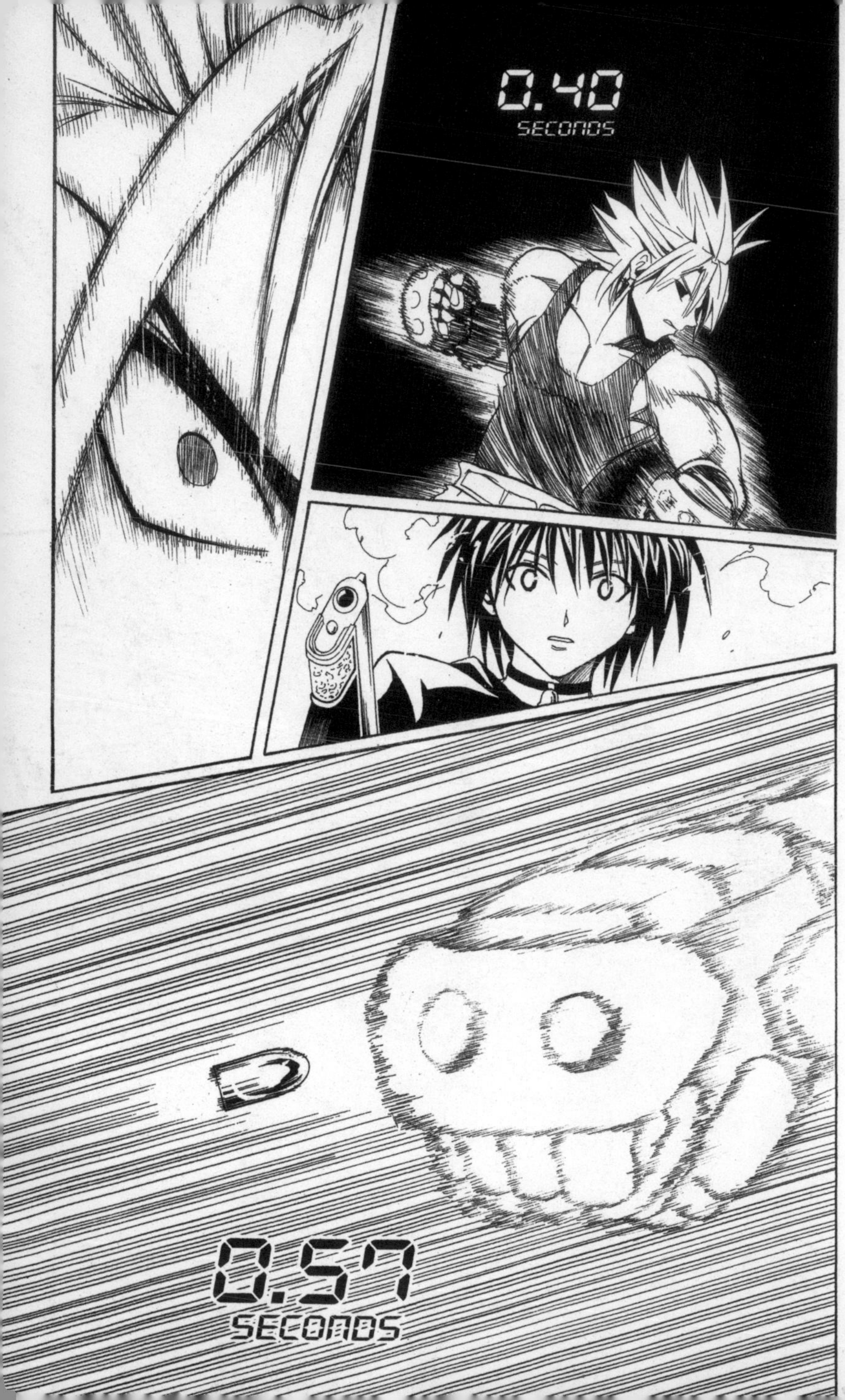
0.40
SECONDS
0.57
SECONDS

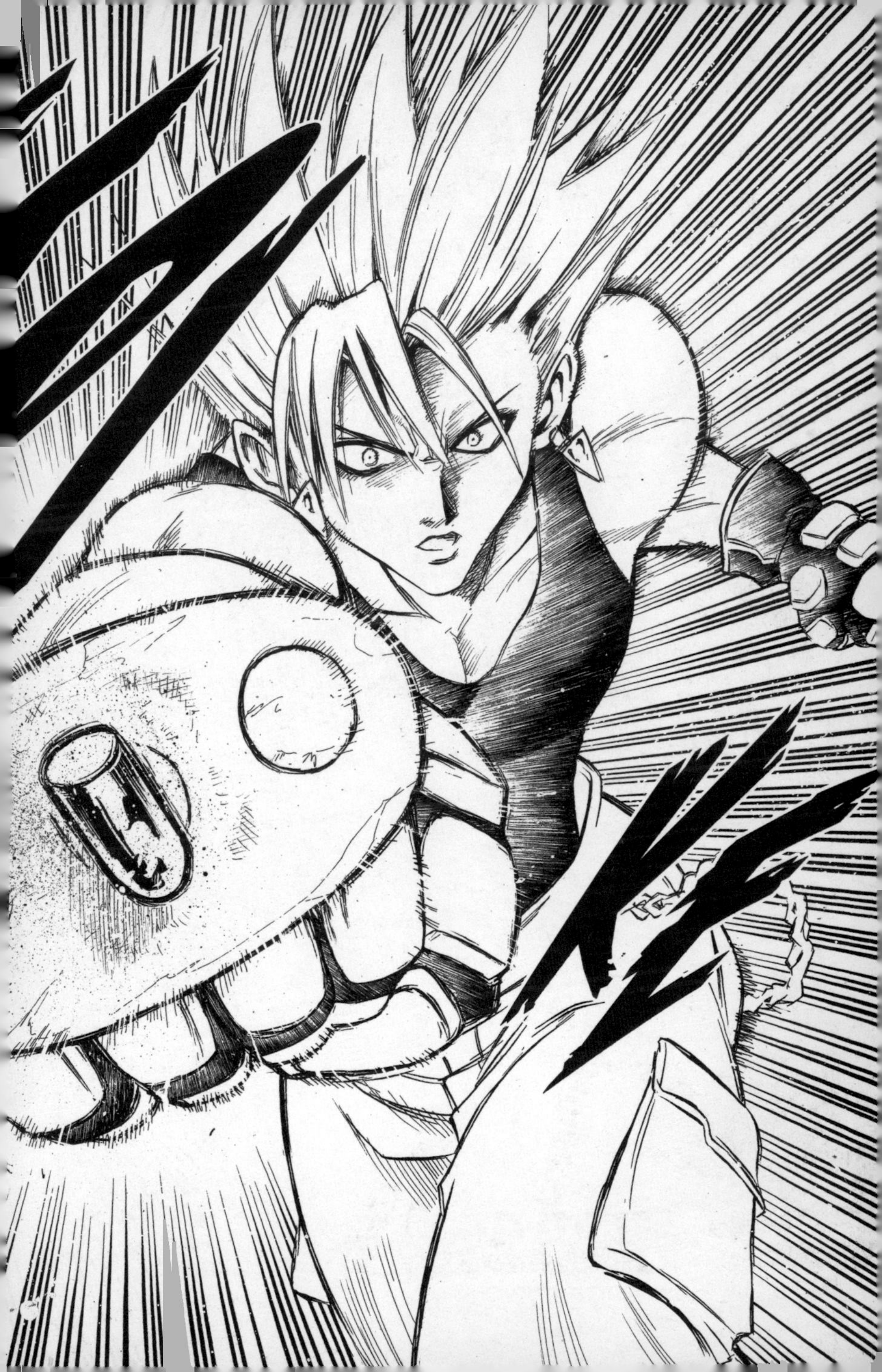

READ THIS WAY

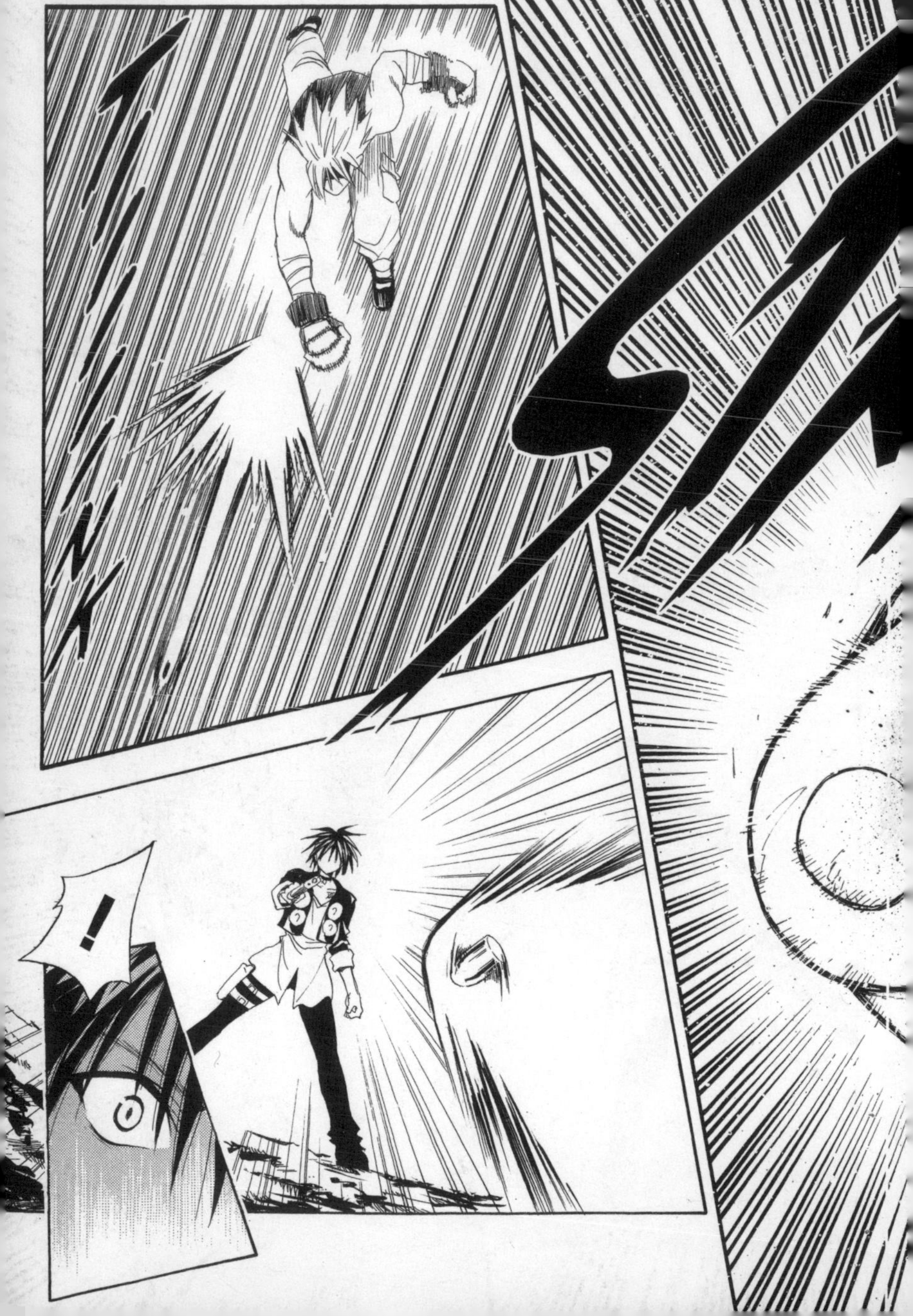
!

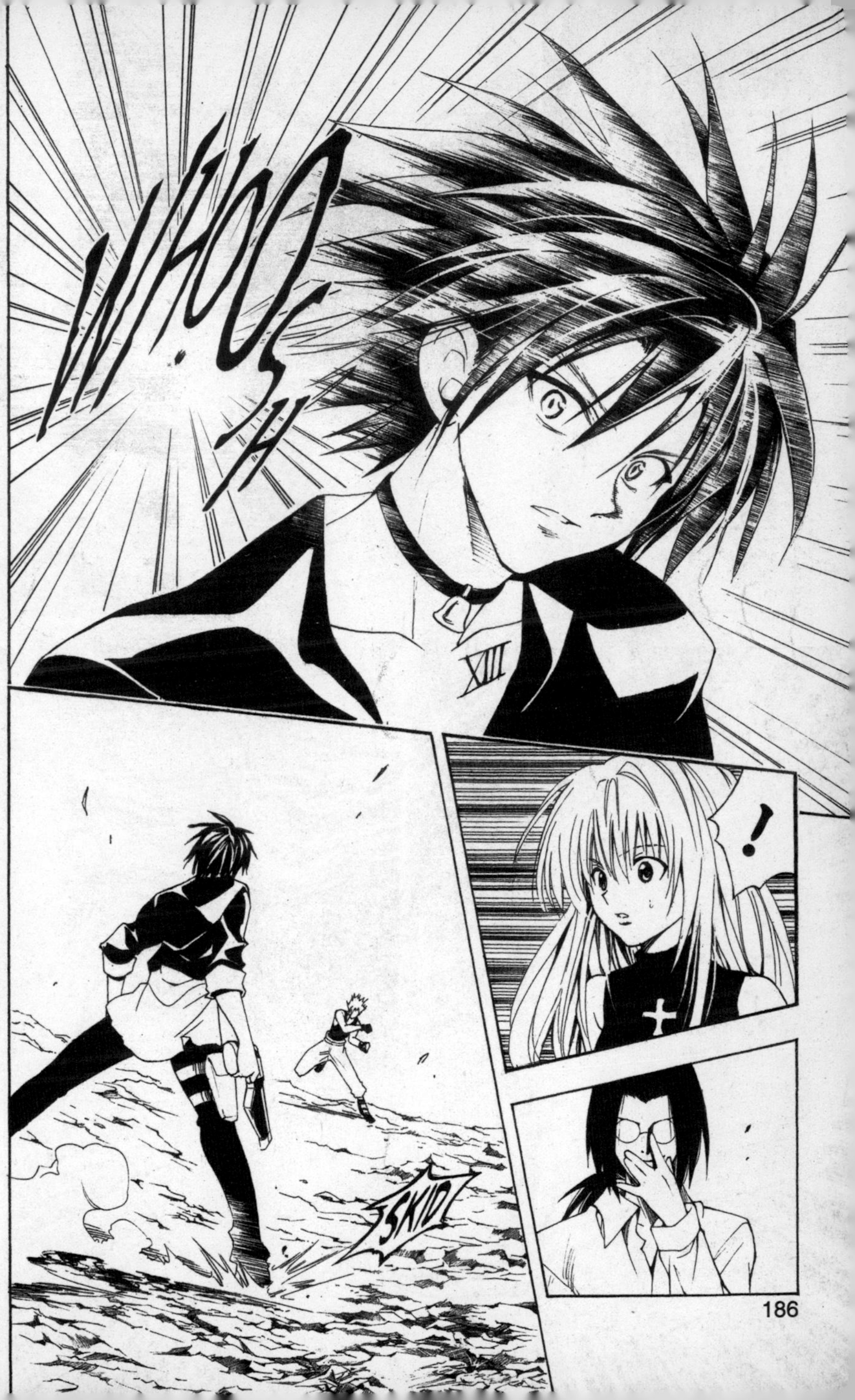
WHOOSH
!
SKID

READ THIS WAY

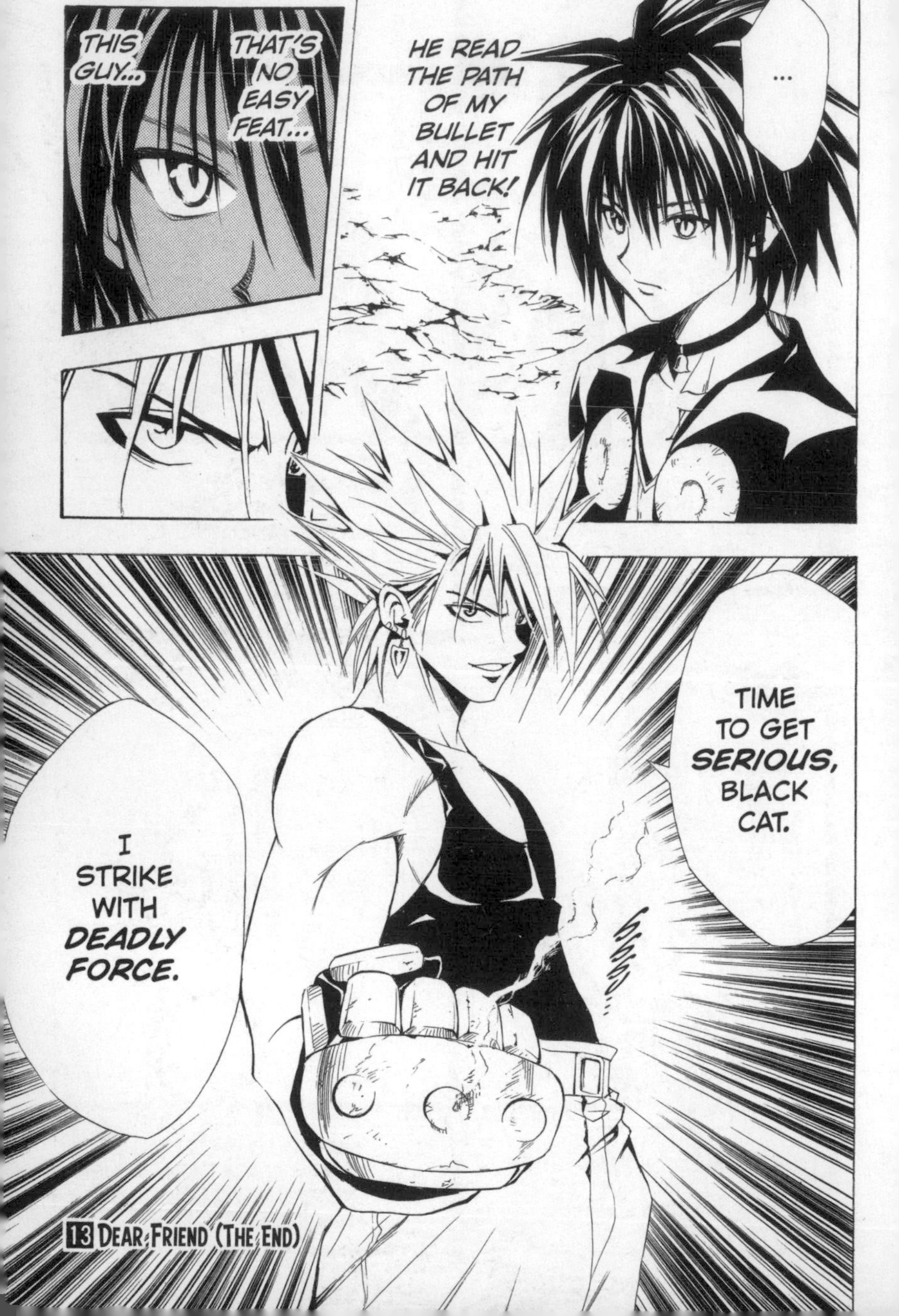
...
HE READ THE PATH OF MY BULLET AND HIT IT BACK!
THAT'S NO EASY FEAT...
THIS GUY...
TIME TO GET *SERIOUS*, BLACK CAT.
I STRIKE WITH *DEADLY* FORCE.
13 DEAR FRIEND (THE END)

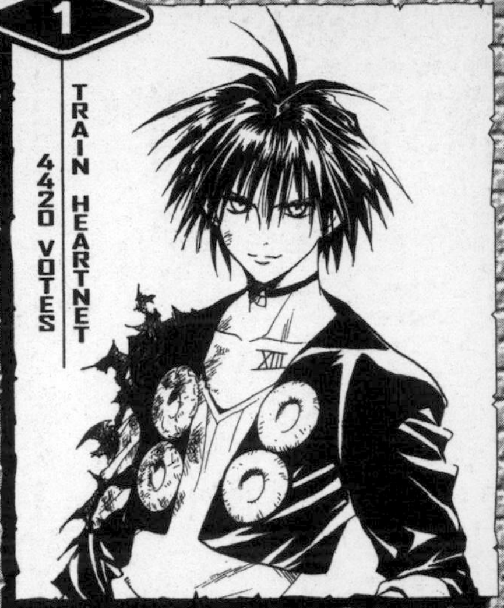
1
TRAIN HEARTNET
4420 VOTES

A POPULARITY CONTEST WAS HELD TO COMMEMORATE OUR FIRST YEAR. I WAS SURPRISED THAT OF THE TOP FIVE, THREE WERE WOMEN AND ONE WAS A CAT! AS EXPECTED, TRAIN CAME IN FIRST.

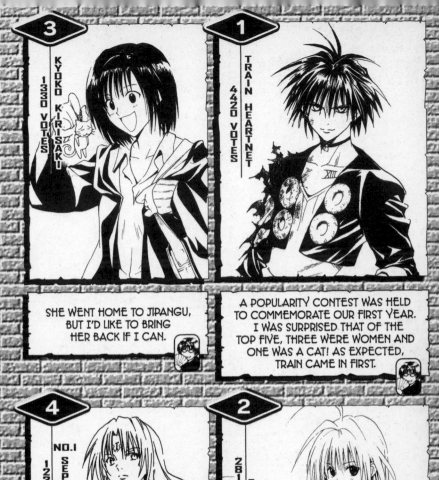

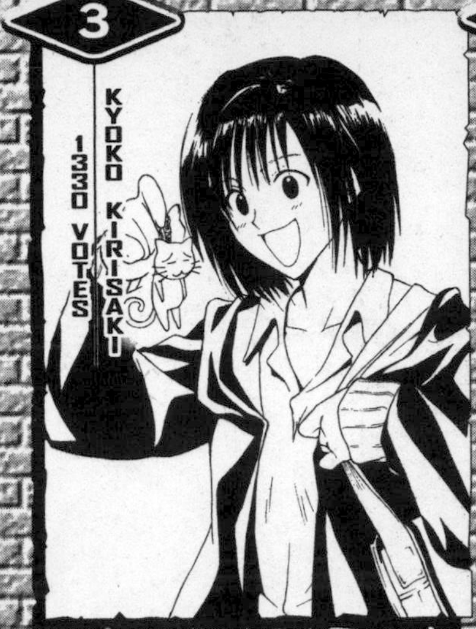
3
KYOKO KIRISAKU
1330 VOTES

SHE WENT HOME TO JIPANGU, BUT I'D LIKE TO BRING HER BACK IF I CAN.

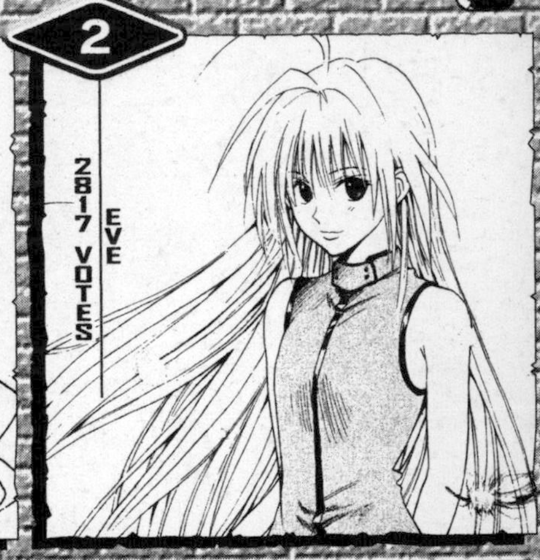
2
EVE
2817 VOTES

BLACK CAT IS ALSO EVE'S COMING OF AGE STORY. A BLACK CAT WAS ALSO MY INSPIRATIONAL IMAGE FOR EVE. FOR SVEN, IT'S A DOG.

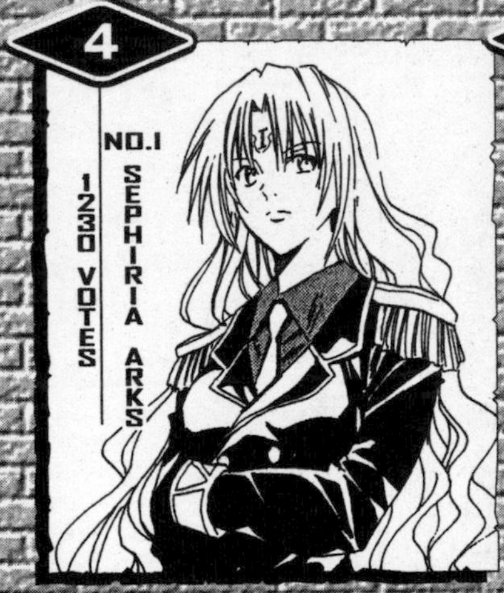
4
NO.1
SEPHIRIA ARKS
1230 VOTES

I KNEW FROM THE START THAT I WANTED A WOMAN TO LEAD THE CHRONO NUMBERS.

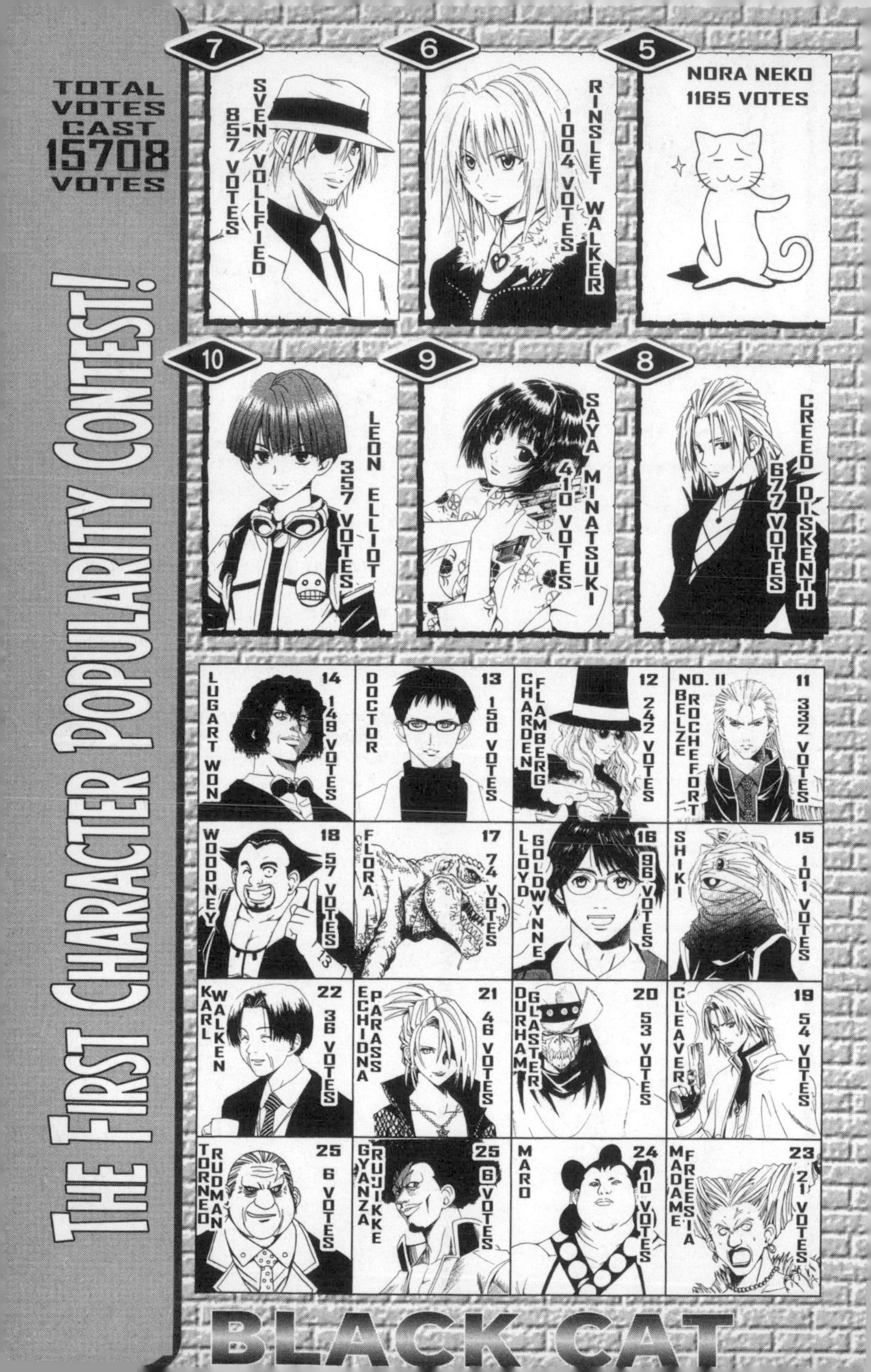
THE FIRST CHARACTER POPULARITY CONTEST!
TOTAL VOTES CAST 15708 VOTES
5
NORA NEKO 1165 VOTES
6
RINSLET WALKER 1004 VOTES
7
SVEN VOLLFIED 857 VOTES
8
CREED DISKENTH 677 VOTES
9
SAYA MINATSUKI 410 VOTES
10
LEON ELLIOT 357 VOTES
11
NO. 11 BELZE ROCHEFORT 332 VOTES
12
CHARDEN FLAMBERG 242 VOTES
13
DOCTOR 150 VOTES
14
LUGART WON 149 VOTES
15
SHIKI 101 VOTES
16
LLOYD GOLDWYNNE 96 VOTES
17
FLORA 74 VOTES
18
WOODNEY 57 VOTES
19
CLEAVER 54 VOTES
20
DURHAM GLASTER 53 VOTES
21
ECHIDNA PARASS 46 VOTES
22
KARL WALKEN 36 VOTES
23
MADAME FREESIA 21 VOTES
24
MARO 10 VOTES
25
GYANZA RUJIKKE 6 VOTES
25
TORNEO RUDMAN 6 VOTES
BLACK CAT

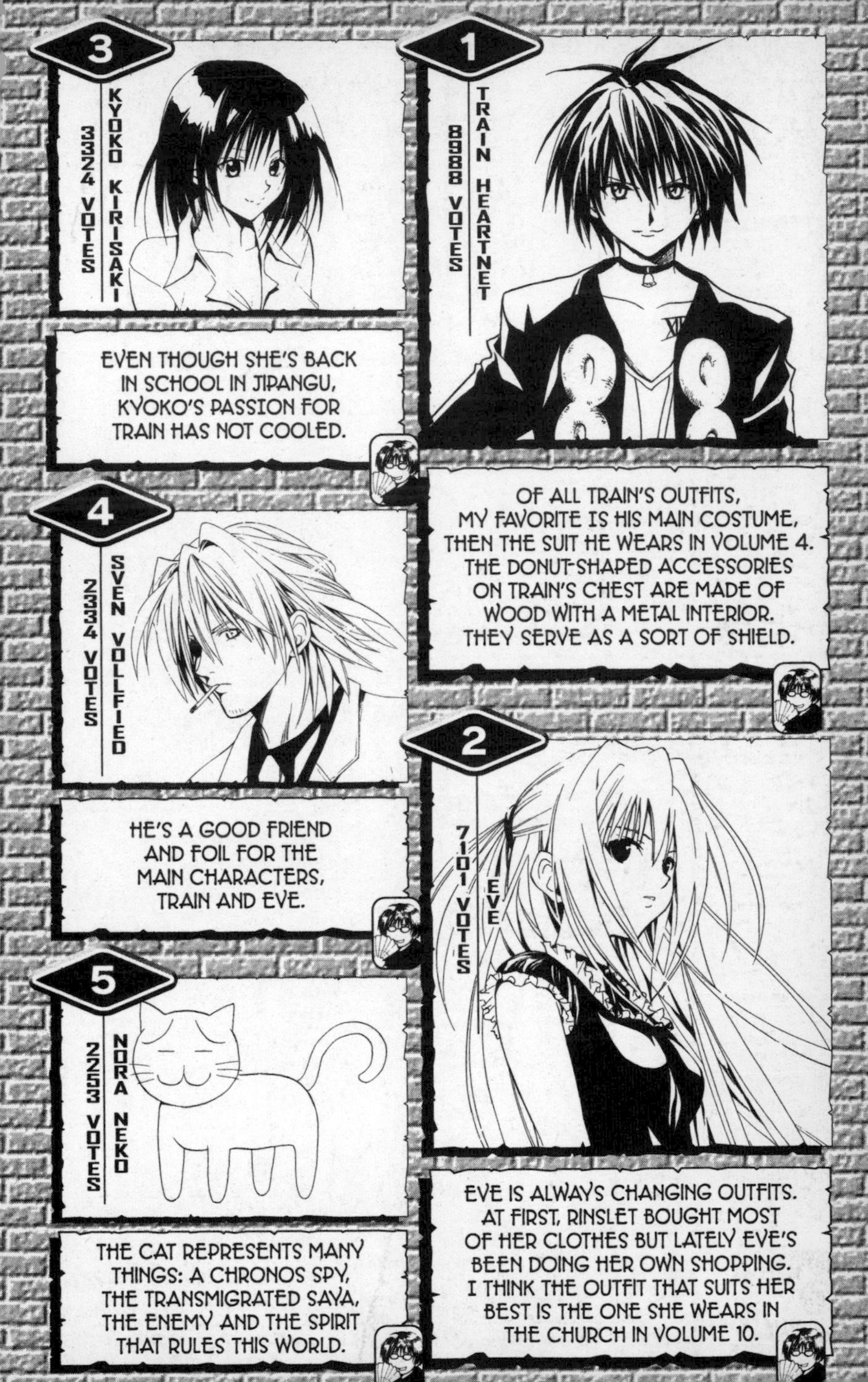
1
TRAIN HEARTNET
8988 VOTES
OF ALL TRAIN'S OUTFITS, MY FAVORITE IS HIS MAIN COSTUME, THEN THE SUIT HE WEARS IN VOLUME 4. THE DONUT-SHAPED ACCESSORIES ON TRAIN'S CHEST ARE MADE OF WOOD WITH A METAL INTERIOR. THEY SERVE AS A SORT OF SHIELD.
2
EVE
7101 VOTES
EVE IS ALWAYS CHANGING OUTFITS. AT FIRST, RINSLET BOUGHT MOST OF HER CLOTHES BUT LATELY EVE'S BEEN DOING HER OWN SHOPPING. I THINK THE OUTFIT THAT SUITS HER BEST IS THE ONE SHE WEARS IN THE CHURCH IN VOLUME 10.
3
KYOKO KIRISAKI
3324 VOTES
EVEN THOUGH SHE'S BACK IN SCHOOL IN JIPANGU, KYOKO'S PASSION FOR TRAIN HAS NOT COOLED.
4
SVEN VOLLFIED
2334 VOTES
HE'S A GOOD FRIEND AND FOIL FOR THE MAIN CHARACTERS, TRAIN AND EVE.
5
NORA NEKO
2253 VOTES
THE CAT REPRESENTS MANY THINGS: A CHRONOS SPY, THE TRANSMIGRATED SAYA, THE ENEMY AND THE SPIRIT THAT RULES THIS WORLD.

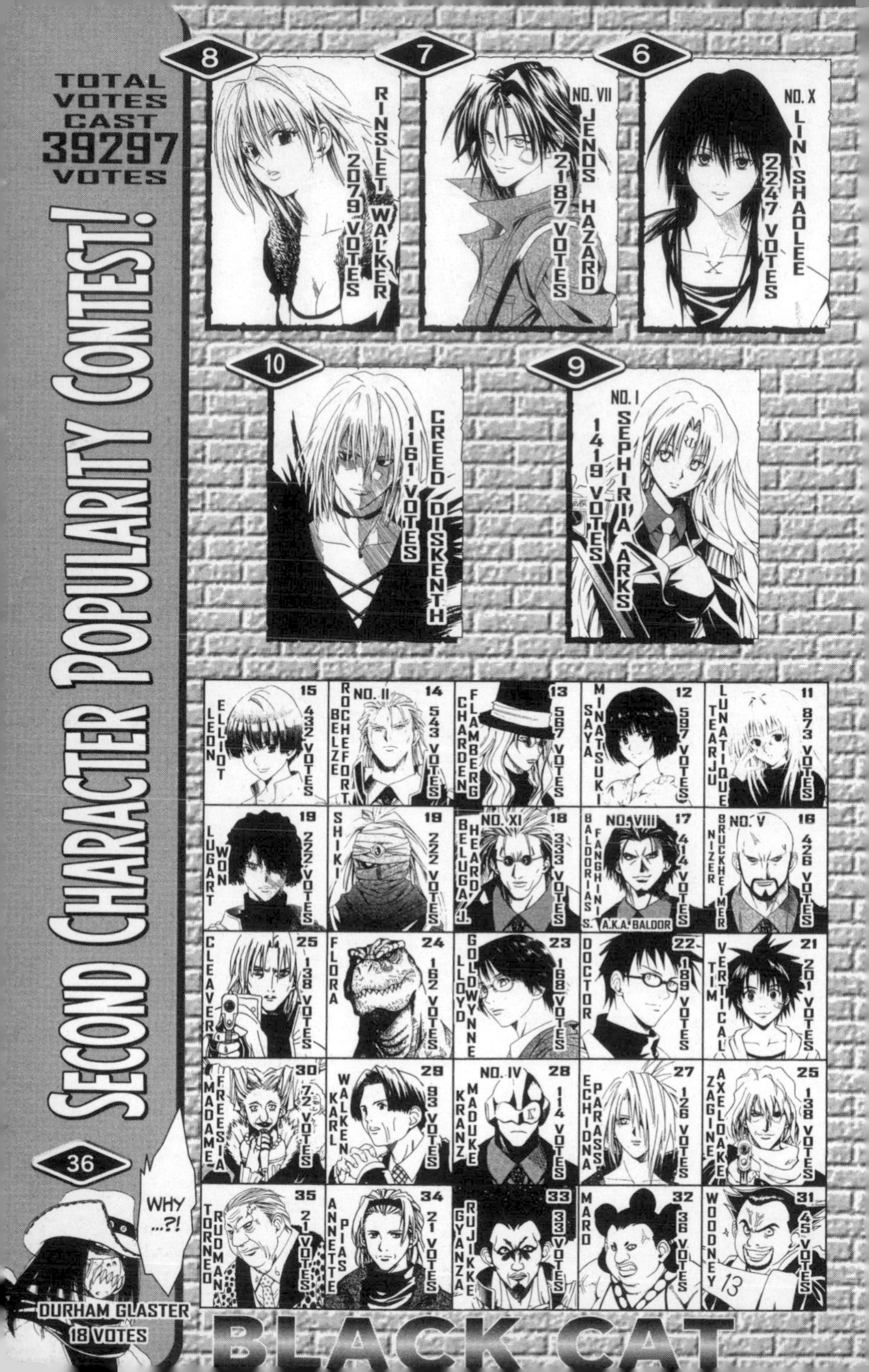
SECOND CHARACTER POPULARITY CONTEST!
TOTAL VOTES CAST 39297 VOTES
6 NO. X LIN SHAOLEE 2247 VOTES
7 NO. VII JENOS HAZARD 2187 VOTES
8 RINSLET WALKER 2079 VOTES
9 NO. I SEPHIRIA ARKS 1419 VOTES
10 CREED DISKENTH 1161 VOTES
11 LUNATIQUE TEARJU 873 VOTES
12 MINATSUKI SAYA 597 VOTES
13 FLAMBERG CHARDEN 567 VOTES
14 NO. II BELZE ROCHEFORT 543 VOTES
15 ELLIOT LEON 432 VOTES
16 NO. V NIZER BRUCKHEIMER 426 VOTES
17 NO. VIII BALDORIAS S. FANGHINI A.K.A. BALDOR 414 VOTES
18 NO. XI BELUGA J. HEARD 333 VOTES
19 SHIKI 222 VOTES
19 LUGART WON 222 VOTES
21 TIM VERTICAL 201 VOTES
22 DOCTOR 189 VOTES
23 LLOYD GOLDWYNNE 168 VOTES
24 FLORA 162 VOTES
25 CLEAVER 138 VOTES
25 AXELDAKE ZAGINE 138 VOTES
27 ECHIDNA PARASS 126 VOTES
28 NO. IV MADUKE KRANZ 114 VOTES
29 KARL WALKEN 93 VOTES
30 MADAME FREESIA 72 VOTES
31 WOODNEY 45 VOTES
32 MARO 36 VOTES
33 RUJIKKE GYANZA 33 VOTES
34 ANNETTE PIAS 21 VOTES
35 TORNEO RUDMAN 21 VOTES
36
WHY ...?!
DURHAM GLASTER 18 VOTES
BLACK CAT

IN THE NEXT VOLUME...

Glin invites Train and his crew to join the Sweeper Alliance in order to destroy Creed and the Apostles of the Stars. But first, Train must pass a test to weed out the weaker sweepers—a test the likes of which Train has never seen!

AVAILABLE MAY 2008!

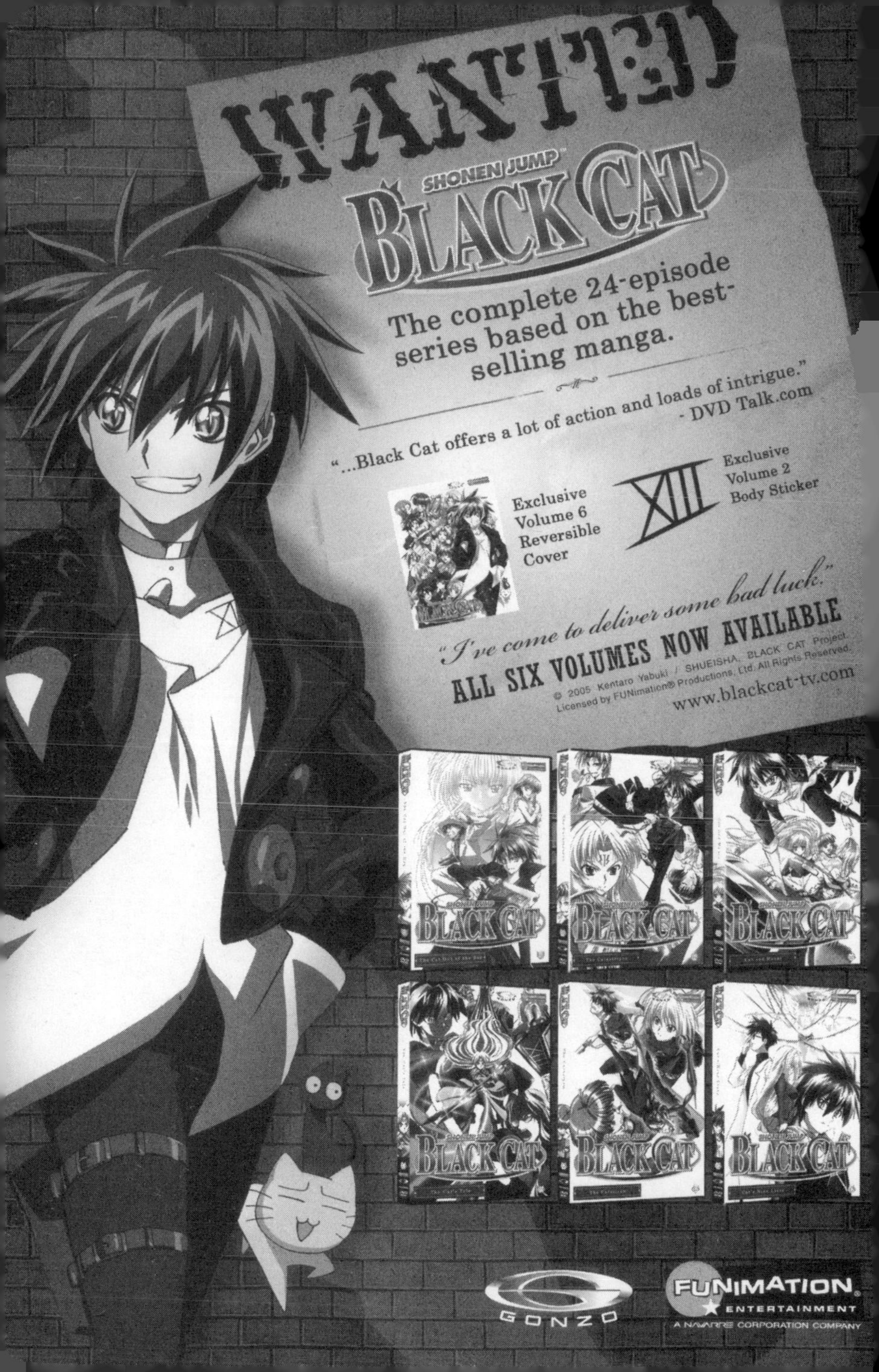
WANTED
SHONEN JUMP™
BLACK CAT
The complete 24-episode series based on the best-selling manga.
"...Black Cat offers a lot of action and loads of intrigue."
- DVD Talk.com
Exclusive Volume 6 Reversible Cover
XIII
Exclusive Volume 2 Body Sticker
"I've come to deliver some bad luck."
ALL SIX VOLUMES NOW AVAILABLE
© 2005 Kentaro Yabuki / SHUEISHA, BLACK CAT Project. Licensed by FUNimation® Productions, Ltd. All Rights Reserved.
www.blackcat-tv.com
GONZO
FUNIMATION®
ENTERTAINMENT
A NAVARRE CORPORATION COMPANY

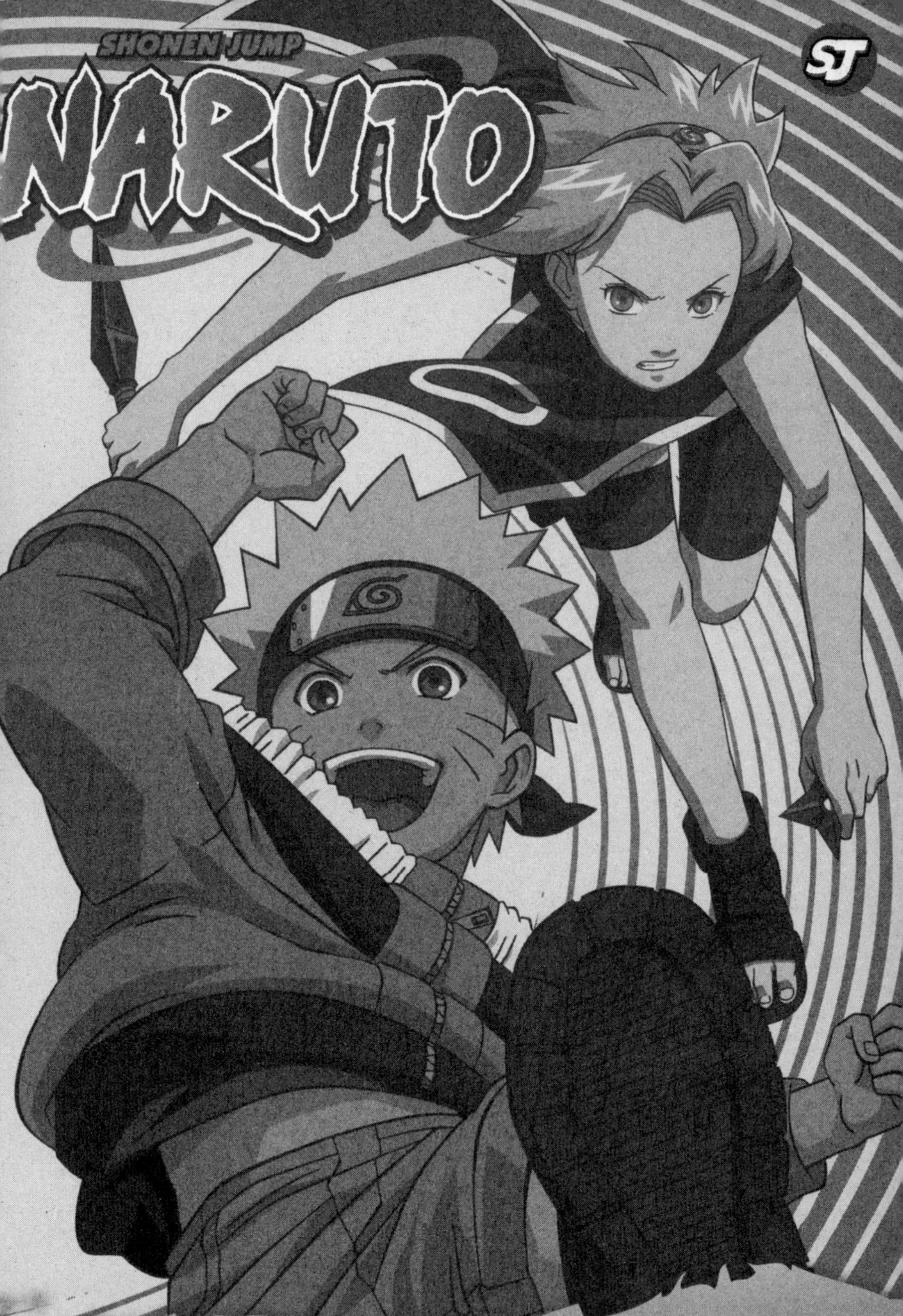
SHONEN JUMP
NARUTO
SJ